Dance in Musical Theatre

Dance in Musical Theatre

A History of the Body in Movement

Edited by

Dustyn Martincich and Phoebe Rumsey

methuen | drama

LONDON · NEW YORK · OXFORD · NEW DELHI · SYDNEY

METHUEN DRAMA
Bloomsbury Publishing Plc
50 Bedford Square, London, WC1B 3DP, UK
1385 Broadway, New York, NY 10018, USA
29 Earlsfort Terrace, Dublin 2, Ireland

BLOOMSBURY, METHUEN DRAMA and the Methuen Drama logo are trademarks of
Bloomsbury Publishing Plc

First published in Great Britain 2024

A catalogue record for this book is available from the British Library.

A catalog record for this book is available from the Library of Congress.

ISBN: HB: 978-1-3502-3553-3
         PB: 978-1-3502-3552-6
         ePDF: 978-1-3502-3554-0
         eBook: 978-1-3502-3555-7

Typeset by RefineCatch Limited, Bungay, Suffolk
Printed and bound in Great Britain

To find out more about our authors and books visit www.bloomsbury.com
and sign up for our newsletters.

Contents

Image List

About the Editors and Authors

Editors/Authors

Dustyn Martincich is Professor of Theatre and Dance at Bucknell University. Her research interests involve investigating narrative, collaborative and interdisciplinary possibilities in theatre and dance performance; as well as musical theatre dance studies that focuses on the work of the ensemble. She has movement directed, choreographed, and performed for concert dance and theatrical stages. She has been recently published in *Studies in Musical Theatre*, and in edited collections like *Gender, Sex, and Sexuality in Musical Theatre* (edited by Kelly Kessler), *Dueling Grounds: Revolution and Revelation in the Musical* Hamilton (edited by Paul Laird and Mary Jo Lodge), and *Toni Morrison: Forty Years in The Clearing* (edited by Carmen Gillespie).

Phoebe Rumsey is Senior Lecturer in Musical Theatre and Course Leader of the BA (Hons) Musical Theatre degree at the University of Portsmouth in the United Kingdom. She received her PhD from The Graduate Center, CUNY, and holds an MA in Performance Studies from NYU, an MA in Theatre from UNLV and a BFA in Contemporary Dance from Simon Fraser University. A scholar and practitioner, her research has been published in *The Routledge Companion to Theatre and Politics*, *Studies in Musical Theatre*, *The Routledge Companion to the Contemporary Musical*, and *Reframing The Musical: Race, Culture, and Identity*. She is the author of *Embodied Nostalgia: Early Twentieth Century Social Dance and the Choreographing of Broadway Musical Theatre*. Along with her engagement in academic studies Dr. Rumsey has worked extensively as a performer and choreographer.

Authors

Benae Beamon is a scholar and artist. Her scholarship focuses on religion, ethics, and culture, specifically Black cultural expressions as they intersect with ritual and reflect moral imagination. Her work has been published in several anthologies, including *Queering Spirituality and Community in the Deep South* and *Silhouettes of the Soul: Meditations on Fashion, Religion, and Subjectivity*. As a tap dancer and performance artist, Benae examines the extraordinary and spectacular in the everyday, focusing on the way that the mundane can be sacred ritual. She has premiered work at various venues, like the Hudgens Center for Arts & Learning and ICA VCU. She holds a BA from Colgate University, an MA in Religion from Yale University, and a PhD in Social Ethics from Boston University.

Bud Coleman is the Roe Green Professor of Theatre and Associate Dean of the College of Arts and Sciences, University of Colorado Boulder. A former dancer with Les Ballets Trockadero de Monte Carlo, Fort Worth Ballet, and Ballet Austin, Dr. Coleman has directed and choreographed many musicals and operas. In 2008, he directed and choreographed the musical *Company* in Vladivostok, Russia, was selected to be a 2009–10 Fulbright Lecturer in Japan, and staged the Thai premiere of *Fiddler on the Roof* in Bangkok in 2017. Publications include *Women in American Musical Theatre* and *Backstage Pass: A Survey of American Musical Theatre* (with Pamyla Stiehl), and numerous articles.

Tomé Cousin is Full Professor of Dance in the School of Drama at Carnegie Mellon University. He received his MFA in New Media Art and Performance from LIU, and his BA in Choreography / Dance History from PPU. He is a childhood discovery of Geoffrey Holder and has appeared on Broadway, Off-Broadway, national and international tours, TV and film. His dance credits include the Physical Theater Project, Tanztheater Wuppertal Pina Bausch, Bill T. Jones and Arnie Zane, Martha Clarke, Meredith Monk, and Mabou Mines. For nine seasons he appeared as Ragdoll Tomé on *Mister Rogers' Neighborhood*. He is the author of *The Total Theater Artist and New Media Performance*, and *The Franklin Project: Interviews, Essays and Articles on Diversity and Non-Traditional Casting for Theatre Performance*, and serves as an artistic supervisor for the Tony Award-winning director Susan Stroman. He has become a leading voice in the conversation of theatrical intimacy education and choreography.

Joanna Dee Das is Associate Professor in the Performing Arts Department at Washington University in St. Louis and an affiliate of the Program in American Culture Studies. She is the author of the award-winning *Katherine Dunham: Dance and the African Diaspora* (2017). With Ryan Donovan, she co-edited the special issue "Dance in Musical Theatre" for *Studies in Musical Theatre*. She has also published articles in *Journal of Urban History*, *Dance Research Journal*, *Theatre History Studies*, *TDR*, and *ARTS*, as well as book chapters in *The Routledge Companion to the Contemporary Musical*, *The Routledge Companion to Musical Theatre*, and *A Critical Companion to the American Stage Musical*.

Ramón Flowers is Associate Professor in the Department of Dance in the Jordan College of the Arts, at Butler University. He began his formal dance training on scholarship at the School for the Pennsylvania Ballet and later attended the School of American Ballet. He was the first male African American dancer to join the Pennsylvania Ballet Company. He moved to Europe as a principal ballet dancer with Maurice Béjart, William Forsythe, and Nacho Duato. He returned to North America to dance with Les Grands Ballets Canadiens. He was also featured in several Broadway shows, national Broadway tours, film, and national TV commercials. During his time away from Butler University, he teaches ballet, and musical theatre jazz at the American Dance Festival at Duke University. He received his BA in French from The City College of New York, CUNY, and his MFA in Dance from The University of Iowa.

Mijiang "M-Jay" He is a Chinese actor, director, choreographer, and musical theater educator. An accomplished triple-threat performer, M-Jay joined the Chinese national production of *Cats* in 2012 and 2013. While continuing to perform, M-Jay added professional directing and choreography credits to his résumé. As an assistant choreographer, he joined *Neverland: Peter Pan* with Broadway Asia and China Broadway Entertainment, as well as productions of *Murder Ballad* and *Fosse*. M-Jay created the original Chinese translation of *42nd Street*, which premiered at the Beijing Dance Academy, China's premier music theatre training program. M-Jay was a visiting professor and director at the Beijing Dance Academy, teaching jazz dance, music theatre history, and musical theatre techniques. He also developed the musical theatre dance curriculum for the Communication University of China musical theatre program. He received an MA in Theatre at Binghamton University, MA in Dance Studies from Beijing Dance Academy, MM from Carthage College, and a BA in Music Education from Hunan Normal University.

Michael D. Jablonski is an Assistant Professor in the School of Performing Arts/Theatre at the University of Central Florida, serving as the Coordinator of the BFA Musical Theatre program with previous academic appointments at Brenau University, Elon University, and Florida State University. Michael serves as Assistant Faculty member of Theatrical Intimacy Education with a focused research in elevating/evolving the consent-based practice in the dance studio/performance. As a professional actor Michael performed in three Broadway productions, eight national tours, and many prestigious theatres throughout the world, performing in fifty states and twenty different countries during his career. He is an award-winning director and choreographer with credits that include *Beautiful*, *Urinetown*, *Fully Committed*, *Footloose*, *Fame*, *Edges*, *Mamma Mia*, *Grease*, *The Producers*, *Hello Dolly*, *Eurydice*, and multiple productions of *West Side Story*. Michael holds a Bachelor of Arts in Theatre and Dance from SUNY at Buffalo and a Master of Fine Arts in Directing from Florida State University.

Nathan James is Managing Director of the Dang Theatre and Dance Syllabus and former Director of HE Programmes at the Urdang Academy, London. A former dancer, he has sailed the high seas for Celebrity and Princess cruise lines, worked in several regional productions, and appeared in the Broadway revival production of *42nd Street* in Stuttgart, Germany. He is an international dance adjudicator for several organisations, an examiner for the ISTD, and has recently created a graded examination syllabus for young performers in Musical Theatre training. He was awarded his MA in Professional Practice from Middlesex University and a PhD in Dance from the University of Roehampton.

Ariel Nereson is an Associate Professor of Dance Studies and Director of Graduate Studies in the Department of Theatre and Dance at the University at Buffalo, SUNY. She is the author of *Democracy Moving: Bill T. Jones, Contemporary American Performance, and the Racial Past* (2022), as well as numerous essays about movement-based performance, race, and embodiment in the United States. Her research has been recognized with the Gerald Kahan Scholar's Prize from the American Society for Theatre Research and, most recently, the Robert A. Schanke Theatre Research Award from the Mid-America Theatre Conference. She is also a practicing choreographer and dramaturg.

Adrienne Gibbons Oehlers recently completed her PhD in Theatre at The Ohio State University and was a recipient of the AAUW American Fellowship for 2022–23. Her research interests are centered on musical theatre and ensemble work, focusing on unison, community, and constructions of gender and race. Her interest in ensembles stems from her professional experience in musical theatre, appearing in numerous regional theatres, national and European tours, as a Radio City Rockette, and on Broadway in the original cast of *The Producers*. Her work has been published in *Studies in Musical Theatre* and the edited collection *Gender, Sex, and Sexuality in Musical Theatre: He/She/They Could Have Danced All Night*. Adrienne teaches musical theatre history, African American theatre history, and race and gender on the American stage as well as voice, movement, and acting.

Amanda Jane Olmstead (she/her) received her PhD in Theatre and Performance Studies from the University of Pittsburgh, MA in Performance Studies from New York University, and BA in Theatre and Dance from the Indiana University of Pennsylvania. She teaches several classes in the Theatre department at the University of Pittsburgh, School of Drama at Carnegie Mellon University, and the English, Communications, and Literature department at Golden Gate University. Her research focuses on theatre history, choreography, embodied dramaturgy, and performance as a tool for communication. She has published an article titled "Développé: Katherine Dunham's Diasporic Dance" in the *Studies in Musical Theatre Journal* and continues to actively practice as a choreographer and director.

Kim Varhola is Assistant Professor of Drama and Musical Theatre at Keimyung University in Daegu, South Korea. She has appeared on Broadway in *Rent*, *Flower Drum Song*, *Thoroughly Modern Millie*, *Pacific Overtures*, and on regional stages throughout the US. As a concert director, she has created events for Broadway Cares/Equity Fights AIDS, East West Players, Kia Motors, Samsung, Sejong Center for the Performing Arts, the National Theater of Korea, and the Seoul Philharmonic. Kim holds an MA in Arts Administration from Columbia University, an MA in Cinema Studies from New York University, and a BS in Theatre from Northwestern University. She resides in Seoul with her husband and two sons.

Alexandra Joye Warren is currently Assistant Professor of Performing Arts at Elon University and a director/choreographer for the Music Theatre program. She is the Founding Artistic Director of JOYEMOVEMENT dance company. JOYEMOVEMENT has performed regionally and toured nationally including Opening Night of the American Dance Festival and at Thomas Jefferson's Monticello in collaboration with activist Bree Newsome. Alexandra performed, choreographed, and taught in New York performing with Christal Brown's INSPIRIT, a dance company. Alexandra has been fortunate to work on projects with Bill T. Jones in development of FELA!, Paloma and Patricia McGregor's Angela's Pulse, Maxine Montilus, Sydnie L. Mosley Dances, Maverick Dance Experience, Van Dyke Dance Group, and the Black On Black Project. She received her BA in Drama with a concentration in Dance/Pre-Medicine from Spelman College and her MFA in Dance Performance from University of North Carolina at Greensboro.

Kevin Winkler enjoyed a career of more than twenty years as a curator, archivist, and administrator at the New York Public Library, prior to which he was a professional dancer. He is the author of *Big Deal: Bob Fosse and Dance in the American Musical*, which won the TLA George Freedley Memorial Award Special Jury Prize, was a finalist for the Marfield Prize, and was cited as an ALA/ACRL CHOICE Outstanding Academic title; *Everything is*

Choreography: The Musical Theater of Tommy Tune; and the forthcoming *On Bette Midler: A Divinely Opinionated Guide*. Kevin served as a consultant for Lincoln Center Education, curating resources to accompany PBS Lincoln Center Live performances available throughout New York City public libraries. He has blogged for the *Huffington Post* and is a MacDowell Colony fellow. Kevin is an on-camera commentator in the documentary *Merely Marvelous: The Dancing Genius of Gwen Verdon*. He holds a BA from San Diego State University, MLS from Columbia University, and MA from Hunter College.

Acknowledgments

We are forever grateful to Dom O'Hanlon and team for his guidance and support through this whole process. We would like to extend our sincere thanks to all our contributors for their expertise, hard work, and patience. The foundational seeds of this project were sown at the American Theatre for Higher Education Conference (ATHE) within the Music Theatre/Dance group whose support is ongoing with their facilitation of discussion and resources and continued contributions to the field. A special thanks to Ryan Donovan, Joanna Dee Das, and dance-focused panels that have brought into question what a musical theatre dance syllabus might look like. We would like to extend our thanks to Elizabeth Wollman and Jessica Sternfeld for their advice on the editing process. We are grateful for the support of the many excellent institutions that have made our work possible especially: The New York Public Library for the Performing Arts Billy Rose Theatre Division and Jerome Robbins Dance Division (Jeremy McGraw, Doug Reside, Annemarie van Roessel, and Arlene Yu), the Theatre on Film and Tape Archive, and the Schomburg Center for Research in Black Culture. Thank you to the University of Portsmouth, UK and the Creative and Cultural Industries faculty and Bucknell University Department of Theatre and Dance and Library and Information Technology for the research time and support; as well as the Bucknell University College of Arts and Sciences Dean's Office and Office of the Provost, who have partially supported this collection through grants and fellowships. A special thank you to all the professional artists and scholars who shared their invaluable knowledge, experiences, and network including Phil Chan, Julio Agustin, Laura Macdonald, Bryan Vandevender, George Burrows, and Ben Macpherson. A special thank you to the detailed work of Jessica Hinds-Bond in the editing process and keeping the direction of the book on track.

We thank our families and friends who have supported us with time and inspiration. Dustyn thanks her mom and dad (in spirit), her grandparents, Gramma Shirley A. Smith, and godmother Jodi-Ann Kasky for laying the foundation for her love and curiosity of musical theatre. She thanks Vida for her light and hours of watching dance clips and car-sing-a-longs, and Joe, for all of the editing and support in the form of time and love. Phoebe is forever grateful to her parents and extended family and friends for their continued interest and love of musical theatre and dance. She thanks Chuck for all his support, curiosity and partnership in life and in the seat next to her at so many wonderful performances.

Introduction

DUSTYN MARTINCICH AND PHOEBE RUMSEY

An ensemble of triple-threat dancers hitting long lines in perfect unison; catch steps and quick footwork executed in decisive patterns that make visible Cole Porter's syncopated notes; the captivating struts and sensuous hips that summon the bump of the drums and the slide of the trombone; the flowing fabric and hand properties that seem to extend from the body, creating, in collaboration with movement, spectacular effects; acting dancers who, through their bodies convey narrative and subtextual emotion, filling the liminal spaces of a production with motion and meaning: these instances all exemplify the fleeting and ephemeral circumstances of live performance that captured us both from an early age. Whether one's childhood memories are of watching family members rehearse for community musical revues or of making that special first trip to Broadway, movement thrills and inspires, imprinting on the body and mind. The delight of this book, we hope, is in its exploration of the visceral feeling of experiencing performance that is uniquely our own and yet is alive among a collective of participants in our shared bodily circumstances. The call of this book is to encourage others—whether spectator or performer, scholar or student—to take up the discussion and reading of dance in musical theatre from both the inside out (the experiences of the dancers themselves) and the outside in (the audience interpretation and critical analysis).

* * *

In planning for this collection, we aspired to offer readers new ways of thinking about dance as well as tools for reading dance in musical theatre. Dance is an essential component of musical theatre, as necessary to address as music and design: in centering it, we seek to uplift the body as a primary communicator of meaning in a musical production. We thus offer models of describing movement in musical theatre with the same kind of specificity that is already offered to music, analysis that moves beyond the aesthetic to consider nonverbal signifiers of identity, culture, time period, and social constructs. Additionally, we bring into focus aspects of labor, highlighting the ensemble both as a group and as individuals who have intrinsically contributed to meaning-making over the history of musical theatre productions. With these goals in mind, this volume's contributors point to the process in which dancers become part of a musical theatre production and work with choreographers to translate ideas, often without credit.

In laying the groundwork for this collection, we started with the acknowledgment that the study of musical theatre dance fuses practice and theory and incorporates embodied knowledge and histories that continue to be central to musical theatre. By taking part in the ongoing scholarly conversation surrounding musical theatre, this book explores (and celebrates) the role of movement and the body in shaping musical theatre, both on a grand historical scale and from show to show (and dancer to dancer). The contributors to this collection offer a variety of critical approaches through fifteen chapters, with the shared aim of creating an intersectional study where the body in motion is seen as an important component of the complex tapestry that is musical theatre where dance is woven together with the music, lyrics, narrative, design, and direction.

We encourage an engagement with musical theatre dance—as its own unique area of study that draws from theatre studies, dance studies, and performance studies—through a spectrum of modes of learning. It is assumed, often, that dance technique and choreography can only be accessed by those who also choose to practice at some level. In this volume, however, we model how practitioners and observers alike can document and discuss what they see using dynamic corporeal descriptions and analyses that open up a critical interrogation of the genre. Perhaps one was fortunate enough to have access to classes with teachers who had lived the experience of the Broadway musical and could share styles and trends, passing history from one body to the next in studios, training centers, conventions, and master classes. Maybe one was exposed to musical theatre dance through community and school theatre productions or YouTube and TikTok videos. Accessibility to, and understanding of, movement in musical productions is varied, and as such we aim to explain what musical theatre choreography *is* and what it can *do* at its core in such a way that encourages engagement with its function and impact on the form.

Key through lines in the collection center the discussion of the body as a site of meaning, one that is able to transmit narrative through its very existence. The unattainability of an exact definition of what a body can do is precisely the rapture of movement, dance, and choreography. Indeed, what a wonder that there is not more documentation of the body in motion in musical theatre throughout history—that is, beyond the precision or aesthetic appearance of a group of dancers, or the virtuosity or perceived sensuality of one soloist. Markedly, the goal of pinning down dance and dancers can never be fully attained; the genre itself revolves around motion and flow; the fleeting and the liminal. With these challenges in mind, we encourage others to interrogate what they see and experience when movement is intentionally employed through choreography in musical theatre.

In order to understand and demystify dance in terms of technical vocabulary, composition, and function for audiences, this volume models how to articulate observations of performance that are both personal and shared, underpinned by an understanding of how one's unique sense of aesthetics shapes their values and mode of interacting with the world. We foreground the work of the ensemble, incorporating firsthand and autoethnographic accounts that intersect with historical and cultural contexts. By centering these stories, we also seek to balance the contributions of the predominantly white men who are named in musical theatre accounts, highlighting practitioners and artists who identify as female and people of color. In so doing, we champion interdisciplinary approaches that contribute to a reframing of history and offer new perspectives.

The chapters in this book explore how the body can be a vehicle for storytelling and can open up discussions of identity, representation, and cultural norms of a time period. Contributors find commonalities in issues of identity, historical context, impact, and collective and collaborative labor. We provide two sections as a point of organization: The first section, "Choreography and Function" begins by offering a framework for how to read dance in a live musical production. This section includes an exploration of the many functions of dance in musical theatre and how musical theatre repertory has been established, alongside a historical contextualization of the shaping of the presence of dance in musical theatre. The second section, "Approaches to Choreography and the Body" explores approaches to musical theatre dance in the contemporary moment. This section looks at styles of dance that create a specific physical language to tell a story. In particular, this section explores the intersection of identity and meaning making and acknowledges the individual bodies performing the many variations of movement.

In each chapter, the experience of viewing and doing dance is discussed through a myriad of case studies, perspectives, and modalities. Our contributors come from varied backgrounds, locales, and careers, but they are united by an attachment to musical theatre dance as a way of thinking and moving through the world. We include interviews with and firsthand accounts from dancers, dance captains, movement directors, and repetiteurs, alongside personal reflection and critical analysis from scholars and practitioners alike. We are fortunate to have so many practitioners and working professionals contribute to this book, both as writers and as interlocutors who took the time to share their lived experiences. We have welcomed author's individual verbiage choices in regards to terms in order to give autonomy to our contributors. We acknowledge that chapters necessarily overlap and invite these happenings as a means to encourage ongoing conversations and considerations of dance and movement in musicals.

We draw the curtain back on the labor of dancers and the role of the dancer in the choreographic process. As such, we read, applaud, watch, listen to, and viscerally connect with bodies both onstage and off. Crucially, we recognize, following Diana Taylor, that the body is an archive.[1] That is, the body is the living archive of its experience, which, in the case of dancers, encompasses training, performances, and cultural influences. Dancers' bodies hold the legacy (and the choreography and movement languages) of those who have come before. Furthermore, the ensemble—understood in this way as a collective of bodily archives—draws on its members' unique body language, style, and embodied presence to translate meaning to the stage. Dancers might also act as muse, giving and finding inspiration in partnership with choreographers— whether this muse is Gwen Verdon to Bob Fosse or the dozens of Black dancers such as the Nicholas Brothers or Josephine Baker whose musicality and originality inspired choreographers to innovate a traditional form and spark new ideas, methods, styles, and ways of moving onstage. Taylor's work helps us understand how the body holds meaning and is rooted in a social and political environment: the body is entangled in debates over representation that will not subside in any visible future. We champion firsthand accounts throughout the book in order to bring to attention to these various actors and the many unique ways in which the dancer and the dancer's body contribute to creating (and to creating meaning in) dance and movement.

We point to important milestones in musical theatre dance and explain in accessible yet critical terms how the legacies of previous choreographers are saluted in homage today, while also problematizing the genre in terms of current social, cultural, and political issues.

---

[1]Diana Taylor, *The Archive and the Repertoire: Performing Cultural Memory in the Americas* (Durham, NC: Duke University Press, 2003).

Contributors interrogate key musical theatre case studies that use dance in a dramaturgically essential manner—that is, productions in which dance is interwoven in such a way as to be indispensable. Though the collection does point to case studies from an established "canon" of musical theatre history, chapters also bring to the fore choreographers, choreographic sequences, and productions that have otherwise been dismissed. It is our hope that looking at these examples in the context of the body points to metaphors they attend to or the representational work they do, as well as to their role in translating productions for new audiences.

This book comes at a time when the need to discuss dance as a primary driver of storytelling in musical theatre is all the more pressing. As choreography includes movement vocabulary and composition necessary to the storytelling, the bodies of performers, each inherently sharing their individual identities and cultural backgrounds, are key to the translation of meaning. Take the musical *Paradise Square* (2022), for example, in which choreographer Bill T. Jones employs classic ensemble dance both as a diegetic part of the musical structure and as a symbol of ethnic and racial identity, national identity, and resistance. The bodies engaging in the physical dialogues are fundamental to the narrative thrust of the show not only to add character information and define the world of the play, but also to dig into and support the subtextual and superficial elements of resistance particularly on the part of the African American enslaved community.

In terms of the historiography of dance in musical theatre, we point to its complex and troubled roots, and we reference how and by whom it has been recorded. The act of documenting dance in more traditional means of writing has captured only part of its history, preserving the legacy of only a few of the key players who have come to shape it as a form. The contributors of this collection engage with a myriad of archives beyond the body itself, including written descriptions of performances, video recordings from the Tony Awards, and holdings in physical archives such as the Theatre on Film and Tape Archive and the Billy Rose Theatre Division, both in the New York Public Library. Where possible, contributors distinguish between performances from the original Broadway cast and related contemporaneous interpretations such as a national tour or filmic version. We champion Liza Gennaro's call that musical theatre dance is a rich and highly varied field that deserves to be investigated as such: "within musical theater dance there exists multiple styles, aesthetics, and choreographic methods that have gone unrecognized in favor of viewing the form as a monolith characterized by chorus girls and boys performing dance combinations of commonly known steps."[2] This book represents a step in the process of righting that monolithic view, treating musical theatre dance as something to be studied in its own right, rather than subsumed under the disciplines of theatre or dance. Accordingly, part of the work of this book is to put forth methodologies for the nuanced study of musical theatre dance.

If musical theatre dance is still a new field, however, it does not exist in a vacuum. We acknowledge those scholars who have paved the way, using dance, theatre, and performance studies to engage in and support critical and historical analysis. This book stands on the shoulders of Genarro and other scholars who have centered the body and

---

[2]Liza Gennaro, *Making Broadway Dance* (Oxford: Oxford University Press, 2021), 218.

dance in musical theatre discourse (including Stacy Wolf, Mary Jo Lodge, Kelly Kessler, and many of the contributors to this collection); dance writers who have centered the body with vivid description in mainstream media (including Joan Acocella, Wendy Whelan, Ruthie Fierberg, and Sylviane Gold); and scholars from a broad range of fields who have pioneered interdisciplinary investigations into dance (including Susan Leigh Foster, Daphne Brooks, Jayna Brown, Lynn Garafola, Susan Manning, Constance Valis Hill, and Ann Cooper Albright).[3] We hope to grow the community around dance, bolster understandings of its role in musical theatre, and encourage others to talk and write about this exhilarating, mystifying, agonizing, exhausting, yet ultimately beautiful art form, one that, in all its many varieties, captivates the soul.

*   *   *

The chapters of this book allow for a broad discussion of historical figures, productions, and topics, providing multiple avenues into the study of musical theatre dance and facilitating additional social and cultural resonances. We encourage readers to enter the discussion wherever they find inspiration, and to note points where chapters work in discussion with one another.

The first chapter considers the various parts and conventions of musical theatre and the function of dance in the production's overall structure. Phoebe Rumsey provides simple and accessible descriptions of movement vocabulary and offers a methodological tool kit for readers to use in forming their own dance analysis and critique. This chapter sets the stage for subsequent contributions, introducing some of the many uses of dance in musical theatre, such as: revealing character psychology, functioning diegetically as part of the story, expressing an unspoken aspect of the libretto, forwarding the narrative, transitioning from scene to scene, and expressing emotions or ideas through metaphor or abstraction.

The second chapter contextualizes the historical formation of the genre of musical theatre dance as drawn from the convergence of a variety of styles and histories. Nathan James explores the roots of the form, from seventeenth- and eighteenth-century Western dance forms to early musical theatre iterations including minstrelsy, vaudeville, and musical revues. James moves on to identify some early practitioners that sought to create a genre of musical theatre dance through composition and movement vocabulary, among them Ned Wayburn, Seymour Felix, Albertina Rasch; and points to the work of practitioners who established training for dancers in musical theatre productions, such as Jack Cole and Luigi. James lays a basic grounding for the development of musical theatre dance that is then taken up and explored in specific directions in further chapters.

In chapter 3, Mijiang He and Dustyn Martincich address musical theatre dance training from a cross-national perspective, looking at approaches and practices in the United States and in China. They look at musical theatre dance as an evolving genre, with its own aesthetics and training methods that prepare performers for the industry. The authors also examine how these aesthetics and methods, through repetition and teaching processes, have

---

[3]Space limits a full listing, however further scholars whose work is essential to the field include, but are not limited to, Ryan Donovan, Bill Everett, Sherril Dodds, Julie Malnig, Brenda Dixon Gottschild, Anthea Kraut, Julia Foulkes, Jessica Sternfeld, Elizabeth Wollman, Millie Taylor, Nadine George-Graves, Thomas F. DeFranz and Dominic Symonds.

codified musical theatre as a dance "style" and established historical repertory. Offering a valuable viewpoint, He recounts his firsthand experiences performing in musical theatre productions in China, developing a training program for the imported art form, and teaching choreography as a function of training, often without the context of a full production.

The fourth chapter, by Adrienne Gibbons Oehlers, takes a historical perspective, centering on the function of the musical theatre dancing ensemble, as well as the social and cultural implications of its staging and compositional spatial formations. Oehlers highlights applications of line and circle and notes the varied ways in which individuals can be featured in a dancing group within a musical. Looking at the chorus "line" as it pertains to identity and cultural values, she further examines the early history of chorus lines like the Ziegfeld "ponies" as well as the Ziegfeld Girls, the dancers in the *Darktown Follies* (1914), the Tiller Girls, and the Radio City Rockettes, and points to trends and aesthetics still relied on today in musical theatre ensembles.

Amanda Jane Olmstead traces the history of reading the ensemble's narrative function in chapter 5, drawing connections from early works such as Katherine Dunham's *Cabin in the Sky* (1940), through contributions from Agnes De Mille and Jerome Robbins, to the contemporary choreographic approaches of Andy Blankenbuehler. Through her exploration of Blankenbuehler's process in creating movement vocabulary, bringing in other voices, and allowing for the creative contributions that tie character to movement, Olmstead asks the reader to consider the implications of imbuing the ensemble body with agency.

In chapter 6, Bud Coleman introduces the dream ballet concept and traces the through line of the convention from its earliest appearances through to the work of Albertina Rasch, Agnes de Mille, and beyond. This chapter includes an analysis of dream ballets of note, such as those in *Lady in the Dark* (1941), *Oklahoma!* (1943), and *Carousel* (1945), with an eye on explaining the role of dance as a plot-forwarding device, among other uses. This chapter also explores how, via the dream ballet, concert and classical dance are inserted into the musical theatre genre.

In chapter 7, Joanna Dee Das examines how dance conveys time on the musical theatre stage. Das argues that dance in musical theatre performances conveys multiple, simultaneous timescapes: not only the temporality of the audience ("real time") and the temporality of the action in the world of the play, but also sometimes the past or future worlds that characters envision, and, in the case of revivals, embodied echoes of the original show. After explaining important concepts related to thinking about temporality and musical theatre dance, such as diegetic/nondiegetic dance, nostalgia, and lyric and linear time, the chapter explores a variety of shows, including *The Pajama Game* (1953), *Anything Goes* (2011 revival), *Memphis* (2009), and *Hamilton* (2015), in which dance communicates overlapping temporalities in distinct ways.

In chapter 8, which starts off the second section, "Approaches to Choreography and the Body," Kevin Winkler explores how Golden Age musical choreographers celebrated the individual body, including the queer body, particularly through diegetic, performative numbers and trio formations. Winkler offers examples of the spectrum of gender expression through physical characterization from Agnes de Mille's choreography in *Oklahoma!* and Jerome Robbins's work in *West Side Story*, as well as instances of choreographers like Ron Field in *Applause* (1970), openly creating movement embracing sexual identity. Winkler then contrasts Bob Fosse's unique movement aesthetic with that of other Golden Age choreographers, examining how they celebrated bodies—and bodies in specific communities—differently, through case studies where Fosse eschewed opposite-sex couple dancing and instead foregrounded the individual body, giving space to envision a stage full of diverse genders and orientations.

In chapter 9, Kim Varhola offers two case studies not typically considered in musical theatre dance: *Pacific Overtures* (1976, 2004) and *Flower Drum Song* (1958, 2002). By examining the choreography and approaches set out for both the original productions and their more recent revivals, Varhola offers readings of the Asian American body staged in musical theatre choreography and ensembles. She looks in particular at what the choreography reveals about the challenges of succumbing to, resisting, and satirizing Asian Americanness in musical theatre productions. Varhola centers her work on questions of identity and the performance of authentic "Asianness," troubling questions of credible storytelling, cultural stereotypes, and representation at the core of choreographic and physical staging approaches in musical theatre productions.

In chapter 10, Benae Beamon foregrounds the subversive work of the chorus, focusing on Black women and their unique instantiation of subjectivity through historical consciousness. Citing examples from *Black and Blue* (1989) and *Shuffle Along, or, the Making of the Musical Sensation of 1921 and All That Followed* (2016), and interviews with ensemble members, this chapter focuses on speaking to the historical trajectory and its consequent impact on black subjectivity. Further, this chapter proposes that the chorus is actually at the center of the story, a shift in perspective that allows the space to engage subjectivity through the collective, particularly in the embrace of Black femininity.

Chapter 11 pointedly addresses the question of why Broadway musicals, like classical ballet, remained exclusively for the white elite for so long. Ramón Flowers points to audition and casting practices that facilitate this exclusivity and protect institutionalized racism. He explores how institutionalized racism remains operative in both musical theatre and concert dance, citing both examples of historical productions as well as his own experiences in both genres as he addresses the problems of stereotyping, typecasting, and tokenism. Flowers interrogates tools and methods to move into a new, more equitable and sustainable dance performance paradigm, uplifting the work of artist advocates like Phil Chan, who, with Georgina Pazcoguin, established the movement Final Bow to Yellowface to interrogate and reimagine systemically racist storytelling practices.

Chapter 12 offers a different approach to dance discussion by centering an interview between dancer and choreographer Tomé Cousin and Dustyn Martincich, with additional contextual framing from Phoebe Rumsey. This interview-style methodology champions the voices of dancers and the collaborative process by way of an exploration of the genesis of Susan Stroman's *Contact* (2000). Cousin draws on his embodied knowledge of the show, from the initial audition to its resetting with different casts, to discuss how *Contact* is at its heart a work of physical storytelling about one's experience in the world and relationships with others. This insider's perspective encourages readers to consider how dance transfers to the stage in a musical, and how a dance-centered musical like *Contact* made its way to Broadway.

Chapter 13, from Ariel Nereson, addresses the use of postmodern dance approaches and values in musical theatre dance through the example of Bill T. Jones's process and product in his work for *Spring Awakening* (2006). She defines the postmodern dance aesthetic as its own genre and in relation to its value and application in musical theatre dance, asserting that the postmodern dance aesthetic brought in by Jones inherently opposes what Elizabeth Wollman terms as the "machinery" of Broadway productions. She points to Jones's work as inspiration and groundwork for Spencer Liff, who choreographed Deaf West's revival of *Spring Awakening* that came to Broadway in 2015, as well as Broadway choreographers like John Heginbotham and Raja Feather Kelly.

In chapter 14, Michael D. Jablonski and Dustyn Martincich tackle movement direction as a distinct approach to dance in musical theatre productions, highlighting the roots of movement direction in early European *Ausdruckstanz*, Rudolf von Laban's work, and physical theatre studies. Translating different dance and theatre approaches to musical theatre stages, the chapter highlights the work of Jerome Robbins, Kate Flatt, and Steven Hoggett before focusing on two recent case studies: Peter Darling's choreography for *Matilda the Musical* (Broadway, 2013) and Kelly Devine's choreography for *Come from Away* (2017). Highlighting Jablonski's personal experience in productions of 2009 Broadway revival of *West Side Story* and Broadway production of *Matilda* as well as an interview he conducted with Kelly Devine, the authors consider the integration of choreography and stage direction, the ways that acting methods support character-driven storytelling, and the implications for choreographic interpretation by the dancers.

The final chapter, by Dustyn Martincich and Alexandra Joye Warren, sets forth a discussion about contemporary musical theatre choreography and approaches to movement, centering the work of Camille A. Brown, who has rethought the possibilities of dance for a deeper, more inclusive understanding of humanity. As new stories are being made for the stage, the chapter explores the importance of cultural consciousness and context in the creative process and rehearsal room, and the ways that dance has integrated identity and representation, often through the use of social dances. As dance continues to be a tool to convey cultural identity and community, the authors look to additional examples from Sonya Tayeh, Spencer Liff, Sam Pinkleton, and Sidi Larbi Cherkaoui, exploring how the choreographers signal and shape identity through movement vocabulary and composition.

* * *

This book is the product of a shared belief that the discussion of dance in musical theatre must involve multiple stakeholders: dancers, choreographers, scholars, and practitioners. This book has brought together those who have been in the trenches doing eight shows a week for many years and those deep in the archives, sleuthing out the records of the impact and presence of dance from the beginning of the genre itself. While we look to honor the work of predecessors, we need to expand the acknowledgment of these predecessors to the laborers who contributed to the history we know now. Though the musical theatre genre is growing, with contemporary practitioners working to create a more inclusive space with new stories and thereby new kinds of movement, its history needs decolonization. Musical theatre's engrained practice and training remain tied to a strictly ballet-based jazz dance form and the styles of very few choreographers and it is our hope that this book introduces new practitioners and influences to the form.

Rather than privileging text, we look at the people, their bodies, their experiences, and the unique perspective they bring. By broadening the focus from choreographers, we reveal erasures of varied influences on dance in musical theatre, whether it be a performer's social dance experiences from their youth or traditional folk dances from their community. We continue to uncover those who have seen their choreographic contributions minimized: like Herbie Harper, who worked with George Balanchine on *On Your Toes* (1936), or Honi Coles and Cholly Atkins, who worked with Agnes de Mille in *Gentleman Prefer Blondes* (1949). In that vein, we recognize that an absolutely essential part of the history of musical theatre that often isn't covered is the creative process of dance. This process can be a meeting point between practice and theory, and looking at how the choreography is created (as many chapters in this volume do) helps inform how audiences might ingest it. Further focus on process will ultimately point to the labor of the ensemble in how dance is created, as well as the dramaturgical support and evidence rooted in how the performers translate character, through movement, to an audience.

This volume also calls attention to the material spaces of musical theatre dance, which is hardly limited to Broadway and West End stages. Scholars must witness, support, and document musical theatre productions off-Broadway, in regional and community spaces, on large and small screens, and in other digital spaces. While live musicals are the subject of this book, the history of stage musicals is influenced by Hollywood, television, and camera movement. Such influences were at the root of Michael Bennett's dream of staging the cinematic transitions of *Dreamgirls* (1981), and inspired Sonia Tayeh to imitate the work of the camera through continuous action in *Moulin Rouge* (2019). Additionally, the transmission of styles and modes of dance in musical theatre fuels continued pursuit of the genre, whether at a professional or an amateur level. Whether one sees a musical live, in a windowless archive, via a smartphone, in a community theatre, or on an app, the continued transmission of the latest styles and trends keeps the pulse of the genre beating with much fervor and that next new production. Kinesthetic quotation and referential choreography have helped define musical theatre history through the bodies that have performed the roles, and through the audiences who took the movement home to make it their own. Accessible and exciting choreography is passed down from the largest stages through dance studio teachers and community theatre and high school directors to their students, casts, and audiences. Furthermore, musical theatre dance can thrive outside of the stage context by ways of revues, cabarets, social media, and other online platforms. As a prime example, Trevor Boffone's new work on social media and Broadway dance, particularly TikTok, sheds light on and celebrates the innovative work being put forth in the digital realm.

* * *

The remarkable production numbers of musical theatre live on in our memories, like the Ballet Bloopers staged by Rob Marshall in the 1994 *Damn Yankees* revival, or the hilarious "On a Sunday by the Sea" from *High Button Shoes* (1947), staged in the 1989 *Jerome Robbins' Broadway*. There are the thrilling opening numbers that immediately hook the audience through movement, like those in Graciela Daniele's *Ragtime* (1998), Kate Prince's *Everybody's Talking About Jamie* (West End, 2017), Lynne Page's *La Cage aux Folles* (2010), and Susan Stroman's *Steel Pier* (1997); high-energy, midshow numbers such as George Faison's "Ease on Down the Road" in *The Wiz* (1975), Christopher Gatelli's "Seize the Day" in *Newsies* (2017), and Peter Darling's meticulous repetition in the "Days" numbers of *Groundhog Day* (2017); and signature closers like Michael Bennett's "One" in *A Chorus Line* (1975) are deeply imprinted on our experience of live performance. Numbers like these provide that "wow" factor that takes our breath away while employing social dance, movement, and gesture to signal a period and a mood. There are star dance moments, like Chita Rivera's captivating versatility in Vincent Patterson and Rob Marshall's *Kiss of the Spiderwoman* (1985), Karen Ziemba's utter joy as the Wife in Susan Stroman's *Contact* (1999), or Michael Berresse's gymnastic feats as Bill Calhoun in Warren Carlye's choreography for *Kiss Me, Kate* (1999). Production numbers such as these (and others) not only make the world of the show move by employing classic, musical theatre dance traditions in form and content, but also offer audiences stylistic movement or virtuosic features that cement the work in its own time period, reminding audiences that movement is a key component to theatricality, merging the past and present in the bodies of dancing performers. As Cynthia Onrubia, legendary Broadway dancer and Robbins's right hand in restaging works for *Jerome Robbins' Broadway*, said in re-creating Robbins's work: "Character first above all else."[4] We see the characters onstage, and they are burned in our memory, whether it is Ariana DeBose's bullet in *Hamilton* (2015), Gabrielle Hamilton's interpretation of the "Dream Ballet" in Daniel Fish's *Oklahoma!* (2018), or Patina Miller's Leading Player in *Pippin* (2013). These performers' sense of nuance, the energy in their little finger: we are enraptured, drawn in, and compelled to write, move, research, share, talk, present, illustrate, uplift, and express our reaction to those performances in a way that is drawn from our own personal and deep reaction to their bodies in motion.

Interdisciplinary connections are vital to understanding musical theatre movement and its impact beyond the borders of the stage. Musical theatre is a socially, culturally driven art form reflective of its time and place. One could study musical theatre, as with so many arts, through a multitude of other lenses: anthropology, sociology, engineering, management, literature, political science, or gender studies. However, in our effort to support musical theatre as its own field of study, we seek to amplify intensive, dedicated study of its practices. This pursuit will better inform future interdisciplinary readings, as well as reshape broader understandings of musical theatre. As Gennaro asserts, "positioning dance at the forefront of musical theatre examination encourages a re-thinking of the musical theatre canon."[5]

Our field has transformed from a time when, as Gennaro notes, "most Broadway choreography was deemed disposable and never properly notated." Today, choreographers, assistant choreographers, dance captains—and dancers—are at the forefront of cultivating space for visibility and inclusivity on the stage.[6] This process involves, in part, acknowledging that the body conveys narrative simply by being in space. This turn in musical theatre dance works in tandem with more inclusive stories being brought to the genre, allowing new and previously disregarded audiences to see themselves onstage.

The depth of physicality in shows such as *A Strange Loop* that debuted off Broadway in 2019 and went on to win the 2020 Pulitzer for Drama or *Head Over Heels* (2019) does more than thrill and tell a story; it reaches out to these broader audiences. And, notably, the bodily impact in each of these mile markers is only just being felt. Though musical theatre has frequently been a space that celebrates queerness—and though queer movement traditions

---

[4]Ruthie Fierberg, "Remounting Jerome Robbins' Historic Choreography for City Center's *High Button Shoes*," *Playbill*, May 6, 2019.
[5]Gennaro, *Making Broadway Dance*, 218.
[6]Gennaro, 3.

are a vital part of many musical theatre and jazz dance–influenced vocabularies—trans and queer actors and dancers are even today rarely cast in musicals. The shows of today are but the start of a renewed legacy for a form that engages with all the complexity and messiness in our society, complexity that can often only be understood by means of the visceral, intuitive, elemental mode of movement. History continues to be uncovered as we learn more stories that have been erased, marginalized, or forgotten. The more we can fill out our history of dance and the moving body in musical theatre, the better we can understand this history's connections to contemporary pieces and shine light on what was not covered by popular media at the time.

We acknowledge that this is only a starting point, particularly in incorporating the research and embodied histories of so many dancers and others who may identify as nonbinary and people of color. We are confident that future research in musical theatre dance will grow as interdisciplinary efforts expand, as embodied knowledge becomes more accepted as a legitimate source worthy of citation beyond ethnographic studies, as identity is further centered in understandings of culture and arts, and as access to musical theatre dance continues to grow through digital spaces. We also call out to the audience members and practitioners who are essential participants in this work, to empower them not only to see the body in dance, but to talk about it as a powerful place of meaning-making in this exciting art form, sharing descriptions with as much care and crafting as one would about any other part of a production.

And, finally, please can we have a Tony Award for ensembles already!

Bibliography

Fierberg, Ruthie. "Remounting Jerome Robbins' Historic Choreography for City Center's *High Button Shoes*." *Playbill*, May 6, 2019.

Gennaro, Liza. *Making Broadway Dance*. Oxford: Oxford University Press, 2021.

Taylor, Diana. *The Archive and the Repertoire: Performing Cultural Memory in the Americas*. Durham, NC: Duke University Press, 2003.

Section I Choreography and Function

1   Reading Dance: The Body in Motion Onstage

PHOEBE RUMSEY

Lights rise on the silhouettes of bodies of all sizes and postures. The thumping of drums inspires a toe-tapping beat, and each person—facing a different focus point, standing or seated, legs crossed, open, or askew—digs their heel into the floor in their own way. Boots thump, running shoes stomp, and the music is loud. The triumphant folk-meets-pop beat is felt in the core. In the individuality of the stomp, the choreography reveals how each character embodies their presence in this tiny town at the far eastern edge of Canada, nicknamed "the Rock." A series of micro-monologues are interspersed throughout the song. The movement, though minimal, is consistent in its time-keeping pulse. Shoulders roll and heels wedge into the floor with increasing emphasis as the music builds toward the chorus of the song. As the lyrics repeatedly claim "I am an Islander," the townsfolk strike the same pedestrian pose: a mid-level crouch, in a parallel position, one foot in front of the other. In unison, they engage in two stamps with the right foot, then replace the right with the left, step back with the left and forward with the right, and clap. In this moment, at the height of the song's chorus in the opening song of the 2017 musical *Come from Away*, multiple influences and styles are visible: a touch of body percussion, a nod toward a jig in the footwork, and a borrowing of rhythmic stomp-heel drops from tap dance. The same sequence is repeated each time the chorus of the song comes around, with growing bodily commitment and insistence in each iteration. The moment is thrilling and welcoming in its homespun grittiness and heart wrenching in its earnestness and its physicalizing of inner strength.

Why does this assemblage of commonplace steps work on so many physical and emotional levels? This choreography, created by Kelly Devine, works in part because an assortment of bodies perform the steps together yet decidedly marked by their own physicality, clear character objectives, full focus, and commitment to their physical engagement with the piece. In the intersection between unison movement and the individual identities and postures that are set forth in the opening of the musical, the roots, beliefs, styles, and passion of a community living in the far-off town of Gander, Newfoundland, come to life. The music and lyrics signify an unbridled pride in place and bring the six-minute opening to a peak. The dozen or so counts of choreography are aesthetically engaging because they mesh together. The embodied resonance of the group launches the performative conceit of the show: kindhearted, no-nonsense, individual goodwill at a moment of global crisis.

Come from Away, the Tony Award–winning musical with lyrics, music, and book written by Irene Sankoff and David Hein, tells the story of a place and people at a very dark moment in history: the terrorist attacks of September 11, 2001. A light in the darkness is focused on

Image 1.1 "Welcome to the Rock," *Come from Away* (2017). Photo by Matthew Murphy.

Gander as the small community had no choice but to welcome approximately seven thousand people to their tiny town when planes had to be grounded due to the closure of North American air space. "Welcome to the Rock," the opening song of the musical, is a tour de force that introduces the characters, the place, and then the "event." The opening offers up a snapshot of the moment when this town, and more broadly the world, tuned into the television or radio and heard of the attacks. Much of the affect is achieved through movement and body language. Devine's choreographic choices pointedly demonstrate how movement can be tied to place, character, and event. The physical and musical dynamics express the sublime moment of realization: the clipped beats transform into an airy soaring melody of long, lifted tones and Devine shifts the hard-hitting movement to more sustained stances; the performers rock slowly forward and back toward the audience in unison. They then point to the ground, indicating the presentness of time and place not to be forgotten. The song splinters into many rhythmic layers of voice and music. Subtle choreographic choices such as the slow shifting of focus from midline to high, along with collective breathing with shoulders rising and falling, illustrate the endurance and hope in the community and, more broadly, connect the audience to that visceral experience of the body in moments of crisis. Musicians take the stage, their own physicality adding to the embodied impact. Performers gesture skyward with open hands that abruptly clamp into fists as heels drop into the floor, resuming the upbeat tempo. The intense commitment to shared physicalized expressions—whether that be precise choreography or individual body language—sustains the possibility for the audience to intuitively connect to the moment.

The embodied tenacity in the vocabulary, composition, and visualization of *Come from Away*, along with the dynamic charge in the simple steps, conveys the power of movement in performance. There is no highly choreographed Broadway-style jazz dance in this musical; the movement signature uniquely suits the group of townspeople. There are no kicklines or virtuosic feats of athleticism, and yet the musical *moves*. Whether it is called dance, physical theatre, movement, or body language, the "fervent use of the body" as described by dance scholar Susan Leigh Foster allows for a unique understanding of our humanity and physical potential distinct from the analysis of the written word or historical artifact.[1] The reading of dance and movement, which Foster defines as "the active and interactive interpretation of dance as a system of meaning," requires a variety of observational tools.[2] This chapter highlights an assortment of approaches to reading dance in an effort to champion the analysis of dance and movement onstage as a key point of meaning-making often overlooked in musical theatre analysis. Musical theatre dance, as described by Liza Gennarro, is a "unique, distinct genre in the history of American dance," and this chapter aims to put forth the tools to recognize, analyze, and ultimately uphold the genre for all it brings to musical theatre and to dance more broadly.[3]

A Space for Dance

In choreography of any kind—whether movements are rooted in the everyday such as that put forward by Devine in *Come from Away*, or, the ballet-based jazz of Jerome Robbins; the sexy, nuanced gestures of Bob Fosse; the urban angles and articulation of Andy Blankenbuehler; the sophisticated patterns of Susan Stroman; the contemporary moves of Camille A. Brown; or the street-style hoofin' of Savion Glover—the body in motion opens up the possibility for a visceral connection to an audience. Expressly, by connecting to the audience on an embodied level, the body makes another layer of meaning available. In 2009, David Savran argued that musical theatre can be a "barometer of cultural and social politics" and a means to comprehend one's place in the world.[4] This mode of thinking has opened the door for musical theatre to be investigated as much more than an entertainment offering. The multifarious uses, roles, devices, tools, and styles of moving bodies onstage are integral pieces of the broader and ongoing desire to understand ourselves in the world. If we are to continue the campaign to bring musical theatre into a critical discourse about social culture, we must galvanize conversations about the body onstage, forge frames of empathy, and understand the body's function outside of the materiality of words and musical scores.

Pointedly, few reviews and critiques of musical theatre describe, evaluate, or interrogate the moving body at any length: there is simply not often the time or space to go into that depth of investigation. As a result, the liminal, or fleeting, quality of movement is often mentioned only briefly, if at all. Critics with experience in dance are more apt to examine the style or quality of moves but still tend to emphasize the book, score, singing, and acting. The goal of this book, as outlined in the introduction, is to model how to read the body in motion onstage and to empower students, scholars, and theatregoers to take on that challenge.

---

[1]Susan Leigh Foster, *Reading Dancing: Bodies and Subjects in Contemporary American Dance* (Berkeley: University of California Press, 1986), xv.
[2]Susan Leigh Foster, 1986, xv.
[3]Liza Gennaro, *Making Broadway Dance* (Oxford: Oxford University Press, 2021), 4.
[4]David Savran, "The Do-Re-Mi of Musical Theatre Historiography," in *Changing the Subject: Marvin Carlson and Theatre Studies, 1959–2009*, ed. Joseph Roach (Ann Arbor: University of Michigan Press, 2009), 230.

Furthermore, the aim is to demystify dance and to offer ideas on how discussions on dance in musical theatre can be better incorporated into critiques, classrooms, and studios. This chapter suggests numerous means to articulate dance effectively, to demonstrate how it entwines with the other elements in performance, and to explore those intersections.

By turning to the body as a critical mode of analysis, and using thick description in connection with the investigation of who is moving and why, one is able to open up a conversation about musical theatre that comes from a place of familiarity and yet recognizes difference. We all have a body, but explicitly not *that* body onstage; we all move, but not in *that* way in front of us. The body is innately familiar, elemental, and intuitive, and yet, by virtue of the distance and unknowability of another's body, the study of bodies in motion can be mystifying. While the tools, language, vocabulary, and observational skills of describing movement may not be readily available to all, there is the potential of shared humanity and a common awareness of how bodies move. In fact, we are perhaps more connected to bodies in motion than we are to the complex musical language of the score or the structure of the libretto. What follows are numerous approaches to investigating dance, as well as suggestions toward starting conversations and formulating ideas around and about dance, movement, and choreography. In essence, as the opening description of *Come from Away* illustrates, a movement-based narrative has the potential to engage, challenge, and inspire readers to think more deeply about performance.

Where Do I Look?

When viewing performance, there is a lot to take in at once. Furthermore, choreography in a musical is much more ephemeral than the score, book, or libretto. While some shows can be watched again on streaming sites, or through excerpts from the Tony Awards on YouTube (where the opening song from *Come from Away* is available for viewing), musicals are rarely available in their entirety on most platforms. Excellent archives such as the Theatre on Film on Tape (TOFT) at the New York Public Library do exist but are often limited in terms of location for those not in New York City. The ephemerality of dance and the difficulty of re-viewing what was witnessed may result in students, critics, and musical theatre enthusiasts backing away from describing dance. It can be much more challenging to rely on memory than on material evidence such as a score or a script. Keen observation of dance in the moment becomes key. And, with that, fundamental challenges emerge.

Common questions arise when one is attempting to describe movement, dance, or choreography: Where do I look? What should I watch out for? How do I interpret what is happening onstage? How do I *read* dance? To start, defining what it is to read the meaning of dance—to use Foster's phrasing—can be helpful toward organizing a methodology for critically analyzing dance.[5] First, there is the question of what a body can do and what it is

---

[5]Dance studies and performance studies offer a plethora of ideas and theories regarding the body as an object of study. This chapter engages with several, though limits of space preclude extensive study. Several resources to look to that explore philosophies of the body in motion include: Susanne Franco and Marina Nordera, eds., *Dance Discourses: Keywords in Dance Research* (London: Routledge, 2007);

capable of. The answer will naturally be different from performer to performer, as well as from audience member to audience member. Despite how much uniformity is valued in dance, a body will never move exactly the same each time, or exactly like another. This understanding can offer a sense of freedom for the observer. Likewise, this recognition of difference may help ease the anxiety felt by many in attempting to assess something they may not be able to do themselves or at least not at the highly accomplished level put forth by performers onstage in a musical. Considering the body as a shifting and transforming object of investigation that happens in the liminal moment of performance helps to pinpoint what the dancing body is *doing* onstage beyond choreographed steps. Furthermore, recognizing how the body is coded (socially and/or politically) given the specific contexts of both the piece and the production fosters critical insight.

For the spectator, the act of sitting in a theatre immersed in all the conventions, thrills, and theatricality of musical theatre can make for a variety of challenges for critical focus. The rapture of an all-singing, all-dancing form with technological feats such as a rotating stage, lifts, onstage musicians, digital enhancements, and projections can distract from maintaining a singular focus on movement. How does one tune in to the dance, the movement, the bodies in this mélange of stimulus, and the collaborative and often integrated nature of the genre? Again, at its most basic—where is one supposed to look?

Pointedly, in working with the director to integrate movement into the songs and narrative, the choreographer is trying to communicate something and has the expectation or hope that spectators will understand their vision, which is translated and augmented by the work of the performers.[6] As such, it is the choreographer's task to bring spectators along, as opposed to it being the spectators' task to figure out what the choreographer wants them to see. In this manner, then, allowing oneself the freedom to watch, interrogate, and pick apart movement that seems interesting can alleviate the pressure to guess the choreographic intention. Pay attention to what your eye is drawn to. Perhaps it is the larger patterns being made onstage by the ensemble, or perhaps it is that one person who is slightly ahead or behind, taller or shorter, similar to one's self or different.

The potential entry points are many. A student recently explained that they prefer analyzing movement based on the kind of shoes the performer is wearing. This point of focus offers an intriguing line of inquiry. Even if the movement/dance technique is unfamiliar, the shoe style worn by a performer can help us connect to the dance style. For example, if performers are wearing high-heeled pumps or character shoes, the situation may be more formal, or as part of a show in the narrative. If the dancers are in bare feet, then the dance style may be more contemporary and grounded, or perhaps the setting is outdoors. Furthermore, the choice of shoes affects the movement quality and the holding and

---

Randy Martin, *Critical Moves: Dance Studies in Theory and Politics* (Durham, NC: Duke University Press, 1998); André Lepecki, *Exhausting Dance: Performance and the Politics of Movement* (New York: Routledge, 2006); and Ann Cooper Albright, *Choreographing Difference: The Body and Identity in Contemporary Dance* (Middletown, CT: Wesleyan University Press, 1997).

[6]One thing to consider, particularly in regard to the presentation of communities onstage, is that areas of the movement or stage blocking can variously be attributed to the director, the choreographer, and the two in collaboration. Furthermore, the performers are often encouraged to offer personal dance styles or movement qualities, particularly if they have training in a style the choreographer does not.

placement of weight. An examination of the musical *Kinky Boots* (2013) from the perspective of footwear might fruitfully connect movement and identity. Perhaps looking at the use of ballet shoes versus miner's work boots in *Billy Elliot* (2008) would make for a productive entry into movement analysis.

Another student mentioned that they were fascinated by dances they had seen their parents do. Here is another potential entry point: identifying social dances in a musical and examining when and where social dance happens can reveal much about the community being explored onstage. Moreover, looking for dances that one's parents or grandparents might have done is a good way to identify social dances from a previous era and begin to consider their historical significance. Discovering the meaning behind those social dances, and looking at how they are weighted and executed,[7] can unveil an entire branch of investigation that is built on the social and cultural meaning of dance.[8] For example, the loose style of the Charleston, along with the unconstrained clothing associated with it, can denote female empowerment and a break away from strict postures and form-fitting clothing. Additionally, movement often works in tandem with other visual factors to signal and enhance meaning within the narrative. As such, looking at how lights change within the dance or how set pieces move alongside or within the choreography can be helpful in understanding the shifting of emotions, ideas, or time frames.

On the whole, anyone who seeks to engage with dance in musical theatre should find an anchor point that interests them to connect to the broader structure of the musical. Dance intersects with all aspects of the musical (the libretto, the music, the design, the acting, and so on); it does not exist on its own. Identifying the movement's connection to the other elements can be a good introduction toward uncovering a more layered interpretation of visual storytelling. Moving forward, this chapter offers a compilation of approaches to reading dance that are accessible and supported by examples from familiar musicals, as well as methods from other practitioners and scholars. The ultimate goal is to give the reader a myriad of options to draw from.

Solos and Ensembles

Musicals commonly incorporate both solo and ensemble dancing. The question of how many people are onstage can be a straightforward place to begin engaging with dance in musical theatre.[9] While solo choreography is rarer (Cassie in *A Chorus Line* [1975] or Louise on the beach in *Carousel* [1945], for example), the use of one person as a building block

---

[7]*Weighted* is a movement term. A dance that is described as being weighted can mean one with much bend in the knee joints and with body weight equal across all four corners of the foot. One's weight can be forward or back if they are mostly on their toes and ball of the foot. Conversely, one's weight can be back, meaning with a heavy heel; in that case they might walk heel toe, rather than toe heel.

[8]Julie Malnig's edited collection Ballroom, Boogie, Shimmy Sham, Shake: A Social and Popular Dance Reader (Chicago: University of Illinois Press, 2009) is an excellent source on context and intertext of social dances and identifying and analyzing social dance from a variety of eras.

[9]For more on formation and ensembles, see Adrienne Gibbons Oehlers's chapter in this volume.

toward a full ensemble dance is a common and effective way to build excitement, tension, or dramatic impact. Dance in this manner works in tandem with the voice as the transition to ensemble is accompanied by the addition of voices, harmonies, multiple solo lines, and rousing choruses, facilitating an emotional build. Examples here include "Tonight" in *West Side Story* (1961) and "One More Day" in *Les Misérables* (1985), where an increase in the number of voices and bodies onstage helps launch the piece to its climax. A unique movement build can be found in the 2019 revival of *Kiss Me, Kate* (1948), specifically in Cole Porter's dynamic piece "Too Darn Hot." Choreographer Warren Carlyle begins with one tap dancer, who is joined by two others, who are by the end joined by the entire ensemble cast, executing exuberant tuck jumps in unison.

Observations of who is moving and who is not can also open up a conversation about character and the question of why some characters "get" to dance in the narrative. A movement analysis of this sort can reveal character relationships and dynamics. For example, if the characters from an older generation are watching the younger generation dance, such as in the song "Shipoopi" in *The Music Man* (1957) or in the Heart Mountain Dance in *Allegiance* (2016), knowledge can be gained about the relationship between generations. Familial tensions might be revealed by reactions to the quality of movements each generation presents as seen in the use of social dance. Investigating that conflict could open the door to a broader sociopolitical discussion and, ultimately, a greater understanding of the musical itself.

Unison and Non-Unison Movement

The distinction between unison and non-unison movements can be a valuable point of focus for those seeking to read what is happening onstage. Have groups of dancers been established? Does one group move differently than another group? In the case of *West Side Story*, for example, the Sharks and Jets have different styles of moving, and those divergent qualities help establish the identity politics between the groups. In fact, *West Side Story* choreographer Jerome Robbins gives each group a dance number of their own in the musical to reinforce their differences via movement. "Cool" is a song and dance moment that fits the Jets' low-to-the-ground and percussive jazz style, and "America" combines punctuated accents with a variety of Latin influences for the Sharks. Comparing and contrasting the two numbers reveals character motives, cultural assumptions, and even the creative team's broader intentions in the musical.

If the performers are not in unison, an examination of the differences in the ways they dance can reveal dramatic intention. Often choreographers use canons to emphasize movements by way of repetition. Similar to a song sung in the round ("Row, Row, Row Your Boat," for example), canon work can create a sort of kaleidoscopic effect in the dance and give multiple layers of movement for interpretation. This effect is easily achieved by having dancers start a movement phrase a couple of counts after one another. *On the Town* (1944) begins with three sailors on shore leave entering one after another doing the same jumping kicks and turns. This choice emphasizes their similarities as members of the Navy, yet it also allows them to add their own character intonations and unique physicality as well as physicalize certain themes and variations in the score.

Revivals and Ghosts of Past Choreographers

Broadway commonly revives musicals. In fact, the revival concept has become so popular that a separate Tony Award for Best Revival of a Musical was added in 1994.[10] This practice leads to fascinating effects as the time and place when a show is revived directly impacts the subtext and undercurrent of the show, no matter when it is set. Studying the context and appearance of revivals can often lead into a discussion of the ongoing developments in society in contrast with the past. Not only do revivals typically have different dancing from the original, but dance is often the only malleable area of a revival, as librettos and scores are commonly fixed.[11] The choreography in revivals can be the most exciting and anticipated change. Liza Gennaro points out how investigating different choreographers' interpretations of musical theatre revivals can lead to a deeper understanding of what movement can do, as well as provide insight into the challenges new choreographers face when working with a show whose original production was quite successful. Gennaro explains, "the ghosts of choreographers past loom heavily just about everywhere: in stage directions, dance arrangements, sound recordings, and cultural memory."[12] Take for example Trevor Nunn and Susan Stroman's 1998 revival of the 1943 musical *Oklahoma!* Though choreographer Stroman specifically requested permission to translate the dances in her own style, the stylings and gestures of original choreographer Agnes de Mille haunt the production by way of contrast, particularly because the 1955 film (choreographed by de Mille) is so broadly known.

Gennaro further emphasizes the potential that Broadway dance, specifically jazz dance, has to express emotion. Though there are many iterations of shows, she writes, dance can be "a rich declaration of human experience that remains current as it morphs through the decades, maintaining a profound and consistent presence in Broadway dance."[13] This brings up the question of stylistic shifts. In *Hamilton* (2015), for example, choreographer Andy Blankenbuehler uses a variety of styles, each suited to a specific moment of dramatic intrigue.[14] When Thomas Jefferson enters in act 2 with "What'd I miss?" he has a light swing-dance sensibility that helps mark a transition out of the high-stakes military battles of the first act and into the formation of government of the second. While, as Gennaro warns, "the juxtaposition between styles is jarring," an awareness of shifts in movement and music styles and how those transitions are handled can be helpful in the analysis of choreography in a musical.[15]

---

[10]The Tony Award for Best Revival of a Play or Musical was introduced in 1977, but musicals were separated out into their own award in 1994. For more on revivals, see Joanna Dee Das's chapter in this volume.

[11]Changes in orchestration or language are sometimes part of the negotiations involved in securing the rights. In rare cases (*West Side Story* is a notable example), the choreography is protected under the copyright and licensing of the musical. Special permission is required to undertake significant choreographic changes in such cases.

[12]Liza Gennaro, "Dance in Musical Theatre Revival and Adaptation: Engaging with the Past while Creating Dances for the Present," in *The Routledge Companion to the Contemporary Musical*, ed. Jessica Sternfeld and Elizabeth L. Wollman (London: Routledge, 2020), 246.

[13]Gennaro, *Making Broadway Dance*, 12–13.

[14]See Phoebe Rumsey, "The Convergence of Dance Styles in the Musical *Hamilton: An American Musical*," in Sternfeld and Wollman, *The Routledge Companion to the Contemporary Musical*, 255–62.

[15]Gennaro, *Making Broadway Dance*, 19. In the case of *Hamilton*, the shift also helps show that Jefferson is a new character, distinguishing him from the first act's Lafayette, who is played by the same actor (Daveed Diggs).

Conventions and Stereotypes

Another critical avenue towards reading dance involves spectators' expectations of what dance should do onstage. How can a spectator recognize their bias or preconceived ideas about bodies moving? Clichés, stereotypes, and conventions swirl around the form, some problematically and others of benefit. Markedly, many choices made onstage by choreographers and movement coaches are picked up on in the media. For instance, a whimsical demonstration of "jazz hands" has become the signature move of the musical theatre. In fact, as this book will discuss, the bold gesture of splayed, often-white-gloved hands shaking in time has a drawn-out and racially inflected history extending back to minstrel shows. Bob Fosse used splayed hands in much of his work, most substantially in the opening of *Pippin* (1972), and more recently the choreographer of *A Strange Loop* (2019), Raja Feather Kelly, hints at minstrelsy by way of "jazz hands."[16] Recognizing and attending to the historical roots of familiar moves in musical theatre, many of which are fraught within structures of white supremacy, helps us contextualize the genre. Exploring why moves become conventions and what that means can help one navigate the challenging task of describing, interpreting, and analyzing the body in motion onstage. As this brief reading of jazz hands has shown, a focus on the inherent meaning and history behind a move can nuance an interrogation of choreographic choices. While some movements are more socially and politically charged than others, all movements, like words, have cultural symbolism and cultural history. Dance in musical theatre moves far beyond production numbers inserted for mere entertainment's sake. Rather, to return to Savran's language, musical theatre is a barometer of the time, and previously expected movement conventions such as male-female partnering fall away to new ways of showing community, such as that outlined for *Come from Away* or seen in *Pippin*, *Kinky Boots*, *Billy Elliot*, or *Everybody's Talking About Jamie* (2021), to name only a few.

Methods and Meaning-Making

Beyond these broadly accessible approaches to reading dance, practitioners and scholars offer numerous options for looking at and reading dance that range from typologies of movement quality to specific analytical tools. Austro-Hungarian dance theorist Rudolph Laban (1879–1958), for example, put forth a complex movement notation system that allows for a categorizing of the quality or flow of the movement, even when the specific names of steps are not known by or available to the observer. The study of Laban's work and Labanotation (his method of notating dance and dance qualities) is vast and beyond the scope of this chapter, but his analytical framework, which examines the space, time, weight, and actions of the dancer, offers some practical vocabulary for describing dance.[17] Laban proposes criteria to use as a lens to determine what a dancer is doing onstage. He asks the

---

[16]For more on Bob Fosse's development of his style and influences see Kevin Winkler's *Big Deal: Bob Fosse and Dance in the American Musical* (New York: Oxford University Press, 2018).

[17]An accessible explanation of the Laban framework of space, time, weight, and action can be found in Theresa Mitchell's *Movement: From Person to Actor to Character* (Lanham, MD: Scarecrow Press, 1998), 65–72.

observer to determine whether the performer's focus in the space is direct or indirect, whether the timing of the movements is quick or sustained, and whether the weight is strong or light. These touchstones allow the observer to begin to understand the concept the choreographer is trying to put forth, using terms that can connect to everyday actions. In Laban's fourth area of investigation, and perhaps the most accessible, he describes simple actions that can identify everyday movement and require no specific training to identify: dab, wring, punch, glide, press, slash, float, and flick. Looking for these eight qualities across the spectrum of movement onstage can help observers ground a description of the dance, particularly if emotional qualities are assigned to the movements. For example, in the stomping action of the opening of *Come from Away*, the movement quality could be described as directly focused using strong weight, with a quick reaction in the foot to the fast music and a punchiness that underpins the resilient attitude of the townspeople. This is only one example of how Laban analysis can allow for the describing of qualities that can lead to more formal unpacking of the movement.

Writing much more recently than Laban, and responding in part to students' observational inquiries, Stacy Ellen Wolf provides a list of questions to ask when analyzing dance. The questions, which appear in an appendix to a 2007 *Theatre Topics* article, range from prompts such as, "What is the relationship between the dance and the lyrics of the song?" to the more general, "Who dances? To or with whom? For what purpose? To what effect?"[18] Returning to the opening of *Come from Away*, we can see these questions in action. To take Wolf's first question: the lyrics of the song relate directly to the movement as the performers stamp on the ground and sing "I am an Islander," with a point to the ground as an indication of place. The lyrics about a place directly correlate to the bodies present in the space, particularly as the musical explores those who "come from away" and the community that welcomes them in. To answer the subsequent chain of questions: the performers move as a group, and the effect of this shows their community spirit and resilience. Notably, they are not dancing as couples or in strict precision but individually. This choreographic choices show from the beginning that each performer has their own story. Asking these sorts of questions offers a way of describing and reading choreography as part of the larger narrative and impression of the musical itself. Wolf offers further questions such as, "Does the dance tell a story? Does it represent conflict? Does the dance develop an emotion? Does the dance embody a changed emotional state?"[19] In "Welcome to the Rock," the movement develops an emotion, specifically pride in place. As the news of the attacks is learned, or recounted, midway through the song, the movement switches to softer gestures, suggesting a changed emotional state. A sense of shock and incredulity is echoed in the body as the stomps stop and upper body postures soften. At the same time, arms rise slowly skyward in an indication of disbelief and despair. Wolf's questions encourage the development of a language to discuss musical theatre dance.

Wolf's questions, Laban's analysis framework, and earlier suggestions for entry points into discussions of dance demonstrate that when we look at the choreography of a musical,

---

[18]Stacy Ellen Wolf, "In Defense of Pleasure: Musical Theatre History in the Liberal Arts [A Manifesto]," *Theatre Topics* 17, no. 1 (2007): 60.
[19]Wolf, 57.

the movement gets parsed through and analyzed for what is specifically happening physically. This sort of observation may uncover the capacity of dance to carry meaning and reveal what it is that dance can *do* in musical theatre, whether that is to reveal character psychology, function diegetically as a part of the story, express an unspoken aspect of the libretto, forward the narrative, transition from scene to scene, or express emotions or ideas through metaphor or abstraction.

Further Analytical Tools

Numerous additional sources and lines of inquiry beyond those outlined above can assist readers in identifying conventions of dance. Elizabeth Titrington Craft and Joanna Dee Das, for example, offer an interdisciplinary approach to the overall analysis of musical theatre that attends to an analysis of dance. They recommend looking at the actual steps being performed in a manner that does not use complicated dance jargon: "Are there lots of turns, kicks, or leaps? What about the shapes the dancers' bodies make—are the movements curved or angular? Do the performers form patterns on the stage?" Furthermore, in order to pull together the observations, they also advocate that observers "take a step back and reflect on how dance and movement serve the show overall."[20]

As was demonstrated at the start of this chapter, and as Craft and Das emphasize, a close description of the body can be helpful in analysis. Details of what one sees specific body parts doing can reveal dramatic intent that is not identified in the narrative. For example, in *Hamilton* there is a moment when the ensemble is circled around Hamilton in a wide lung toward him. The men and women of the ensemble align their torsos diagonally from their back heel to the tip of their head. This pose creates a ramp up to Hamilton's face. The performers' hands are against their sides, emphasizing the diagonal line, their hands in strong fists against their hips. These moves highlight the center point, demonstrate strength, and guide the viewer toward Hamilton. Further, as they are in a deep lunge, they perform lower status than the protagonist. The ensemble does not overwhelm him but rather support and enhance his stature. Likewise, as the men and women are portraying his army, the movement emphasizes the military structure with one in command and others in obeisance. This instance demonstrates how a single pose can reveal the meaning in a piece. An examination of the shapes and lines bodies make onstage can be a productive analytical tool toward reading the physicalized semiotics of the musical.

Blankenbuehler's ensemble staging for *Hamilton* models how the bodies onstage can be part of the building blocks of the narrative.[21] Reading the ensemble in this manner demonstrates how different components of the musical can be looked at alongside one another. Dustyn Martincich points to the possibilities of the ensemble in *Hamilton* when she describes how Blankenbuehler, "mobilizes the ensemble to drive the narrative by activating

---

[20]Elizabeth Titrington Craft and Joanna Dee Das, "Interdisciplinary Approaches to Studying the Stage Musical," in *A Critical Companion to the American Stage Musical*, ed. Elizabeth L. Wollman (London: Bloomsbury, 2017), 240.
[21]Thank you to Lisa Anne Brain for extended discussions about the intricacies of Andy Blankenbuehler's choreography in *Hamilton*.

the liminal spaces in and between the scenes."[22] In our larger quest to highlight the body, we have the possibility of reframing the analysis, redirecting the emphasis from the text and score, and drawing attention to what the body is doing within those frameworks. Much time has passed since dancers were merely moving props or figures who facilitated the scene changes. In fact, over the past several decades, shifts between scenes have become an opportunity to physically engage in transforming the space with bodies at the helm. As Martincich explains, the choreography between scenes shows the passing of time and, importantly, "fill[s] out the necessary storytelling elements of the piece."[23] By following how an object such as a chair or table is moved through the space, we watch choreography in motion. Particularly in a show like *Hamilton*, where the set changes are highly choreographed, the watching of the journey of one object can reveal the machinery of the whole musical.[24]

Dance can function in numerous other ways as well, as Mary Jo Lodge traces in "Dance Breaks and Dream Ballets: Transitional Moments in Musical Theater." Just as there is a sense of suspended disbelief when a character breaks into song, so too is there when one goes from stasis to dancing. These transitional moments offer a key window into the choreographer's work and styles of reception. As Lodge explains, "the musical itself is also transformed as new modes of communication are introduced . . . and disrupt the stability of the form that had been previously established."[25] While the dance break and the dream ballet, Lodge's central objects of analysis, will be discussed at length in upcoming chapters, suffice to say here that it is in these moments historically that dance has been investigated for its depth of meaning as well as its possibilities in the genre.[26]

The Dancer's World

Finally, a reading of the many nuances of dance must encompass a focus on the dancers themselves. For example, the motivation and process a dancer uses (much as one would identify the actor's process) can help support what movement is doing whether overtly or covertly. Ryan Donovan describes how "subtext always supports the movement and gives dancers motivation for each phrase," particularly in the work of Bob Fosse.[27] Getting at the subtext or motivation for dancers can be quite difficult, but digging deep here, just as one would for an actor's process, can be fruitful. An opportunity to talk to (or consult interviews with) a performer in a show, or the choreographer behind a show, can round out any analysis.

---

[22]Dustyn Martincich, "Revolutionary Movement: 'Non-Stop' Ensemble Choreography at Work," in *Dueling Grounds: Revolution and Revelation in the Musical "Hamilton,"* ed. Mary Jo Lodge and Paul R. Laird (Oxford: Oxford University Press, 2021), 149.

[23]Martincich, 149.

[24]This is also expertly accomplished in Michael Bennett's choreography of set changes in *Dreamgirls* (1981) and in Christopher Wheeldon's choreography and direction in *An American in Paris* (2014).

[25]Mary Jo Lodge, "Dance Breaks and Dream Ballets: Transitional Moments in Musical Theater," in *Gestures of Music Theater: The Performativity of Song and Dance*, ed. Dominic Symonds and Millie Taylor (Oxford: Oxford University Press, 2014), 78.

[26]Dance breaks are discussed in numerous chapters across this volume. For a thorough discussion of the dream ballet, see Bud Coleman's chapter.

[27]Ryan Donovan, "Style as Star: Sixty Seconds That Changed Broadway," in Sternfeld and Wollman, *The Routledge Companion to the Contemporary Musical*, 49.

For instance, Jerome Robbins was deeply invested in using method acting in his work, going so far as to keep the performers playing the Jets and the Sharks in *West Side Story* apart to foster a sense of competition and rivalry outside the show. Bob Fosse, particularly as he became a choreographer/director, was dedicated to having dance serve the specific intentions of the story, and this began with the dancer building character from an internal embodied interpretation and then moving outward.[28]

*   *   *

Overall, the body has an opportunity to communicate in ways that modes of language cannot. When we consider choreography and movement in this manner, the body becomes one of the focal points of performance, inviting the audience in to commune and interpret based on their own understanding of bodily codes and physical experiences. Importantly, unlike the book, libretto, or lyrics, dance (and the accompanying music) allows one to think and feel in the moment.[29] Dance can summon ideas, emotions, and experiences that the text and score cannot. Though dance, movement, and gesture are by no means universal, there is a sense that if the body is "speaking" in its performance, it is using a language that has an unspoken level of communicative possibility in our shared bodily engagement. In *Come from Away*, when Mayor Claude (Joel Hatch) takes his ending step in the opening song, his right foot forward, it is distinct from the police constable Oz (Geno Carr)—the mayor has a confident yet careful step, while the policeman uses a strong and authoritative action. While Beulah Davis (Astrid Van Wieren) has the same intent and direction as Annette (Jenn Colella), their execution of the choreography sets forth the distinctiveness in their character: Beulah has a grounded sense of experience, where Annette is more lifted and unsure. Pointedly, the movement variations become crucial throughout the musical because each actor plays numerous characters, and their embodiment of movements and staging allows for that choice to work. When Colella takes on the role of Beverley Bas, the first female captain for American Airlines, her movements are assured and proud, and the contrast with the movement of her other character allows for Colella's layered and complex performance to be put forth in the show.[30] By discovering and unfolding these kinds of physical engagement with choreography and movement, we open up a range of opportunities toward understanding ourselves in an physicalized mode. The tools presented in this chapter provide some suggestions toward articulating movement and, ideally, inspire the development and sharing of individual methods, techniques, and systems of analysis not yet considered in the reading and support of dance in musical theatre.

---

[28]For a detailed investigation of how the director/choreographer role transform dance into an additional language see Michael Jablonski's chapter 14 in this volume.

[29]This study does not allow for an extensive examination of the role of music in musical theatre, even though, as subsequent chapters will show, music and dance are a shared and integrated part of musical theatre. Weaving together theories from musicology and composition is equally important in the analysis of a collaborative art form like musical theatre.

[30]Colella received a Tony nomination for Best Featured Actress in a Musical and won the Helen Hayes Award for Outstanding Supporting Actress, the Drama Desk Award for Outstanding Featured Actress, and the Outer Critics Circle Award for Outstanding Featured Actress in a Musical.

Bibliography

Albright, Ann Cooper. *Choreographing Difference: The Body and Identity in Contemporary Dance*. Middletown, CT: Wesleyan University Press, 1997.

Craft, Elizabeth Titrington, and Joanna Dee Das. "Interdisciplinary Approaches to Studying the Stage Musical." In *A Critical Companion to the American Stage Musical*, edited by Elizabeth L. Wollman, 237–50. London: Bloomsbury, 2017.

Donovan, Ryan. "Style as Star: Sixty Seconds That Changed Broadway." In *The Routledge Companion to the Contemporary Musical*, edited by Jessica Sternfeld and Elizabeth L. Wollman, 48–57. London: Routledge, 2020.

Foster, Susan Leigh. *Reading Dancing: Bodies and Subjects in Contemporary American Dance*. Berkeley: University of California Press, 1986.

Franco, Susanne, and Marina Nordera, eds. *Dance Discourses: Keywords in Dance Research*. London: Routledge, 2007.

Gennaro, Liza. "Dance in Musical Theatre Revival and Adaptation: Engaging with the Past while Creating Dances for the Present." In *The Routledge Companion to the Contemporary Musical*, edited by Jessica Sternfeld and Elizabeth L. Wollman, 246–54. London: Routledge, 2020.

Gennaro, Liza. *Making Broadway Dance*. Oxford: Oxford University Press, 2021.

Lepecki, André. *Exhausting Dance: Performance and the Politics of Movement*. New York: Routledge, 2006.

Lodge, Mary Jo. "Dance Breaks and Dream Ballets: Transitional Moments in Musical Theater." In *Gestures of Music Theater: The Performativity of Song and Dance*, edited by Dominic Symonds and Millie Taylor, 75–90. Oxford: Oxford University Press, 2014.

Malnig, Julie, ed. *Ballroom, Boogie, Shimmy Sham, Shake: A Social and Popular Dance Reader*. Chicago: University of Illinois Press, 2009.

Martin, Randy. *Critical Moves: Dance Studies in Theory and Politics*. Durham, NC: Duke University Press, 1998.

Martincich, Dustyn. "Revolutionary Movement: 'Non-Stop' Ensemble Choreography at Work." In *Dueling Grounds: Revolution and Revelation in the Musical "Hamilton,"* edited by Mary Jo Lodge and Paul R. Laird, 149–63. Oxford: Oxford University Press, 2021.

Mitchell, Theresa. *Movement: From Person to Actor to Character*. Lanham, MD: Scarecrow Press, 1998.

Rumsey, Phoebe. "The Convergence of Dance Styles in *Hamilton: An American Musical*." In *The Routledge Companion to the Contemporary Musical*, edited by Jessica Sternfeld and Elizabeth L. Wollman, 255–62. London: Routledge, 2020.

Savran, David. "The Do-Re-Mi of Musical Theatre Historiography." In *Changing the Subject: Marvin Carlson and Theatre Studies, 1959–2009*, edited by Joseph Roach, 223–37. Ann Arbor: University of Michigan Press, 2009.

Winkler, Kevin. *Big Deal: Bob Fosse and Dance in the American Musical*. New York: Oxford University Press, 2018.

Wolf, Stacy Ellen. "In Defense of Pleasure: Musical Theatre History in the Liberal Arts [A Manifesto]." *Theatre Topics* 17, no. 1 (2007): 51–60.

2 Dancing Genre: Influences on Dance in Musical Theatre

NATHAN JAMES

As an expressive art form, dance and movement have been intertwined within the development of musical theatre since its late nineteenth-century beginnings. As a defined *style* of dance, musical theatre movement and choreography are a complex combination of many different influences. A theatricalized form of jazz dance would be a mainstay of dance in musicals for much of the twentieth century and become a widely identified element within musical theatre. This chapter gives an overview of the movement genres that had a significant influence on musical development of dance in musical theatre from its foundations through the early 1950s, when dance in Broadway musicals found a clearly defined physical identity. The chapter begins with early genres of dance that combined social and formalized forms, with special attention on influential choreographers including Ned Wayburn, Sammy Lee, Bobby Connolly, and Seymour Felix; and early dance stars such as Marilyn Miller and Bill "Bojangles" Robinson. This chapter also gives attention to the influence of minstrelsy on the genre. From there, the discussion turns towards the influence of classical ballet through the work of choreographers Albertina Rasch and George Balanchine. Finally, the chapter surveys the significant influence of classical and modern dance on the genre, and closes with the introduction of theatrical jazz dance and its early teachings by various teachers and choreographers such as Robert Alton, Katherine Dunham, Jack Cole, Matt Mattox, and Luigi. While the overall focus is on stage performance, the discussion brings in examples from key Hollywood musicals as the genre of film provides an archive of what stage dance would look like and showcases some of the main influences at the time. In all, this chapter explores numerous branches of the history of development of musical theatre dance that is expanded upon in upcoming chapters.

Dance in musical theatre is an amalgamation of many styles and social forms, some of which require specialized training. In the early twentieth century, musical theatre dance was often entwined with social dance trends, such as the Charleston, the Black Bottom, and the foxtrot. These popular dance crazes provided theatre choreographers with a way to entice audiences, in turn broadening the reach of social dance styles. Be that as it may, dance in musicals has often been disregarded, relegated to the realms of low art because of its commercial nature.[1] However, there is much to be explored regarding how the development

---

[1]For a detailed definition of commercial theatre see chapter 12.

of dance in musical theatre worked in tandem with the dominant aesthetics and social politics of the time.

In the early musicals of the twentieth century, stage dancing, as defined by choreographer Ned Wayburn in his 1925 manual *The Art of Stage Dancing*, was a form of dance that drew away from social dance forms because it could be commercialized.[2] Yet, further expansion of "stage dancing" is rather vague. Early influences saw the inclusion of comedic and pantomime ballet, styles that drew from the vernacular movement of other cultures, tap dance, and ballroom, alongside the rise of the kickline and precision chorus, dances that became a staple in early musical theatre. Dance was certainly a central element of the performance, but its main purpose was to provide visual spectacle, making it a somewhat frivolous element in these early musical comedies.

During the 1920s, Broadway musicals saw a rise in dancing stars, many drawn from the vaudeville circuits, who possessed a varied range of unique and idiosyncratic performance styles, tap dance being one of the most prominent. Of these performers, a small number— Ray Bolger, Bill "Bojangles" Robinson, Charlotte Greenwood, the Nicholas Brothers and Cholly Atkins to name a few — had their work captured on film as the emergence of the Hollywood musical saw the studios entice performers and choreographers away from Broadway. This early work established what musical theatre dance would be at the time. The 1930s would witness a greater influence from classical ballet, particularly with the work of George Balanchine, which would have a lasting effect on the shaping of dance movement on the stage.[3] As musical styles evolved and performances became more cohesive, with all elements (book, lyrics, score) working for the same purpose, choreographers such as Agnes de Mille and Jerome Robbins significantly changed the landscape and purpose of dance, contributing to character development through an infusion of classical and modern dance vocabularies. Dance in musicals during the 1940s went through monumental changes, brought about in part by the evolution of musicals by Richard Rodgers and Oscar Hammerstein II. In contrast, the work of dancer and choreographer Jack Cole infused the musical theatre genre with "modern jazz dance," which seemed well suited to the type of musicals that were emerging at this time. Cole's articulation of the body and movement composition would incorporate a wider range of cultural influences including South Asian and African American vernacular movement. Importantly, the work of Katherine Dunham, drew on authentic African dance movement and broadened the movement vocabulary that early choreographers had utilized.[4]

For the purpose of this chapter, "theatre dance" encompasses a fusion of dance styles in a theatrical setting, as in a revue show or musical play. Theatre dance draws on many influences, significantly jazz, ballet, and tap genres during the early period of its development, and has become identifiable with the Broadway musical, particularly through theatrical jazz dance (a term that more broadly encompasses all styles of jazz that are performed before

---

[2] Ned Wayburn, *The Art of Stage Dancing* (1925; New York: Belvedere, 1980), 23.
[3] See Bud Coleman's chapter in this volume for more on Balanchine's work, particularly the dream ballet.
[4] See Amanda Jane Olmstead's chapter in this volume for more on Katherine Dunham.

an audience). Here, I focus particularly on those styles of dance that pertain to early commercial theatrical productions and musical theatre.[5]

Early Dance Influences

Drawing on the movement and gesture of pantomime, dance as used in early theatre productions primarily took the form of ballet divertissement between acts and served little purpose other than providing another form of entertainment for audiences.[6] Classical ballet, an art form originating in the sixteenth century, established itself in opera productions at the Paris Opera in 1671. One of the earliest forms of dance to establish a codified technique in the Western world, ballet would eventually find its own voice apart from operatic productions, utilizing narrative to develop choreographic movement that could convey meaning, purpose, and story to an audience. In London in 1734 ballet dancer and choreographer Marie Sallé would present the story of sculptor Pygmalion.[7] Her interpretation, along with several other interpretations of the same theme, would provide a springboard from which a theatricalized art form would find its own identity and a body could tell a story. Ballets, as a cohesive narrative production, would proliferate in the theatrical world during the late 1800s, becoming increasingly popular throughout the nineteenth century, which would see the creation of some of the most influential productions of the genre, such as *Giselle* (1841), *Swan Lake* (1877), and *Sleeping Beauty* (1890). Susan Leigh Foster states that ballets of this period offered "dramatic interpretations on stage [that] came to be less based on the hierarchies of status, class, and profession, and more on the exchanges of heartfelt emotion." In this consideration, the balletic movement vocabulary would rely heavily on mime and gesture that communicated with the audience.[8]

Much of the classical ballet canon of the nineteenth century is characterized as being in the romantic style, perhaps reflecting the influence of the wider nineteenth-century arts and literature movement known as Romanticism. Romantic ballet can be delineated as giving greater prominence to the female dancing body and to pointe work, providing a more ethereal and magical quality to the movement. The romantic tutu, with a hemline falling just below the knee, highlighted the footwork, with more fluid use of the arms and upper body, often emphasized by a rounder arm position and slight forward lean of the body.[9] The formulaic structure of ballet from this era provided a template that worked well within musical theatre.

---

[5]For broader definitions of the jazz dance idiom, see Lindsay Guarino and Wendy Oliver, eds., *Jazz Dance: A History of the Roots and Branches* (Tallahassee: University Press of Florida, 2014). For a historical overview of vernacular dance styles that evolved into early forms of jazz dance, see Marshall Winslow Stearns and Jean Stearns, *Jazz Dance: The Story of American Vernacular Dance* (1968; New York: Da Capo Press, 1994).

[6]Gerald Bordman, *American Musical Theatre: A Chronicle* (New York: Oxford University Press, 2001), 7.

[7]Susan Leigh Foster, *Choreography and Narrative: Ballet's Staging of Story and Desire* (Bloomingfield: Indiana University Press), 1–12.

[8]Susan Leigh Foster, *Choreography and Narrative: Ballet's Staging of Story and Desire* (Indianapolis: Indiana University Press, 1998), 8, and see 1–8.

[9]Deborah Jowitt, "In Pursuit of the Sylph: Ballet in the Romantic Period," in *The Routledge Dance Studies Reader*, ed. Alexandra Carter and Janet O'Shea (London: Routledge, 2010), 214.

Another important precursor to musical theatre and its use of dance is minstrelsy.[10] From the mid-1800s to the early 1900s, minstrel shows were one of the most popular forms of entertainment in America. As early as 1767, Black dances had been appropriated and performed by white entertainers and appeared in theatrical productions.[11] In 1828 a white performer named Thomas Dartmouth Rice would become synonymous with blackface minstrelsy and the perpetuation of African American stereotypes with his alter ego, Daddy "Jim Crow" Rice. In the years to come, as Brenda Dixon Gottschild notes, even though minstrelsy was essentially about white power and supremacy, African Americans "had no choice but to step into a white-constructed mirror that distorted their reflection. Yet they introduced genuine black presence, invention, and creativity into the genre." This resulted in Black dancers, to some effect, reclaiming this act of cultural appropriation and offering a more culturally authentic quality to the performances. As abhorrent as this was, to some extent the reclaiming of these minstrel stereotypes would ultimately provided a platform in which Black performers could gain more attention and recognition as entertainers alongside their white counterparts.[12]

Minstrelsy's significance for dance is monumental because of its amalgamation of cultural influences, including African vernacular dance, Irish reel and jig, and Lancashire clog, all of which would become part of the later jazz and tap idioms. Additionally, minstrelsy provided a significant shift in compositional styles of music, using rhythms drawn from African American influences and becoming a precursor to the jazz music genre.[13] Minstrelsy's painful portrayal of African American stereotypes, through an overly caricatured performance style in blackface, is certainly not to be celebrated: it is a tarnish on social and political history that can never be undone. However, as a form of performance, it provided dancers both white and Black with a rich movement vocabulary that informed both tap and jazz dance. One of the most popular dancers of this period was the freeborn William Henry Lane, whose alter ego, Master Juba, would compete against minstrel dancers to assert his skill and proficiency. His dance characteristics drew from the form's many cultural influences, with his leg movements revealing the Irish influence, and his single and double shuffles suggesting the African American presence. What made his dance displays stand out was his rhythmic beating of his feet on the floor.[14]

Even though the white-dominated minstrel shows would continue for decades, Black artists would find ways to make a name for themselves. The cakewalk, one of the most influential dance styles to have evolved during the mid- to late nineteenth century, provided a gateway for Black performers to join the predominately white theatrical world. The Cakewalk was featured in the early twentieth century performances of Aida Overton Walker, a Black dancer

---

[10]For further information on minstrelsy, see Stearns and Stearns, *Jazz Dance*; Megan Pugh, *America Dancing: From the Cakewalk to the Moonwalk* (New Haven, CT: Yale University Press, 2015); and William J. Mahar, *Behind the Burnt Cork Mask: Early Blackface Minstrelsy and Antebellum American Popular Culture* (Urbana: University of Illinois Press, 1999).

[11]Jacqui Malone, *Steppin' on the Blues: The Visible Rhythms of African American Dance* (Urbana: University of Illinois Press, 1996), 51.

[12]Brenda Dixon Gottschild, *Digging the Africanist Presence in American Performance: Dance and Other Contexts* (Westport, CT: Greenwood Press, 1996), 82–3. For more on Black identity in performance, see Ramón Flowers's chapter in the present volume.

[13]Stearns and Stearns, *Jazz Dance*, 43–7.

[14]Stearns and Stearns, 46–7; Malone, *Steppin' on the Blues*, 54.

who starred in all-Black musicals that evolved as a breakaway from the formulaic structure of minstrel shows. As a form of dance, it mocked and parodied the upper class (or, originally, white plantation owners) and consisted of a pigeon-chested posture, a strutting action with the legs sometimes kicking up in front of the body. Although the cakewalk's stature was diminished as white Americans relegated it to an almost cartoonish portrayal of Black dancers in society settings, it nonetheless gained notoriety and respect as an American national dance created by enslaved African Americans.[15] In the larger development of dance, the cakewalk also meant that Black performers were instrumental in integrating dance as a more focused part of the overall performance along with the song and text. Many Black performers would distance themselves from the racial stereotyping that became associated with this dance, becoming independent artistes with styles of dance that opposed such caricatures in movement.[16]

Vaudeville and Revues

Vaudeville and revue shows, building on the format of minstrelsy and an ever-changing program of performers, gained quickly in popularity in the early twentieth-century and gave greater exposure and prominence to the dancer in theatrical productions. Gerald Bordman explains the difference in forms: vaudeville, whose productions traveled across the US bringing a plethora of talent to local audiences and presenting shows with interchangeable lineups and no cohesive link, were one of the most popular forms of theatrical entertainment of the era; revues, cohesive and elaborate productions that became a mainstay of Broadway theatre, were more erudite and had less appeal to mass audiences outside of New York.[17] The king of all revue shows in New York was the *Ziegfeld Follies*, an annual production of theatrical producer Florenz Ziegfeld Jr., which began in 1907 and made stars out of many of the performers showcased. Chief among these were the female chorus dancers, known as Ziegfeld Girls. In one of her last interviews, *Follies* dancer Doris Eaton Travis explained that Ziegfeld dancers were categorized as either *hoofers* or *showgirls*, with the latter having more status. Travis was a hoofer, while her sister Mary was a showgirl, and Ziegfeld was more concerned with the visual allure of his showgirls than the hoofers. In describing the significance of a Ziegfeld revue, Travis stated, "the great quality of the Ziegfeld Touch was elegance, refinement, radiance, and wonderful humour—it wasn't vulgarity—it was funny. The whole theatre was a romantic interlude for anyone that would come to see the show."[18] Travis also acknowledged the early twentieth century influence of dance and music styles of the Harlem Renaissance. She felt that tap dance during this period was the most significant development because it used increasingly popular syncopated rhythms.[19]

---

[15]Pugh, *America Dancing*, 15–23. For a wider discussion and overview of the cakewalk, see Pugh, *America Dancing*; and Gottschild, *Digging the Africanist Presence*.

[16]Stearns and Stearns, *Jazz Dance*, 285.

[17]Gerald Bordman, *American Musical Revue: From "The Passing Show" to "Sugar Babies"* (New York: Oxford University Press, 1985), v.

[18]Doris Eaton Travis, interview by Michael Kantor, May 7, 2002, New York, Theatre on Film and Tape (TOFT), Performing Arts Research Collections, New York Public Library.

[19]For more on the influence of tap dance, see chapters 4 and 11. For more on the *Ziegfeld Follies* see chapter 4 and 6.

Situated in upper Manhattan, the neighborhood of Harlem was a melting pot of talent through its all-Black musical and revue productions. One of the most significant was *Darktown Follies of 1914*, which Constance Valis Hill identifies as bringing multiple dance forms, many of them Black, onto the popular stage: the strut, the tango, ballin' in the jack, traditional time steps, acrobatics, and even Russian folk-dance steps.[20] While primarily designed as an entertainment form for Black audiences, the production garnered the attention of white audiences, including producers such as Ziegfeld. This would mark an instrumental change in performative practices, with all-white productions publicly "borrowing" from Black productions, while all-Black revues and musicals relied less on all-white theatrical conventions and developed their own formats. The complexity of this appropriation is under scrutiny in the twenty-first century as we grapple with the clear reign of white supremacy in the entertainment world and across cultural history more broadly. Much debt needs to be repaid to the countless Black artists whose legacies are given scant attention due to the cultural and political tensions of the era. In the wider dance world, the act of "borrowing" steps was a common practice, but the cultural theft in theatre and dance has long marred the evolution of both popular dance and music forms.[21]

It is during this era that Hill identifies a significant shift in dance practices—the rise in jazz—influenced both by indigenous Black dance vocabularies and rhythmic structures and by the Irish and Lancashire clog that proliferated in the all-white musicals featured on Broadway.[22] *Shuffle Along*, a 1921 all-Black musical revue, brought this momentous change to Broadway theatre when it was produced on Broadway rather than being relegated to the uppermost streets in Harlem. The musical production introduced white audiences to an extensive range of Black dance styles and forms, set to the music of composer Eubie Blake and lyricist Noble Sissle. Chief among these new forms, as jazz dance historians Marshall Winslow Stearns and Jean Stearns state, was jazz: the syncopation and pulsating rhythms of the music and the spirited dancers.[23] Female performers were prominent throughout the cast in both principal roles and the three separate dancing ensembles; a young, pre-stardom Josephine Baker was featured. While *Shuffle Along* was not given the deluxe treatment in production that the Ziegfeld revues experienced, its success with audiences enabled it to run for 504 performances.[24]

The vaudeville productions that toured the United States gave rise to the star dancer as seen in ballet. Free of any narrative constraints, theatre of the early twentieth century was rich with dancers who exhibited specialist skills and idiosyncrasies that set them apart from

---

[20]Hill, *Tap Dancing America: A Cultural History* (New York: Oxford University Press, 2010), 47.
[21]For more on this topic, see Hill, *Tap Dancing America*; Jayna Brown, *Babylon Girls: Black Women Performers and the Shaping of the Modern* (Durham, NC: Duke University Press, 2008); and Anthea Kraut, *Choreographing Copyright: Race, Gender, and Intellectual Property Rights in American Dance* (Oxford: Oxford University Press, 2016).
[22]Hill, *Tap Dancing America*, 49.
[23]Stearns and Stearns, *Jazz Dance*, 136. In 2016 the Broadway musical *Shuffle Along, or, The Making of the Musical Sensation of 1921 and All That Followed*, explored the complex development of the 1921 production while showcasing the choreography of tap dancer Savion Glover, who attempted to create tributes to the dance evolution of that original production. For more on the original production see chapter 6, for more on the 2016 production, see chapter 11.
[24]Brown, *Babylon Girls*, 197–8.

other performers. While much focus was placed on the large dance ensembles in musical productions, the freedom of the vaudeville format was generative. Solo dance and specialty dance acts facilitated the development of a diverse range of dance styles and performances that did not conform to the unity or precision of chorus line dancing.

Among the most successful all-Black touring revue shows were those produced by the Whitman Sisters, which featured some of the highest paid Black performers of the era. Alice, the youngest of the sisters, was considered by her peers to be one of the most talented and versatile performers of the troupe. She did not conform to the chorus line formation and was among the few leading female soloist tap dancers outside of Broadway.[25] Another significant Black dancer and choreographer from this era was Buddy Bradley, who worked on Broadway staging dances often without credit for the major revue shows of the time, before, in 1931, heading to London to choreograph productions there. While in London he would work with dancer Jessie Matthews and Royal Ballet choreographer Frederick Ashton. He also ran a UK dance studio, where he no doubt heavily influenced the style of tap dance that infused the syncopated rhythms in the American productions.[26]

Bill "Bojangles" Robinson, considered to be one of the most influential tap dancers of the early twentieth century, rose through the ranks of vaudeville to become a headline soloist on the most successful and well-regarded vaudeville circuits in America. In 1918 Robinson introduced his stair dance, a solo that revolved around small, neat footwork as he ascended and descended a portable staircase.

With only a simple piano accompaniment, as well as heavy use of stop-time and tacet, Robinson's articulation and clarity of beats and rhythmic patterns were showcased. Film footage from 1932 captures the entire sequence and demonstrates a dancer with crystal-clear tap beats that are light and precise, with clean, crisp footwork on the balls of the feet. Hill suggests that Robinson's style, a breakaway from the more traditional flat-footed buck style, was most likely influenced by Irish dance.[27] Along with his articulated style of tap dancing, Robinson honed a distinctive performance style that engaged audiences wherever he performed. Greater attention to the line and hold in the upper body helped create focus in coordination with the complexities of the footwork. Robinson would eventually dance on Broadway (beginning with the revue show *Blackbirds of 1928*, when he was fifty) and then go on to Hollywood, where his tap dance style would be captured permanently on celluloid. Although the transition to Hollywood films would have a profound effect on the revue show format—causing it to lose popularity toward the end of the 1930s—film enabled the immortalization of Robinson's legacy for future generations. He received worldwide recognition for his appearances with child star Shirley Temple, creating another stair dance with Temple in the 1935 film *The Little Colonel*.[28]

[25]Hill, *Tap Dancing America*, 58–9.
[26]*Harlem World*, "Harlem's 'Buddy' Bradley, Tap Dancer and the First African-American to Run a British White Company," posted April 23, 2018, https://www.harlemworldmagazine.com/harlems-buddy-bradley-tap-dancer-first-african-american-run-british-white-company.
[27]Hill, *Tap Dancing America*, 63–7.
[28]Jim Haskins and N. R. Mitgang, *Mr. Bojangles: The Biography of Bill Robinson* (New York: William Morrow, 1988), 99–189.

Image 2.1 Bill Robinson (Bojangles) in *Blackbirds of 1928*. Billy Rose Theatre Division, The New York Public Library Digital Collections.

The freedom of the revue and vaudeville format nurtured a generation of "eccentric" dancers, defined by Stearns and Stearns as dancers who have "their own non-standard movements and sell themselves on their individual styles."[29] Some of these dancers included George M. Cohan, Jack Donahue, Hal Le Roy, Charlotte Greenwood, and Ray Bolger. Finding his feet in vaudeville, and more remembered today for his performance as the

[29]Stearns and Stearns, *Jazz Dance*, 232.

Scarecrow in the 1939 film *The Wizard of Oz*, Bolger combined elements of tap dancing, comedy, and seemingly rubber-made legs that slid in and out of the splits with undemanding ease. Bolger's charisma and dance talent allowed him to break free of being typecast purely as a specialty dancer. He was able to hone his musical skills as an actor and singer to such a degree that he was a staple of theatrical productions and early Hollywood musicals at MGM. One of his most significant dance roles was in the 1936 Broadway musical *On Your Toes*, discussed later in this chapter.

Among the plethora of dance styles that proliferated during the 1920s, one particularly identifiable element of revue and musical productions was the precision dancing done by a chorus of women. Established in the United Kingdom in the early 1900s, the Tiller Girls would become synonymous with precision line dancing, kicking the legs to the same height with military exactness. There was no place for individuality; every dancer would look similar and dance in the same fashion. While precision dances of both Black and white choruses are explored in detail in subsequent chapters, a brief outline helps to understand how the style influenced dance in musical theatre.

Founded by John Tiller, the Tiller Girls would make their Broadway debut in 1918, starting a militaristic trend in the chorus line.[30] Albertina Rasch, whose contribution is discussed later in this chapter, would be influenced by this formula, albeit utilizing classical and modern dance vocabulary within her choreography. While racial tensions pervaded America, and segregation meant many prohibitory measures for Black performers, the all-Black chorus girl line became a staple of Black musical theatre and also attracted particular attention in 1920s European revue shows, where it suggested sometimes primitive, sometimes sexually alluring titillation for audiences.[31] While precision lines in all-white productions evoked a sense of militant unity, the all-Black precision lines influenced change by blending movement drawn from a rich cultural history, demonstrating flexibility in new surroundings, and drawing from the jazz music idiom to effect changes in rhythmic structure. The enduring legacy of dance from Black culture would help shape a whole new generation of dance styles in the mid-twentieth century.

Ned Wayburn and His Contemporaries

As a teacher and dance director, Ned Wayburn was one of the most influential creative forces in the development of dance in musical theatre at the start of the twentieth century, predominantly because of his work with theatre impresario Florenz Ziegfeld Jr. between 1915 and 1930. Today, what is perhaps most significant about Wayburn is his written contribution to the understanding of dance and its inclusion in musical theatre: his 1925 manual *The Art of Stage Dancing*. This manual provides the reader with an understanding of the approach to dance training and choreography that was utilized during the early twentieth century and defines modern stage dancing as "differ[ing] from social or ballroom dancing in

---

[30]Eugenia Voltz Schoetter, "From a Chorus Line to 'A Chorus Line': The Emergence of Dance in the American Musical Theatre" (PhD diss., Kent State University, 1979), 52–4.

[31]Brown, *Babylon Girls*, 210–23. By "Black musical theatre," I mean theatrical works that were created and performed solely by Black performers. For more on chorus lines and ensemble and precision dancing, see Adrienne Gibbons Oehlers's chapter 4 in this volume.

that it is the kind of dancing that one can commercialize."[32] Wayburn explains the following dance styles as features of this genre of dance: musical comedy dancing, tap and step dancing, acrobatic dancing, exhibition dancing (ballroom), and modern American ballet dancing. The first two styles were the most prominent during the 1920s and 1930s. Musical comedy dancing, which Wayburn defined as containing elements of tap dance incorporating kicks and turns alongside balletic movements, was the type of dancing he taught to Fred and Adele Astaire. He identifies tap dancing (a term some dance historians claim he coined),[33] conversely, as an American art form that relies on the syncopated rhythms of the footwork. Wayburn developed his own codification of tap dancing technique by identifying the different uses of the foot and the way it can create different sounds.[34] Many styles and components of Wayburn's stage dancing would become passé as ballet technique became more influential in the overall aesthetic of the musical theatre dancer, yet his systematic approach to training dancers at his school would provide a clear model for the period.

Wayburn was involved in musical theatre at one of the most pivotal times in its development, although he perhaps overstated his own contributions to the field in one key area. The overview of his career that appeared in his 1925 manual claimed that he had introduced ragtime and syncopation to audiences across the United States when he toured in vaudeville,[35] an account that obscures and minimizes the significant contribution of Black dancers in alternative touring productions such as *Shuffle Along* and *Runnin' Wild* (1923). Beyond this, Wayburn's work, also delved into the presentation of movement from other cultures, including Indian, Turkish, and Egyptian aesthetics, demonstrating, like other white performing artists at the time, appropriated non-white cultural dance forms.[36]

Wayburn's influence would also help give rise to the dance star, who would be elevated from a chorus line position and placed in a leading role. One such dance star was Marilyn Miller, a child star who appeared as part of a family vaudeville act that would be introduced to Broadway audiences in *The Passing Show of 1914*, a revue show produced by Lee Shubert. Miller attended the Wayburn school and became conversant in a variety of dance styles, tap being one of her specialties. She would eventually go on to appear in the revue shows of Ziegfeld and was featured in musicals tailored around her dance talents, such as *Sally* (1920) and *Sunny* (1925).[37] Film versions of both musicals would allow audiences the opportunity to see Miller's musical skills for themselves, albeit somewhat limited by the static filming techniques of these early musicals. An accomplished tap dancer who exhibited a delightful energy, she was an adept hoofer who also showed a flair for characterization and comedy.

---

[32]Wayburn, *The Art of Stage Dancing*, 23.

[33]Hill considers the publication of Wayburn's techniques in 1925 to be one of the first uses of the term *tap dance* in relation to musical theatre (see *Tap Dancing America*, 81). Sharon Park Arslanian observes that while this may be the first time the term appeared in print as an associated dance form, Wayburn does not acknowledge his own labeling. Even so, she writes, the term seems to have come into popular use in the 1920s. See Arslanian, "History of Tap Dance in Education: 1920–1950" (PhD diss., Temple University, 1997), 162. See chapter 11 for more on tap dance.

[34]Wayburn, *The Art of Stage Dancing*, 58.

[35]Wayburn, 31.

[36]Barbara Stratyner, *Ned Wayburn and the Dance Routine, from Vaudeville to the Ziegfeld Follies* (n.p.: Society of Dance History Scholars, 1996), 48.

[37]Warren G. Harris, *The Other Marilyn: A Biography of Marilyn Miller* (New York: Arbor House, 1985), 32–77.

Two other significant tap dancers of the 1920s were Ruby Keeler and Eleanor Powell, both of whom would become prominent film stars and influence the evolution of the dance musical as a genre, particularly Powell, who was one of the leading dance stars of the 1930s. Keeler established herself as a Broadway star during the mid-1920s and would feature in the Ziegfeld show *Whoopee* in 1928, though she did not make it to opening night.[38] She would make her film debut in the 1933 film *42nd Street* and later feature in a series of backstage film musicals. Her style of tap merged elements of buck and wing dance, with a lighter, more balletic influence in her film work with dancer Paul Draper. Powell made her Broadway debut in 1929, working with choreographer Bobby Connolly. Initially a balletic and acrobatic dancer, she would incorporate these dance influences into her work as she rose to become one of the most successful female tap dancers of the period. Powell's influence on the tap genre is incomparable, merging a fluidity and graceful quality of movement with sheer athleticism and unparalleled technique in her footwork. Significantly, despite an initial lack of training in tap dance, Powell would choreograph all her own work and would often spend her days in an empty theatre developing her terpsichorean skills.[39]

While Wayburn was perhaps the most prominent dance director of the era,[40] several of his contemporaries (all white) also had noteworthy influence on the development of dance genres on the Broadway stage. Key among these were Dave Bennett, George White, Bobby Connolly, Sammy Lee, and Seymour Felix. Bennett, who worked exclusively in the theatre (rather than in vaudeville), would substantially advance dance during the 1920s, elevating the complexity of tap dance combinations within his chorus choreography to break away from formulaic step combinations and thus requiring more skilled tap dancers in his dance ensembles. While footage of musical numbers of the 1920s is scarce, Bennett, like many, would find himself in Hollywood. His choreography for "In a Girl's Gym" in the 1930 film *Paramount on Parade* with dancer and actress Zelma O'Neal utilizes a chorus girl ensemble to foreground O'Neal's star turn. The choreography makes use of stop-time and staccato rhythms from the ensemble while O'Neal's rhythms are overlaid and are more complex in their phrasing. Despite tap dance being the dominant technique, elements of legomania (use of high kicks) and acrobatics are also present.

George White was uniquely well rounded in his contribution to musical theatre in that he worked as a performer, director, writer, and producer, establishing *George White's Scandals* as an alternative to the *Ziegfeld Follies* revue productions. White is known for having popularized the Charleston in 1924 and the Black Bottom in 1926, two dances that would become international trends outside the musical theatre, becoming social dances danced in public settings and forever identified with the 1920s.[41] These dances both have roots in

---

[38]Nancy Marlow-Trump, *Ruby Keeler: A Photographic Biography* (Jefferson, NC: McFarland, 1998), 29–47.
[39]Larry Billman, *Eleanor Powell: A Bio-Bibliography* (Westport, CT: Greenwood Press, 1994), 5. See "I'll Take Tallulah" from the MGM film *Ship Ahoy* (1942) as one of many examples of Powell's dance style and technical virtuosity.
[40]For much of this early period of creating dance in musicals, the choreographer credit usually read "dances by" or "musical numbers staged by," and the customary title was dance director. The phrase "choreographed by" was first used in 1936, to identify the contribution of George Balanchine to the musical *On Your Toes*. The role of the choreographer/dance director in theatre has long held more recognition than in film, and a union, the Stage Directors and Choreographers Society, was formed in 1959.
[41]Robert Darrell Moulton, "Choreography in Musical Comedy and Revue on the New York Stage from 1925 through 1950" (PhD diss., University of Minnesota, 1957), 31–9.

Black vernacular dances, with the Charleston first being witnessed in the Deep South in 1905 and the Black Bottom harking back to song lyrics from 1907. Essentially African American folk dances that had been passed on through an ever-growing cycle of dancers who traveled the United States, they would be popularized in theatre productions as new dance crazes.[42]

Dance director Bobby Connolly was particularly associated with tap dance. In his study of the rise of the director-choreographer in musical theatre, Gregory Dennhardt describes Connolly's style as, "rhythm tap; it emphasized a perfect union between the dancer's toe work and the musical beats. The tapper attempted to match or supplement the orchestral percussion. . . . He was the only dance director to emphasize skill over beauty.[43] Several scholars emphasize Connolly's background as a hoofer prior to becoming an established dance director, but an assistant, dancer Dona Massin, suggests that his own dance ability might have been overstated: "I worked mostly with Bobby Connolly . . . he was wonderful, didn't know his left foot from the right . . . actually most of your dance directors didn't dance very much, they knew what they wanted but they couldn't do it themselves. They knew dancing when they saw it . . . whatever I did he used to take and use it."[44] Connolly was an assistant and teacher for Wayburn in New York, which suggests that he certainly had some dance ability (although no film footage exists to confirm this). But rhythm tap goes beyond the basic structure of most early tap dances of this period and requires greater musical and rhythmical comprehension. Some technical proficiency in tap would be necessary to adapt to the syncopation and use of dropped heel beats that are part of this style.

Sammy Lee was one of the most prolific dance directors of the 1920s due to his involvement with several successful Broadway productions, including *Lady, Be Good!* (1924), *No, No, Nanette* (1925), and *Show Boat* (1927). From 1922 until 1929 Lee would stage several productions a year, until he received an offer from Hollywood, where he became one of the busiest dance directors in early film musicals. A short film clip from 1932 presents Lee seemingly auditioning and rehearsing a small group of female dancers. At one point in the footage, he gets up to demonstrate the required steps, showcasing secure rhythmical footwork.[45] Utilizing the tap genre, his rhythmic patterns show a varied range and rarely repeat. Lee also contributed two dances to the first all-talking, all-singing, all-dancing film, MGM's 1929 *The Broadway Melody*, which would mark his debut in film choreography.[46] Though visual records of dance in the 1920s are limited, such early films provide audiences with a snapshot of what dance on the musical theatre stage looked like. Like all elements of these early musical films, the capturing of dance was in its infancy, and so the filming often consisted of a stationary camera positioned in the front. The choreography in the title

---

[42]Stearns and Stearns, *Jazz Dance*, 111–14.
[43]Gregory Dennhardt, "The Director-Choreographer in the American Musical Theatre" (PhD diss., University of Illinois at Urbana-Champaign, 1978), 47–8.
[44]Dona Massin, interview, 2001, TCM Archival Project, Mary Pickford Research Center, Academy Award Film Archive, Los Angeles. For an extended investigation into ownership and copyright of dance please see Anthea Kraut's *Choreographing Copyright: Race, Gender, and Intellectual Property Rights in American Dance. Oxford University Press, 2016.*
[45]Sammy Lee, choreog., "1932 Choreographer Sammy Lee," film clip, 2:21, Producers Library, accessed October 15, 2022, https://producerslibrary.com/preview/V-0219_009.
[46]Frank W. D. Ries, "Sammy Lee: The Hollywood Career," *Dance Chronicle* 11, no. 2 (1988): 141.

number exemplifies Lee's use of the traditional chorus line setting and basic, repetitious content. The tap choreography follows a three-and-a-break format, where the same step and/or rhythmic pattern is repeated three times followed by a step (the break) to change the rhythm and finish the phrase. Interspersed are elements of musical comedy dancing, including high kicks and some rather ungainly holding of the leg as high as the dancers can achieve (to varying levels of success). The dancing's only purpose is entertainment, especially evident when a dancer enters and proceeds to tap dance *en pointe*, for no other reason than to showcase a virtuosic skill. That said, the use of soloist dances in Lee's work did change the standard chorus line dance numbers and allow for individuality in the dance routines by showcasing the skills of specific dancers in front of the chorus line.

Choreographer Seymour Felix had an extensive grounding as a performer in the vaudeville circuit and contributed dance numbers to many musicals during the 1920s. Felix, more than any other dance director discussed here, choreographed with a purpose to integrate dance by working more closely and collaboratively with the writers of the book and lyrics. At a time when dance was mostly provided for enjoyment or a playful interlude, Felix recognized that specialty dances bore little relevance to musicals and sought to make changes to the chorus line structure. First, he gave more individual opportunities or identifiable traits to his chorus line, and second, he developed dances that created a sense of atmosphere rather than just visual spectaculars. In breaking the conventions of precision line ensembles, he allowed the audience to make stronger connections with the performers onstage. His choreography relied on variations of the time-step, a repetitive rhythmic structure (often in patterns of two or six bars and then a break to signal its end) that has become a staple of the Broadway style tap dance.[47]

Tap dance dominated this early period of musical theatre in part because it allowed choreographers to create movement that was free of characterization or plot mechanism. The dance in musicals was, up until this time, essentially for showmanship, bearing only a fleeting connection to the plot or lyrics. With ensembles, tap in unison is exciting, providing an auditory experience of pulsating and military precision beats, unlike any other form of dance, because the sounds created by the dancers work in harmony with the existing musical accompaniment. As chorus and precision lines were still very much part of the structure of a musical's ensemble in the 1920s and 1930s, tap as a genre fit the formula well. However, tap as a genre in musical theatre is most often intrinsically linked to the emerging jazz rhythms. As musical styles changed leading into the 1940s, particularly in the work of Oscar Hammerstein II and Richard Rodgers, the score offered little voice for tap dancers and gave a much wider opportunity for the ballet idiom.

Classical Convergence and Integration

While classical ballet maintained its high art status, crossover dancers and choreographers brought elements of classical technique to early musical theatre dance. The use of ballet in musical theatre was for visual effect, rather than any serious effort to develop or integrate the art forms. Most choreographers did require their dancers to have some formal training, but

---

[47]Moulton, "Choreography in Musical Comedy and Revue," 49–52.

the use of ballet, particularly "toe" dancing, which would feature the dancer *en pointe*, was limited to specialty interludes.

One of the few women choreographers in theatre at the time, Albertina Rasch was foremost among those musical theatre choreographers whose dance works were completely molded in the classical ballet idiom. Drawing on the codified technique of ballet, Rasch capitalized on the commercial nature of the precision lines and utilized large ensembles executing ballet vocabulary in exciting unison patterns. Rasch's earliest work was a crossover between concert ballets and vaudeville that built on her European roots and dance training with modern dancers Mary Wigman and Émile Jaques-Dalcroze. Her extensive use of the classical ballet genre established her apart from the tap-dancing chorus lines that dominated the theatres.[48] The utilization of ballet and modern dance presented a stark contrast to the formulas derived by her male counterparts, and her approach to staging dance would further showcase that musical theatre offered opportunities for a range of dance styles to be integrated into the dance work. Rasch would follow her choreographic journey to Hollywood, where much of her choreography captured on film is in line with the more traditional precision line dances of the 1920s, albeit utilizing a clearly identifiable repertoire of steps drawn from the classical canon. Much of the emphasis is on pointe work, with a focus on the feet and lower legs executing a series of *relevé passés*, *echappés*, and *grande battements*. Some later work, captured by British Pathé news while her dancers were in London in 1932, showcases experimentation with modern dance and balletic movements, certainly contrasting with the plethora of tap choreography of the time.[49]

In terms of classical influence, Russian-born choreographer George Balanchine would significantly contribute to the integration of ballet into musical theatre during the 1930s. During this time musical theatre went through its own metamorphosis. Leaving the frivolity of the 1920s musicals behind, particularly with the work of Lorenz Hart, Richard Rodgers, and George and Ira Gershwin, productions were starting to move toward a more serious tone. Musical theatre now required something more substantial in its dance, and choreographers were beginning to realize the importance of dance as a means of communication. Despite his Russian heritage and influential career with the Ballet Russe de Monte Carlo, Balanchine would, along with Lincoln Kirstein, establish the New York City Ballet and give classical ballet a true American identity. Balanchine's work in musical theatre involved revue shows, musicals, and films between the 1930s and 1950s. His erstwhile assistant Barbara Horgan claimed that Balanchine's American education came from his involvement in musical theatre, particularly through the rhymes of lyricist Lorenz Hart.[50]

Balanchine is one of only a handful of choreographers whose work has been studied and researched extensively,[51] and whilst the majority of his influence was in the evolution of American ballet, his contribution to musical theatre was significant through his ability to interweave classical ballet with other American dance forms, such as tap and jazz dance. I

---

[48]Frank W. D. Ries, "Albertina Rasch: The Broadway Career," *Dance Chronicle*, 6, no. 2 (1983): 95–105.
[49]See Bud Coleman's chapter 6 in this volume for further investigation into the work of Rasch.
[50]Cited in Jessica Dunning, "Balanchine's All-American Dedication," *New York Times*, November 20, 2001.
[51]The Broadway choreographers who have received the most focused examinations in dance and musical theatre scholarship are Balanchine, de Mille, Robbins, Gower Champion, Bob Fosse, Tommy Tune, and Michael Bennett.

focus narrowly here on a single ballet, "Slaughter on 10th Avenue" from the 1936 Richard Rodgers and Lorenz Hart musical *On Your Toes*. A show-within-a-show ballet number that skillfully interweaves ballet, jazz, and tap vocabulary into the overarching narrative, the ballet serves the dramatic function of the musical. It originally featured Tamara Geva and Ray Bolger, but no footage of their performance is available. A slightly truncated form of the original choreography exists in the 1939 film adaptation featuring Vera Zorina and Eddie Albert, and archival footage exists of the 1983 Broadway revival, which reconstructed the original Balanchine choreography. In the former, Zorina displays much stronger technical training in classical ballet than the dancers featured in footage of Rasch's choreography. Albert is not an accomplished dancer, however, and much of his tap footwork seems to be danced by a dance double, as the more complex steps are filmed with only legs in view. The choreography portrays a different style and sensibility to the dance form as previously seen in musical theatre, and the pas de deux between the two dancers has much more freedom and abandon, influenced by the heavy brass-laden orchestrations, than expected in a classical pas de deux. The use of tap dance is no longer limited to a specialty act; here it helps convey the mood of nervousness following the onstage death of two characters and motivates the character to keep dancing. By repeating rhythmic patterns at increasing speed, the character can delay the threat of the gangsters until they are successfully captured. The purpose of the dance is twofold, providing characterization (particularly as the original dancer, Ray Bolger, was a specialty tap dancer) and continuing the plot. Balanchine generated a new wave of choreographic input into musical theatre dance that was influenced by classical ballet and amalgamated with a variety of other dance forms.

One choreographer who is seldom mentioned in dance in musical theatre is Robert "Bob" Alton, who was a major force in the musical comedy of the 1930s prior to attaining a successful career at MGM during the 1940s. Unlike such contemporaries as Balanchine, de Mille, and Robbins, Alton was among the choreographers who did not seem to achieve noticeable idiosyncrasies in their movement vocabulary and choreographic output, leaving little evidence of their contributions to dance in theatre.. A notable exception here is the 1940 Rodgers and Hart musical *Pal Joey*, which offers a window into Alton's creative work and was significant for several reasons: its topic was far more cynical and acerbic than the usual romantic entanglements of musical comedy, it marked a personal success in Alton's choreography, and it made a star of its dancing lead, Gene Kelly. Alton fashioned, alongside his peers such as de Mille, an integrated form of dance for the musical, with the lead character's choreography becoming a part of the overall dramaturgy and a physical realization of the character. Kelly had a wide range of training in dance forms such as classical ballet, tap and modern dance. His technical dance training provided a platform in which to utilise his own personal dance style to expand the unsavory attributes of the character Joey through movement and establish him as an antihero rather than the traditional romantic lead. Part of this characterization was developed and enhanced throughout the musical through the means of dance and physical movement. On his working relationship with Alton, which would continue at MGM, Kelly said,

> "Bob would take a group and always stop a show cold with a chorus. But the choruses learned a lot from him, but they learned in a quasi-balletic way. In other words, Bob never invented a new style of dance the way [jazz dancer] Jack Cole did or the way I have always tried to do. What he did, the fusion of the styles that remained there, was

so excellent, was so good, he should be given far more credit, I think. I think just watching him work has helped many, many young dancers, and I know it helped me."[52]

As a choreographer, Alton utilized tap dance even when his peers had abandoned the genre for classical and modern dance styles. His contributions on the Broadway stage included several *Ziegfeld Follies* productions, *Anything Goes* (1934), *Hellzapoppin!* (1938), and *Me and Juliet* (1953).[53] John Martin, critic for the *New York Times*, observed that Alton interwove the dance elements in *Pal Joey* with such skill that "the whole production is so unified that the dance routines are virtually inseparable from the dramatic action."[54] In a 1952 interview about his choreographic methods, Alton stated, "I study the script, listen to the music, and then go away and dream about it for a while. When I have the ideas I need, I get together with the designers, begin rehearsals, and work out from there the final arrangements of both dances and music."[55]

As Alton explained, he expected his dancers to possess the highest technical caliber of ability across a broad range of dance styles. Working with Kelly in *Pal Joey*, Alton had versatility at his fingertips. Kelly was a teacher, dancer, and choreographer in his own right, and he was well versed in a range of dance styles thus establishing a professional persona through movement and his own unique style.

Silent video footage exists of the original production of *Pal Joey*, with excerpts from several dance numbers.[56] What this footage reveals is Alton's ability to interweave the dance so that it conveys location, time, and space: his chorus girl numbers epitomize the tawdry and lewd performances of the nightclub setting through revealing costuming and brash and suggestive choreography. While it is hard to separate Kelly's contribution from Alton's, Alton fashioned a role for the choreographer as an integral part of the creative team and enabled dance to be seen as a conveyor of meaning through multiple genres. The integration of the upper body, jazz and balletic influences, and the tap dance vocabulary became strongly associated with musical theatre dance and its adoption and adaptation of multiple styles of dance.

Broadway Finds Its Choreographic Identity

During the 1940s balletic and modern dance vocabularies infused dance in musicals, as exemplified in works such as *Oklahoma!* (1943) and *Carousel* (1945), choreographed by de Mille, and *On the Town* (1944), choreographed by Robbins. Dance in musicals had found a new identity, that would give dance a much greater focus than in the previous two decades. Newer choreographers found a voice, often drawing on their own training and performance experience in a field that had grown to require technically proficient dancers with formal dance training. One such influential choreographer was Katherine Dunham, an African

---

[52]Gene Kelly, interview by Marilyn Hunt, March 10–14, 1975, Beverly Hills, CA, Oral History Project, Dance Collection, New York Public Library.
[53]For a discussion of dance and temporality in *Anything Goes*, see Joanna Dee Das's chapter 7 in this volume.
[54]John Martin, "The Dance: Pal Kelly," *New York Times*, June 8, 1941.
[55]Richard Kislan, *Hoofing on Broadway: A History of Show Dancing* (London: Simon and Schuster, 1987), 63.
[56]For video please see: "Pal Joey—Gene Kelly on Broadway" in bibliography.

American dancer whose work was heavily influenced by her anthropological studies of dances and customs witnessed in the Caribbean. With an intellectual approach, Dunham introduced audiences to an authentic representation of various cultural dances, remaining true to their original form rather than trying to capture the "spirit." According to biographer Joanna Dee Das, Dunham "broadened the horizons of her dancers and audience members, opening them up to a thriving Black world outside the United States."[57]

Dunham's work appeared in both Broadway musicals and Hollywood films before she opened a school in New York and codified her technique, which would influence later figures such as dancer Alvin Ailey and performer Eartha Kitt. Dunham's technique was broad and encompassed a variety of influences from several cultures.[58] She emphasized the use of isolations, fluidity through the spine and torso, and a focus on the movements of the hip. While all these elements would be integral to other methods, Dunham's focus was deeply rooted in her own anthropological studies.[59]

Whilst the development of Dunham technique is more aligned to the modern dance style, her influence in musical theatre in productions such as *Cabin in the Sky* (1940) would expose audiences to other musical and dance styles, particularly those drawn from other cultures. New musical styles including Latin-inspired rhythms began to proliferate in popular music and feature in Broadway musicals. After almost forty years, the early theatre composers of the twentieth century were becoming less active, much of the creative talent and performers had relocated to the West Coast to work in Hollywood films, and audiences had begun to seek more from Broadway theatre. All these elements contributed to a period of creation and exploration that would lay the foundations for theatre dance to find an identity and, most importantly, an audience.

One foremost contributor to theatrical dance is jazz dancer Jack Cole, whose work appeared in nightclub acts, film, and Broadway musicals. While Cole's jazz was closely aligned with the syncopated rhythms of jazz music, his movement vocabulary was drawn in part from the more vernacular branch of jazz, combined with modern and East Indian dance. These influences would contribute to a new identity for jazz dance, one that integrated seamlessly into a more theatrical setting. While Cole failed to have any long-running musical theatre productions, his style would influence later choreographers who worked within the jazz dance idiom, among them Bob Fosse, whose work is instantly recognizable even today due to its continual use in stage choreography some thirty-five years after Fosse's death. It is oft stated in dance history that Cole is the "father of modern jazz dance," an accolade that even he grappled with. In a 1963 interview, his disdain for being so limited by a specific label—particularly one that he described as "Broadway Commercial"—was abundantly clear. By his own definition, jazz dance was "anything that was danced to jazz music," and his focus was "stylized theatre dance which uses syncopated rhythms."[60]

---

[57]Joanna Dee Das, *Katherine Dunham: Dance and the African Diaspora* (Oxford: Oxford University Press, 2017), 57.

[58]Das, 6.

[59]Saroya Corbett, "Katherine Dunham's Mark on Jazz Dance," in Guarino and Oliver, *Jazz Dance*, 94. For further investigation of Dunham, see Amanda Jane Olmstead's chapter 5 in the present volume. For more on Dunham in this collection see chapter 6.

[60]Clayton Cole, "'It's Gone Silly': Jack Cole Explodes on the Subject of Modern Jazz Dance" (1963), in *Anthology of American Jazz Dance*, ed. Gus Giordano (Evanston, IL: Orion, 1975), 72–3.

Cole established a repertory company of dancers who fully embodied his style, including Gwen Verdon, Buzz Miller, Alex Romero, and Carol Haney, all of whom had significant dance or choreographic careers and would become closely associated with Fosse and his stylistic development. With a strong sense of exoticism and sensuality in his work, Cole often came under scrutiny under the Hollywood Production Code. Although Cole continually challenged these restraints through his creative output, he did little to fight the restrictions directly during his Hollywood career, yet greater freedom was granted his theatre work where there was less restriction in terms of censorship of Cole's movement vocabulary.

Cole's work was heavily influenced by a range of dance styles, particularly Bharatanatyam and East Indian techniques, alongside African American influences of the Lindy Hop, which would provide the foundations for the rhythmic and dynamic isolations that would become so associated with his style. Cole established a movement vocabulary that responded to the rhythmic pulses in the music, using the beats within the bar to define and dictate the quality of the movement. Within the style there is no reference to the lengthened and held posture of ballet, and the movement is grounded, with bent knees and the body shaped to allow the music to be expressed throughout the body as a whole (although separate parts of the body may move rhythmically at any one time). Jazz dance often explores the rhythms of the music in more depth, like tap dancing, by utilizing the complex note values within each bar of music. The Cole style, Bob Boross describes, "include[s] dancing in *plie*, with isolated body movements, with compressed or stored energy, and with a keen sense of manipulating rhythm, spatial levels, and attack."[61]

One unique example of Cole's dance influences can be witnessed in the choreography for "Not Since Ninevah" from the Broadway musical *Kismet* (1953), captured on film by MGM in 1955. The choreography demonstrates elements of the East Indian style, with a deep plié, hold of the torso, and rhythmic beating of the footwork. The number would become recognizable as part of Cole's "Hindu Swing"[62] oeuvre, a combination of social dance forms, swing music, and dance from Indian culture. Featuring a heavily accented and syncopated rhythmic structure, the music displays a clear sense of jazz in its driving energy. Throughout the number the dancers have a strong sense of depth in their movement and an articulated and angled use of the arms in coordination with the footwork. Isolations of the head abound, and as the music builds, the energy and size of the movement gradually increases. Repetition is evident in the stylized port de bras and long low runs, which work in varying formations as the dancers move around their enclosure in the performance space. Cole's contribution is significant because he fashioned a series of physical traits, as mentioned above, in jazz dance that are still utilised within the teaching of the genre's technique in the twenty-first century.

Shifting Approaches in Teaching

As identified in some of the cases above, the shift in the aesthetics of the dance vocabulary required by dancers in musical theatre paved the way for a new generation of teachers,

[61]Bob Boross, *Comments on Jazz Dance, 1996–2014* (n.p.: privately published, 2014), 129.
[62]Constance Valis Hill, "From Bharata Natyam to Bop: Jack Cole's 'Modern' Jazz Dance", *Dance Research Journal*, 33, No. 2 (2001), pp 29–31.

particularly those who specialized in the style and rhythmic demands of theatrical jazz dance. One of the earliest teachers to deviate from the regime of the classical ballet method was Eugene Loring, a Hollywood choreographer who integrated elements of jazz and modern dance into his pedagogy. Matt Mattox and Eugene Louis Faccuito, the latter known professionally as Luigi, were two of the most significant teachers in New York, both establishing a significant following and international recognition of their individual styles and codified techniques.[63] Luigi danced in several Hollywood musicals of the 1940s and 1950s and states that when he was working as a contract dancer, his individual style was recognized by Alton. Luigi started his own classes in 1951, with a focus on developing the musicality of the dancer. In defining jazz dance, Luigi stated, "jazz dancing is an interpretation of sound and America's cultural contribution to the world of dance."[64] Unlike his contemporaries, Luigi focused on the continuum of the movement rather than the isolation of the body.[65] Mattox, similar to Luigi, was schooled in classical ballet and featured in several Hollywood film musicals, notably as a dancer with Cole's repertory company. He began teaching in New York in 1956, integrating several forms of dance and pushing back on the label of "jazz" teacher. While his use of the upper body and arms were more closely related to ballet technique, the use of plié and depth in the movement were more derivative of the jazz dance style of Cole.[66] These early teachers of the jazz dance method would become recognized pioneers in theatre jazz technique and would provide a springboard for aspiring Broadway dancers, many of whom were trained in classical ballet and tap, to develop and hone their skills in preparation for the challenges thrown at them by Broadway choreographers.

The evolution of dance genres in musical theatre dance during the early part of the twentieth century is certainly far from linear. More than any other form of dance, the dance in musical theatre had a development entombed in cultural, political, and artistic forces and is often overlooked in writings about dance history. It is also inherently commercial: even in its most theatrical and extravagant of settings, its success is wrapped up in financial viability and it is directed at the mass audience, which often reduces its status in the wider dance sphere. Yet, in a traditional musical that heavily relies on dance, the audiences will often celebrate and remember their emotional and physical connection with the frenetic life force that dancers can project across the footlights. Much of the genre's foundations were established during the early twentieth century, but it is during the golden age of the Broadway musical, as described in this chapter, that musical theatre dance found its voice, drawing on the many cultural and social influences that proliferated through the arts.

While the twenty-first century has seen a wave of new choreographers making their mark on the theatrical stage and the interweaving of more current dance styles, theatre dance is

---

[63]Other significant teachers of jazz dance in the United States, beyond the present discussion, include Gus Giordano, Donald McKayle, Frank Hatchett, Sue Samuels, and JoJo Smith. For more discussion, see Boross, *Comments on Jazz Dance 1996–2014*. N.p.: privately published, 2014; Wendy Oliver, Carlos RA Jones, and Lindsay Guarino's *Rooted Jazz Dance: Africanist Aesthetics and Equity in the Twenty-first Century*. University Press of Florida, 2022. For further discussion of training methods see chapter 3 in this volume.
[64]Luigi [pseud.], interview by Sarah Franklin and Lorraine Kriegel, November 1, 1993, and May 22, 1994, New York, Oral History Project, Dance Collection, New York Public Library.
[65]Patricia Cohen, "Luigi, Jazz Dance Icon," in Guarino and Oliver, *Jazz Dance*, 114–16.
[66]Boross, *Comments on Jazz Dance*, 230–1.

still indebted to the profound developments of the start of the twentieth century, with the influence of Black rhythms and a dance vernacular that significantly shaped jazz and tap forms. From the 1940s onward, when theatre dance emerged as a key contributor to the musical theatre form, wider vocabularies of dance were utilized, creating an amalgam of influences. Like the genre of musical theatre itself, dance in theatre maintains its relevance and appeal, not only paying homage to its lineage but also continuing to evolve and be influenced by the world in which it is created.

Bibliography

Arslanian, Sharon Park. "History of Tap Dance in Education: 1920–1950." PhD diss., Temple University, 1997.

Billman, Larry. *Eleanor Powell: A Bio-Bibliography*. Westport, CT: Greenwood Press, 1994.

Bordman, Gerald. *American Musical Revue: From "The Passing Show" to "Sugar Babies."* New York: Oxford University Press, 1985.

Bordman, Gerald. *American Musical Theatre: A Chronicle*, Third Edition, New York, Oxford University Press, 2001.

Boross, Bob. *Comments on Jazz Dance, 1996–2014*. N.p.: privately published, 2014.

Brown, Jayna. *Babylon Girls: Black Women Performers and the Shaping of the Modern*. Durham, NC: Duke University Press, 2008.

Cohen, Patricia. "Luigi, Jazz Dance Icon." In *Jazz Dance: A History of the Roots and Branches*, edited by Lindsay Guarino and Wendy Oliver, 113–18. Tallahassee: University Press of Florida, 2014.

Cole, Clayton. "'It's Gone Silly': Jack Cole Explodes on the Subject of Modern Jazz Dance." In *Anthology of American Jazz Dance*, edited by Gus Giordano, 72–3. Evanston, IL: Orion, 1975.

Corbett, Saroya. "Katherine Dunham's Mark on Jazz Dance." In *Jazz Dance: A History of the Roots and Branches*, edited by Lindsay Guarino and Wendy Oliver, 89–96. Tallahassee: University Press of Florida, 2014.

Das, Joanna Dee. *Katherine Dunham: Dance and the African Diaspora*. Oxford: Oxford University Press, 2017.

Dennhardt, Gregory. "The Director-Choreographer in the American Musical Theatre." PhD diss., University of Illinois at Urbana-Champaign, 1978.

Dunning, Jessica. "Balanchine's All-American Dedication." *New York Times*, November 20, 2001.

Foster, Susan Leigh. *Choreography and Narrative: Ballet's Staging of Story and Desire*. Indianapolis: Indiana University Press, 1998.

Gan, Vicky. "The Story behind the Failed Minstrel Show at the 1964 World's Fair." *Smithsonian Magazine*, April 28, 2014. https://www.smithsonianmag.com/history/minstrel-show-1964-worlds-fair-180951239/.

Gottschild, Brenda Dixon. *Digging the Africanist Presence in American Performance: Dance and Other Contexts*. Westport, CT: Greenwood Press, 1996.

Guarino, Lindsay, and Wendy Oliver, eds. *Jazz Dance: A History of the Roots and Branches*. Tallahassee: University Press of Florida, 2014.

Harlem World. "Harlem's 'Buddy' Bradley, Tap Dancer and the First African-American to Run a British White Company." Posted April 23, 2018. https://www.harlemworldmagazine.com/harlems-buddy-bradley-tap-dancer-first-african-american-run-british-white-company/.

Harris, Warren G. *The Other Marilyn: A Biography of Marilyn Miller*. New York: Arbor House, 1985.

Haskins, Jim, and N. R. Mitgang. *Mr. Bojangles: The Biography of Bill Robinson*. New York: William Morrow, 1988.

Hendy, David. "The Black and White Minstrel Show." *BBC 100*. Accessed June 19, 2022. https://www.bbc.com/historyofthebbc/100-voices/people-nation-empire/make-yourself-at-home/the-black-and-white-minstrel-show.

Hill, Constance Valis. *Tap Dancing America: A Cultural History*. New York: Oxford University Press, 2010.

Jowitt, Deborah. "In Pursuit of the Sylph: Ballet in the Romantic Period." In *The Routledge Dance Studies Reader*, edited by Alexandra Carter and Janet O'Shea, 209–20. London: Routledge, 2010.

Kelly, Gene. Interview by Marilyn Hunt. March 10–14, 1975, Beverly Hills, CA. Oral History Project, Dance Collection, New York Public Library.

Kislan, Richard. *Hoofing on Broadway: A History of Show Dancing*. London: Simon and Schuster, 1987.

Kraut, Anthea. *Choreographing Copyright: Race, Gender, and Intellectual Property Rights in American Dance*. Oxford: Oxford University Press, 2016.

Lee, Sammy, choreog. "1932 Choreographer Sammy Lee." Film clip, 2:21. Producers Library. Accessed October 15, 2022. https://producerslibrary.com/preview/V-0219_009.

Luigi [pseud.]. Interview by Sarah Franklin and Lorraine Kriegel. November 1, 1993, and May 22, 1994, New York. Oral History Project, Dance Collection, New York Public Library.

Mahar, William J. *Behind the Burnt Cork Mask: Early Blackface Minstrelsy and Antebellum American Popular Culture*. Urbana: University of Illinois Press, 1999.

Malone, Jacqui. *Steppin' on the Blues: The Visible Rhythms of African American Dance*. Urbana: University of Illinois Press, 1996.

Marlow-Trump, Nancy. *Ruby Keeler: A Photographic Biography*. Jefferson, NC: McFarland, 1998.

Martin, John. "The Dance: Pal Kelly." *New York Times*, June 8, 1941.

Massin, Dona. Interview, 2001. TCM Archival Project, Mary Pickford Research Center, Academy Award Film Archive, Los Angeles.

Moulton, Robert Darrell. "Choreography in Musical Comedy and Revue on the New York Stage from 1925 through 1950." PhD diss., University of Minnesota, 1957.

"Pal Joey—Gene Kelly on Broadway." Uploaded by Mostlydaydreaming, August 25, 2020. YouTube video, 6:39. https://www.youtube.com/watch?v=LSX1YHZR614&t=53s.

Pugh, Megan. *America Dancing: From the Cakewalk to the Moonwalk*. New Haven, CT: Yale University Press, 2015.

Ries, Frank W. D. "Albertina Rasch: The Broadway Career." *Dance Chronicle* 6, no. 2 (1983): 95–137.

Ries, Frank W. D. "Sammy Lee: The Hollywood Career." *Dance Chronicle* 11, no. 2 (1988): 141–218.

Schoetter, Eugenia Voltz. "From a Chorus Line to 'A Chorus Line': The Emergence of Dance in the American Musical Theatre." PhD diss., Kent State University, 1979.

Stearns, Marshall Winslow, and Jean Stearns. *Jazz Dance: The Story of American Vernacular Dance*. 1968. New York: Da Capo Press, 1994.

Stratyner, Barbara. *Ned Wayburn and the Dance Routine, from Vaudeville to the Ziegfeld Follies*. N.p.: Society of Dance History Scholars, 1996.

Thomas, Tony. *The Films of Gene Kelly: Song and Dance Man*. Secaucus, NJ: Citadel Press, 1974.

Travis, Doris Eaton. Interviewed by Michael Kantor. May 7, 2002, New York. Theatre on Film and Tape (TOFT), Performing Arts Research Collections, New York Public Library.

Wayburn, Ned. *The Art of Stage Dancing*. 1925. New York: Belvedere, 1980.

3 Musical Theatre Dance Training: Approaches in the United States and China

MIJIANG HE AND DUSTYN MARTINCICH

Musical theatre training has increasingly grown in popularity and access in the United States and across the globe. Amy Osatinski and Bud Coleman comment in "Musical Theatre Training in the Twenty-First Century" that "around the world in the twenty-first century," training opportunities are now found "in and beyond traditional instruction in high schools and universities, to include workshops, academies, conservatories, audition preparation, and online instruction."[1] As such there is a market to codify the training methods and techniques necessary to cultivate performers who can dance, sing, and act, in order to meet the demands of today's musical theatre productions. Many training programs now offer courses in musical theatre dance, which are directed toward two constituencies: actors who require instruction in key movement/dance vocabulary or period-style choreography seen in first-rate musical theatre productions, and dancers who want to pursue musical theatre performance and are already familiar with more Eurocentric dance forms like classical or contemporary ballet or ballet-based jazz dance and/or Africanist rooted forms like tap dance.

This chapter examines training approaches to musical theatre dance across two key sites: the United States, which has driven new developments in musical theatre from its infancy to today, and China, where the demand for large, romantic, Western-style musical theatre has boomed in the twenty-first century. The two case studies complement each other due to the divergent histories of musical theatre training across the two nations: in the United States, musical theatre training grew up alongside musical theatre itself, as dancers searched for ways to pass down embodied knowledge of the evolving forms of dance through training and practice; in China, in contrast, such programs have had to be created to meet the demands of an imported blockbuster industry that integrates Western movement traditions. For each country, the chapter centers the studio teaching practices that are used to define a more codified "theatre dance" or "musical theatre dance" genre, contextualized in the development (or arrival) of musical theatre dance in that country. Additionally, this chapter looks at instances where "repertory," meaning the teaching of previously, professionally choreographed numbers, is used in training to kinesthetically pass on embodied knowledge, enforce common aesthetics, and reinforce a lineage of canonically established choreographies.

This chapter takes a transcultural approach because the cultural and historical context in which musical theatre dance training takes place can affect that training itself – particularly

---

[1]Amy S. Osatinski and Bud Coleman, "Musical Theatre Training in the Twenty-First Century: A Primer," in *The Routledge Companion to Musical Theatre*, ed. Laura MacDonald and Ryan Donovan (New York: Routledge, 2023), 179.

in regards to the very expectations of what skills might be acquired through certain methods. Looking at approaches to dance training specific to musical theatre career preparation in the United States and China, the chapter considers how musical theatre dance continues to evolve as its own genre—both within a national tradition and in the global theatre market of the twenty-first century. This discussion also gives insight into how musical theatre dance is defined through training as well as the repetition of dominant styles seen in musical theatre productions around the world.

Musical Theatre Dance Training in the United States: Supporting an Evolving Genre

An understanding of US (and Chinese) training practices necessitates first that we address musical theatre dance as it is labeled as a teachable genre. Scholars Joanna Dee Das and Ryan Donovan suggest that musical theatre dance does not exist "as its own codified form," saying that it instead "borrows openly from various codified genres including, but not limited to, jazz, ballet, tap, modern and postmodern dance."[2] This borrowing is certainly evident in the evolution of musical theatre choreography over the decades: what was once a string of entertaining dance numbers that featured precision-based vocabulary from ballet, tap, and social dances had become, by the so called Golden Age of musicals, movement that served a core narrative, alongside music, book, and design (for example, Agnes de Mille's work in *Oklahoma!* (1943) and Jerome Robbins' work in *On the Town* (1944)). Still later, the genre of the dance form began shifting to fit the needs of the production and social and concert dance styles of the time. For instance, George Faison's original choreography for *The Wiz* (1974) was rooted in jazz dance movement vocabulary, which by the 1970s freely incorporated soul and other Motown-inspired movements. Training for musicals has had to adapt from classes in ballet, tap, and other "various codified genres," (early musical theatre training included training in Flamenco or Bharatanatyam, for instance) in order to prepare dancers to meet the physical aesthetics of the dominant choreographers' styles of the day. In essence then, musical theatre dance *has* become something of a codified form with training programs adhering to some core general aesthetics, often tying aspects of ballet technique to jazz dance musicality and expression.

In the United States, then, musical theatre dance has come to be treated as a trainable genre in its own right, a genre that established itself as a primarily ballet-based jazz dance technique through the choreographic aesthetics that became popular in musical theatre of the 1940s and 1950s and classes of notable, mostly New York City-based, master teachers. Inextricably linked, jazz and tap dance, rooted in Africanist diasporic movement traditions, have also remained at the core of musical theatre dance. Musical theatre classes have also been heavily influenced by cultural social dances of a particularly period, like mambo or disco. Though contemporary musical theatre choreography has extended beyond these traditional perceptions of musical theatre dance, many musical theatre dance classes have remained mostly tied to this aesthetic.

---

[2] Joanna Dee Das and Ryan Donovan, "Dance in Musical Theatre," *Studies in Musical Theatre* 13, no. 1 (2019): 4.

In the United States, the codification of musical theatre dance training evolved as musical theatre became a staple of entertainment, responding to demand from performers and even audience members wishing to take classes. Dancers and early choreographers could become entrepreneurs, capitalizing on particular "expertise" and industry connections to offer a wide variety of dance classes and train the next big performer. In the 1920s, as Liza Gennaro writes, "ballet, tap, eccentric, acrobatic, precision lines, jazz, and exhibition ballroom were among the most popular styles dominating stages and dancing schools from New York to California."[3] "Musical comedy" was also a popular offering. Biographies of legendary choreographers such as Bob Fosse, Agnes de Mille, Katherine Dunham, and Jerome Robbins cite their early starts at theatre schools and dance studios from a young age. Notable musical theatre dancer Gwen Verdon reported being put into dance class to recuperate from polio, and she was not alone.

As described by Nathan James in this collection, Ned Wayburn, who worked with Florenz Ziegfeld on his dance lines, was one of the first to codify Broadway training into his own method, one rooted in "Americanized Ballet," which ultimately rejected the length of time it took to classically train. Along with Wayburn, other early dance directors like Albertina Rasch in New York and John Tiller in the United Kingdom, as well as lesser-credited Black dance directors like Buddy Bradley and Charlie Davis, trained dancers to perform an evolving fusion of ballet and American jazz and tap dance styles in precision lines. Dance directors often brought social dance styles from ballrooms and nightclubs to the stage, further interpreting and codifying movements that were then disseminated to audiences and often other dancers. It was not uncommon for aspiring dancers to learn moves by watching others perform, then self-training for auditions.

Throughout the twentieth century, musical theatre dance training in the United States, like early modern dance training, increased in rigor and centered on the styles and protocols of key, mostly white, male individuals. In efforts to create unified aesthetics for a "company" of dancers performing in Hollywood movie musicals, Jack Cole created a "modern jazz dance" training system that allowed dancers to learn his style and then quickly learn choreographed numbers in the same style. Undoubtedly influenced by his training at the Denishawn School with modern dance giants Ruth St. Denis and Ted Shawn, Cole had been exposed to methods that appropriated cultural dance forms and integrated aesthetics and training with forms seen around the United States. His style incorporated Indian Bharata Natyam and African American Lindy Hop with ballet vocabulary and modern dance compositional methods, and he brought in teachers like Uday Shankar and white, American-born La Meri to teach classes, further solidifying a training regimen that centered isolations, "get down", and syncopated footwork in exercises.[4]

---

[3]Liza Gennaro, *Making Broadway Dance* (Oxford: Oxford University Press, 2022), 9.
[4]For more information on Jack Cole, see Constance Valis Hill, "From Bharata Natyam to Bop: Jack Cole's 'Modern' Jazz Dance," *Dance Research Journal* 33, no. 2 (2001): 29–39; Rohini Acharya and Eric Kaufman, "Turns of 'Fate': Jack Cole, Jazz and Bharata Natyam in Diasporic Translation," *Studies in Musical Theatre* 13, no. 1 (2019): 9–21, and chapter 2 in this collection. Robert Farris Thompson in his book African Art in Motion: Icon and Act in the Collection of Katherine Coryton White (Los Angeles: University of California Press, 1974), and as Julie Kerr-Berry describes, "get down" as "giving weight in which the knees act as springs that release into and rebound from the earth." Kerr-Berry, "Africanist Elements in American Jazz Dance," in Rooted Jazz Dance: Africanist Aesthetics and Equity in the Twenty-First Century, ed. Lindsay Guarinao, Carlos R. A. Jones, and Wendy Oliver (Gainesville: University Press of Florida, 2022), 85.

As integrated musicals from director-choreographers like Jerome Robbins and Bob Fosse began to expect dancers to act and sing, training shifted accordingly. In the mid- to late twentieth century, training programs began to center the classical concert jazz dance styles of Luigi, Gus Giordano, and Matt Mattox.[5] These programs offered dancers training in ballet-based jazz dance technique, giving dancers a versatile style, emphasizing the importance of musicality, and implementing a set rotation of exercises that featured polyrhythmic upper- and lower-body sequences, get·down, and stretches to increase flexibility. By the time Fosse and Michael Bennett were bringing in the new Broadway jazz dance styles in shows like *Pippin* (1972), *Cabaret* (1966), and *A Chorus Line* (1975), training centers such as Luigi's Dance Center, established by jazz dance teacher Luigi in the 1960s, Phil Black Dance Studio, which was established in 1968, and JoJo's Dance Factory, which was founded in the 1970s by JoJo Smith and Sue Samuels Smith, were offering dancers coming to New York a place to train in ballet, jazz, and tap. These centers were open to all levels of dancers, from youth to adult beginners to previously-trained dancing professionals. Classes by master teachers who were themselves performers and choreographers, were specifically crafted for singing, acting dancers looking to enter the professional industry. These spaces gave way to the now epicenters of professional training for aspiring musical theatre dancers: Broadway Dance Center, formally JoJo's Dance Factory, which was founded by "Doctor Jazz" Frank Hatchett in 1984, and Steps on Broadway, NYC, which was founded by Carol Paumgarten and Patrice Sorier in 1979 and is now run by leading jazz dance instructor Joe Lanteri.

Today, US-based university programs that offer musical theatre training typically focus on growing skills of acting, voice, and movement. Markedly, when theatre training is paired with a strong dance program, students will take a range of classes including ballet, jazz, and tap, and potentially modern, hip-hop, or social dance. Continued training in specific dance genres not only provides musical theatre performers with a more diverse set of movement vocabulary, but also fosters in them an adaptability between styles and approaches. For instance, in a ballet class, dancers execute variations on standardized exercises that promote individual practice and mastery of aesthetics that include line, flexibility, and liftedness, whereas dancers in a tap class work in a community, as musicians would, sharing common vocabulary rooted in call-and-response, polyrhythm, and get down. Both methods are valuable in musical theatre, depending on the needs of a production. Furthermore, training in university programs ideally allows students to apply and synthesize lessons from individual classes in full musical theatre productions or cabarets, joining dance training to voice and acting, as well as working with props, sets, and costumes.

Intensive programs outside of universities, such as those at Jacob's Pillow, Broadway Theatre Project, and CAP21 (Collaborative Arts Project 21), offer training to students interested in preparing for the industry that further defines musical theatre dance in the context of broader musical theatre training. These programs often focus not on the basic steps of dance, but instead on the application of previously acquired technique to musical theatre choreography. In this way, training focuses on the practice of quickly picking up choreography, something that is necessary in many musical theatre production auditions

---

[5]For more on Luigi and Matt Mattox, see chapter 2.

and rehearsals. In addition to picking up specific movements, dancers must also focus more on style—the quality of the movement and the approach to musicality.[6] Style, not necessarily technique, and signature aesthetic components are what link the choreography to a specific choreographer and make it identifiable as musical theatre dance. Being able to adapt to a specific style or choreographic signature serves a musical theatre performer well as a production will often draw from the aesthetics of a particular narrative. For instance, Gower Champion's choreography for *42nd Street* (1980) requires a very different style from Savion Glover's choreography for *Shuffle Along, or, the Making of the Musical Sensation of 1921 and All That Followed* (2016), though both are identified as tap dance. Champion's style is more uplifted and his vocabulary can be readily translated from dancer to dancer by sharing names of the steps as well as rhythm. The work is meant to be performed in unison by a large ensemble. Glover's style, rooted in the lineage of greats like Henry LeTang, is grounded with complex rhythmic structures and singular virtuosities, much like a jazz music session. It is shared primarily through conveying rhythm and feeling, trading sounds between dancers, shifting from communal performance to individual features. Though dancers may train in specific, non–musical dance genres like ballet, modern, and tap, the ability to adapt to the stylistic needs of the choreography and then integrate it into the larger narrative picture of the production has made musical theatre dance unique and has come to be a central point of focus in training programs in the United States today.

In the United States, musical theatre dance has benefited from a "master class" model of training (both inside and outside university programs), where students take classes from teachers who worked with a specific choreographer in an original cast of a show and thus hold a bodily archive of that style. A performer's embodied history can translate style in the classroom. For instance, Lee Becker Theodore, who originated Anybodys in *West Side Story* (1957), taught "theatre dance" that was "grounded in the ballet-based jazz techniques of Robbins and Cole . . . every day the class warm up unfolded in a rigorous and codified progression from barre to centre and classic jazz isolations—including Jack Cole's 'Hindu swing' jazz isolations."[7] Furthermore, teaching the choreography from a specific production— with the cues, vocabulary, and coaching methods that were used by the choreographer or original dancer in the role—has become a common method to train particular styles. Gwen Verdon, for example, even during and after her performance career, rehearsed with dancers in Bob Fosse's productions, "translating his choreographic vision for other dancers and putting movement into understandable physical and verbal language they could interpret and execute."[8] Dancers, in this way, have concretized choreographic styles in musical theatre more so than choreographers.

Dancers, associate choreographers, and dance assistants can teach the choreography from a production, lifting it out of its context for the benefit of training and further establishing

---

[6]Though often an amorphous word encompassing a choreographic signature, *style*, as suggested by Adrienne L. Kaeppler, refers "to persistent patterning in ways of performing structure—from subtle qualities of energy to the use of the body parts as recognized by people of a specific dance tradition." Kaeppler, "Dance and the Concept of Style'," *Yearbook for Traditional Music* 33 (2001): 62.
[7]Acharya and Kaufman, "Turns of 'fate'," 10.
[8]Dustyn Martincich, "Stepping Out of Line: (Re)Claiming the Diva for the Dancers of Broadway," *Studies in Musical Theatre* 12, no. 1 (2018): 87.

this sort of "repertory" model for musical theatre dance, though this is not without challenges. First, the ephemeral nature of choreography in musical theatre productions means that the archive of musical theatre dance often rests in the dancers themselves, who act as embodied historians. Second, musical theatre dance, especially after the mid-twentieth century, has tended to be integrated into a production, not something that can stand on its own (although exceptions exist: dance revues like *Fosse* [1999] and musicals like Twyla Tharp's *Movin' Out* [2002] and *Come Fly Away* [2009] offer ways to excerpt a choreographer's style because dance is the primary narrative communicator). Additionally, US copyright is exceedingly difficult for dance and may prevent repertory work from being circulated because of notions of ownership and authorship.

In an effort to create a physical archive of musical theatre dance, Lee Becker Theodore formed the American Dance Machine in 1976. This organization recorded dancers performing signature pieces from over eighty works by key Broadway choreographers. Working with Margo Sappington, Theodore restaged pieces, extracted from their original productions, with as much context necessary to preserve the work's intention, including costumes, sets, and props. Well-documented choreographers Cole, de Mille, Fosse, Robbins, Champion, and Bennett, whose work is often pointed to in musical theatre dance texts, were preserved, and so too were choreographers whose work is less discussed in their influences in creating musical theatre dance as a genre like Donald McKayle, Geoffrey Holden, Patricia Birch, Henry LeTang, and Tommy Tune. Works were restaged directly by the choreographer who had created them or by the dancers who had performed in or coached the role. Dancer Robert LaFosse, for example, restaged Jerome Robbins's choreography for "Mr. Monotony" and "Charleston" from *Billion Dollar Baby* (1945), while Donna McKechnie, who originated the role of Cassie in *A Chorus Line*, restaged Michael Bennett's choreography for the number "Music and the Mirror."

American Dance Machine was a performing company, and it was Theodore's intention to host a training space that would operate along the master class model that has since become more common, where budding musical theatre dancers can take classes in specific styles from dancers who can translate the vocabulary from established choreographers.[9] This practice is now seen on the dance convention circuits and in well-established training spaces. The Verdon Fosse Legacy organization for example, formed with the mission to disseminate a codified version of Fosse dance technique, something Bob Fosse never established for himself. This organization, supported by the Fosse estate, has worked to codify what can actually be called "Fosse technique," in the same way modern dance companies have preserved the works and technique of Martha Graham or Alvin Ailey. Organizations like American Dance Machine and the Verdon Fosse Legacy have thus solidified musical theatre dance technique according to the particular needs of a certain style.

---

[9]American Dance Machine was resurrected in 2012 as AMD21 (American Dance Machine for the 21st Century) to feature and catalog the work of choreographers like Jerry Mitchell, Susan Stroman, Rob Ashford, Andy Blankenbuehler, and Mia Michaels, with the help of their associate choreographers. The organization, led by Nikki Feirt Atkins and Cathy Folgelman, also shared dance film interpretations of numbers like "The Music and the Mirror" from *A Chorus Line* and "Cool" from *West Side Story* over the 2020–1 Covid pandemic lockdown.

Today, this kind of repertory-style training has become a cornerstone for many evolving musical theatre training markets, around the world, particularly as musical theatre has grown as a cultural and economic "export." Dancers have long taken their embodied experience to teaching opportunities, training future dancers in the style or even specific numbers of a production. This has gone a step further, where today dance studio teachers, dance teams coaches and captains, or school glee clubs who do not have direct experience try to replicate aspects of choreography they see online, captured from Broadway, *So You Think You Can Dance*, or dance competitions. The questions of copyright and authenticity certainly are raised, however; in the US choreographic copyright is hard to obtain, prove, and enforce.[10]

In the case of China, repertory-learning has been an embedded practice in much of dance training, where students often train to replicate, with precision, the movement, quality, and style of the choreographer who has been deemed a "master" of the form as an act of respect, both for the teacher and the form. The tradition of passing training, choreography, and movement traditions, often appearing in master/apprentice models of learning, puts emphasis on historical lineage and honoring the work and choreography with an exact replica. When it comes to musical theatre, however, and other Western forms, translating the movement and style, though still taught as repertory, are learned instead by watching video or bringing additional teachers in to craft the movement as closely to the original as possible. In what follows, coauthor Mijiang He speaks about the growth of musical theatre dance and its training methods in China, drawing on his personal experience of musical theatre's arrival to China and his performance as a member of the cast of *Cats,* as well as his own work in building a musical theatre dance program at the prestigious Beijing Dance Academy. In creating a curriculum for dancers to train in, repertory-based methods were necessary to align with the structures of other forms, as well as to create a legitimate training program that would prepare dancers for the industry standards and aesthetics in China. To start, in order to contextualize this autoethnographic narrative, we will offer some background of how Western forms like musical theatre integrate into traditions of Chinese performance.

A Brief History of Chinese Musical Theatre

The earliest roots of Western-style musical theatre in China extend to the 1980s, the decade after the Cultural Revolution (1966–76) ended, when China went through a period of reform and opening up policy. Though China's economy underwent rapid growth over the next twenty years, the musical theatre industry did not develop as quickly. In fact, through the end of the century and into the following decade, commercial theatre in China largely existed in the form of propaganda shows presented by national and provincial theatre groups. Most of these "musicals"—which took the form of a story with songs and dances— were supported by government funding and were developed to promote government-approved messages of strong moral values, a practice common for many Chinese popular

---

[10]For a historical contextualization and critical discussion of choreographic copyright see Anthea Kraut's *Choreographing Copyright: Race, Gender, and Intellectual Property Rights in American Dance* (Oxford: Oxford University Press, 2016).

art forms. The productions reinterpreted Chinese stories and drew on the music and physical language of traditional Chinese dramas. The content revolved around themes that rarely related to contemporary, urban Chinese life. Overall, they were mostly unpopular and had little to do with musical theatre as we understand it today.

Toward the end of the twentieth century, Chinese theatre creators began looking for opportunities to bring popular global theatre trends and (non-Soviet) theatrical productions to Chinese audiences. Chinese musical theatre pioneers were particularly attracted to musicals from Broadway and the West End that sonically aligned with Chinese music traditions and could be produced with government approval. Beginning in the early 2000s, a number of Western musicals came to China on tour but in untranslated productions. Tours of *Les Miserables*, *Cats*, and *Phantom of the Opera* found success with Chinese audiences, likely because of some sonic similarities to Chinese traditional music and core love stories.

In 2004, Songlei International (China·Songlei Industries Group Co., LTD) established the first musical theatre company to be backed by private investors: Die-Zhi-Wu Musical Theatre Company (蝶之舞音乐剧团). Its objective was not to host tours of foreign-language productions but to produce Chinese-language musical theatre that aligned with the globally popular form. In September 2007, its first original musical, *Butterflies* (蝶), premiered at the Beijing Poly Theatre. Li Dun produced the show, with music and lyrics by San Bao and Guan Shan and book by Guan Shan and Xu Qing. The production team was led by Canadian directors Gilles Maheu and Wayne Fowkes and UK choreographer Darren Charles. Touted in advertisements as China's "first world-class musical," *Butterflies* had a successful run both domestically and overseas. It presented a traditional Chinese story in a modern way with music, dance, and acting styles that departed from traditional Chinese drama practices and instead offered popular music and vocal stylings of the time period as well as technological additions typically seen in concerts, with spectacular lighting and scenic elements. After *Butterflies*, Songlei International produced more musicals, like the Chinese jukebox musical *Love U, Teresa* (2010), which was based on the music of pop star Teresa Teng, and *The Vagrant Life of Sanmao* (2011), which was based on a popular Chinese cartoon character.

Though Songlei's musicals garnered audience attention, it would be the Chinese-language production of *Mamma Mia!*, which premiered in Beijing in 2011 (twelve years after its English-language, West End debut), that signaled the real emergence of Broadway-style musical theatre in China, along with a concomitant rise in privately backed production companies. *Mamma Mia!* was the first endeavor of United Asia Live Entertainment, which had the vision of translating a successful Western musical into Mandarin and casting Chinese performers. Although some critics were against translating the lyrics, audiences clearly enjoyed being able to understand this Western-style musical production from beginning to end, indeed humming lyrics when they departed the theatre. Due to the production's success, United Asia Live Entertainment backed a Chinese-language touring production of *Cats* (West End premiere, 1981) in 2012–13, taking it to six cities: Shanghai, Beijing, Guangzhou, Xi'an, Wuhan, and Chongqing. Though United Asia Live Entertainment dissolved two years later, the tour cemented musical theatre's place in China's two biggest cities, Beijing and Shanghai, with a fast-growing market. In 2015, One World Culture Communication purchased a touring production of *The Phantom of the Opera* (West End premiere, 1986). The international touring production "played Beijing and Guangzhou and took in a total box office of approximately 17 million USD during its two-month run," which was considered a tremendous success at the time.[11]

These musical successes from 2011 to 2015 stimulated more producers and performing companies to try musical theatre as a performance genre. Companies like Sevenages, Shanghai Media Group, CCstage, A.C.Orange, ENNOVA Culture, Poly Performing Arts, and iMusical are now producing three categories of musicals in Beijing and Shanghai: international tours from the United States, United Kingdom, Australia, France, and South Korea; Chinese Mandarin-language productions of overseas musicals; and original Chinese musicals. In the 2017–18 season, for example, nearly fifty shows toured the big cities in China, among them the international tours of *Wicked*, *The Producers*, West Side Story, *Legally Blonde*, *Jersey Boys*, *Sister Act*, *Rent*, and *Chicago*; Mandarin-language productions of *The Lion King*, *Jekyll* and *Hyde*, *A Gentleman's Guide to Love* and *Murder*, *Into the Woods*, *The Sound of Music*, *Man of La Mancha*, *Beauty* and *Beast*, and *Next to Normal*; and original musicals *Secret* (不能说的秘密), *Mr.& Mrs. Single* (隐婚男女), *Papa, I Only Sing for You* (酒干倘卖无), *Firmly Happiness* (稳稳地幸福), *Destroying Opium at Humen* (虎门销烟), *Journey under the Midnight Sun* (白夜行), and *In the Mood for Sorrow* (《马不停蹄的忧伤》).[12] From this one season's offerings, it is clear that the Chinese musical theatre industry was continuing to evolve—and that Chinese audiences loved the variety of shows. Speaking about this season, the *South China Morning Post* reported in September 2019 that "ticket sales in China for imported musicals grew almost 150 percent last year, driving overall revenue growth for musicals by over 90 percent. More Chinese versions of Western musicals, and Chinese originals, are being staged."[13] But as the popularity of these diverse musical productions grew, so too did the demand for performers who could sing, dance, and act, not only in Western techniques, but in Chinese traditional styles as well. Musical theatre education in China evolved as a new genre of study built to prepare performers for this growing field.

Musical Theatre Training in China

Musical theatre training in China primarily exists in programs that offer a four-year university education. Most musical theatre performers graduate from one of three types of universities: professional academies (similar to conservatories); comprehensive universities, which offer classes in a range of disciplines, including acting, singing, and dancing, with a focus not just on practice but also on theory and pedagogy; and public universities and colleges, which are less geared toward pedagogy and theory, and where informal, student-led clubs offer students performance opportunities outside of formal class offerings. This section will primarily focus on conservatory training, but it is useful to consider how each program

---

[11]"A Look at Imported Western Musicals in China," *China Stage Connection*, accessed January 10, 2023, https://www.chinastageconnection.com/imported-western-musicals.
[12]"Why Musicals Are So Great in China in 2017" [2017中国音乐剧为什么这么厉害], Sohu.com, January 4, 2018, https://www.sohu.com/a/214720011_760269.
[13]Snow Xia, "From *Cats* to *Chicago*, China Is Loving Western Musicals, But What of Its Own?," *South China Morning Post*, September 18, 2019.

considers "training" and how the musical theatre industry in China has been supported by these programs.

While many professional academies in China provide musical theatre education, four academies account for most musical theatre graduates: Shanghai Conservatory of Music, Beijing Dance Academy, Shanghai Theatre Academy, and the Central Academy of Drama. These professional academies began to offer musical theatre training in the 1990s, developing performing arts majors in acting and music with courses in singing, dance, acting, and speech. In 2002, the Beijing Dance Academy became the first university in China to develop a musical theatre department, for which, like for its other programs, students wishing to enroll must engage in a competitive audition process. Shanghai Conservatory of Music and the Central Academy of Drama have also established musical theatre departments, while the Shanghai Theatre Academy nests musical theatre under the acting department. These four academies have formed a systematic four-year undergraduate curriculum that centers the study of musicals from the United Kingdom and the United States. Studies are supplemented by training in original Chinese musicals. Together, training in these styles offers students a comprehensive curriculum in terms of styles of singing, dancing, and acting. Courses are directed at making students proficient in the kind of musical theatre audiences expect to see, with specific courses including, for example, vocal technique, song coaching, sight singing, ear training, music theory, and choral class.

Many comprehensive universities have also established majors in acting, singing, and dancing, among them the Communication University of China, Shanghai Institute of Visual Arts, Communication University of Zhejiang, and Capital Normal University. Geared toward training students interested in teaching, schools such as these brought in musical theatre training in order to meet the needs of students. Their majors in musical theatre focus on pedagogy and theoretical research in music, singing, acting, and dance. Many of these institutions have been successful in their endeavors as many students have completed the programs prepared to join the industry.

Public universities and colleges do not offer performing majors, but many students who are interested in musicals and plays have established amateur theatre troupes and clubs of various sizes on campus. As Laura MacDonald points out, "the majority of C9 league institutions (China's Ivy League) have musical theatre clubs, and draw members studying subjects as varied as journalism, languages, finance, medicine and engineering."[14] At universities like Peking University, Tsinghua University, and Shanghai International Studies University, among others, students who do not have the opportunity to receive professional training in musical theatre develop skills in acting, singing, and dance through self-produced musical theatre shows of various sizes. Some students also transition into industry jobs after graduation, even after earning degrees in another discipline. Ultimately, no matter the training program, students have multiple pathways to study musical theatre, or at the very least to pursue interest in this new art form in China. In the sections that follow, coauthor Mijiang He talks about his own trajectory from traditional Chinese dance to musical theatre

---

[14]Laura MacDonald, "Seasons of Love: Chinese Millennials' Affective Amateur Musical Theatre Performances," *Performance Research* 25, no. 1 (2020): 112.

and, ultimately, to the Musical Theatre Department at the Beijing Dance Academy, where he worked to train the next generation of musical theatre dancers.

A Performer's Perspective: Mijiang He on His Musical Theatre Training Trajectory

"As a musical theatre performer, my practice starts with my connection to music," He says.[15] After studying music and dance in middle school, He attended Hunan Normal University, majoring in Chinese dance. After completing his studies, he moved into the performance industry as a Chinese dancer and teacher. In his mid-twenties, pop music, theatre dance, Hollywood movies, and American TV dramas caught his attention. He explains, "Hollywood musicals in particular opened up a new world for me." After watching a pirated DVD of the filmed staging of the *Les Misérables* twenty-fifth anniversary concert, he was hooked. In 2011, He enrolled at the prestigious Beijing Dance Academy to pursue a master's degree, focusing on musical theatre choreography. While enrolled in the program, he heard of a call for dancers for the Chinese-language production of *Cats*. "After four rounds of auditions and callbacks, I became a cast member. . . . My supervisor [at the Beijing Dance Academy] thought joining a professionally produced musical would be a better way to learn musical theatre dance, so the academy allowed me to complete my studies while on tour."

Being a performer in *Cats* marked the shift for He from a Chinese dancer and teacher to a professional musical theatre performer. "The challenge was enormous," He explains. "My dance training was mainly Chinese classical dance, Chinese ethnic and folk dance, and some ballet and modern dance. I had never learned ballroom, jazz, tap, hip-hop, etc." He notes that he had little experience in the style of jazz ballet and theatre dance that Gillian Lynne uses in the choreography for *Cats*. He describes,

> First of all, Chinese dance and musical theatre dance are different in their aesthetics. Chinese dance follows the core [elements] of Chinese traditional art, which are Jing (精, essence), Qi (气, energy), and Shen (神, spirit). When a dancer starts to move, the inner energy goes first, and it drives her muscles and joints to transmit the spirit to her movements. The whole dance shows her essence from the inside out. In musical theatre, the function of dance is to tell a story and entertain the audience. Dancers trained in Chinese traditional dance are not very good at communicating external narratives to audiences. Even when a dancer faces the auditorium, she usually looks into the distance of nothingness. In musicals, actors must completely release their energy and passion to all spectators. In some scenes, they build a connection with the audience in the first few rows. This is a difference between performers in concert dance and those in musical theatre. The characteristic of Chinese dance is that a scene is pre-set first, and then the dancers are immersed in an isolated world, dancing like no one is watching. It is very similar to modern dance because, on the one hand, many

---

[15]The rest of this chapter, which bridges autoethnographic and (auto)biographic forms, is drawn from a conversation between Mijiang He and Dustyn Martincich on He's musical theatre training in China. All quotations from He come from this discussion.

early pioneers of Western modern dance were influenced by Chinese traditional art, and, on the other hand, contemporary Chinese dance has been influenced by modern dance since its inception.

New Chinese dance aesthetics also share similarities with and draw inspiration from ballet. He describes the dance form as combining ballet technique and composition with traditional arts such as Peking Opera, martial arts, and calligraphy, as well as ancient Chinese murals, literature, and paintings. He asserts: "Chinese classical dance, which combines the training of ballet and the core of traditional Chinese aesthetics, has become the most critical training system in dance schools, dance companies, and amateur training institutions." The new Chinese dance aesthetics predominantly extend upward, revealing a sense of sacredness and grace that is infinitely close to the celestial realm and defies gravity. Additionally, like in ballet, some vocabulary and qualities are assigned by gender. For instance, female dancers embody qualities of lightness and elongation, while male dancers are assigned certain acrobatic movements that showcase strength and athleticism.

He explains that his primary obstacle in learning choreography in those early rehearsals for *Cats* was learning the movement without mood or expression—the execution of the dance vocabulary and style was the primary focus. Lynne's style and vocabulary for the production are grounded in ballet-based jazz dance, with physical homages to significant Broadway choreographers. For instance, Jo-Anne Robinson, who was the dance captain of the original UK production and associate director and choreographer of the production in China, aligned the honky-tonk qualities seen in "Macavity: the Mystery Cat" with Bob Fosse's style. She also cited certain fight sequences as inspired by Jerome Robbins's work from *West Side Story*. All of this was different from what He was familiar with from Chinese classical dance, but he learned it quickly without time for exploration, because Lynne's choreography was already created and simply being translated onto different performers for the new production.

Another shift of focus and practice that He noticed in rehearsals was the change in the body's center of gravity. Jazz dance technique, rooted in African American vernacular dance forms, requires a low center of gravity. Dancers may walk on their heels (instead of lifting up on the balls of their feet), with their pelvis dropped between the knees, never locking at the joints to allow for movement at the hips, spine, and chest. Jazz dance conveys a sense of life that is relaxed and closer to the earth. For dancers who trained in Chinese classical dance, it is not easy to lower the center of gravity in choreography. He noticed, however, that dropping his weight and relaxing the knees, hips, stomach, and chest allowed him to adjust in preparation to speak and sing. The aesthetic was as much visual as it was functional for a musical theatre performer.

He further observed a difference from Chinese dance in the choreography's use of isolation and its relation to the music. Where Chinese dance emphasizes graceful movement with a sense of extension and fluidity, anatomical isolations (for example, shoulders articulating the individual percussive instruments or ribs shifting side to side with a beat) are featured heavily in jazz and musical theatre dance to reflect musicality and create angular physical shapes. For He, lyrical music ties directly to Chinese dance in terms of lightness and elegance. "Traditional Chinese music is mainly melodious or poignant," He says. "Melodic and sad songs dominate the popular music developed in the 2000s, where up-tempo dance music has never been the first choice for Chinese mainstream media and audiences." He notes that this aesthetic orientation is codified in Chinese dance training, where instructors purposefully connect lyrical music and a strong sense of melody to smooth and seamless movement. As a performer in *Cats* who was not trained in isolations, He recalls, "I often unconsciously ignored the rhythm of the choreography." He continues, "When the choreographer and music director required us to focus on specific aspects of the music, the syncopated and compound rhythm became a significant challenge for Chinese dancers like myself."

Lastly, prior to his casting in *Cats,* He was not trained to sing while dancing. Andrew Lloyd Webber's music set to lyrics inspired by T. S. Eliot's poetry required actors to sing the multipart chords in complex harmonies while performing Lynne's choreography, which included making spectacular jumps and leaps and standing in poses often on half-toe (or, in ballet, *demi-pointe*). "Most of the dancing was accompanied by singing in this show," He says. "Learning how and when to breathe became one of the most critical aspects to the choreography." His training in Chinese dance was the same as ballet, which requires dancers to tighten their abdomens and mostly use thoracic respiration. As He explains, "Chinese classical dancers hold their breath as long as possible to support the movements and make them more extended and flowing. The rhythm of breathing is wholly based on the dancer's physical movement." Lynne's complex and athletic choreography required proper breathing to ensure enough stamina to shift from dance to singing quickly, or to execute both at once.

He performed with the company of *Cats* for more than two hundred performances between May 2012 and January 2014. He finished the master's program in 2014 and became a professor in the Musical Theatre Department of Beijing Dance Academy. In that time, He has worked to establish the kind of musical theatre dance training that supports the experience he had as a performer in an effort to prepare the next generation of performers for the industry.

Developing Musical Theatre Dance Training at the Beijing Dance Academy

He developed his approach to musical theatre training within the existing structure of training practices in Chinese arts schools like the Beijing Dance Academy.[16] He began with the class cohort of 2014, starting the curriculum with Appreciation of Musical Theatre and "basic" or introductory technique courses in individual dance genres, voice, and acting. After the first year, He followed curricular protocol to develop "integrated" courses where skills are combined in class exercises. For instance, students both sing and dance. As most students had previous dance experience, with backgrounds in Chinese classical and folk dance, ballet, contemporary, and ballroom, He could create courses focusing on specific styles, not just technique, of musical theatre dance. In addition to designing courses, He was responsible for deciding the musical repertoire studied each session and directing the class

---

[16]A brief explanation about Chinese art school structures: different from practices in the United States, Chinese university art education course offerings are based on a fixed class group. Students of the same major who entered the college in the same year form a fixed group. For the four academic years, the students of this cohort take all courses together and live together on campus. In the Beijing Dance Academy, each class group has a head teacher, who is responsible for mentoring students and teaching some courses.

Image 3.1 Students at the Beijing Dance Academy performing an excerpt from the musical *Cats* for their showcase. Photo by Weija Zhao.

group in productions that would both showcase skills and actively train dancers in applying classroom skills to formal performance. The curricular trajectory was intended to culminate in a final, full-length performance.

He developed a Musical Theatre Repertoire class, using as his first assignment a low-tech, eighty-minute adaptation of *Cats*. Not only did he know Lynne's choreography firsthand, but the selection provided a challenge for acting through dance. He observed among his students the same obstacles he had experienced: "the students' previous dance training did not include enough jazz dance." He incorporated isolations into warm-ups and added exercises to help dancers drop the center of their weight and refocus their breathing patterns to be able to sing while dancing. He coached dancers in musicality and performance qualities outside of "exaggerated facial expressions, overly dedicated hand shapes, excessively flared hips, and locked knees," which were stylistic techniques acquired from classical Chinese dance. Instead, he helped dancers build and translate character, which, along with music led their reason to move.

He, eager to further develop the 2014 cohort's knowledge of musical theatre technique and styles, went on to translate Bob Fosse's movement vocabulary. Fosse, particularly through his work in *Chicago* (1975), which he directed and choreographed, became one of the most important references for the students of what was seen as "musical theatre dance." As He did not have firsthand Fosse training, he researched videos, books, and movies to select twenty-two numbers, which he then learned himself in order to teach to the students. Among these, the number "Sing, Sing, Sing" from *Fosse* (1999) proved the most challenging for students, with its complex entrances and exits, constantly changing formations, and an unfamiliar swing rhythm. However, in studying and embodying so much of Fosse's repertoire in these reconstructions, He found that the students gained a new understanding of how to act in musical theatre, improving their expressive qualities in translating the choreography

Image 3.2 Students at the Beijing Dance Academy performing in a Fosse-style showcase.

and tying the movement into a larger narrative. Students also improved their ability to pick up choreography and execute attributes specific to Fosse's style. He notes that for his students, "Broadway jazz felt like a rebellion against classical dance aesthetics." He's students present their Fosse-style revue in a formal presentation for the teachers and students of the Central Academy of Drama, Shanghai Theatre Academy, Shanghai Conservatory of Music, and other traditional schools.

Beyond the question of style, He acknowledged the diversity of dance genres that are encompassed by musical theatre dance. As He notes, tap dance is relatively unfamiliar to Chinese musical theatre teachers, actors, and choreographers, and due to its complex musical rhythm and techniques it has not often been taught in Chinese musical theatre curriculums. He learned basic tap skills for his performance in *Cats* and, taking that knowledge, incorporated tap into his musical theatre dance syllabus. In the cohort's first year, He taught the students the *Cats* scene "The Old Gumbie Cats and her Beetles' Tattoo." The scene gave the students only brief exposure to tap as a dance genre, so in their second year, He brought in Chinese tapper Zhu Haifeng to teach basic tap vocabulary akin to Broadway's on-your-toes style, including specific routines from Susan Stroman's choreography from *Crazy for You* (1992) and Randy Skinner's choreography from the 2001 revival of *42nd Street*.[17] He wanted to immerse his students in a full, tap-based musical, so

---

[17]Skinner's choreography was based on Gower Champion's original 1980 choreography, on which Skinner is credited as Dance Assistant.

he persuaded the Musical Theatre Department to procure the copyright for *42nd Street*. It was the first time Beijing Dance Academy had purchased the copyright of a full-length musical theatre work from abroad.

He invited Zhu to choreograph or, rather to reconstruct the original choreography by listening to the sounds of the taps and watching the original and revival choreography on film. He translated the script and lyrics to Mandarin with friend and fellow *Cats* company member Yumeng Chen, allowing the students to work with the text in their own language in order to, as He says, "understand every line and be freer to create their characters onstage." The production, which was presented in October 2017, was the final project of this twenty-five-student cohort. It gave the students the opportunity to demonstrate basic skills in individual techniques, as well as integrated and applied skills that would not have been possible outside of a production setting.

When He was hired at the Beijing Dance Academy, a musical theatre curriculum had been set in place, and it was already a practice to engage students in this repertory-based learning. However, with his cohort, He wished to eventually acquire rights for works and bring in other professionals who could build the students' range of styles as well as professional network. Based on his experience cultivating this cohort and developing a more repertory-focused curriculum for musical theatre dance at his university, He reflects on the needs of today's musical theatre performers. For He, a well-trained musical performer must have what He calls "a multifunctional body." "Performers cannot train in every style," He explains, though he advocates for training to include as many styles as possible. "The [training] process is long and requires dancers to continue learning new vocabularies, new rhythms, to make their bodies adaptable for any style in a production, both in contemporary musical theatre and in the future." He acknowledges the competition for jobs, and the need for dancers to be tenacious, persistent, and malleable in order to move in the way needed to convey a story.

Image 3.3 Students at the Beijing Dance Academy performing in *42nd Street* for their showcase. Photo by Weija Zhao.

Since 2011, musicals have increasingly become the dominant art form in the theatre market in China's metropolises. However, industry jobs are often not posting for triple threats or even dancers. Dance-heavy musicals are less popular in China, and very few have been produced, though international tours like *An American in Paris* and *Cats* were acclaimed by Chinese audiences. This lack of interest in more dance-based musicals could reflect the appeal of the familiar, as original Chinese musicals and the popular Mandarin productions of Western musicals are more focused on singing—but that does not mean that the industry will not develop in this direction. He believes that the long-term success of future musical theatre performers in China necessitates a strong grounding in musical theatre dance. In 2017, He joined the faculty of the Communication University of China to establish a musical theatre major based on the practices he cultivated at the Beijing Dance Academy. Since he left, the Beijing Dance Academy has shifted its focus into integrating more Chinese musicals into its curriculum. He continues to choreograph and train actors and amateurs in musical theatre dance, now in the United States as he pursued master's degrees at Carthage College in Wisconsin, and Binghamton University in New York. While choreographing *Sweet Charity*, *Ride the Cyclone*, and *Songs for a New World* for Carthage, He had to shift from the Chinese practice of imitating Western musicals to developing original choreography and personal style—and so his trajectory continues to evolve.

Musical Theatre Dance Training: Homage and Innovation

Musical theatre dance training has necessarily evolved with the needs and aesthetics of the shows being produced. The movement, as part of the visual narrative, also reflects the culture in which the show is being performed. Globally, musical theatre dance has become identified as a technique associated with choreographic style, mostly that of a ballet-based jazz or tap. As seen in China and the United States, learning choreography serves as a method of accessing an embodied history, similar to how one kinesthetically learns social dances or how one might learn to sing from a recorded piece of music.

As He observes from his own experiences, the practice of using repertory as a means of teaching musical theatre dance as a genre offers teachers a ready-made curriculum and allows students a chance to have an embodied understanding of stylistic aesthetics and key movement vocabularies of established choreographers. However, there are repercussions to this method, namely that some choreographers' styles are necessarily omitted, either due to copyright, movement requirements, or idiosyncrasy vis-à-vis the now-developed musical theatre style. If musical theatre dance, like modern dance, has become defined by key choreographic styles, it is useful to look at how those styles are performed, documented, and further disseminated, thereby ensuring the legacy of certain choreographers. Who can and should be teaching repertory? And how is repertory communicated outside of the context of a production? As YouTube, TikTok, and other digital resources have helped grow the musical theatre fan base, the repetition of certain styles further concretizes audiences' and trainees' perceptions of the form, and may even solidify the form itself.

As He points out, musical theatre performers who specialize in dance have had to be adaptable. Training beyond the musical theatre repertory is necessary in order to gain exposure to the kind of dance genres outside of the ballet-jazz or tap that undergirds musical theatre style. Performers must continue to train in acting and voice, as well as dance forms that prepare them for work in pieces by choreographers and movement directors like Bill T. Jones or Camille A. Brown. Additionally, as musical theatre dancing bodies have historically been athletic and able-bodied, one must also encourage the incorporation of movement study that allows for bodies who may not traditionally be identified as "dancers" or even "trainable" dancers.

This examination of musical theatre dance training in the United States and China reveals evolving trends. As a cultural export from the United States, Canada, the United Kingdom, and other Western countries, musical theatre transfers not only just the music and lyrics, but a whole visual narrative, often embodied and translated through the movement of the performers. The body is then read, conveying identity markers as well as narrative to audiences. In training performers to be more articulate and fluent in multiple physical languages associated with musical theatre, educators must continue to evolve with the needs of the stories being told.

Bibliography

Acharya, Rohini, and Eric Kaufman. "Turns of 'Fate': Jack Cole, Jazz and Bharata Natyam in Diasporic Translation." *Studies in Musical Theatre* 13, no. 1 (2019): 9–21.

Das, Joanna Dee, and Ryan Donovan. "Dance in Musical Theatre." *Studies in Musical Theatre* 13, no. 1 (2019): 3–7.

Gennaro, Liza. *Making Broadway Dance*. Oxford: Oxford University Press, 2022.

Harris, Diana Dart. *Beginning Musical Theatre Dance*. Champaign, IL: Human Kinetics, 2016.

Hill, Constance Valis. "From Bharata Natyam to Bop: Jack Cole's 'Modern' Jazz Dance." *Dance Research Journal* 33, no. 2 (2001): 29–39.

Kaeppler, Adrienne L. "Dance and the Concept of Style." *Yearbook for Traditional Music* 33 (2001): 49–63.

"A Look at Imported Western Musicals in China." *China Stage Connection*. Accessed January 10, 2023. https://www.chinastageconnection.com/imported-western-musicals.

MacDonald, Laura. "Seasons of Love: Chinese Millennials' Affective Amateur Musical Theatre Performances." *Performance Research* 25, no. 1 (2020): 112–20.

Martincich, Dustyn. "Stepping Out of Line: (Re)Claiming the Diva for the Dancers of Broadway." *Studies in Musical Theatre* 12, no. 1 (2018): 79–91.

Osatinski, Amy S., and Bud Coleman. "Musical Theatre Training in the Twenty-First Century: A Primer." In *The Routledge Companion to Musical Theatre*, edited by Laura MacDonald and Ryan Donovan, 172–86. New York: Routledge, 2023.

"Why Musicals Are So Great in China in 2017" [2017中国音乐剧为什么这么厉害]. Sohu.com. January 4, 2018. https://www.sohu.com/a/214720011_760269.

Xia, Snow. "From *Cats* to *Chicago*, China Is Loving Western Musicals, But What of Its Own?" *South China Morning Post*, September 18, 2019.

4 Ensembles in Motion: Formations, Spectacle, and Unison

ADRIENNE GIBBONS OEHLERS

When I sit in the audience of musical productions, I cannot help but follow the ensemble. I have been fortunate to have worked consistently as a professional performer in musical theatre, auditioning alternately as a "dancer who sings" or a "singer who moves well." As a result, my resume includes a wide range of shows—from *Sweeney Todd*, a vocally demanding show with no dancing, to the *Radio City Christmas Spectacular*, a highly challenging dance show with no required singing for the Rockettes. It has also meant that my career has been spent in countless ensembles.[1] As I watch performances, I find myself considering how the director or choreographer configures the people onstage, and whether they move in graphic shapes, are arranged to create focal points, or are used as transitions. Other times, I get lost in the choreography of the ensemble—the movement quality, the gestural or abstract vocabulary, and the use of unison, improvisation, and variation. These compositional elements coalesce to help make meaning and aid interpretation of the choreography's dramatic intent. Yet, these elements are rarely examined individually as tools for staging ensemble dance in musical productions. This chapter is dedicated to the ensemble and the way it functions through dance in musical theatre. I focus on both historical and contemporary musicals, with a particular interest in analyzing compositional structure to interpret group movement. I examine how basic formations like the line, the circle, and the trio can generate anticipation, cohesion, or narrative substance in a show. I draw on the early history of the chorus—which I differentiate from the concept of ensemble—and its various iterations and intersections to demonstrate its foundational significance in terms of spectacle, spatial formations, group dynamics, and the value of unison. These elements articulate group identities within the story of the musical as well as reflect real-life cultural and social codes.

Scholars routinely point to choreography of the Golden Age musicals, particularly Agnes de Mille's work for *Oklahoma!* (1943), as the period in which dance began to advance the story and contribute to the idea of the integrated musical.[2] However, prioritizing integration

---

[1]To avoid confusion, I do not include the dates of the Broadway premieres in the discussions of my own performance, lest it suggest I appeared in these original casts. *Sweeney Todd* opened on Broadway in 1979, and the Radio City Rockettes appeared at the inauguration of Radio City Music Hall in 1933.

[2]While the dates are frequently contested between scholars, the Golden Age of American musicals has been routinely cited as beginning with *Oklahoma!* in 1943 and ending with *Fiddler on the Roof* in 1964. Recent work such as Liza Gennaro's *Making Broadway Dance* and Sarah Whitfield's edited collection *Reframing the Musical: Race, Culture, and Identity* have begun to restore less studied figures into the narrative, blurring those historiographic date markers.

has positioned those musicals as superior and created a rift between pre– and post–Golden Age musicals. I submit that "post-integrated" musicals have clear connections to choreographic structures from earlier decades through spatial formations, spectacle, and unison. I join Bradley Rogers, who refutes the idea of integration as a marker of a successful musical and instead claims "bursting into song" as musical theatre's strength, tracing its foundations to the nineteenth-century genres of melodrama, minstrelsy, and burlesque.[3] I emphasize the ties between theatrical eras by using case studies from musicals before and after the Golden Age in order to connect later musicals to their historical roots. Because the early history of musical theatre is racially divided, due to the impact of legalized racial segregation and the inequities of Jim Crow laws, I first examine line and precision in historically white companies such as the Ziegfeld Girls and the Radio City Rockettes and then address how Black-created musicals such as the *Darktown Follies* (1914) were attentive to circle and community.[4] The signature aspects of differing ensembles illuminate the values of their respective communities, which continue to inform contemporary musicals. Before looking at historical cases that show the origins of formations as well as their reflection of social and cultural values, I begin by examining how ensembles function in production numbers in more recent musicals. These more familiar examples offer a framework to see ensembles within their comprehensive lineage.

As noted by Phoebe Rumsey in her chapter of this collection, movement onstage is often shallowly described in reviews and theatre scholarship, leaving gaps in how to interpret dance in musicals as well as how to envision choreography in musicals that did not leave recorded documentation. Throughout my work, I adhere to dance scholar Susan Leigh Foster's call to "vivify" the body, centering the body as discourse and movement as a representational practice.[5] I address what movement looks like on musical stages, even as I consider historical musicals with little or partial documentation of this.[6] To reconstruct a fuller history of what happened onstage in earlier musicals, I rely on interviews, photographic records, and instructive song lyrics, alongside contemporaneous reviews and essays, taking snippets from different sources to draw a clearer picture of how the chorus functioned. As well as serving as a historical restoration, tying past and present ensembles together, these examples provide a framework to see the ensemble as a primary communicator and demystify the embodied messages within movement.

It is worth taking a moment to consider the semantic and operational differences between the terms *ensemble* and *chorus*. In line with the terms' historical distinction, I use *chorus* in my review of early United States dancing troupes and *ensemble* in my examination of musicals from the Golden Age through today. Millie Taylor reasons that early musicals and revues positioned the chorus as "an anonymous mass without opportunities to articulate

---

[3]Bradley Rogers, *The Song Is You: Musical Theatre and the Politics of Bursting into Song* (Iowa City: University of Iowa Press, 2020).

[4]The Radio City Rockettes remained an all-white organization until Japanese American dancer Setsuko Maruhashi was hired in 1985. The organization Rockettes of Color Alumnae aims to spotlight the racial inequities so long in practice.

[5]Susan Leigh Foster, *Corporealities: Dancing, Knowledge, Culture, and Power* (New York: Routledge, 1996), x.

[6]Scholars who have influenced my thinking on historical reimaginings of early Black performance include Jayna Brown, Daphne Brooks, and Saidiya Hartman, among others.

individual identities," in contrast to more recent musicals, which tend to cast the ensemble as a "community of individuals—where the community articulates diverse identities."[7] However, in practice, the terminology used by production teams today still varies, depending on factors such as directorial preference, the period of the show, or the structure of the company.[8] I have performed in large anonymous "choruses," such as *42nd Street*, as well as shows like *Cabaret*, where the "ensemble" is made up of distinct individuals, often identified by name in the script. In this way, my professional experiences performing with different cast configurations illustrate how these distinctions are not as clear in practice as the linguistic divide I employ here.

Production Numbers and the Ensemble Effect

Ensemble numbers contribute to the world of the musical and heighten the audience's affective response by adding a physicalized component to the music and bolstering the visual appeal. Scott McMillin named this amplification the "ensemble effect," pointing to the emotional impact of a group number and the way the collective effort in dance and song lifts the intensity of the moment.[9] Effective ensemble choreography serves the needs of the show and is crafted in response to the requirements of style, the size of the cast, and the configuration of the theatre seating. The ensemble can direct the audience's attention, elevate the emotional moment, or clarify the dramatic intent. McMillin identifies the ensemble number as the "heart of the musical," where the form of the musical reaches its fullest potential through unison lyrics and choreography.[10] The climactic number that often ends each act builds to its finish, and the "expansion of a number into a united ensemble" can be read as "a dramatic event in itself."[11]

The ensemble effect is demonstrated in the number "Everybody Say Yeah," the first act finale of *Kinky Boots* (2012), choreographed and directed by Jerry Mitchell. Two seemingly incompatible ensemble groups—the conventionally old-school factory workers and a posse of flamboyant drag queens—are at odds, both in their inability to work together and in the way they dress and move. As the number progresses, the workers get caught up in the excitement of the new direction of the factory, mixing in with the drag queens to clap and jump as if at a rave, surrounding the two leads, who march down the conveyer belt turned runway. Together, the two ensembles face the audience to perform simple turns and step touches as a cohesive team, clearly ready to work together. By the end, everyone is united in the common goal of making shoes, and as the entire cast moves together with a joint vocabulary, their unison suggests they are also moving toward acceptance of the strangers in their midst.

---

[7]Millie Taylor, "Singing and Dancing Ourselves: The Politics of the Ensemble in *A Chorus Line*," in *Gestures of Music Theater: The Performativity of Song and Dance*, ed. Dominic Symonds and Millie Taylor (Oxford: Oxford University Press, 2014), 279.
[8]Actors' Equity Association (the union for stage actors) continues to use the term *chorus* in its contracts and audition language.
[9]Scott McMillin, *The Musical as Drama* (Princeton, NJ: Princeton University Press, 2006), 80–1.
[10]McMillin, 9.
[11]McMillin, 79–80.

Production numbers have utilized the elements of unison, spectacle, and formation as structural hallmarks throughout musical theatre history. Unison dancing moves the attention from the singular to the whole, presenting movement as pattern, shape, and dynamic. Much like dynamic markings in musical notation, changes in the expressive style of choreography (for example from abrupt to fluid transitions) can communicate a different emotional state or narrative theme. When bodies are moving together, a change in movement quality magnifies a change in the effect of the meaning. Breaking from this synchronicity can not only spotlight the individual emancipated from the group but also reveal the workings of the group itself. Additionally, choreography can convey group identity through the use of, or departure from, unison and formations, highlighting boundaries of belonging. Jerome Robbins masterfully utilized dance and formations to highlight the tensions between various social groups in *Fiddler on the Roof* (1964). In "To Life," for example, the Jewish and Russian men interweave and encircle each other in progressive comradeship on the dance floor to celebrate an engagement, which only heightens the harsh division that later arises between them.

Production numbers generally utilize the entire ensemble, if not the whole cast, and amplify the impact of a song through dynamic group movement. Large ensembles contribute to the sense of spectacle, adding a corporeal and kinesthetic dynamic to the materiality of sets and costumes. Spectacle, a hallmark of many Broadway musicals, is a visual and aural smorgasbord, providing an overriding sense of pleasure and wonder. The sheer mass of bodies onstage heightens this perception, as does the display of the female body and the ensemble's combined movement, ranging from technical virtuosity to group unison.[12] For example, Casey Nicholaw's *Something Rotten!* (2015) celebrates famous moments in musical theatre history in its wonderfully overwrought six-minute number "A Musical." Alongside the seemingly endless cascade of musical references found in the score and lyrics, the number captures iconic dance moments such as the trombone playing in *The Music Man* (1957), the sensual hip thrusts and wrist curls of *Chicago* (1975), and the final kickline of *A Chorus Line* (1975).

Musical theatre faces the common criticism that spectacle—while exciting—is more about entertainment and therefore should be seen as superficial and less meaningful.[13] Although the majority of spectacle in musical theatre is primarily for entertainment purposes, it can also operate within a range of atmospheres, expanding narrative significance or underlying themes. For example, Bill T. Jones's use of juba dance and step dancing in the choreography of *Paradise Square* (2022) expresses the differences between the tight-knit communities of African Americans and Irish immigrants. In both *Oklahoma!* and *Carousel* (1945), Agnes de Mille choreographs journeys of nightmarish fears and difficult sexual escapades in spectacular dream ballets, which intensify the emotions of the narrative through extended dance sequences and offer examples of how ensemble dance can tackle

---

[12]For more reading on the chorus girl as spectacle, see Lois W. Banner, *American Beauty* (Chicago: University of Chicago Press, 1983); Susan A. Glenn, *Female Spectacle: The Theatrical Roots of Modern Feminism* (Cambridge, MA: Harvard University Press, 2002); Jayna Brown, *Babylon Girls: Black Women Performers and the Shaping of the Modern* (Durham, NC: Duke University Press, 2008); and Linda Mizejewski, *Ziegfeld Girl: Image and Icon in Culture and Cinema* (Durham, NC: Duke University Press, 1999).

[13]See John J. MacAloon, *Rite, Drama, Festival, Spectacle: Rehearsals toward a Theory of Cultural Performance* (Philadelphia, PA: Institute for the Study of Human Issues, 1984).

disturbing themes.[14] In addition, even the most delightful spectacle is reflective of deeply encoded cultural beliefs surrounding gender, race, and sexuality.[15] In its technicolor world, *Guys and Dolls* (1950) is considered an emblematic show that "defines Broadway dazzle," yet Michael Kidd's buoyant choreography defined the Hot Box Girls and the male gamblers, conveying 1950s gender dichotomies for a certain class of white New Yorkers.[16]

In terms of design, choreographers and dance directors use formations to create visual interest as the dancers move in and out of recognizable patterns.[17] Ensemble dancers are required to work together, paying simultaneous attention to their own execution of choreography and to the group as a whole. Large configurations carry the risk of falling apart, with an individual's misstep able to ruin the effect. This challenge makes it even more pleasing when they are successfully performed, the accomplishment reinforcing a sense of cohesion and joint effort. In music, the term *dissonance* correlates to feelings of "disagreeableness and a need of resolution," while *consonance* denotes "perceived agreeableness and stability."[18] This same tension is felt in dance as formations dissolve and re-form, generating a sense of satisfaction and completion. Formations create abstract geometric shapes, organizing dancers to be seen as units rather than individuals, and the degree of technical prowess to move as one is recognized as virtuosic.

Spectacle and unison formations can be detailed and intricate or big and bold. The musical *42nd Street*, directed and choreographed by Gower Champion in 1980, was a reworking of the Busby Berkeley 1933 film of the same name. Alongside the meticulous tap choreography created by assistant Randy Skinner, Champion reimagined the choreographic excess of Berkeley's kaleidoscopic camera effects and insanely large casts.[19] Champion mirrored the spectacle of the earlier choreography and dancers in formation in the film through large-scale movement onstage, often utilizing simple unison and techniques from early chorus formations, such as rows of parading women in "Dames." Furthermore, in "Lullaby of Broadway," Champion blocked the entire cast across the floor, up the staircases, and into the balcony of the train station set. The ensemble and leads moved together, step touching from side to side with arms stretched up to the sky in an overhead V with splayed fingers. Their raised arms extended the physical space of the individual body, and the whole stage moving together provided a visualization of the pronounced downbeats, building the excitement as the cast moved as one. Likewise, movement reinforced the narrative arc that follows the company's reunification for "Pretty Lady," the show-within-the-show. As a musical from the 1980s that was based on films and movement styles of the 1930s, *42nd Street* offers homages to classic chorus lines alongside contemporary interpretations of

---

[14]For more details on the dream ballet, see Bud Coleman's chapter in this book.

[15]Anthony Wilden and Rhonda Hammer, *Women in Production: The Chorus Line 1932–1980, with The Rules Are No Game: The Strategy of Communication* (London: Routledge, 1987).

[16]Frank Rich, "Guys and Dolls: Damon Runyon's New York Lives Anew," *New York Times*, April 15, 1992.

[17]The term choreographer was first used in 1936, to credit George Balanchine's work in *On Your Toes*. Before then, dance composition was nearly always credited under "dance direction," "staging," or "directing," if at all.

[18]Imre Lahdelma and Tuomas Eerola, "Cultural Familiarity and Musical Expertise Impact the Pleasantness of Consonance/Dissonance but Not Its Perceived Tension," *Scientific Reports* 10, no. 8693 (May 26, 2020): 1, https://doi.org/10.1038/s41598-020-65615-8.

[19]Frank Rich, "Musical '42nd Street': A Backstage Story," *New York Times*, August 26, 1980.

ensemble movement, such as the signature fragmentation of the dancing feet by the partially raised curtain at the top of the show.

Spectacularizing Unison in White Chorus Lines

Expectations of spectacle and formation can be seen throughout early musicals, creating frameworks for production numbers in later musicals. At the turn of the twentieth century, musicals were routinely structured as revues, which featured discrete numbers without regard to an overall narrative and placed celebrity acts, dance sequences, comedic numbers, and chorus girls sporadically throughout a vague plot. The chorus line was commonplace as a way to celebrate uniformity, going so far as to mechanize and standardize white female dancers in particular. During the turbulent decades of the Progressive Era in the United States (1890s–1920s), the chorus exemplified how the radical upheaval surrounding social codes for women and standards for public decency were instantiated. In considering ensembles, we must look at how the appearance of women and dance added to spectacle in early iterations of the chorus.

The Black Crook (1866), arguably claimed by many scholars as the first American musical, was a chance amalgamation of a French ballet company and its extravagant sets with a melodrama being developed in Niblo's Garden in New York City. As discussed by Bud Coleman and Nathan James in their respective chapters in this collection, the resulting performance was a pastiche of dance, melodrama, and stage machinery; it was not a cohesive or original work but rather one constructed from isolated entities that, taken together, became the hallmark of the spectacle-extravaganza. While the French ballet company was trained in ballet technique, the American producers hired additional inexperienced girls to perform simple marching drills in mass formations on the stage to create pleasing effects.[20] The practice of using large groups of women to create stage shapes that would appear and dissolve became an essential element of the spectacle-extravaganzas, which grew in popularity from the mid-nineteenth century.

The six-hour phenomenon of *The Black Crook* was a runaway hit. This has been historically credited to the (then) scandalous nature of the short skirts and flesh-colored tights for the female chorus, under the direction of David Costa.[21] The figure of the "chorus girl" became a popular character, appearing at the center of public controversies in American media over her appearance and perceived immodesty. The chorus girl presented a dominant prototype of the idealized woman—white, young, and beautiful—while being simultaneously scorned for her public display. *The Black Crook* further solidified cultural imagining of the chorus girl through the sheer number of similar-looking women who appeared onstage (touted to be seventy in advertisements), as well as their dissemination to a wide audience through the longevity of the show's run and its spread across the United States during its touring years.

---

[20]Kristina Gintautiene, "*The Black Crook*: Ballet in the Gilded Age (1866–1876)" (PhD diss., New York University, 1984), 31.
[21]See Banner, *American Beauty*; and Faye E. Dudden, *Women in the American Theatre: Actresses and Audiences, 1790–1870* (New Haven, CT: Yale University Press, 1997).

The iconography of the chorus girl was further cemented in the popular consciousness decades later by legendary theatrical producer Florenz Ziegfeld Jr., whose famed marketing skills and lavish productions ensured the influence of his *Ziegfeld Follies*, which ran nearly annually from 1907 through 1931. Subscribing to the show's motto, "Glorifying the American Girl," the Ziegfeld Girls became renowned for their attractiveness and elegance, which further entrenched connotations of whiteness with beauty.[22] While much has been written about these women, I want to consider the legacy of other chorus divisions that handled the choreography. Like other producers of the time, Ziegfeld hired multiple choruses to perform different functions, which permitted the Ziegfeld Girls to remain solely as statuesque beauties, leaving the dancing to other groups. For example, the *Ziegfeld Follies of 1917* featured a "Garden of Girls" in which singular showgirls rose through trapdoors to represent different flowers, while the first act finale featured a specialized female chorus that performed precision drills while dressed as a troop of Continental soldiers.[23]

The duties of the dancing chorus, customarily divided by gender, expanded and formalized as vaudeville shifted into revue formats.[24] Choreographer Ned Wayburn developed a system that he utilized in his work for Ziegfeld to divide the women of the chorus into groups by height, size, and specialty techniques. The greatest prestige was held by the Ziegfeld Girls, alternately referred to as the *A girls* or "showgirls", the tallest women who wore ornate costumes and headdresses as they gracefully walked across the stage. Dances that required acrobatics, ballet, tap, buck and soft-shoe technique were performed by the *C girls*, also called "chickens," who ranged in height from five feet two to five feet six inches. The *E girls*, or "ponies," were the shortest set of dancers, made up of women of between five feet and five feet three inches in height, and were the group that specialized in precision dance. The idea of tap dancing performed in unison by many dancers, instead of the typical solos and duos, was a novelty happening across theatres in the 1910s, and a precursor to later precision troupes like the Rockettes.[25] In Wayburn's instruction manual, *The Art of Stage Dancing* (1925), he explains his methods of teaching a broad range of movement styles to young women so that they would have a "repertoire of fancy steps and neat dance routines." He considered "true Musical Comedy dancing" to include numerous dance styles, combining "pretty attitudes, poses, pirouettes, and the several different types of kicking steps . . . full of happy surprise steps . . . that arouse the interest as they quickly flash by."[26] The *E girls* were responsible for the most difficult choreography but did not enjoy the glamor or prestige of the "glorified" Ziegfeld Girls. The use of various large formations of white attractive women trained in simple unison drills in both *The Black Crook* and Ziegfeld's chorus divisions demonstrates the creation of spectacle through scope, bodily exposure, and disciplined dance routines.

---

[22]Mizejewski, *Ziegfeld Girl*.

[23]Richard E. Ziegfeld and Paulette Ziegfeld, *The Ziegfeld Touch: The Life and Times of Florenz Ziegfeld, Jr.* (New York: H. N. Abrams, 1993), 245.

[24]For more on the variety of revues, see Gerald Bordman, *American Musical Revue: From "The Passing Show" to "Sugar Babies"* (New York: Oxford University Press, 1985).

[25]Barbara Cohen-Stratyner, *Ned Wayburn and the Dance Routine: From Vaudeville to the "Ziegfeld Follies"* (Madison, WI: Society of Dance History Scholars, 1996).

[26]Ned Wayburn, *The Art of Stage Dancing: The Story of a Beautiful and Profitable Profession* (New York: Ned Wayburn Studios of Stage Dancing, 1925), 85.

Precision in Line

In consideration of historical contextualization, precision dance was evident in the military-inspired unison and use of formations in groups like the British Tiller Girls, who then influenced the creation of the Radio City Rockettes. As early as 1889, John Tiller made headlines with his traveling troupes, showcasing a new style of "tap-and-kick." Tiller was a cotton broker who selected unskilled northwestern English farm girls as young as eight or ten to train in his dance schools. Tiller utilized his knowledge from the manufacturing world to teach movement, and drew inspiration from military tactics to organize working-class girls and teenagers into lines of kicking and marching dancers. He found that by having the dancers link up together, they could better coordinate their jumping and the kicks would stay in rhythm. In addition to the kickline, Tiller's specialty was creating formations that rearranged themselves into surprising patterns. He created multiple groups from twelve to thirty-two dancers, all matching in height and physique, whose ability to coordinate their moves catapulted them to worldwide fame.

The Tiller Girls are well-studied, particularly in the work of Siegfried Kracauer, a German philosopher and cultural critic who used the example of the Tiller Girls to engage with the intersection of popular culture and the masses as a critique of capitalism.[27] As "the perfect analogy for industrialization," the abstract group formations of the Tiller Girls could be seen as an assemblage of disembodied parts or alternately as part of a working, moving unit.[28] This form of athletic dance freed female performers from their sole function as objects of beauty, which was a radical change from their familiar positions in beauty revues. Although looks were still a major factor in getting these positions, dancers in precision chorus lines were viewed differently than the parading Ziegfeld Girls, whose individualized costumes and slow procession across the stage invited appraisal as an imaginary ideal. The spectacle of precision dancers was less fixated on the female body but shifted to the larger formations, the creation of abstract patterns, and the rigor required to successfully perform the choreography.

The Radio City Rockettes are a direct descendant of the Tiller Girls. In 1922, dance director Russell Markert, inspired by a *Ziegfeld Follies* performance that showcased one of the British Tiller Girl troupes, created a company that featured "sixteen American girls—taller—kicking higher and doing lots of tap dancing."[29] Markert combined the visual hallmarks of the Ziegfeld Girls—tall, white, slim—with the kickline and precision of the Tiller Girls, plus required dance abilities in a variety of movement styles. When Radio City Music Hall opened in 1932, its massive stage and house of 6,200 seats necessitated a continuation of the stage spectacle from its predecessors at Niblo's Garden and the Hippodrome. What began as a team of sixteen women in the Missouri Rockets grew to a line of thirty-six Radio City Rockettes, who were unified in figure, costume, and movement style across the "Great Stage." The Rockettes embraced the designation of spectacular, with dancers in sparkling

---

[27]Siegfried Kracauer, "Ornament der Masse (The Mass Ornament)," in *The Mass Ornament, Weimar Essays*, trans. and ed. Thomas Y. Levin (1963; Cambridge, MA: Harvard University Press, 1995).
[28]Kara Reilly, *Automata and Mimesis on the Stage of Theatre History* (New York: Palgrave Macmillan, 2011), 146.
[29]Russell Markert, collection, Rockettes, Miscellaneous Manuscripts, Special Collections, Library for the Performing Arts, New York Public Library.

costumes, larger-than-life visual effects, and complex group choreography designed to be more impressive from a distance than up close.

For two seasons, I performed with the Radio City Rockettes, perfecting the details of the crisp, athletic, and energetic choreography. In rehearsal, a single count of movement would be frozen, and the body positioning picked apart, ensuring that if a photo were taken at any point in the number, all thirty-six dancers would appear identical. The reliable applause generator in nearly every number was the kickline, which requires technique, flexibility, and skill to execute with mechanical exactness. The gathering of an ensemble into a visible line, linked together and moving as one, signals a satisfying feeling of community. The buildup of the "ensemble effect," the extreme synchronicity of the Rockettes' kickline, and the scale of thirty-six women lined up across the stage all culminate in creating the anticipated "spectacular" final number. The meticulous attention to detail is the defining factor of precision dance and requires a subsummation of the individual to the group.

Image 4.1 Radio City Rockettes have performed with clear precision since 1932. Enrique Shore/ Alamy Stock Photo.

Precision and unison share many characteristics but remain distinguishable by their performative goals. Precision, drilled for exactitude and sameness, emphasized the geometric shapes and the virtuosity of achieving near-perfect uniformity. The Rockettes epitomized the "illusion of perfection" and valorized the dancers performing "the exact same step, with the exact same timing, *and* with uniformity of interpretation."[30] The wide-ranging popularity of indistinguishable female dancers moving as if one mechanized unit speaks to the significance placed on industry, compliance, and perfection in white culture. In contrast, unison dance, or moving together, opens a window for slight variation in both how the choreography is executed and who is doing the dancing, sometimes allowing a sense of the individual dancer to be present through spontaneity or improvisation. In examining the chorus lines in racially segregated casts, the divergent choreographic values offer insight into the forces that shaped each cultural community.

Black Cultural Roots and Community

In early chorus lines, the concept of unity was not relegated to the choreography but also extended to the dancers' race. While Broadway locations were primarily dominated by white productions, Black performances were equally prolific but were confined to the Harlem community, which was becoming the epicenter of Black artistic development.[31] Nightclubs sprung up around the new "Great *Black* Way," bringing popular dance and its new ways of articulating the body to the forefront.[32] Black musicals were restricted from Broadway between the years 1910 to 1917, called the "term of exile" by James Weldon Johnson, a writer, activist, and prominent figure in the shaping of the Harlem Renaissance.[33] Having a "significant measure of control over every aspect of their productions," Black artists enjoyed a time of nurturing without needing to satisfy anyone outside of their own community, as "the vast majority of black performers and their songs and dances were seldom seen by white audiences."[34] The rival Lafayette and Lincoln Theatres were key uptown spaces that employed artists across the theatrical spectrum: the vernacular residue of vaudeville; musicians exploring the ragtime phenomenon and the beginnings of jazz; serious dramatic troupes who recast the white canon with Black actors; and a variety of musicals, some of which were still steeped in stereotypes from blackface and minstrelsy.

The Lafayette Theatre was home to the 1914 smash production of *Darktown Follies*. The theatre packed the house with desegregated (although primarily Black) audiences, churned out stars, and used satire to promote the emerging changes in racial identity. The chorus of *Darktown Follies* was a primary strength of the production by embodying expressive movement rooted in African traditions moving away from white imaginings of what Black movement looked like. In the foundational work *Jazz Dance: The Story of American Vernacular Dance*, Marshall

---

[30]John Alliotts, "Precision Dancing," *Dance Magazine*, December 1982, 42 (original emphasis).

[31]I use the term "Black" to include dark-skinned people who identified themselves or were classified and cast as Black.

[32]Jervis Anderson, *This Was Harlem: A Cultural Portrait, 1900–1950* (New York: Farrar, Straus and Giroux, 1982) (emphasis added).

[33]James Weldon Johnson, *Black Manhattan* (New York: A. A. Knopf, 1930), 170.

[34]Henry T. Sampson, *Blacks in Blackface: A Source Book on Early Black Musical Shows* (London: Scarecrow Press, 1980), 20.

Winslow Stearns and Jean Stearns articulate four basic characteristics of African American dance that were carried from the soil of Africa to the boards of America—improvisation, the shuffle, the counterclockwise circle dance, and the call-and-response pattern—and in so doing, highlight how these qualities attend to the interconnected issues of rhythm, choreography, and voice.[35] All four of these characteristics can be found in "At the Ball, That's All," the show-stopping production number filled with complex rhythms that spurred vibrant and vocal recognition between the performers and the audience of *Darktown Follies*.

This finale included a circular dance with the performers "shuffling in a circle" across the front of the stage, through the stage-left wings, behind the scenery, and around and back out onto stage via the stage-right wings.[36] Circle dances have a long history across various cultures and in different social spheres, often performed to celebrate community, special occasions, or religious ceremony. Commonly found in folk dance, the circle ranges in complexity of configuration, but as a social event it is usually simple enough for nondancers to learn quickly. This choreography harked back to ring shout formations in the African traditions of dance, and the resultant back-and-forth vocalizations between cast and audience echoed the familiar call-and-response patterns intrinsic in African music. Dancers' "a-prancing, right and left a-glancing," followed prescribed choreography in the lyrics, which became a blueprint from which each dancer could move as instructed (stepping forward on alternating feet while holding on to the dancer in front of them) while retaining some freedom in the manner in which they moved.[37] The visceral manner in which the cast of *Darktown Follies* connected with its

Image 4.2 "Scene from the stage production of *Shuffle Along*, 1921." White Studio (New York), Billy Rose Theatre Division, New York Public Library Digital Collections.

---

[35]Because reviews rarely give detailed movement description, many dance scholars are indebted to the vast array of artist interviews done in this book. See Marshall Winslow Stearns and Jean Stearns, *Jazz Dance: The Story of American Vernacular Dance* (1968; New York: Da Capo Press, 1994).
[36]Stearns and Stearns, *Jazz Dance*, 31.
[37]J. Leubrie Hill, *At the Ball, That's All*, sheet music, 1914, Music Division, New York Public Library Digital Collections, Catalog ID b14533237.

audience points to what was inherently understood between the Black cast and its largely Black audience at a theatre situated in their own community. The language of the bodies onstage was familiar to the audience as it reflected the vernacular vocabulary of social dance; the structural patterns were a part of their cultural heritage. By restaging dances that were "encoded moments of historical memory," dancers could speak to audiences with a certain point of reference, bringing a dance language from the past to both remember its origins and create new meanings.[38] The ensemble as a collective body reflected the audience's history and experience, and they responded vociferously as an answering assembly. If the audience liked the performance, they might "scream, stomp, and applaud until the whole building shook," replying with what blues singer Ethel Waters called a "communal response."[39]

Unlike the Tiller Girls and the Radio City Rockettes, who had to adhere to the exactness of precision dance, the dancers in *Darktown Follies* were not only allowed but encouraged to interpret the group choreography with individual flair. Ethel Williams exemplified such "improvisatory disobedience" in performance, marking her place at the end of the chorus line with outrageous and humorous reactions to the rest of the chorus.[40] Williams herself described doing "anything but" what was being done by the line of dancers ahead of her, kicking higher than the rest of the line and playing for laughs.[41] Williams's dancing at the end of the line was an improvised response to the chorus line's set choreography, adhering to some constraints of the dance (following the line and staying in rhythm) while blatantly disregarding others (kicking too high and undulating through her entire body). Her ability to both be part of the line and stand out as a soloist influenced other dancers who paired their good looks and talents with comic effects, such as Josephine Baker. Baker, who began her career as the end chorus girl in *Shuffle Along* in 1921, became popular as the chorus girl who would flagrantly disregard the rules of staying in her place. In 1924, she was billed as "That Comedy Chorus Girl" in *The Chocolate Dandies*.[42] With this mischievous lack of compliance, both Ethel Williams and Josephine Baker found a way to stand out in or, rather, despite the ensemble.

Shuffle Along was the first show to break the "drought" of Black musicals on Broadway, and with its 1921 success came a legitimization of the Black-produced and Black-performed musical.[43] Its dancing chorus was perhaps most influential in the way the three chorus groups—the Jazzy Jasmines, the Happy Honeysuckles, and the Majestic Magnolias—translated the score by embodying emerging jazz sensibilities, employing a sense of improvisation and spontaneity within the prescribed choreography.[44] "Above all," claim Stearns and Stearns, "musical comedy took on a new and rhythmic life, and chorus girls

[38]Brown, *Babylon Girls*, 161–2.
[39]Donald Bogle, *Heat Wave: The Life and Career of Ethel Waters* (New York: HarperCollins, 2011), 28.
[40]Brown, *Babylon Girls*, 163.
[41]Stearns and Stearns, Jazz Dance, 125.
[42]*The Chocolate Dandies*, 1924, Clippings Folder, Special Collections, Library for the Performing Arts, New York Public Library.
[43]Allen Woll, *Black Musical Theatre: From Coontown to Dreamgirls* (Baton Rouge: Louisiana State University Press, 1989). Multiple factors determined the historical significance of *Shuffle Along*, including the way it became a breeding ground for breakout stars and daringly showcased a romantic plotline for the two Black leads.
[44]John Jeremiah Sullivan, "'Shuffle Along' and the Lost History of Black Performance in America," *New York Times*, March 24, 2016.

began learning to dance to jazz."[45] Reviewers point to the energetic vitality of the chorus girls in particular, for "to have a chorus of lithe brown-skinned girls dancing before you with an orderly abandon that can come only from training and talent is unusual to say the least."[46] The success of the show opened the door for a flood of new Black musicals, with twelve shows opening in the next seven years. Although blackface and other demeaning characterizations that perpetuated harmful stereotypes were present in *Shuffle Along*, it also enabled the rhythms and movements of Black culture to finally have an entry into the white-dominated spaces of Broadway. Henry T. Sampson argues that "the fast-stepping, high-kicking ladies of the modern chorus lines are a direct off-shoot of the beautiful bronze beauty chorus girls that flashed across the stage" in Black musicals from 1900 to 1940.[47] Although the performers were relegated to separate stages, the transmission of dance crossed many boundaries, including racial lines.

Formations as Metaphor and Meaning

The choreography and performance of chorus lines of the early twentieth century have had lasting impact, with trends in contemporary musical theatre dancing ensembles following similar structures of composition, group dynamics, use of spectacle, and connection to audiences. It is useful to see how the composition of the line continued as a major component in creating spectacle, offering disciplined consistency in appearance as well as in synchronized movement. The line has been used to meld individuals into one mass ensemble but also to break down individual hierarchies into a semblance of community. One example is *Cabaret*, a musical that aims to amuse the audience only to then subvert their expectations. The second act begins with the Emcee decked out in drag, in a blonde wig and costume that is indistinguishable from those of the now identically dressed Kit Kat Girls.[48] The music is vibrant; the mood is silly. The Master of Ceremonies has been subsumed into the group. Linked together, they all lean forward and backward as one being, evoking traditional cancan choreography. The dancers jump and kick, divide into two lines, and join again to execute a raucous version of a classic kickline. Slowly, the music changes, the lights become stark, and the bounce disappears from the line. The kicks slow down and straighten out. Feet become flexed, and arms are released down and extended through the elbows. The frivolous and slightly sexualized kickline has morphed into goose-stepping, and the Emcee steps forward to reveals his/her/their identity.[49] In this three-minute segment, the company has offered an embodied translation of the insidious nature of the Nazi Party. Almost before the audience has realized the dance has changed, the kickline has morphed from fun into something else, signaling how easy it is to slide from one way of moving—and of living—to

---

[45]Stearns and Stearns, *Jazz Dance*, 139.

[46]"Big Hit: No. 2 Company of 'Shuffle Along' Gets Fine Press," *Chicago Defender*, December 9, 1922, 6.

[47]Sampson, *Blacks in Blackface*, 131.

[48]Both the original 1966 production, directed by Hal Prince and choreographed by Ron Field, and the 1998 revival, directed by Sam Mendes and choreographed by Rob Marshall, included this kickline, although the song title "Kick Line" did not appear in the original program. The 1972 movie, directed and choreographed by Bob Fosse, includes a version of this number entitled "Tiller Girls," in reference to the troupes discussed earlier in this chapter.

[49]The role of the Emcee has traditionally been performed by male actors, although the sexuality/gender of the character is often portrayed as fluid or undefined.

another. The Emcee conforms to the group both in choreography and in image, offering a metaphor for submission (rather than deception) in society writ large.

The most overt example of the literal and metaphorical use of a line is Michael Bennett's direction and choreography in the musical *A Chorus Line*. Throughout the show, the cast stands along a white line painted across the edge of the stage, which becomes the base of the narrative structure, calling attention to the tension between the individuality of each dancer and the need to mold into a unified, indistinguishable group. The show is set up as a window into a chorus audition, and the actors are each asked questions about their backgrounds by the primarily unseen director, Zach. The dancers break from the line to perform each solo number, but always return to their same spots and their signature character stance, rejoining the line as a hopeful auditionee. The breaking apart and re-forming of the line demonstrate that no matter how gifted (or troubled) each dancer is, those individual differences do not belong in the ensemble that Zach is looking to hire. As Zach cautions his ex-lover Cassie, who has had a career as a "star" performer but now needs a job, she cannot "pop the head" if she expects to fit in with an ensemble that requires unison first and foremost. *A Chorus Line* illustrates a style for successful chorus dancing through disciplined synchronicity, contrasting with the welcomed improvisation of *Darktown Follies*. Notably, the desire for Josephine Baker—and the character of Cassie—to move in a more individualized way suggests an inherent drive for solo attention. In *Darktown Follies*, that dichotomy was welcomed; in the narrative of *A Chorus Line,* it was shunned.

The finale, "One," is a sequin-filled production number that the dancers have been learning during the "audition." Dressed in a gold outfit and top hat, each dancer steps from the wing, raises their hat, and takes a bow before continuing on to join the now identically costumed ensemble members. After dancing in near-perfect unison in a circle and then re-forming into an inverted triangle, the ensemble links up along the white line, kicking together as the lights go down, and as if they will keep kicking in perpetuity. If *A Chorus Line* had been the story of individual dancers, then the end celebrated the sense of community and subsumption of individuality to the good of the group. This expression of group primacy is highlighted through the matching costuming and choreography, morphing the cast from an ensemble of characters lined up into a chorus of indistinguishable dancers. The line itself structures the dancers, and as they link together in the kickline, they echo the precision lines of the undifferentiated Tiller Girls and Rockettes.

Although the circle appears briefly as a transitional shape in *A Chorus Line*, this formation has a history steeped in social and folk dance, regularly illustrating the bonds within a community. With its implications of fellowship, the circle employed in "Dance at the Gym" in *West Side Story* (1957) has a prominent narrative function. Interrupting the dancing at the neighborhood social, Glad Hand, one of the few well-meaning adults in the musical, attempts to engage the Sharks and Jets in a dance/game designed to help the rival gangs intermingle. The boys form an outer circle while the girls form an inner circle. The male leaders of each gang take their places, with their girlfriends accompanying them in their respective circle. With a signal from their leaders, the remaining gang members and girls fall into their spots in the circles. When the music begins, the boys and girls start walking in opposite directions. When the music freezes, each member of the Jets and Sharks is standing across from a member of the other gang. Rather than pairing up in this new, socially varied assortment, the leader of each group—Bernardo and Riff—reaches over and returns his established girlfriend to his side, refusing the get-together game and customs of the social dance. The integrated circles, momentary formations with comingled identities, disperse. The dancers form separate groups, utilizing lines to push back opposing groups and return to semicircle formations to feature a dance challenge forming around each gang leader and his respective girlfriend. The two circles split the stage evenly and keep the two competing groups apart. Throughout *West Side Story*, director and choreographer Jerome Robbins and co-choreographer Peter Gennaro used dance as a major narrative tool, creating gestures and movement styles to articulate struggles with identity and belonging and often turning to formations such as the circle to illustrate boundaries.

Focus on Scale

Formations for large numbers of dancing individuals help viewers identify collective values and illustrate cohesion or conflict. Additionally, smaller formations like trios are often used to spotlight performers as identifiable characters who can quickly step in and out of the company as featured performers. Trios in musicals are most often established as three featured members of the chorus or as two people flanking a leading actor. Trios offer a microcosm of the ensemble function but spotlight a small-enough number for audiences to easily see them as individuals rather than a group. Consequently, any staging that magnifies tension or imbalance between the characters or within the community is more readily noticed by audiences. At the same time, the trio offers many of the same functions as larger group choreography but provides an intimate scope. Trios can appear within a full-scale number as a special dance feature or appear as a unit alone to provide a visual change from a busy, populated stage.

An example of effective trio staging can be seen in the 1981 musical *Dreamgirls*, directed and choreographed by Michael Bennett, where the struggle for status between the three Black women in a Motown-style girl group is the crux of the story. As they transition from backup singers to headliners themselves, they perform diegetic numbers whose choreography and staging alter with the shifts in their group dynamic. The characters transition between moving in unison and following choreography that differentiates the lead singer from her two backup singers as their bookings change. When the Dreamettes begin their career at a talent competition, Effie sings the lead vocal, standing in front of the other two women and joining in on the choreography intermittently. Later, the girls are hired as backup singers for Jimmy Early, and here they are directed to move in unison, as all three of them are equal to one another, in service of setting off the headliner. After landing their own group, now reimagined as the Dreams, Deena moves into the lead position. The other two flank her, presenting a picture of unison in dresses that match hers, but a hierarchy is signaled through Deena's featured singing and dancing against the duo's background performance.

As with many jukebox and biographical musicals, the choreography for the Dreams re-created era-appropriate dance inspired by real-life figures, such as former rhythm tap dancer and vaudevillian Cholly Atkins, who was responsible for what recently has been termed the "vocal choreography" of Motown groups.[50] As part of the continuous sampling and

---

[50]The Dreams are speculated to be based on the Supremes, and several parallels are apparent between the two groups. However, this link is routinely denied by the show's creators, supposedly to avoid litigation issues.

borrowing found across performance, Atkins called on his knowledge of vernacular jazz dance to create stylized movement specifically for singers, in particular drawing from "black chorus line dancing of the twenties, thirties, and forties."[51] Black female trios in musicals—such as the Hunnies in *Jelly's Last Jam* (1992), the urchins in *Little Shop of Horrors* (1982), and the Dynamites in *Hairspray* (2002)—function as a mini-chorus or extended narrator, using choreography that echoes the dynamics found in the Black pop trios popular in the Motown era to signify them as a unit. As they sing, the women sway and pulse to the music, articulating their shoulders, ribs, and hips, and suggesting polish and class by making their movements subtle and smooth. Often their dance vocabulary relies on stylized girl group choreography from Motown just as their three-part harmony leans on that era's musical stylings.

Trios can replicate what a larger ensemble can do but on a miniature scale, with two bodies being sufficient to create a frame around the focal performer. They offer feature moments for smaller roles to shine, like the three secretaries in the infamous "Turkey Lurkey Time," the wildly nonsensical finale to the first act of *Promises, Promises* (1968). An early example of Michael Bennett's habitual use of formations, "Turkey Lurkey Time" takes place in the office Christmas party, and the acrobatic choreography that seems to call for rubber necks and backs culminates in a drunken frenzy with the rest of the office partygoers. The dance is so difficult, so epically 1960s, and so iconically performed by original cast members Donna McKechnie, Baayork Lee, and Margo Sappington, that it has become a cult classic on its own, despite the infrequency of the show's revival. The number is an example of how an energetic finale of an act can be constructed, building in intensity from a focus on a featured group into the inclusion of the entire cast.

Conversely, other trios are a focus within the show itself, using dance and the small group both to move the narrative forward and to express thematic motifs. In *Sweet Charity* (1966), Charity—the down-on-her-luck dance hall hostess with a heart of gold—leans on her two best friends as they fantasize about getting out of their demeaning jobs and "moving up" in the world. Their discussion turns into song and then into dance in "There's Gotta Be Something Better Than This," which takes place in their dressing room as the three friends create an "ecstatic" number in which we see them perform an "imaginative utopia of a different place and a different life."[52] Charged with Bob Fosse's percussive choreography, Charity, Nikkie, and Helene burst into unison dancing with a wild abandon that conveys their dreams of this unrealized life. Charity remains at the center point of the formation, and the synchronicity of choreography with her two friends shows their equal support of one another and the commonality of the lives and dreams they share. They charge across the space to the flamenco-inspired music, as if both bullfighter and bull, creating poses with a strong carriage and curved arms raised overhead. They trade this in for tiny feminine movements, holding their skirts politely raised and tilting their heads from side to side as if little bobblehead dolls, before aggressively clapping rhythmically, catapulting their bodies into a C-curve, and flicking their wrists as they cry "phooey!" Rejecting controlled civility for passionate freedom, the trio begins a section of sweeping steps, taking up the space as they practically skip

---

[51]Cholly Atkins and Jacqui Malone, *Class Act: The Jazz Life of Choreographer Cholly Atkins* (New York: Columbia University Press, 2001), ix.
[52]Stacy Wolf, "'Something Better Than This': *Sweet Charity* and the Feminist Utopia of Broadway Musicals," *Modern Drama* 47, no. 2 (2013): 309–32.

across the stage in a wide arc, as if there were no more containing their bodies than their dreams. The dance sequence allows their fantasies to take flight, as they finally begin to leap off the floor and dance more dynamically with skirts swishing and legs flicking, leading up to their final pronouncement, "I'm gonna get up, get out, and live. Live it!" The choice to write this number as a trio distinguishes Charity and her two friends from the rest of the "taxi-dancers," as they break apart from the trap of their dead-end jobs and embody another type of living, if only for a few moments.

Conclusion

Whether in a group as small as three or in a mass exhibition of hundreds, dance presented by an ensemble is interpreted differently than that of a soloist. Large gatherings inherently offer the potential for spectacle, and mass unison prompts a sense of cohesion, accomplishment, and unity. Precision can be amplified through the use of formations, from complex configurations to the simplicity of a line, and the work toward perfect synchronicity emphasizes the group over the individual. Patterns break apart and re-form, building tension and adding dynamics to the number through anticipation and resolution. Whether a mass of pure rhythmic delight or subtle atmospheric shifts, collective movement is integral to the "ensemble effect" as it amplifies the impact of the moment.

Overviews of dance ensembles in American musical theatre often describe a simplified story of early musicals and revues as featuring non-diegetic, entertaining dance numbers that have no connection to the later narrative-driven dance features that some say began with the *Oklahoma!* dream ballet. But the truth is more complex: foundational structures of composition and elements of choreography in the early twentieth century can be identified as building blocks that still exist in later musicals and serve as a map to make meaning of group movement onstage. Rooted in spectacle, spatial formations, and unison dancing, contemporary production numbers are linked to their artistic antecedents and still use these traits to illustrate metaphorical and thematic concepts, able to add narrative substance or create sensational performance events.

By introducing choreographic analysis alongside archival research, I bring forward the performing body as it exists in a group to illuminate connections between historical and modern uses of the ensemble in musical theatre. Early interest in lavish presentation was intensified due to the enormous stages that were built as the American musical was taking shape and created the form of the "spectacle-extravaganza." Reviewing early iterations of the chorus line demonstrates how women's bodies have been positioned as spectacle, but also how mass precision moves the emphasis from the individuality of the female form to the larger stage picture. From the chorus lines of the Tiller Girls and the Rockettes to *A Chorus Line*, synchronized dance has proven to captivate and entertain audiences. Unity in performance also articulates the boundaries and connections of communities onstage, occurring in the joyous dance train in *Darktown Follies* as well as in the refusal to integrate in *West Side Story*. Ensemble dance in musical theatre offers an extra layer of meaning through corporeal synergy; this kinesthetic information expands the capacity for an enhanced experience with the show. By "vivifying" the dancers in musicals across different eras, such examples of dance and embodiment studies interrupt and deepen discussions of musical theatre history.

Bibliography

Alliotts, John. "Precision Dancing." *Dance Magazine*, December 1982, 42–4.

Anderson, Jervis. *This Was Harlem: A Cultural Portrait, 1900–1950*. New York: Farrar, Straus and Giroux, 1982.

Atkins, Cholly, and Jacqui Malone. *Class Act: The Jazz Life of Choreographer Cholly Atkins*. New York: Columbia University Press, 2001.

Banner, Lois W. *American Beauty*. Chicago: University of Chicago Press, 1983.

Bogle, Donald. *Heat Wave: The Life and Career of Ethel Waters.* New York: HarperCollins, 2011.

Bordman, Gerald. *American Musical Revue: From "The Passing Show" to "Sugar Babies."* New York: Oxford University Press, 1985.

Brown, Jayna. *Babylon Girls: Black Women Performers and the Shaping of the Modern*. Durham, NC: Duke University Press, 2008.

Chicago Defender. "Big Hit: No. 2 Company of 'Shuffle Along' Gets Fine Press." December 9, 1922.

The Chocolate Dandies. 1924. Clippings Folder, Special Collections, Library for the Performing Arts, New York Public Library.

Cohen-Stratyner, Barbara. *Ned Wayburn and the Dance Routine: From Vaudeville to the "Ziegfeld Follies."* Madison, WI: Society of Dance History Scholars, 1996.

Dudden, Faye E. *Women in the American Theatre: Actresses and Audiences, 1790–1870*. New Haven, CT: Yale University Press, 1997.

Foster, Susan Leigh. *Corporealities: Dancing, Knowledge, Culture, and Power.* New York: Routledge, 1996.

Gennaro, Liza. *Making Broadway Dance*. New York: Oxford University Press, 2022.

Gintautiene, Kristina. "*The Black Crook*: Ballet in the Gilded Age (1866–1876)." PhD diss., New York University, 1984.

Glenn, Susan A. *Female Spectacle: The Theatrical Roots of Modern Feminism*. Cambridge, MA: Harvard University Press, 2002.

Hill, J. Leubrie. *At the Ball, That's All*. Sheet music, 1914. Music Division, New York Public Library Digital Collections. Catalog ID b14533237.

Johnson, James Weldon. *Black Manhattan*. New York: A. A. Knopf, 1930.

Kracauer, Siegfried. "Ornament der Masse (The Mass Ornament)." In *The Mass Ornament, Weimar Essays*, translated and edited by Thomas Y. Levin, 75–88. 1963. Cambridge, MA: Harvard University Press, 1995.

Lahdelma, Imre, and Tuomas Eerola. "Cultural Familiarity and Musical Expertise Impact the Pleasantness of Consonance/Dissonance but Not Its Perceived Tension." *Scientific Reports* 10, no. 8693 (May 26, 2020). https://doi.org/10.1038/s41598-020-65615-8.

MacAloon, John J. *Rite, Drama, Festival, Spectacle: Rehearsals toward a Theory of Cultural Performance*. Philadelphia, PA: Institute for the Study of Human Issues, 1984.

Markert, Russell, collection. Rockettes, Miscellaneous Manuscripts, Special Collections, Library for the Performing Arts, New York Public Library.

McMillin, Scott. *The Musical as Drama.* Princeton, NJ: Princeton University Press, 2006.

Mizejewski, Linda. *Ziegfeld Girl: Image and Icon in Culture and Cinema*. Durham, NC: Duke University Press, 1999.

Reilly, Kara. *Automata and Mimesis on the Stage of Theatre History*. New York: Palgrave Macmillan, 2011.

Rich, Frank. "Guys and Dolls: Damon Runyon's New York Lives Anew." *New York Times*, April 15, 1992.

Rich, Frank. "Musical '42nd Street': A Backstage Story." *New York Times*, August 26, 1980.

Rogers, Bradley. *The Song Is You: Musical Theatre and the Politics of Bursting into Song*. Iowa City: University of Iowa Press, 2020.

Sampson, Henry T. *Blacks in Blackface: A Source Book on Early Black Musical Shows*. London: Scarecrow Press, 1980.

Stearns, Marshall Winslow, and Jean Stearns. *Jazz Dance: The Story of American Vernacular Dance*. 1968. New York: Da Capo Press, 1994.

Sullivan, John Jeremiah. "'Shuffle Along' and the Lost History of Black Performance in America." *New York Times*, March 24, 2016.

Taylor, Millie. "Singing and Dancing Ourselves: The Politics of the Ensemble in *A Chorus Line*." In *Gestures of Music Theater: The Performativity of Song and Dance*, edited by Dominic Symonds and Millie Taylor, 276–92. Oxford: Oxford University Press, 2014.

Wayburn, Ned. *The Art of Stage Dancing: The Story of a Beautiful and Profitable Profession.* New York: Ned Wayburn Studios of Stage Dancing, 1925.

Whitfield, Sarah, ed. *Reframing the Musical: Race, Culture, and Identity*. London: Red Globe Press, 2019.

Wilden, Anthony, and Rhonda Hammer. *Women in Production: The Chorus Line 1932–1980, with The Rules Are No Game: The Strategy of Communication.* London: Routledge, 1987.

Wolf, Stacy. "'Something Better Than This': *Sweet Charity* and the Feminist Utopia of Broadway Musicals." *Modern Drama* 47, no. 2 (2013): 309–32.

Woll, Allen. *Black Musical Theatre: From Coontown to Dreamgirls*. Baton Rouge: Louisiana State University Press, 1989.

Ziegfeld, Richard E., and Paulette Ziegfeld. *The Ziegfeld Touch: The Life and Times of Florenz Ziegfeld, Jr*. New York: H. N. Abrams, 1993.

5   Dancing Narrative: Storytelling through the Ensemble Body

AMANDA JANE OLMSTEAD

At a talk for *Words on Dance* at Symphony Space in New York in 2019, choreographer Andy Blankenbuehler proclaimed, "The ensemble MUST be the lens of the piece. The ensemble MUST focus the principal storyline so that no matter where your eye goes in the show, you see refracted back what the principal is going through."[1] His prioritization of the ensemble as crucial to understanding the action within a show consequently positions the ensemble body as an indispensable element through which the audience gains vital text and subtext. In *Hamilton: The Revolution* (2016), Blankenbuehler is quoted saying, "There are very few times when I really want the audience to look at dance. . . . Dance is just meant to be a framing device that matches emotionally what I want the audience to feel."[2] By utilizing the ensemble body as lens, his choreography coordinates what information the audience receives and how.

My project considers how the chorus and ensemble have affected storytelling throughout musical theatre history.[3] This brief genealogical study of choreography within musical theatre leads to an examination of how Blankenbuehler's work itself not only illuminates the evolution of musical theatre dance aesthetics but amplifies the role of the chorus or ensemble. The chorus and ensemble move beyond spectacle and functional additions to a production (set movers, supporting characters, etc.), and become individual pieces of the puzzle essential to how the narrative, nuances, and world of the show are communicated to and understood by an audience.

This chapter looks at historical examples that have made an impact on how the chorus/ ensemble functions within musical theatre. I then analyze some of Blankenbuehler's earlier choreography, for *In the Heights* (Off-Broadway, 2007; Broadway, 2008), to interrogate how dance in musical theatre connects the ensemble bodies with one another and aggrandizes their potential, allowing bodies to speak without "text," thereby creating the ensemble body as doing and being within the world of a production. In privileging character and story over virtuosity and spectacle, the ensemble body can connect with social meaning beyond an

---

[1] Andy Blankenbuehler and Sarah L. Kaufman, "Words on Dance" (discussion at Symphony Space, New York, October 21, 2019).

[2] Quoted in Lin-Manuel Miranda and Jeremy McCarter, *Hamilton: The Revolution* (New York: Grand Central, 2016), 134.

[3] For the purposes of this chapter, chorus and ensemble will be used as two distinct vocabulary terms. The distinctions will be defined later in the piece.

anatomical display of athleticism, and use stylistic movement vocabulary to offer meaning or socio-historical context. By prioritizing the ensemble as the lens by which an audience views a piece while illuminating the individual ensemble body, Blankenbuehler's choreography has the ability to expose an unlimited number of layers to a story.

Theorizing the Ensemble Body

First, to theorize and define the ensemble body, it is important to build a foundation regarding how bodies are read by or communicated to a viewer. Susan Leigh Foster identifies two essential ideas when discussing the body in relation to dance: the notions of the body's autonomy and interiority, and that of the body's virtuosity. The first suggests the ability to produce feelings and reproduce those feelings for a viewer. The latter is the mastery of a technique, the capacity to exhibit the choreographer's vision. After the codification of ballet in the 1600s, dance practitioners tested the limits of the body's capabilities; thus, virtuosity began to triumph in importance over autonomy and interiority. Foster points out that the dancing body became "detached from its social moorings and objectified through scientific investigation."[4] The operative word here is *detached*. Though, for some, the dancing body has indeed been detached from any previously cultivated sense of self in favor of virtuosity, the identifications associated with that body have not disappeared. Social conscriptions on the body can be ignored, but they do not disappear.

Furthermore, the *performativity* of a body can just the same be ignored but not escaped. According to Dennis Waskul and Phillip Vannini's conceptions of bodily impression, "From a dramaturgical perspective, bodies are *necessarily* performative—which is to say that bodies are always in motion and, hence, a perpetual site of action—the fundamental unit of dramaturgical analysis and the most essential element of any drama."[5] They argue that because the body is produced, manipulated, and presented in accordance with socially constructed situations:

> at all times, bodies are actively inscribed with any one or more of the physical markers of powerful social institutions including age, gender, race, ethnicity, sexuality, and religion . . . the body is clearly the site of enormous expressive and impressive appearance management as well as a focal point for significant ritual activity—two dynamics that are, without question, foremost to dramaturgical analysis.[6]

A viewer can see and read this body, gathering clues that connect it to broader contexts outside of itself. This dramaturgical body is a corporality written with social inflections, cultural memory, and lived experiences: it *does* and *is*. However, what happens when this dramaturgical body performs or becomes a character? What happens when this dramaturgical body is acknowledged rather than erased or detached from its social moorings due to the triumph of virtuosity over autonomy and interiority? And, what happens when this

---

[4]Susan Leigh Foster, *Choreography and Narrative* (Bloomington: Indiana University Press, 1996), 9.
[5]Dennis Waskul and Phillip Vannini, "The Performative Body: Dramaturgy, the Body, and Embodiment," in *The Drama of Social Life: A Dramaturgical Handbook*, ed. Charles Edgley et al. (Farnham: Taylor and Francis, 2013), 200 (original emphasis).
[6]Waskul and Vannini, 197.

dramaturgical body is grouped together with other dramaturgical bodies in something like a chorus or ensemble?

Traditionally in musical theatre, the chorus member has been scripted and staged as an anonymous entity, supplemental to the milieu of a show. Relatively unmediated by specified characteristics of personality or biography, those in the chorus have been subject to generalized groups such as townsfolk, repudiating any sense of individuality or uniqueness. Still, in much of modern popular culture, the words *chorus* and *ensemble* have become synonymous. The chorus in scholarship has sustained its position as a generalized, unified group used to support a production. The ensemble was implemented as a philosophy to discuss individual characters with biographical information and unique characteristics working together to communicate ideas and narrative. It seems, then, that the terms *ensemble* and *chorus* are neither synonymous nor interchangeable, as the ensemble activates individualization within the group cast as generalized supporting characters (or as a singular supporting character).

Furthermore, my project identifies an imperative element of the ensemble substantially absent from musical theatre scholarship, the ensemble body. In many ways, Blankenbuehler has reattached the dancing body to its interiority by exposing the dramaturgical body as a vital element of a musical production. By embracing the dramaturgical body of those in the chorus, Blankenbuehler has developed a complex, discernible ensemble that provides nuance and elucidation to a production. Through the shaping, framing, and choreographing of the chorus member body in a way that considers its dramaturgical body, the ensemble body emerges as a type of dramaturgical body that may be cast as a generalized supporting character, but that remains unique. Moreover, the ensemble body functions as a crucial lens through which the audience can receive and comprehend information related to the piece, rather than merely functioning as background support.

Historicizing the Ensemble Body and Choreographic Storytelling

Historically, in US-based musical theatre, there has been a paradox regarding how the chorus/ensemble is conceptualized alongside the narrative of a production as well as in relationship to the audience; it is both fixed and transformed. Foundational concepts of the chorus/ensemble, such as its functions, have remained unchanged for hundreds of years. Yet, particularly through the twentieth century, there have been key moments of evolution and development regarding who makes up an ensemble and how their bodies are or are not activated. With *The Black Crook* (1866), the line between the chorus, dancer, and character became blurred. Dancers were no longer just seen as moving figures in a section of an opera to add entertainment value or distract from a variety of situations; they were now relevant characters, and their bodies, identified by markers of gender and race, affected an audience's understanding of the world of a production. Across the early twentieth century, there was a dramatic shift from choruses that feature female bodies to a unified chorus of realistic male and female characters. Additionally, Black and white chorus bodies began to be integrated onstage, affecting audiences' recognition of a show's sociological milieu.

From the beginning of the Golden Age of musical theatre (1943–59) onward, the chorus populated theatrical worlds as a collective group of villagers, townsfolk, sailors, farmers, cowboys, seamstresses, and party guests. Their function was essentially to bolster the narrative of a production, and they were a connection between the audience and the show through song, dance, and transitions. Famed choreographers such as Katherine Dunham, Agnes de Mille, and Jerome Robbins utilized the chorus as character in tandem with their choreography to further the narrative, highlight overarching themes or emotions, connect scenes, and create a "wow" factor. In the 1960s and 1970s, Bob Fosse challenged the aesthetics of dance in musical theatre to promote a more abstract, atmospheric, and often gender-neutral effect on a production through the chorus. Additionally, Donald McKayle fostered embodied narratives surrounding social consciousness and humanity, subsequently uplifting bodies of color within the Broadway arena. I analyze these moments of evolution with regard to the function of the chorus along with the function of the dance/choreography to articulate further *how* this change affected the landscape of musical theatre.

Following the musical extravaganza *The Black Crook*, musical farces and comedies propagated what was affectionately called the "leg business"—female chorus–centered productions. In 1909, inspired by the 1869 French Folies Bergère, Florenz Ziegfeld Jr. developed a production that further inscribed such a notion of the "chorus girl" into US entertainment. The Ziegfeld Follies was a grand musical revue that presented synchronized dance and pageantry of beautiful chorus girls. Ziegfeld's chorus became more than just background filler in a production; he positioned the collective of chorus girls as the revue's primary focus. The productions did not promote any specific narrative; instead, the very premise was to present feminine sexuality as pure spectacle and entertainment.[7]

Linda Mizejewski argues that Ziegfeld commodified the female body to sell such displays of sexual imagery in a seemingly high-class, respectable manner as a form of entertainment for the middle class.[8] The chorus girl body became an icon in American culture; it became a symbol of the ideal, authentic, "American" woman. As Mizejewski firmly asserts, the ideal, authentic Ziegfeld Follies dancer body was distinctly white. She quotes historiographer Robert C. Toll: "He [Ziegfeld] never said it, but they had to be Caucasians. . . . Of some three thousand women he chose to be Ziegfeld Girls," there were no people of color.[9] Ziegfeld's production of whiteness onstage and its association with glamor and idolatry hold a specific weight in the grand narrative that has been, and in some ways still is, the performing body in musical theatre.

However, in 1921, a new revue-style musical production would challenge such construction of whiteness onstage: *Shuffle Along*. With an all-Black American creative team—music by Eubie Blake, lyrics by Noble Sissle, and book by F. E. Miller and Aubrey Lyles—*Shuffle Along* helped legitimize the presence of Black artists on Broadway.[10] In

---

[7]For more on the *Ziegfeld Follies* and chorus girls, see chapter 4 in this collection.
[8]Linda Mizejewski, *Ziegfeld Girl: Image and Icon in Culture and Cinema* (Durham, NC: Duke University Press, 1999), 3. The first person of color to join the Ziegfeld Follies cast was Bert Williams, in 1910. Williams was a famous Black vaudeville and minstrel performer—though, he performed in blackface.
[9]Mizejewski, 9.
[10]Allen L. Woll, *Black Musical Theatre: from Coontown to Dream Girls* (Baton Rouge: Louisiana State University Press, 1989), 78.

opposition to the pageantry and idolatry of white female sexuality in the Ziegfeld Follies, *Shuffle Along* positioned its female performers in a way that would significantly affect the future of musical theatre. The sixteen girls in the chorus of *Shuffle Along* "were these stomping, sexy, incredible dancing women."[11] As jazz and tap made their palpable entrance on the Broadway scene, the female chorus reattached itself to associations of skill and athleticism that had waned behind the presentation of sexuality and glamour.[12] With *Shuffle Along* and other all-Black revues, white producers saw the potential for Black bodies and Black cultural forms onstage to enhance entertainment value outside of minstrel-like comedy sketches, and sought to "incorporate" ideas into their own shows—appropriating the Black revues' sound, aesthetics, and even plot elements. The Black chorus women of *Shuffle Along* were even subsequently hired by several white producers and directors to teach white women how to execute their jazz, hoofing dance style.

Ziegfeld, for instance, staged "It's Getting Dark on Old Broadway" in the 1922 Follies revue with "a lighting effect [that] caused the chorus girls and their white costumes to take on a brown tint as they danced."[13] The number in some ways appeared similar to acts performed in blackface, which was used throughout the Follies in different instances: the lighting allowed these white bodies to take on color as a performative tool, calling attention to an increasingly race-conscious Broadway and fetishizing Black female bodies for a white audience. These white performers possessed the agency and privilege to maintain their elegance and voguish status, fetishizing the Black body without having to endure the racism and stigma associated with being Black.

As the form of musical theatre grew, the concepts of racial integration and gendered faculties, specifically for the chorus, remained in flux. However, when musical productions began to lean into theatrical practices of realism, they were challenged with reinventing how the chorus would function and who would be included in the chorus. *Show Boat* (1927) is hailed as marking a critical moment for the metamorphosing musical comedy genre as it took on a more serious narrative. Its complex chorus highlighted a shifting social consciousness regarding race in the United States. Instead of acting as spectacle, a presentation of feminine sexuality, or generic background filler, the now racially integrated, realistically costumed chorus was structured as a representation of US society, drawing particular attention to the racial segregation of the 1880s–1920s. Such a shift in the use of the chorus is worthy to note in this genealogical study because, although the move has not been explicitly tied to the way dance was utilized in the chorus in general, how *Show Boat*'s chorus functioned in the narrative necessarily affected the way a chorus would function for decades. The way *Show Boat* viewed the overall chorus did, indeed, alter how future musicals would implement the chorus in service of their narrative. Still, the production did little to shift how the *dancing* chorus would function. The Broadway stage would not see that change until about a decade later.

---

[11] "Audra McDonald and George C. Wolfe | Interview | TimesTalks," uploaded by New York Times Events, February 23, 2016, YouTube video, 51:31, https://www.youtube.com/watch?v=oJDbK03o6d8.
[12] Marshall Winslow Stearns and Jean Stearns, *Jazz Dance: The Story of American Vernacular Dance* (New York: Macmillan, 1968), 139.
[13] Mizejewski, *Ziegfeld Girl*, 129.

A Part of the Play: Integrating Dance and the Chorus as a Narrative Tool

Dance in musical productions leading up to the 1940s predominantly served those three functions (spectacle, display of sexuality, or filler). Correspondingly, the chorus had functioned as spectacle or background support and was only just starting to become a narrative element. The traditional use of ballet or Eurocentric social dances had most often been for situations where there needed to be a waltz or a show-within-a-show production number. Jaw-dropping tap numbers had significant entertainment value. Dance had yet to become a seamlessly spoken language within a production. As the idea of the "book musical" was growing in popularity, creative teams reimagined the integration of dance within these productions. Choreographers such as Katherine Dunham, Agnes de Mille, and Jerome Robbins would play with the relationship between dance and spectacle, dance and metaphor, dance and psychology, and dance and narrative, all of which featured the chorus, and its members, as essential character(s).

Cabin in the Sky (1940), choreographed by Katherine Dunham and George Balanchine (who also directed), uniquely integrated dance, and thusly the chorus, into the book musical. In 1936, on the heels of her intensive ballet training, Dunham was awarded a fellowship to conduct research on the islands of Haiti, Jamaica, Martinique, and Trinidad, from which she brought back various dance techniques rooted within the African diaspora. Following her studies Dunham developed a dance style (later known as Dunham Technique) that combined Eurocentric concert and social dance with Afro-Caribbean dance philosophies such as polyrhythm, torso isolations, and spiritual awareness, which she would subsequently activate in *Cabin in the Sky*.

Cabin in the Sky revolves around Little Joe, who, after being murdered for high gambling debts, is given six more months to save his soul and transcend to Heaven. For the production, Dunham used dance to create a social atmosphere that conveyed the predominately Black American, southern town setting of the show. Her hybrid dance style for the people living in this world allowed dance to become integrated as an essential part of their everyday vocabulary. Combining genres from their diasporic heritage as well as the culture of the United States allowed for the social and performance worlds to collapse in on each other. The movement began to affect how the people living in the world of the show thought, spoke, and traveled.

For *Cabin in the Sky*, Dunham entwined Caribbean Carnival dances, where movement was often a line connecting the material world with the spiritual world, with American socially accepted dances such as square dance, swing dance, and cakewalks. By combining movements and ideas she gleaned from Carnival dance, she was able to capture, legitimize, and contain said spiritual connection, sexual stimulus, and release. This allowed her to codify and create a hybrid aesthetic that would be familiar and yet peculiar for the typical 1940s, white, Broadway audience. Moreover, her work brought the reading of Black bodies by these white audiences out of previously ascribed roles of violently stereotyped primitivism, hypersexuality, or perversion and into a space of diasporic ownership and veridical identity.

In one scene, the demon Lucifer Jr., determined to bring Little Joe to Hell, sends the temptress Georgie Brown to take him to a nightclub, Jim Henry's Paradise. One article reported, "Miss Dunham's dancers form an odd group. In a hell scene they contort in the

Image 5.1 Katherine Dunham and her group of dancers rehearse for *Cabin in the Sky*, a musical comedy, at the Martin Beck Theatre. Photo by Pat Candido/NY Daily News Archive via Getty Images.

manner of dervishes, but in the café scene they are in action first with what is billed 'lazy steps' and then the better known 'boogie woogie.'"[14] Another said, "the dancing, which practically accompanies all the scenes, is simply one variation after another of the *danse du ventre*."[15] As reported by reviewers, the recognizable and unrecognizable dance styles were intriguing, different from the large balletic numbers the reviewers typically saw. The combination of Carnival dance with American social dance (both Eurocentric and from the Black American vernacular) often practiced in nightclubs at the time generated a conversation that pointed to connections between dance and action, dance and scene, and dance and atmosphere. Dunham's new dance genre not only allowed the characters to present themselves as they entered the space, but also metaphorically offered ideas or feelings of temptation, lust, and freedom.

As the members of the chorus, paired into couples, enter Jim Henry's Paradise, they use varied combinations of step touches, abstract body positions, and theatricalized walking, similar to moves used in a cakewalk.[16] As they enter the dance space, the couples jump

---

[14]Ibee [Jack Pulaski], "Legitimate: Plays on Broadway—*Cabin in the Sky*," *Variety*, October 30, 1940, 56.
[15]Elizabeth Jordan, "Theatre," *America*, November 16, 1940, 166. At the time, *danse du ventre* was translated literally as "dance of the belly." It has become the nickname given to more scandalous and provocative movement of the (female) body. See Ainsley Hawthorn, "Middle Eastern Dance and What We Call It," *Dance Research* 37, no. 1 (2019): 1–17.
[16]Because there is little visual evidence of the 1940 production, the 1943 film version of *Cabin in the Sky* serves as the best hint of how the original movement looked. Both film and stage production were choreographed by Dunham. See "'Cabin in the Sky,' a Musical Fantasy, with Ethel Waters, at Loew's Criterion," *New York Times*, May 28, 1943; review of *Cabin in the Sky*, *Variety*, December 31, 1942.

into a mix of recognizable square dancing, swing dancing, and the Lindy Hop. Between movements, there are hints of swaying hips and cha-cha-like steps. Additionally, isolations of the hips and torso, bent knees, shoulder shrugs, and small foot stomps (all lightly improvised by the individual dancer) are evidence of Carnival dance aesthetics from the Caribbean. The chorus bodies, here, collectively function to invite the audience into the seemingly salacious club with movements that are familiar, then add in unique steps typically practiced outside of the white gaze. The entrance of this dance arguably underscores Little Joe's vulnerability to be tempted and surrender to Lucifer Jr. as the dancers have given themselves over to the music that moves them.

Soon after *Cabin in the Sky*, Dunham's choreographic practices—in style and structure—would influence Agnes de Mille's choreography in *Oklahoma!* (1943).[17] In a 1999 interview with Constance Valis Hill, Dunham reflected on de Mille and the connections between their work, saying, "I was really annoyed with her [de Mille] because I think her idea came from something called the plantation dances, not in *Cabin in the Sky*, but in our concerts. I had prided myself on using my work and my discoveries for establishing certain things about black dance."[18] It's certainly possible that Dunham's "plantation dances," which combined ballet with African American, Afro-Caribbean, and American social dances, in her previous ballets *L'Ag'Ya* (1938), *Tropics* (1939), *Le Jazz Hot* (1939), and *Rites de Passage* (1941) may have directly influenced de Mille's choreography in numbers such as "The Farmer and the Cowman" or "Laurey Makes Up Her Mind." What is crucial to understand is that the very idea that creating hybrid dance styles and placing them onstage in a way that served the narrative, style, and themes of a production was arising in multiple spheres at this time.

While Dunham's dance did not *forward* the plot in the same way we see de Mille's do in *Oklahoma!*, it was an essential element to understanding the culture and world of the characters. It was "a part of the play," capturing the sociocultural/socioeconomic milieu of the characters.[19] Even de Mille reflected on Dunham's work, saying that "her large scenes with many people always seemed spontaneous."[20] De Mille's choreography for *Oklahoma!*, likewise, establishes the locale of "the West" and the spontaneous essence within a large scene, perhaps best seen in the number "The Farmer and the Cowman."

At the opening of act 2, the audience is welcomed into the box social, where the "territory folks" engage in a large square dance. "The Farmer and the Cowman" reestablishes the locale of *Oklahoma!*, providing insight into the social relations among community members. After the Civil War, square dance became embedded into the culture of the US Southwest. Not long into the dance, the farmers and the cowboys—two distinct groups in the chorus—begin to squabble over fences, cattle ranges, wealth, resources, and women. During the choruses of the song, the square dance resumes. There is great fluidity between dancing,

---

[17]Balanchine was billed as "co-choreographer." However, Dunham asserts, "I think he did pretty much trust me for the choreography, especially since the company was mine. I couldn't tell you [whether he helped choreograph the number]." See Constance Valis Hill, "Collaborating with Balanchine on *Cabin in the Sky*: Interviews with Katherine Dunham," in *Kaiso! Writings by and about Katherine Dunham*, ed. Vèvè A. Clark and Sarah East Johnson (Madison: University of Wisconsin Press, 2005), 245.
[18]Hill, 242–3.
[19]John Martin, "The Dance: De Mille's *Oklahoma!*," *New York Times*, May 9, 1943, X6.
[20]Agnes de Mille, *Leaps in the Dark: Art and the World*, ed. Mindy Aloff (Gainesville: University Press of Florida, 2011), 69.

dialogue, and song. A fistfight even ensues, until Aunt Eller, the matriarch of the community, shoots a gun to break up the fight and instructs the men to sing and get along. As excitement grows, the choreography integrates recognizable realist square dance vocabulary, which then evolves into a more extensive ballet mixed with stylized square dance movements. This hybridization/theatricalization of square dance helps blur the line between social dance and performance.

Now, prior to "The Farmer and the Cowman" is the act 1 finale, titled "Laurey Makes Up Her Mind" / "Out of My Dreams," commonly known as the dream ballet.[21] This infamous dream ballet would open Broadway audiences up to the idea that dance could tell a piece of the story within a musical production and solidify the chorus as a vital element of it. The ballet embodies Laurey's subconscious thoughts, making them vital character(s) in the story. Leading up to *Oklahoma!*, it was common practice to use a distinct dancing chorus and a distinct singing chorus as opposed to integrating said performers into a unified cast. De Mille followed suit and used an entirely different dancing chorus to perform the large numbers in *Oklahoma!* In performance, this meant that for the dream ballet, there was a second, "dream" Laurey that the "real" Laurey watched experience her nightmare. As Mary Jo Lodge points out, the use of an entirely different dancing chorus "creatively reinforced the idea that the sequence was a fantasy, happening outside of the realm of the relative reality of the rest of the show."[22]

The separation of skills and thus the separation of singing chorus and dancing chorus would begin to dissolve with the popularization of the director-choreographer role. Prior to *Oklahoma!* most productions typically had a director responsible for the concept and the scenes and a choreographer accountable for the movement, specifically the dancing chorus. However, heading into the 1950s, some productions began to combine these roles.[23] The rise of the director-choreographer role would come to fundamentally shift the dancing chorus as a standalone entity and transition them into a more integrated element of a production.

When You're a Jet, You're a Jet All the Way: Choreographing Character in the Chorus

Director-choreographer Jerome Robbins and his work with *West Side Story* (1957) caused a paradigm shift in the way (most of) the chorus functioned within the world of a production. Robbins's ambitious dance score, necessary for articulating plot and character, relied on an aggressively male-heavy, triple-threat chorus. He used dance to emphasize the athleticism and physical power of the men of both rival gangs. Through the Golden Age, the dancing male chorus was beginning to gain traction, and Robbins's choreography took a momentous step toward staging more complex masculinities through dance.

---

[21]For an extended discussion of the dream ballet see chapter 5 in this collection.
[22]Mary Jo Lodge, "Dance Breaks and Dream Ballets: Transitional Moments in Musical Theatre," in *Gestures of Music Theater: The Performativity of Song and Dance*, ed. Dominic Symonds and Millie Taylor (Oxford: Oxford University Press, 2014), 87.
[23]Lodge, 82.

Robbins's emphasis on individual characters within the unified, integrated singing, dancing, and acting chorus added additional layers of conflict and personality to the narrative through choreography. The prologue is nearly seven minutes of pure choreography, introducing the audience not only to the power dynamics and hierarchies between and within the Jets and the Sharks but also to the individual personalities of Jet members. Robbins ensured there were "no anonymous chorus boys and girls; they all had names"— and often character descriptions as well, in Arthur Laurents's book.[24] For instance, Riff was "glowing, driving, intelligent, slightly whacky"; Diesel, Riff's lieutenant, was "big, slow, steady, nice"; and the youngest is Baby John, "awed at everything, including that he is a JET, trying to act the big man."[25] Each character had their own individualized choreographic score. Robbins capitalized on dance's ability to influence how an audience understood narrative, emotion, and character development, using ballet and jazz techniques to give power (or take power) from certain characters or groups of characters.

Nevertheless, there is a firm dissonance in the individualized (white) Jet choreography and the generic or common (Latinx) Shark choreography, which was co-choreographed by Peter Gennaro. Alberto Sandoval-Sánchez argues, "the drama articulates a binary and hierarchical opposition of power relations, and this binarism establishes the dominant paradigms of the musical: Jets/Sharks; US/Puerto Rico; center/periphery, empire/colony; native/alien; identity/alterity; sameness/difference."[26] This "sameness/difference" suggests that the Jets are the "same" as white Americans, whereas the Sharks are people of color and are therefore different. For the chorus, the idea of sameness versus difference provides agency and identity to the Jets while further marginalizing the Sharks as a collective Other within the plot.

In a similar vein, Robbins and Gennaro attempted to use Latinx-based dance steps as a crucial part of the Sharks' vocabulary in numbers such as "America" and "The Dance at the Gym" as a direct contrast to the pure ballet/jazz of the Jets' choreography scores. This binarism further scripted conceptions of Other onto the Sharks' chorus—a chorus primarily made up of white bodies in brownface. Contrary to Katherine Dunham, who used dance as a cultural product to establish a collective social atmosphere uplifting unfamiliar movement styles and Black bodies, Robbins and Gennaro used generalized Latinx steps as signals of difference. While this choice indisputably promotes distance between the two groups, the Jets eventually appropriate the generic mambo steps, reflecting the popular dance trends of the 1950s, into their choreography, further perpetuating an erasure of cultural identity for the performing bodies. Where for Dunham the Lindy Hop was used as a bridge between worlds, reifying the notion that this Black dance was now practiced across cultures, Robbins and Gennaro employed the mambo to signal a transference or taking of power.

Despite these challenges, which deserve more interrogation than possible here, Jerome Robbins, as a director-choreographer, made a major identity shift for the chorus, taking it

---

[24]Deborah Jowitt, *Jerome Robbins: His Life, His Theater, His Dance* (New York: Simon and Schuster, 2004), 275.
[25]Arthur Laurents, Leonard Bernstein, and Stephen Sondheim, *West Side Story: A Musical* (New York: Random House, 1958), 1.
[26]Alberto Sandoval-Sánchez, *José, Can You See? Latinos on and off Broadway* (Madison: University of Wisconsin Press, 1999), 67–8.

from a group of dancers who play generalized cowboys, villagers, and partygoers to a group of more individualized characters. The utilization of dance as an equal mode of communication in *West Side Story* also thrust musicals into a new era of possibility, one where the label of *ensemble* entered the conversation.

Rhythm of Life: Chorus as Metaphor

Seemingly counter to Robbins's prioritization of the individual, in the 1960s, Bob Fosse challenged the aesthetics of dance in musicals, prioritizing its function as metaphor and abstraction over its function as collective narration or characterization. He also challenged long-standing gendered choreographic techniques of dance. From the decline in the quintessence of the male ballet dancer in the late 1700s to the male dancing body's resurgence in the chorus in Robbins's work, choreography practices had, for the most part, continued to separate male and female dancers. Fosse employed asymmetrical movements, contorted wrists, and inverted knees to decenter how the body was "supposed to" move and what it should look like regardless of gender identity. He applied his gender-fluid dance style to a collective chorus, prompting a more unified, embodied voice regardless of narrative. Fosse's collective dancing chorus moved to abstractly proffer ideas and hyperbolize a production's atmosphere and mood.

While Fosse choreographed for a vast assortment of productions, his unique approach to the chorus is legible in every production on which he worked. Fosse gravitated toward narratives that played with what he felt were society's secrets and desires, and toward characters whose movement did not need to be confined to realism in gesture. One of his most iconic numbers is "Rich Man's Frug" from *Sweet Charity* (1966). *Sweet Charity* tells the story of a young taxi dancer, Charity Hope Valentine.[27] In the scene where film star Vittorio Vidal takes her to the exclusive Pompeii Club to spite his mistress, Fosse establishes the atmosphere of the posh and satirical club—quite the opposite of the dance hall at which Charity works—particularly through the movement of the chorus members, who are dancing in the show-within-a-show for the club patrons. An analysis of the number's choreographic score highlights the tensions between gender binarism and fluidity in the narrative and style. The chorus is costumed in a conspicuously gendered way, with the female chorus members in sparkly shift dresses, and the male chorus members in tuxedos. Additionally, Fosse's choreography frequently groups together or organizes the bodies onstage according to gender. Apart from these elements, however, the dance movements maintain gender-neutral comportment.[28]

The choreographic score of "Rich Man's Frug" is broken up into small sections that feature varied groups of chorus members within the collective chorus. Aesthetically the movement energizes small isolations of the hands, hips, and heads while playing with various contortions and elongations of the arms, legs, and torso for all the chorus bodies. Virtually any recognizable ballet-based dance aesthetic is avoided, favoring instead signature

---

[27]"Taxi dancers," or paid dance partners at a dance hall, began to fall out of popularity in the 1950s and 1960s.

[28]For more on Fosse and gender, see chapter 8 in this collection; see also Kevin Winkler, *Big Deal: Bob Fosse and Dance in the American Musical* (New York: Oxford University Press, 2018).

Fosse moves like the "Fosse walk," "monkey down," "mechanical boxer," "pecking chug," "cranking at the hip," and "fur coat." Some movements are deliberate and controlled; others are convulsive and erratic.[29]

The chorus members individually function as performers in the club, but they also establish ambiance. While the dance within the narrative of the production elevates the pompous, spectacular nature of the Pompeii Club itself, the chorus members hold stoic facial expressions to highlight that the Pompeii Club's offerings are just another ordinary engagement for the regular patrons. A stark juxtaposition is curated to situate the vivacious Charity as an atypical participant. Fosse's choreography, set on the eccentrically moving collective of chorus bodies, promotes sensuality and nonchalance within frivolity. As seen in other Fosse productions, the chorus characters are aesthetically scripted with gendered associations, though his neutral dance style shifted the priority focus onto more abstract ideas and nuances of a scene or production rather than dance's virtuosity or narrative capacity.

Interrogating Humanity in the Chorus

Moving beyond abstract and metaphorical conventions, Donald McKayle is a Black choreographer whose work also spanned concert dance and Broadway in the 1960s and 1970s, and would raise concerns regarding the humanity of the performer/character in musical theatre dance. Hailed as creating through his choreography "socially conscious work that exposed the black experience in America," McKayle used a myriad of genres (jazz, ballet, modern, and Afro-Caribbean, among others) to elevate character and narrative.[30] He activated isolated movements to bring about emotion or text and employed repetition to draw attention to a particular idea or laboring body. Regarding the chorus specifically, McKayle's work tends toward synchronous movement, using groups of dancers to collectively convey moments or ideas. Occasionally he would spotlight individuals, when their separation from the chorus was necessary to create tension or juxtaposition within the narrative.

In the musical *Raisin* (1973), for example—based on Lorraine Hansberry's play *A Raisin in the Sun* (1959)—McKayle supports the dramatic narrative, allowing the movement to "grow and develop out of Miss Hansberry's emotionally charged text and story. It is this refreshing marriage of lean, spare realism with the releasing and dynamic flow of song and movement that gives 'Raisin' its particular impact."[31] McKayle's conceptions of choreography and humanity, and his resistance to the use of the body as a design element, point to a larger social conversation regarding the humanization of Black bodies on the Broadway stage. As he said, "I always begin a project with the knowledge that I am dealing

---

[29]Only one gesture seems to suggest any sense of gender specificity. From the beginning of the number onward, the male ensemble members frequently use "teacup fingers" while holding a cigarette. The "teacup fingers" are a Fosse favorite where one "simply touches the tips of the thumb and forefinger together so that a circle or an oval is formed. . . . The remaining three fingers are played." See Debra McWaters, *The Fosse Style* (Gainesville: University Press of Florida, 2008), 8.
[30]Lindsay Guarino and Wendy Oliver, *Jazz Dance: A History of the Roots and Branches* (Gainesville: University Press of Florida, 2014), 167.
[31]Quoted in John Gruen, "With 'Raisin,' He Rises to the Top: Donald McKayle Triumphs as Broadway's First Black Director-Choreographer," *New York Times*, November 4, 1973.

with people—with individuals, with human beings. . . . When I choreograph, I never use people merely to create a design. . . . My work has always been concerned with humanity, in one way or another."[32] McKayle's statements are central to what we know about his work, and help contextualize his work when archival footage is sparse.[33] Even the *Raisin* numbers presented at the 1974 Tony Awards, "Sidewalk Tree" and "A Whole Lot of Sunlight," are not flashy like those of other productions. However, viewing the Tonys' recorded coverage, in which principal characters walk down the street or rock in a chair, suggests that rather than inserting choreography as spectacle or even narration, McKayle must have instead positioned Black chorus bodies within the narrative to call attention to their lived experience and not simply their capacity to entertain.[34]

From the end of the twentieth century through the beginning of the twenty-first, Broadway choreographers continued implementing the functions of dance in musical theatre curated by their predecessors. Choreographers like Onna White (*Carmen Jones*, 1956), Gower Champion (*Hello, Dolly!*, 1964), Michael Bennett (*A Chorus Line*, 1975), and George Faison (*The Wiz*, 1975) activated large choruses in their productions, building on dance techniques and styles that came before them. Steven Hoggett would enter the choreographic sphere using pantomime and heightened gesture to move forward plot and ideas in plays such as *The Curious Incident of the Dog in the Night-Time* (2012). Sergio Trujillo's work on *Memphis* (2009) and *Ain't Too Proud* (2015) activated 1950s and 1960s Black American, African diasporic, and theatrical jazz in a space of electric communion. Similarly, Camille A. Brown's work on *Once on This Island* (Broadway revival, 2017) elevated Caribbean-centric movement in ways akin to Katherine Dunham, to develop a concrete sense of staged authenticity for the fictional island world of the story. All these artists and more have continued the work of their predecessors, using the chorus as a crucial part of the narrative and engaging dance as a storytelling element. Still, the dramaturgical body of those residing in the chorus/ensemble has yet to be fully interrogated within musical productions.

Blankenbuehlerized Storytelling: *In the Heights*

Influenced by his predecessors and building on the complex history of the chorus's role and the chorus member's body in a musical, Andy Blankenbuehler would begin a transition toward ensembleizing—or establishing uniquity and individuality for—the entire chorus with his work on *In the Heights* (Off-Broadway, 2007; Broadway, 2008). Blankenbuehler activates the individual bodies cast in these supplemental roles so that they each affectively operate within the production. His choreography actuates emotion, transfers energy, and prompts intellectual engagement both for the performer and for the audience. Although Blankenbuehler has also worked on productions such as *9 to 5* (2009), *Annie* (2012), and *Cats* (2016), where he implements choreographic practices that maintain a more conventional or long-established understanding of the chorus, his work with *In the Heights*, *Bring It On: The*

---

[32]Quoted in Gruen.
[33]The ephemerality of dance—and, perhaps more importantly, the ephemerality of productions developed by people of color, as seen with *Cabin in the Sky*—poses particular challenges to any specific analysis.
[34]See Liza Gennaro, *Making Broadway Dance* (Oxford: Oxford University Press, 2021), 164–70.

Image 5.2 Lin-Manuel Miranda and cast of *In the Heights* (2008). Photo by Joan Marcus.

Musical (2012), *Hamilton* (Off-Broadway, 2015; Broadway, 2016), and *Bandstand* (2017) would help him curate a choreographic style that prioritizes the ensemble and the ensemble body as a fundamental production element. Melding pedestrian movement with hip-hop, jazz, and ballet in a fusion of dance genres, he promotes dance and the dancing body as communication tools to connect the audience to the sociological metanarratives that surround the productions on which he works.

In the Heights creator Lin-Manuel Miranda "wanted to create something that shows Latinos in the everyday mode [he's] used to, and not just in gangs."[35] The production has been praised for being the first Broadway musical about Latinx stories written by Latinx artists—Lin-Manuel Miranda and Quiara Alegría Hudes. Conversations about casting practices, new audiences, cultural hybridity, and "authenticity" have surrounded the musical since its inception some twenty years ago (in the early 2000s), when Miranda was a young student writing its first iterations. In order to choreograph Miranda's vision of a musical showcasing Latinxs in "everyday mode," Blankenbuehler needed to learn movement and music styles (hip-hop, salsa, merengue, etc.) not traditionally incorporated into musical theatre productions or even his personal vocabulary.

In a 2008 interview promoting *In the Heights*, Blankenbuehler remarked, "It's all about communication . . . about translating the kernel of an emotional idea to the audience . . . it

---

[35]Quoted in Mark Blankenship, "No Fear of 'Heights': Producers Take Risk on Tyro Talent," *Variety* 405, no. 13 (2007): 55.

comes from understanding life."[36] Believing that lived experience is essential to successfully communicating a story or idea allowed him to capture the performer's body itself as a storytelling apparatus. In this way, the body—every body—is a tool that can help establish an environment onstage that a viewer may identify as being "authentic." For *In the Heights*, the individual ensemble body becomes a foundational entity in creating the "authentic" world of the musical. The ensemble body is the lens by which the audience gains access to the layered, complex social world that is the staged Washington Heights. Through collaborative creation between ensemble and choreographer and an overall emphasis on action over spectacle, this ensemble body is choreographed in performance to frame the society from the ensemble members' individual perspectives, transporting the audience into a heterogeneous world that might have otherwise seemed superficial. The ensemble body becomes an essential part of the dramaturgy of the piece. Individualized choreographic scores in the musical numbers "In the Heights," "The Club," and "Carnaval del Barrio," for example, produce sociological milieus specific to the social and physical environments of this staged Washington Heights.

Before moving into these specific numbers further, it's worth pausing on what it means to stage authenticity or attempt to stage authenticity, particularly through dance. In order to include and subsequently codify culturally rooted social dance, and in order to avoid essentialization or misappropriation, Blankenbuehler relies on his diverse cast and associates to bring their own experiences into the space, creating both difference and uniquity within the choreography score. For some, that means drawing on their identity as Latinx individuals, for others, it means showcasing their unique experience living in the staged Washington Heights. The character's authentic self may be a hip-hop dancer or an actor living in New York City. Writing in *Movmnt Magazine*, Jayzel Samonte reports, "Blankenbuehler's talent of conveying a dance landscape seemingly true to the streets required dancers whose abilities interpreted these gyrations authentically. It's that authenticity from every level of the creative team that makes *Heights* such a captivating evening."[37] Authenticity suggests that something is real, bona fide, genuine. If something is labeled "authentic," it is thought to be based on facts, giving it a heightened level of authority or believability. Western tourist culture, in particular, thrives on notions of authenticity: certificates of authenticity, authentic cuisine, or authentic experiences.

Samonte's identification of the *In the Heights* dance landscape demands dancers whose abilities can authentically interpret movements. Because of the production's call for a dramaturgy attuned to "Latinos in the everyday mode," the *In the Heights* creative team manufactured a world in which the characters, and their choreography, become products of staged authenticity.[38] Processes of staging authenticity within the theatrical setting entail the adaptation of social and cultural practices so that they become codified for repetition. The now-codified product then produces a symbol of the original social/cultural practice rather than genuinely enacting that practice. For *In the Heights*, including Latinx social dance

---

[36]"MOVE TV—Andy Blankenbuehler—In the Heights," uploaded by MoveTVnetwork.com, February 20, 2012, Vimeo video, 2:58, https://vimeo.com/37156545.
[37]Jayzel Samonte, "Heightened Exposure: *In the Heights*," *Movmnt Magazine*, June 29, 2008.
[38]See Dean MacCannell, "Staged Authenticity: Arrangements of Social Space in Tourist Settings," *American Journal of Sociology* 79, no. 3 (1973): 589–603.

throughout the production emphasizes the importance of dance within the culture of Washington Heights. Blankenbuehler's choreography allows for flexibility with interpretation and remains open to notions of diversity that are at the root of the story, and the cast. The ensemble body is both dramaturgically authentic and dramaturgically contextualized within the production; it is not one or the other.

Blankenbuehler is a white choreographer tasked with choreographing a show about a community of color—predominantly Latinx—using movement styles with which he did not have previous experience. His choreography is a contemporary blend of aesthetics rooted in jazz and tap techniques, but he has acquired additional dance vocabulary from hip-hop and Latinx social dance traditions.[39] Above all, he is open and willing to accept the expertise of associates and ensemble members whose experiences and training bring authenticity and individual expression to the physical storytelling and help develop his fusion-dance genre. The exchanges of choreographic ideas foster a collective, embodied understanding of a cultural product that he then communicates to ensemble members, who in turn enhance the story with their personalization of the movement, thereby generating a textured and diversified choreographic score. This collaboration further encourages complex and layered dramaturgical narratives as the ensemble body provides a lens through which the audience is to access this staged authenticity. Similarly, situating Latinx-rooted dance movements as requisite to the daily activities of staged Washington Heights creates an illusion of an unmediated encounter with a cultural product.

For example, during "Carnaval del Barrio" the community members celebrate the assortment of countries they come from by waving their flags and dancing Latinx social dances. In this case, dance is directly used to accentuate staged authentic identifications of nationality and ethnicity. The dances in "Carnaval del Barrio" appear organic, almost improvised at times. There is little codified synchronous choreography. The individual doing the dancing shapes the choreography. The staging of Latinx social dance by a white choreographer not trained in these forms risks misappropriation and exoticization, not dissimilar to the "Dance at the Gym" scene in West Side Story. However, the dialectics created by the community of assistants, associates, dance captains, performers, and characters have the potential to intervene in these challenges.

Blankenbuehler engaged the work of assistant chorographer and ensemble member Luis Salgado to stage a moment of salsa. Salgado, whose background is as a trained salsa dancer, does not dance the steps precisely created by Blankenbuehler; he has the freedom to use Blankenbuehler's idea and make it true to his body and his experience, fluidly connecting movements using a salsa vocabulary to score the number and avoid a generalized interpretation. Blankenbuehler's collaborative proclivity allowed for individual cast members to have agency over their characters and the development of community in the production.

By bringing in multiple collaborators' voices, especially those with the kind of embodied experience necessary for authentic, physical storytelling, Blankenbuehler's choreographic ideas can connect in a way far more personal to the specific bodies of the performers. Broadway dancers are typically highly skilled in ballet, jazz, and tap dance, but the foundational vocabulary

---

[39]Lyn Cramer, *Creating Musical Theatre: Conversations with Broadway Directors and Choreographers* (London: Bloomsbury Methuen Drama, 2013), 39.

of hip-hop and break dance in the musical *In the Heights* does not engage ballet training's upright aesthetic. Therefore, dancers proficient in styles outside the typical training are featured in Blankenbeuhler's choreography. In blending different dance genres, he can create a dance vocabulary and choreography that support the narrative, and a physical score that provides opportunities for individuals to show off their skill set through their embodied character.[40] By allowing for the flexibility of individual interpretation, he also allows ensemble bodies to communicate lived experience. A dialectical relationship is created between Blankenbuehler's body, the performer's body, and their character's body. Such tangible corporeality through dance can lead to a viewer's perception of an authentic embodied presence, even though the presence itself is manufactured and staged through this dialectical relationship.

To highlight how this all works together, I will conduct a close reading on a few key choreographic moments within *In the Heights*. Let us begin this process by taking a look at the opening beats of "In the Heights" from a few different perspectives. To start, the opening of the libretto reads:

It is July 3rd—Sunrise.

A beat comes in. In the shadows, **Graffiti Pete** *is revealed painting various walls in the neighborhood. Enter* **Usnavi** *from his stoop.*

Usnavi   Yo, That's my wall!

Graffiti Pete   Pshh . . .

Graffiti Pete *runs away.* **Usnavi** *turns to us.*[41]

Now, let us imagine that moment again, but choreographed by Blankenbuehler. It is July third, sunrise. Graffiti Pete, played by Seth Stewart, is walking down the street to find his next target. He places his boom box on the ground, pauses to look at Usnavi's bodega, and rubs his hands together as he comes up with a plan. Pete pulls out his spray cans and pumps one into the air, then takes three backward steps on the beat shift into the next song on the radio—to the syncopated rhythm of one, (pause) two, and three—analyzing the canvas he is about to develop. Electronic dance music plays as he jumps into second position (a position of believing in something), shrugs his shoulders, and lunges right, lifting one spray can and looking at it—the creative juices are beginning to flow. Spinning the spray can in his left hand, he leans left, then jumps to cross his legs, and jumps out into second position once more with his arms out in the shape of a T—getting pumped up. He turns over his right shoulder, slowly drags his foot around as he looks left, then looks back at the bodega—double-checking no one is around. Pete lunges to his right, alternating his arms (punch out with right/pull left into a bent elbow), holding his palms up with spray cans, switch, switch, switch (to the eight-note rhythm one, and, two, and)—the vision is almost prepared. Once more, he lunges, but this time it is forward into a fourth position (a position of action), before activating his cans behind him and completing a three-step turn toward the bodega storefront—the plan is in motion; the art is blossoming. He jumps into a backward

---

[40]Andy Blankenbuehler, pers. comm.
[41]Quiara Alegría Hudes and Lin-Manuel Miranda, *In the Heights: The Complete Book and Lyrics of the Broadway Musical* (Milwaukee, WI: Applause Theatre and Cinema Books, 2013), 1.

lunge, facing the bodega and analyzing his work, and leaps back to the front to keep going before Usnavi comes outside and scares him away.

Graffiti Pete is the first character the audience sees in the world of *In the Heights*. In the prologue-style opening, it would have been simple to have the character walk out, spray a little paint, and get caught by Usnavi, and then have the opening number, "In the Heights," begin. It would have been just as easy not to have the character at all. Even so, what Blankenbuehler, and the creative team, did was heighten this moment to dictate its importance. The moment itself is not necessarily the "important" part, though Pete does come back later in the show to paint a beautiful mural of Abuela Claudia. What is important is the idea that the body performing Graffiti Pete is unique, even though he is not a principal character. Pete's ensemble body dancing movements, which fall, arguably, under the genre of hip-hop, establish a vocabulary of the piece that is notably different from other Broadway shows at the time. This body says, *In the Heights* is going to move in this way. It informs the audience that bodies other than principal characters will be essential for creating the world of staged Washington Heights. From the very first movement, an ensemble member is established through choreography as a lens for the audience to understand the show's milieu. The ensemble body is immediately set up as essential to the dramaturgy of the world.

To elevate the tangibility of the ensemble body, Blankenbuehler prioritizes communication of ideas (narrative, metaphorical, subtextual, theoretical, or philosophical) over virtuosity and spectacle. Arguably, the most palpable example is when he uses heightened pedestrian or pantomimic movement. In the opening number, "In the Heights," the character Usnavi narrates an introduction to Washington Heights through hip-hop-based music as the neighborhood comes to life around him. The number begins by using quotidian movement to introduce the audience to the idea of the staged city and slowly incorporates abstract ideas within the choreography. A metro worker dawdling on his way to work walks from stage right past the *pirangüero*, who is selling shaved ice, goes up the steps located center stage, and exits. As the city continues to wake up, other people begin to walk down the street, entering from stage left, stage right, or upstage center. The number ebbs and flows between individualized choreography scores, synchronized choreography scores, and small breakout scenes to introduce the audience to this unique world and its vocabulary.

As the staged social world of Washington Heights comes alive through the lens of the entire company's performer/character bodies, the dancing ensemble body becomes increasingly crucial to forming a milieu with a complex, layered history. Lin-Manuel Miranda remembers, "with *In the Heights*, we were very much trying to convey a community. We wanted it to feel like you could follow that person down the block, and there's another musical happening."[42] Let us take Miranda's suggestion and follow ensemble member Nina Lafarga halfway through "In the Heights." The lyrics act as a guide map for understanding the constellation of events that occur:

---

[42]Quoted in Mo Brady, "Writing for Ensembles (*Hamilton*, *In the Heights*—Featuring Lin-Manuel Miranda)," July 2, 2020, in *The Ensemblist*, produced by Broadway Podcast Network, audio podcast, 21:10, https://broadwaypodcastnetwork.com/the-ensemblist/181-from-the-vault-lin-manuel-miranda-on-ensembles/.

All (*except* **Nina**)   In the Heights

Piragua Guy/Carla/Daniela/Others   I flip the lights and start my day

All   There are fights

Carla/Daniela/Women   And endless debts

Kevin/Benny/Piragua Guy/Men   And bills to pay

All   In the Heights

Benny/Kevin/Piragua Guy/Others   I can't survive without café

Usnavi   I serve café

All   'Cuz tonight seems like a million years away!

En Washington—[43]

Lafarga, who is in the ensemble, enters upstage center and walks directly to Rosie Lani Fiedelman. They exchange a few words; it is no coincidence that they meet on the word "fights." Luis Salgado leaves the bodega area and crosses to Fiedelman, sending Lafarga into an evasively quick chaîné turn toward downstage right, her arms in a "touchdown" shape (hands in fists). On the downbeat before "In," her arms flip so her fists are toward the ground, then flip back to touchdown shape on "In" and back to the reverse with legs bent and back curved on "the." Ending the movement sequence, posing with one leg beveled facing the audience, she pauses, looking back at Salgado and Fiedelman, who are now paired center. They salsa together straight down center stage on "I can't survive." As they salsa, once again drawing attention to notions of staged authenticity within this Latinx community, everyone else onstage is in their point of pause, making them the only moving entity. On "café," Salgado and Fiedelman continue their duet, and the others onstage pick up where they left off. By isolating these three ensemble members, allowing Lafarga's action to drive the plot, the choreography reveals a love triangle. There may not be a story here, but it feels like a story. When this sequence becomes the focus, the movement (quotidian and danced) accumulates into a narrative completely separate from the central plot of *In the Heights*, but still fundamental to receiving a complex, staged society.

Blankenbuehler's choreographic landscape continues to breathe between brief moments of synchronization and moments of individuality to highlight the uniting principles of this group of people but acknowledge each performer/character's unique personalities. The linkage of movement, music, and text by the ensemble bodies during these moments of unity speaks to Miranda's question, "What is something that everyone in this neighborhood is feeling at the same time?"[44] The mediation of all the bodies onstage is a point of connection. The fluidity of the ensemble body in moving between mediated and unmediated phases creates an intricate environment that promotes the community atmosphere of Washington Heights as well as the sense of staged authenticity.

The ensemble body in *In the Heights* yields an array of recognizable shapes that can then attach to emotional states, character attributes, or narrative. Interpreting these postures

---

[43]Hudes and Miranda, *In the Heights*, 4.
[44]Quoted in Brady, "Writing for Ensembles."

and gestures through the individual ensemble bodies enacting them generates a complex sociological environment within the world of the production. The individual ensemble bodies portray individual characters living in staged Washington Heights and reveal the socioeconomic effects on their community. The staged authenticity of this world is established as the individual ensemble bodies move in uniquely personalized ways. Particularly when framed by Latinx social dance, the individual ensemble bodies are read by the audience as a dramaturgically Latinx body and become understood as presenting an unmediated encounter with a cultural product. Blankenbuehler's choreography adapts the milieu of the production into an embodied narrative (literal, supplemental, or nuanced) in service of manufacturing a lens through which these bodies and characters can transport the audience to a heterogeneous, translocal community. He activates the real, individual, and diverse ensemble body as an essential storytelling component. In prioritizing the ensemble as lens, then, Blankenbuehler contains a century-old lineage of chorus and dance implementation practices while revolutionizing the chorus's storytelling capacity.

Conclusion

Historically, the dancing body, the chorus body, and the chorus in musical theatre productions have developed in concert with transitions in sociocultural thought and praxis. In the twenty-first century, a time when conversations on racism, sexism, and equitability are at the forefront of our sociocultural/sociopolitical consciousness, Blankenbuehler's shift toward the recognition of individuality and embodied knowledge within the chorus/ensemble has created a link between a production and the audience that promotes sociological metanarratives beyond the show itself. His work builds on Dunham's activation of the chorus as social world creation, de Mille's use of the chorus as plot driver, Robbins's individualization of members within the chorus, and McKayle's humanization of the chorus character, among other concepts and practices that came before him. Whether the chorus/ensemble body is presenting a Black community in the 1940s southern United States, a group of cowboys and farmers in rural Oklahoma, or the community of staged Washington Heights, it can become a microcosmic metaphor for society, historically or contemporarily.

Blankenbuehler's emphasis on the ensemble as the lens for a piece positions the individual ensemble bodies within the generalized group of supporting characters as each being important for an audience to encounter and understand a show. The audience receives information either implicitly or explicitly through the lens of the ensemble. For *In the Heights* the audience gains access to a complex social world by bearing witness to the individual ensemble bodies communicating the effects of, response to, and resistance toward processes of gentrification and homogenization. Dance and choreography's ability to frame the ensemble (body) as the lens of a piece can similarly shape how the audience reads the group or the individual enacting the movement.

How can admiring the ensemble body provide performers with agency, voice, and respect? Susan Leigh Foster argues, "by inviting viewers into a specific experience of what the body is, they also enable us to contemplate how the body is grounded, its function in remembering, its affinity with cultural values, its participation in the construction of gender and sexuality, and the ways in which it is assimilating technologies so as to change the very definition of the human."[45] The body is unquestionably integral to past, present, and future musical theatre productions. Attaching the body within the ensemble to its social moorings strengthens the potential for the audience to receive complex layers of a production. The ensemble (body) can be the lens by which audiences gain clarity and productions permeate affect. In honoring the profound potential of the ensemble body to reveal a principal character's psychology, tell a piece of the story, express an unspoken aspect of the libretto, transition to another scene, allow characters to express themselves, present ideas metaphorically or abstractly, perform spectacle, connect the audience to an identifiable human experience, and activate a show's sociological metanarrative, we can amplify the reflective embodied voices of the unique individuals who tell the story.

Bibliography

"Audra McDonald and George C. Wolfe | Interview | TimesTalks." Uploaded by New York Times Events, February 23, 2016. YouTube video, 51:31. https://www.youtube.com/watch?v=oJDbK03o6d8.

Blankenbuehler, Andy, and Sarah L. Kaufman. "Words on Dance." Discussion at Symphony Space, New York, October 21, 2019.

Blankenship, Mark. "No Fear of 'Heights': Producers Take Risk on Tyro Talent." *Variety* 405, no. 13 (2007): 55.

Brady, Mo. "Writing for Ensembles (*Hamilton*, *In the Heights*—Featuring Lin-Manuel Miranda)." July 2, 2020. In *The Ensemblist*, produced by Broadway Podcast Network. Audio podcast, 21:10. https://broadwaypodcastnetwork.com/the-ensemblist/181-from-the-vault-lin-manuel-miranda-on-ensembles/.

Cramer, Lyn. *Creating Musical Theatre: Conversations with Broadway Directors and Choreographers*. London: Bloomsbury Methuen Drama, 2013.

De Mille, Agnes. *Leaps in the Dark: Art and the World*. Edited by Mindy Aloff. Gainesville: University Press of Florida, 2011.

Foster, Susan Leigh. *Choreographing Empathy: Kinesthesia in Performance*. London: Routledge, 2011.

Foster, Susan Leigh. *Choreography and Narrative*. Bloomington: Indiana University Press, 1996.

Gennaro, Liza. *Making Broadway Dance*. Oxford: Oxford University Press, 2021.

Gruen, John. "With 'Raisin,' He Rises to the Top: Donald McKayle Triumphs as Broadway's First Black Director-Choreographer." *New York Times*, November 4, 1973.

Guarino, Lindsay, and Wendy Oliver. *Jazz Dance: A History of the Roots and Branches*. Gainesville: University Press of Florida, 2014.

Hawthorn, Ainsley. "Middle Eastern Dance and What We Call It." *Dance Research* 37, no. 1 (2019): 1–17.

Hill, Constance Valis. "Collaborating with Balanchine on *Cabin in the Sky*: Interviews with Katherine Dunham." In *Kaiso! Writings by and about Katherine Dunham*, edited by Vèvè A. Clark and Sarah East Johnson, 235–47. Madison: University of Wisconsin Press, 2005.

Hudes, Quiara Alegría, and Lin-Manuel Miranda. *In the Heights: The Complete Book and Lyrics of the Broadway Musical*. Milwaukee, WI: Applause Theatre and Cinema Books, 2013.

Ibee [Jack Pulaski]. "Legitimate: Plays on Broadway—*Cabin in the Sky*." *Variety*, October 30, 1940.

---

[45]Susan Leigh Foster, *Choreographing Empathy: Kinesthesia in Performance* (London: Routledge, 2011), 218.

Jordan, Elizabeth. "Theatre." *America*, November 16, 1940.

Jowitt, Deborah. *Jerome Robbins: His Life, His Theater, His Dance*. New York: Simon and Schuster, 2004.

Laurents, Arthur, Leonard Bernstein, and Stephen Sondheim. *West Side Story: A Musical*. New York: Random House, 1958.

Lodge, Mary Jo. "Dance Breaks and Dream Ballets: Transitional Moments in Musical Theatre." In *Gestures of Music Theater: The Performativity of Song and Dance*, edited by Dominic Symonds and Millie Taylor, 75–90. Oxford: Oxford University Press, 2014.

MacCannell, Dean. "Staged Authenticity: Arrangements of Social Space in Tourist Settings." *American Journal of Sociology* 79, no. 3 (1973): 589–603.

Martin, John. "The Dance: De Mille's *Oklahoma!*." *New York Times*, May 9, 1943.

McWaters, Debra. *The Fosse Style*. Gainesville: University Press of Florida, 2008.

Miranda, Lin-Manuel, and Jeremy McCarter. *Hamilton: The Revolution*. New York: Grand Central, 2016.

Mizejewski, Linda. *Ziegfeld Girl: Image and Icon in Culture and Cinema*. Durham, NC: Duke University Press, 1999.

"MOVE TV—Andy Blankenbuehler—In the Heights." Uploaded by MoveTVnetwork.com, February 20, 2012. Vimeo video, 2:58. https://vimeo.com/37156545.

New York Times. "'Cabin in the Sky,' a Musical Fantasy, with Ethel Waters, at Loew's Criterion." May 28, 1943.

Samonte, Jayzel. "Heightened Exposure: *In the Heights*." *Movmnt Magazine*, June 29, 2008.

Sandoval-Sánchez, Alberto. *José, Can You See? Latinos on and off Broadway*. Madison: University of Wisconsin Press, 1999.

Stearns, Marshall Winslow, and Jean Stearns. *Jazz Dance: The Story of American Vernacular Dance*. New York: Macmillan, 1968.

Variety. Review of *Cabin in the Sky*. December 31, 1942.

Waskul, Dennis, and Phillip Vannini. "The Performative Body: Dramaturgy, the Body, and Embodiment." In *The Drama of Social Life: A Dramaturgical Handbook*, edited by Charles Edgley, Phillip Vannini, Simon Gottschalk, and Dennis Waskul, 197–210. Farnham, UK: Taylor and Francis, 2013.

Winkler, Kevin. *Big Deal: Bob Fosse and Dance in the American Musical*. New York: Oxford University Press, 2018.

Woll, Allen L. *Black Musical Theatre: From Coontown to Dream Girls*. Baton Rouge: Louisiana State University Press, 1989.

6 Storytelling through Dance: The Rise of the Dream Ballet

BUD COLEMAN

Melissa is having trouble with her boyfriend. After an odd musical encounter with a German baroness (with echoes of *The Sound of Music*), Melissa scans the countryside. She sees a woman walking dreamily toward her through mist (which suddenly appears on this sunny day), wearing the same dress and hair style as Melissa. At the end of her emotional rope, Melissa vents her frustration to the world:

> Oh no, is this a dream ballet? We're not having a dream ballet. They're annoying and stupid and slow everything down. Nobody loves a dream ballet—nobody!

With that, her doppelgänger disappears. In *Schmigadoon*, a big-hearted satirical television valentine to musical theatre, where seemingly every trope, convention, cliché, and gimmick from the canon is trotted out for a cameo, there is one that is missing: the dream ballet.

What is a dream ballet, and why in this popular 2021 TV series on Apple+ would the convention be so summarily dismissed as being unworthy of satire? For a musical theatre component that dates almost all the way back to the first "musical comedy" productions, the term *dream ballet* seems to have escaped a set definition. Adding to the challenge is that the dream ballet has manifested itself in different ways over time. Nevertheless, a working definition of the dream ballet can be a movement or dance sequence, integrated (or not) with the production's plot, which is usually realized without spoken dialogue. The dream ballet is separate from the reality of the story; it can be a dream or fantasy of a character, a flashback, an alternate reality, or even a lie. The movement vocabulary of the dream ballet does not need to be rooted in ballet, and can showcase the virtuosity of one or many dancers. In order to further explicate the dream ballet in musical theatre, this chapter explores its antecedents in depth, tracing how ballet became its first dance vocabulary via *The Black Crook* (1866), and how it flowered in such works as *The Band Wagon* (1931), *Babes in Arms* (1937), *Pal Joey* (1940), *Lady in the Dark* (1941), and *Oklahoma!* (1943).

The Dream Ballet as a Convention of Musical Storytelling

While every production has permission to write its own rules, popular song, spoken word theatre, and story ballets present dramaturgical options to the creators of musical theatre. What theatrical conventions is the production going to employ? What modes of storytelling is it going to embrace: spoken word? instrumental music? sung lyrics (and what kind of vocal style)? rap? dance (and what kinds of dance)? puppets? and so on. And, of course, each production decides when in the musical to roll out these choices. In the first three minutes of *Hamilton* (2015), we learn that this show will have direct address, rap, hip-hop, a mixed-race cast telling a story predominately about Caucasians, variations on circa 1760s costumes in ivory tones, and dance used as a counterpoint to the narration, sometimes illustrative but mostly abstract, often delivered in unison by an ensemble of highly skilled performers.

Of course, a production does not have to introduce all its modes of storytelling in its first three minutes. But waiting can come with a cost as the audience might feel alienated: initially informed that the aesthetic experience would be of a certain type, then suddenly learning that the storytelling is going to be delivered in a nonverbal way. For some theatregoers, a musical stretches their willing suspension of disbelief as they are unwilling to go on the journey from spoken word to song. For others, the transition from song to narrative dance is where they want to get off the bus, as they either do not want to see the story told through movement or feel that they will not be able to understand a story told through the medium of dance. Usually, dance does not appear in *Oklahoma!* until the third song, when Will Parker sings "Kansas City" and teaches two-step and ragtime to the ensemble, who join in. And, since there is typically no signal that a dream ballet will appear later in the evening, this is where *Schmigadoon*'s Melissa pops into the frame to remind us that the dream ballet is never welcome, at least not in her musical world.

Of course, there are some musicals which are written to present dance early on: *West Side Story* (1957), *A Chorus Line* (1975), *Cats* (1981), *Ragtime* (1996), *Head Over Heels* (2015), etc. And revivals of works which did not originally introduce dance in the early part of the musical can be re-thought. In the 1992 revival of *Carousel*, director Nicholas Hytner and choreographer Kenneth MacMillan establish dance during the overture, after the audience first views the dreary mill where Julie and Carrie work. As the mill disappears, we see vibrant social dance as a carnival comes to town and a carousel is built right in front of us. In addition to being a stunning production number, this lets the audience know that dance will take on a major part of the storytelling of this production.

The Fascination with Dreams in the Nineteenth Century

Because musical theatre as a genre grew out of other performance modes in the nineteenth century, it is instructive to look at how and where dream sequences began to appear in entertainment at this time. While scientific and technological innovations and the Industrial Revolution brought enormous changes, some in society sought greater value in emotions and the irrational world of dreams and their meanings. Writers such as Honoré de Balzac, Charles Baudelaire, Charlotte Brontë, Emily Brontë, Charles Dickens, Victor Hugo, Gustave Flaubert, Fyodor Dostoyevsky, Arthur Rimbaud, Ann Radcliffe, and Mary Shelley explored the causes behind dreams, the relationship of dreams to madness and creativity, the difference between dreams and memory, and other topics. Many nineteenth-century ballets, often based on literary sources, also used the dream state as a narrative device: *La Sylphide* (1836), *Don Quixote* (1869), *Sleeping Beauty* (1890), *The Nutcracker* (1892), and others. The romantic era embraced the supernatural and fantasy, symbolic and allegorical meanings, with the female dancer in pointe shoes seen as the epitome of the ethereal. While these romantic story ballets could be seen often on stages in Russia, Italy, France, and Denmark, their impact on traditional theatre was limited.

Just as the dream ballet in musicals made its first appearance well before *Oklahoma!* (1943), so too did the scientific exploration of dreams precede Sigmund Freud's *The Interpretation of Dreams* (1899). The European and US popular culture obsession with dreams also began well before 1913, when Freud's works were first translated into English. Dream books—linking dreams with "lucky" numbers—were developed by the gambling and lottery industry early in the nineteenth century. These were constantly updated to reflect contemporary inventions; in 1935, Prince Max Lowenstein published *What Does My Dream Mean?*, purportedly an assemblage of all existing dream theories that was aimed at correlating dream subject matter to lotto numbers.[1] Other examples of the fascination with dreams can be seen in the 1874 publication of Wilhelm Wundt's *Principles of Physiological Psychology* and the more than two dozen films featuring a dream sequence that were created by German producers between 1895 and 1906.[2] The pioneering French filmmaker Georges Méliès might have been the first to combine dance with a dream sequence in film, with *The Balletmaster's Dream* (1903) and *The Clockmaker's Dream* (1904).

The Black Crook and the Popularization of Ballet

An ungainly marriage of melodrama and Parisian ballet, *The Black Crook* (1866) was an extravagant spectacle with spoken words, songs, dance, and lots of scenery and special effects. For audiences, the kinesthetic power of seeing more than a hundred performers onstage in this ballet-infused extravaganza must have been impactful at a time when ballet was rarely seen by the American public, save for the occasional solo act on the vaudeville circuit. Beyond its incorporation of ballet, the extravaganza, as Raymond Knapp points out, also popularized many components of early musical theatre: a central story; music that combines classical and popular song; dance that includes solos as well as a female ensemble performing synchronized movement; and elaborate costumes, scenery, and lighting that frequently changes throughout the production.[3] *The Black Crook* is often called the "first" musical, but it actually opened several months after the first known entertainment to call itself a musical comedy: a double bill titled *The Black Domino / Between You, Me, and the Post* (1866). As neither the score nor the libretto is extant for this earlier production, we can only speculate as to its contents, but its embrace of this new label of "musical comedy" surely meant that some new form was emerging. With its popularity, longevity, and impact on producers and theatre creators, *The Black Crook* cements this impression.

American producers Henry Jarrett and Henry Palmer were negotiating to bring a Parisian ballet to the New York Academy of Music but were prevented from doing so when the Academy burned down in the summer of 1866. Titled *La Biche au Bois*, the ballet is set in a forest and featured various dances where flowers, sea creatures, masked revelers, and

[1]Lydia Marinelli, "Screening Wish Theories: Dream Psychologies and Early Cinema," *Science in Context* 19, no. 1 (2006): 95.
[2]Marinelli, 90.
[3]Raymond Knapp, *The American Musical and the Formation of National Identity* (Princeton, NJ: Princeton University Press, 2005), 29.

more first threaten and then ultimately rescue the featured romantic couple. Fortuitously, the ballet's storyline featured certain similarities with a melodrama titled *The Black Crook* that had been written by Charles M. Barras and that was also scheduled to open in New York at Niblo's Garden that year. Barras teamed up with Jarrett and Palmer (who also had bought an elaborate transformation scene from a British pantomime). Adding on a full score of music, the new work alternated ballet numbers with scenes from the melodrama, which resulted in a work Kurt Gänzl describes as "a highly attractive if reasonably incoherent and lengthy opéra-bouffe féerie entertainment."[4] As the extravaganza clocked in at more than five hours, everything about the piece at Niblo's Garden was epic in this grand theatre seating over three thousand patrons, located on Broadway at Prince Street.

As *La Biche au Bois* was already choreographed, there was no initial attempt to integrate the movement sequences with the plot of the melodrama. The appeal (for men in the audience) was not the story, but rather the display of the female form, packaged as "art." Besides foregrounding classical ballet (and teenage girls in flesh-colored tights and costumes with bare arms), the production helped popularize transformation sequences. For example, when Rodolphe finds himself surrounded by Hertzog's fiends, he kisses a magical ring given to him by the Fairy Queen, who then appears with her entourage to save him. The convention of the transformation scene would become a staple in early dream ballets such as the ones in *The Band Wagon*, *Lady in the Dark*, and *Pal Joey*.

As the production script of *The Black Crook* continued to morph throughout its original run of 475 performances and subsequent tours, there is no such thing as a fixed script of *The Black Crook*. In the script held at the New York Public Library (based on the 1866 promptbook), act 2, scene 4, takes place in a grotto where the Fairy Queen of the Golden Realm has brought the young lover, Rodolphe, to keep him safe from the clutches of Hertzog, a vile crook-backed master of the black arts. Rodolphe is convinced he must be dreaming as he gazes on golden stalactites, silver waters, masses of emerald and gold, fairies, and gnomes. At the end of the musical play, Rodolphe and his beloved, Amina, are safely reunited. Interestingly, act 4, scene 6, is wordlessly concluded in dance, and act 4, scenes 7 and 8, depend exclusively on dance to finish the narrative. (There was no dream ballet in the original *Black Crook*, but one might have appeared in a later iteration or knock-off.)

Amid the conservative Victorian mores of the era, the scantily clad young dancers attracted negative editorials in New York papers, free publicity (which sold more tickets), and decades of imitators. Just at Niblo's Garden, there were a dozen facsimiles between 1866 and 1887.[5] Subsequent extravaganzas often evoked the European roots of their source material or performers, counting on the esteem of "Parisian ballet" to give the imprimatur of taste to a display of female flesh, a spectacle that might have gotten the production closed down if the public thought there were American girls onstage. (In point of fact, the sixty-two women who originally appeared in what was advertised as the "Grand Parisienne Ballet Troupe" was

---

[4]Kurt Gänzl, "Double-Treat: 'The Black Crook' from New York to London," *Encyclopedia of the Musical Theatre*, Operetta Research Center, last updated October 4, 2001, http://operetta-research-center.org/double-treat-black-crook-new-york-london/.
[5]Knapp, 23.

comprised of thirty-nine Americans and twenty-three British.)[6] *The Black Crook* imitators were not confined to the United States as productions also appeared in the United Kingdom.

The first British production of *The Black Crook* opened in 1872, featuring a story that hewed closely to the one in *La Biche au Bois* (tossing out Barras's play), with new music by Frederic Clay and Georges Jacobi. Several different versions of *The Black Crook* also toured the United States during the 1870s and 1880s.[7] Due to the high visibility of the production, seemingly every minstrel and burlesque troupe took a turn at creating a parody: *The White Crook* made rounds on the vaudeville circuit, for example, and *Black Cook* toured the country.[8] A silent film version of *The Black Crook* was released in 1916. Across all these iterations, the extravaganza and its imitators popularized spectacle with elaborate costumes and scenery, transformation scenes, narrative told through dance, and the display of the female body in the form of a large chorus of ballet dancers.

The Dream Ballet and Freud

As the nineteenth-century obsession with dreams played out in literature, science, and early film, it was only a matter of time before it began to appear in musical theatre. Pamyla Stiehl argues that the first dream sequences appeared on Broadway in *Tillie's Nightmare* (1910) and *Peggy-Ann* (1926).[9] With the latter based on the plot of the former, both musical productions featured a woman who has flamboyant dreams of a glorious life but cannot seem to gain control over her nightmares. Vaudevillian in structure, the musicals contained a weak plot and were made up of multiple individual dance acts, in this case, dreams. Herbert Fields wrote the libretto for *Peggy-Ann*, with a score by Richard Rodgers and Lorenz Hart. Its choreographer, Seymour Felix—credited with its "musical staging"—acknowledged publicly that the traditional bag of tricks of kick lines, backbends, cartwheels, splits, and such no longer suited the modern musical: "the chorus interlude became a colorful but negative interruption to the action or comedy of the musical comedy book."[10] As a great deal of *Peggy-Ann* takes place in the ingenue's dreams of New York—a yacht, a wedding, and an escape to Cuba—Felix was able to create musical stagings that advanced the plot and character development. Although versed in many dance forms, Felix chose a more balletic vocabulary to tell this story rather than sticking to the more standard Broadway dance vernacular.[11] There were clearly many elements about the production that audiences found compelling as *Peggy-Ann* ran for 333 performances. *Tillie's Nightmare* and *Peggy-Ann* mark the beginning of Broadway productions that were created by authors intrigued by the theories of Freud and his contemporaries about the dream state.

---

[6]Gänzl, "Double-Treat."

[7]Thomas Postlewait, "The Hieroglyphic Stage: American Theatre and Society, Post–Civil War to 1945," in *The Cambridge History of American Theatre*, ed. Don B. Wilmeth and Christopher Bigsby, vol. 2 (Cambridge: Cambridge University Press, 1999), 152.

[8]Gänzl, "Double-Treat."

[9]Pamyla Stiehl, "The Dansical: American Musical Theatre Reconfigured as a Choreographer's Expression and Domain" (PhD diss., University of Colorado, Boulder, 2008), 39.

[10]Robert G. Dame, "The Integration of Dance as a Dramatic Element in Broadway Musical Theatre" (master's thesis, University of Nevada, Las Vegas, 1995), 41.

[11]Frederick Nolan, *Lorenz Hart: A Poet on Broadway* (New York: Oxford University Press, 1994), 92.

Ballet began to appear more regularly in musicals in the 1930s, courtesy of choreographers Albertina Rasch, George Balanchine, José Limón, and Agnes de Mille, who had already made a name for themselves in the world of concert dance. The dream ballet depended on a high level of dance technique in order not only to carry the narrative weight of the scene, but to meet the audience's expectations of virtuosity (expectations based on soloists they saw in vaudeville). Acclaimed during the late 1920s and 1930s as the "Czarina of Broadway," dancer/choreographer Rasch (1891–1967) was hired to be the "dance director" on more than thirty Broadway musicals and revues, almost single-handedly creating what came to be known as musical theatre dance in the 1920s. She began her career as a professional ballerina (prima ballerina at the Vienna Ballet, and later guest star with the Chicago Opera and the Metropolitan Opera), but her choreographic output was not limited to one style or movement vocabulary; rather, it was shaped and informed by the world of the musical or revue. After touring on the vaudeville circuit in the United States and Europe, she returned to New York in 1923 and opened her first dance studio. While she continued to perform on concert stages and in opera houses, she was hired to create dance routines for the Keith-Orpheum vaudeville circuit. Her first venture was successful, a ballet for fifty girls on the vast stage of the Hippodrome. More offers came, and she began to train and send out dancers in companies of six to twenty girls, under the moniker the Albertina Rasch Girls or the Albertina Rasch Dancers. (Other dance masters created their own troupes of precision dancers who performed in vaudeville and revues, such as the Tiller Girls, who first arrived in New York in 1900.) Rasch's school in New York was popular, and by 1925 she had 150 dancers performing (under her masthead) on vaudeville stages around the country.[12] While vaudeville had been home to a number of solo dancers, the sight of a highly trained corps de ballet was new to American audiences. (The first professional ballet company in the United States, George Balanchine's American Ballet, would not appear until 1935.) As a sign of the artistic license granted to Rasch, she was engaged to create a jazz ballet for George Gershwin's *Rhapsody in Blue* as part of the vaudeville bill at the Hippodrome in 1925. Dance historian Carrie Gaiser Casey suggests that *Rhapsody in Blue* was one of Rasch's first experiments creating a hybrid form from classical ballet and American jazz dance.[13]

In a world dominated by men, Rasch was at last able to begin her Broadway career in 1924, after she was invited to create the choreography for a few specialty numbers in *George White's Scandals of 1924*. Early dream ballets include the "Beggar Waltz" in *The Band Wagon* (1931), starring Fred and Adele Astaire and ballerina Tilly Losch. In this intimate revue with a score by Arthur Schwartz and Howard Dietz and libretto by Dietz and George S. Kaufman, a beggar (Fred Astaire) falls asleep outside of the Vienna Opera House and dreams of performing onstage with the ballet star and chorus, only to wake up back where he started. The revue contained other fantasy sequences staged by Rasch, and their daring and innovation were noticed by critics. "After 'The Band Wagon,'" Brooks Atkinson warned in the *New York Times*, "it will be difficult for the old-time musical show to hold up its head."[14]

---

[12]Richard and Paulette Ziegfeld, *The Ziegfeld Touch: The Life and Times of Florenz Ziegfeld, Jr.*, New York: Harry N. Abrams, 1993.
[13]Carrie Gaiser Casey, "The Ballet Corporealities of Anna Pavlova and Albertina Rasch," *Dance Chronicle* 35, no. 1 (2012): 12.
[14]Frank W. D. Ries, "Albertina Rasch: The Broadway Career," *Dance Chronicle* 6, no. 2 (1983): 116.

Prominent dance critic John Martin (*New York Times*) cited Rasch's choreography for *The Band Wagon* as evidence that her body of work was raising the caliber of dance on Broadway.[15]

Rasch's work was not only popular with audiences, but she also won over the Broadway "establishment." Producer Max Gordon hired Rasch to choreograph seven Broadway productions, Florence Ziegfeld engaged her to choreograph five, and Sam H. Harris for four. While Rasch could choreograph using a wide range of dance vocabularies, she was often engaged to stage a piece using classical ballet with women *en pointe*. Formally trained in the grandest traditions of European ballet, Rasch reasoned that American audiences would rather see "dynamic surprises, accentuated action and syncopated sensations."[16] Rasch dubbed this hybrid of classical ballet with popular music, American jazz, and syncopated rhythms the New World Ballet (later American Ballet). This artistic amalgamation of American popular forms of music and dance with classical ballet became her trademark. The influential critic Robert Benchley – self-described as "anti-ballet Bob" – wrote that his anti-ballet stance changed when he saw the Albertina Rasch dancers in the musical *Rio Rita* (1927) and in *The Ziegfeld Follies of 1927*.[17]

While there is a paucity of written descriptions of her work on Broadway, Rasch's many Hollywood films provide a rich visual archive of a versatile and much-in-demand choreographer. Works like *Devil-May-Care* (1929), *Broadway Melody of 1936,* and *The King Steps Out* (1936), feature sixteen to twenty-four Albertina Rasch Dancers on pointe, performing highly synchronized movement at a lively clip. The pointe number in *Hollywood Revue of 1929* features the twenty-four dancers in classical tutus, but they are performing to a big band ballad and executing synchronized precision choreography that includes a kick line and fan kicks. Indeed, the camera angles showing the women are on pointe with framing that could be used in a TV commercial for the Radio City Rockettes. (Rasch also used an overhead camera in order to create a kaleidoscope effect using her dancers, years before Busby Berkley made this camera shot his signature.) As a sign of Rasch's status, in the MGM trailer for *The Merry Widow* (1934), the Albertina Rasch Dancers are named after the five starring performers.

An interesting article appeared in the December 1929 *Photoplay* magazine that describes the type of chorus girl now hired by the major studios for film musicals: "Small, active, and pretty."[18] The author notes that "The Albertina Rasch girls at M-G-M are a bit different," as they "are larger and apparently stronger than the others."[19] What the author does not explain is that the Albertina Rasch "girls" were most likely older than the studio lot chorines, who were often teenagers, and a lot more seasoned in their level of dance technique. Once Rasch had trained a dancer to her specifications, she was loyal to them, hiring them gig after gig. To give an example of their versatility, in *The Merry Widow,* the twenty-four Albertina Rasch Dancers each led a group of ballroom dancers in one

---

[15]John Martin, "The Dance: Number for Our Revues," *New York Times*, October 18, 1931, 110.
[16]Qtd. in "Albertina Rasch" in the "Dimitri Tiomkin, the official website." https://dimitritiomkin.com/biography/albertina-rasch/
[17]Ziegfeld 142.
[18]Qtd. in Frank W. D. Ries, "Albertina Rasch: The Hollywood Career," *Dance Chronicle* 6, No. 4 (1983), 295.
[19]Ibid.

number, then performed an acrobatic can-can set in Maxim's, and then executed mazurka steps in a Russian dance.

Moving back and forth between California and New York, Rasch was tapped to create a dream ballet for the Broadway musical *The Cat and the Fiddle* (1931), with music by Jerome Kern and book and lyrics by Otto Harbach. In "Dance in Phantasy," a young classical composer dreams about his high ambitions to conquer the musical world. Rasch has not received her due in histories of musical theatre, no doubt the result of the assessment of writers like Cecil Smith. Writing in 1950, Smith described Rasch's choreography as "modish pseudo-modernity" and "stylized convolutions," whose significance was only in paving the "way for the triumphal entry of George Balanchine onto Broadway."[20] A standard trope of musical theatre history is that most productions before the Golden Age were artistically "inferior," with exceptions being made only for works by Irving Berlin, the Gershwins, Cole Porter, Dorothy Fields, Jerome Kern, and George Balanchine.

During Rasch's ascendency to Broadway choreographer, Freudian analysis began to directly affect the work of American playwrights. Eugene O'Neill underwent psychoanalysis in 1927, which had a profound influence on his construction of *Strange Interlude* (Pulitzer Prize, 1928) and *Mourning Becomes Electra* (1931). Other playwrights who used psychoanalysis in the construction of their plays include John Howard Lawson, Elmer Rice, Sidney Howard, and Lynn Riggs. Even Philip Barry, who is known primarily for excelling in comedy of manners, used psychoanalysis, doing so in order for his characters to analyze their past and liberate themselves from its tentacles, resulting in plays like *Hotel Universe* (1930). Not surprisingly, as psychoanalysis became part of the national conversation, satires began to appear that mocked the new fad: the 1906 film *Dr. Dippy's Sanitarium* and Susan Glaspell and George Cram Cook's 1915 play *Suppressed Desires*.

Freudian analysis, in its popularity, came to influence musical theatre creators. In preparation for an upcoming meeting, Jerome Kern wrote to Oscar Hammerstein II in 1933 about their collective desire to push the boundaries of musical theatre. Kern exclaimed, "we are reaching in the air for ideas, [a] form of musical play of any texture" and proceeded to write out a scenario where a "beautiful spinster" dreams of children she never had, after which the scene dissolves and we are back to the routine life of the characters.[21] Kern was

---

[20]Cecil Smith, *Musical Comedy in America* (New York: Theatre Arts Books, 1950), 108, 353. Smith was not a big fan of most musical theatre choreographers (or dance directors) who predated Balanchine, but he did speak well about a few figures. He describes Robert Alton (1902–57) as "one of Broadway's breeziest choreographers," noting Alton's work for *Pins and Needles* (1939) and crediting him with creating "exciting dances" for *The Ziegfeld Follies of 1943* (289, 315). Ned Wayburn (1874–1942) fares better, with Smith referring to him as "one of the slickest masters of slow-dance routines" (186). (Wayburn's extensive credits include being the dance director for annual editions of *The Passing Show*, 1912–24). Gertrude Hoffman (1883–1966) is lauded for reinstating ballet in musical comedy in the 1920s, and Julian Mitchell gets a nod for knowing how to "stage some of the most sumptuous production numbers on the New York stage" in his work for Weber and Fields and *The Ziegfeld Follies* (108, 172). Smith does not even mention Seymour Felix. As one of the first histories of musical theatre, Smith's *Musical Comedy in America* (1950) had a profound influence on subsequent histories, which often give short shrift to the work of choreographers in musical theatre.
[21]Quoted in Stephen Citron, *The Wordsmiths: Oscar Hammerstein 2nd and Alan Jay Lerner* (New York: Oxford University Press, 1995), 201.

clearly interested in exploring the possibilities of the dream ballet, as it was included in all three of the remaining Kern and Hammerstein collaborations: *Three Sisters* (book and lyrics by Hammerstein, London, 1934), *Gentleman Unafraid* (book and lyrics by Hammerstein and Harbach, 1938), and *Very Warm for May* (book and lyrics by Hammerstein, 1939). As none of these productions attracted critical or popular acclaim, they have tended to disappear from the history books. About all we know about the dream ballet in *Very Warm for May*, staged by Rasch and Harry Losee, is that Atkinson of the *New York Times* considered it "an imaginative ballet of psychological phantoms."[22]

George Balanchine and Jerome Kern

Remembering the success of *Peggy-Ann*, Rodgers and Hart decided to experiment with the dream ballet again when they set down to pen *Babes in Arms* (1937). Starting with an original idea by Hart, the resulting work is the quintessential let's-put-on-a-show musical, with group of vaudeville performers' children banding together to create a show in order to avoid being put in the workhouse while their parents are on tour. Featuring a cast of primarily teenagers (including a young Alfred Drake), *Babes in Arms* was the Broadway debut of the Nicholas brothers, Fayard and Harold. Even though the show included serious themes like communism and racism, the critics chose to focus on the score by Rodgers and Hart, who were at the apex of their powers. *New York Times* critic Atkinson's only mention of Balanchine's choreography is that he created "an ingenious dream ballet"—"Peter's Journey"—which lets us know that the dream ballet was no longer considered a novelty in the late 1930s.[23] In the dream, Peter runs into famous people (Rockefeller, Marlene Dietrich, Greta Garbo, etc.) as he travels around the world.[24]

Trained in Russian ballet, Balanchine was already at work on creating a new American ballet idiom when he was employed on Broadway and in Hollywood in the 1930s. His work on Broadway was more expansive, including social, tap, modern, jazz, and world ("ethnic") dance vocabularies. While there is no disagreement about Balanchine's genius, he could not personally choreograph tap dance, a form he did not know, so he delegated the task to tap choreographers like his Black associate Herbie Harper, who created the tap dances for *On Your Toes* (1936). Balanchine worked with the Nicholas brothers twice, in the 1936 edition of the *Ziegfeld Follies* and *Babes in Arms*. Fayard Nicholas remembered that Balanchine made suggestions and offered ideas but did not create steps. According to Liza Gennaro, for *Babes in Arms*, "his Black tap assistant Johnny Pierce 'arranged all of the tap dances' and again the Nicholas Brothers 'choreographed their own tap material.'"[25] Neither Harper nor Pierce received program credit for their work. In addition to making dream ballets

---

[22]Brooks Atkinson, review of *Very Warm for May*, Alvin Theatre, New York, *New York Times*, November 18, 1939, 23.

[23]Brooks Atkinson, review of *Babes in Arms*, Schubert Theatre, New York, *New York Times*, April 15, 1937, 18.

[24]The George Balanchine Foundation incorrectly identifies "Peter's Journey" as the first dream ballet on Broadway. George Balanchine Foundation (website), catalog entry #175 (Babes in Arms), accessed May 2, 2022, https://www.balanchine.org.

[25]Liza Gennaro, *Making Broadway Dance* (New York: Oxford University Press, 2022), 26.

popular, the eighteen Broadway musicals Balanchine choreographed had a significant impact on other choreographers and the public, whose newly formed expectations of what musical theatre dance could do meant that they were no longer willing to settle for mediocre dances.

Rodgers and Hart decided to write their own libretto again for *I Married an Angel* (1938), which was based on a Hungarian play by Johann Vaszary. Impatient with the imperfections of mortal women, successful banker Count Willie Palaffi vows that the only girl he can marry is an angel. The gods decide that Palaffi needs to be taught a lesson, so they send a real angel, played by Balanchine's then wife, Vera Zorina. She appears, all is bliss, and they marry. However, unable to lie, Angel begins to create problems for the banker (socially and in business) as she speaks honestly about everything. *I Married an Angel* contained two dream ballets choreographed by Balanchine, one in each act. The first is an actual dream where the couple imagines they are visiting a zoo where animals do specialty dances for them before they end up in a snowy Norway. Zorina was a former dancer with Ballet Russe de Monte Carlo and was partnered by Charles Laskey (American Ballet Theatre), so the technical level of the choreography was very high.[26] (Curiously, this "Snow Ballet" is one of the few in the musical theatre canon that is positioned as a dream and is choreographed using classical ballet as the movement vocabulary.)

The second act dream ballet, "Roxy's Music Hall," was a surreal psychological divertissement invoking Salvador Dali and Freud as it satirized variety acts at local movie theatres. Balanchine created a "wickedly funny parody" of novelty acts, using only a chorus line of two women.[27] With a cast of fifty-one, staging by Josh Logan, and choreography by Balanchine, *I Married an Angel* was a rousing success, running 338 performances.

Jerome Kern biographer Stephen Citron argues that Kern "played a crucial part" in the development of the dream ballet in American musicals, asserting that Kern agreed with Kurt Weill that "part of a theater composer's job [is] to create for himself the vehicle which he needs for his music," which could include an extended instrumental section where dance takes over the narrative.[28] Indeed, either the librettist or the composer might be the one to suggest a dream ballet as the most effective way to develop the story, to explore character, or to create a different kind of production number. Kern and Hammerstein, along with Rodgers and Hart, were early musical theatre collaborators who regularly included a dream ballet in their works. Likewise, Rasch, Balanchine, Harbach, Robert Alton, Felix, and George Abbott all experimented with the form of the dream ballet years before Hammerstein and Rodgers created *Oklahoma!*

Just as various antecedents became components of early musical comedy, so too did elements of story ballets, the romantic era's fascination with dreams, early psychological theories, and contemporary dance forms helped shape the creation of dream ballets. A clear sign of the dream ballet's increased importance to musical theatre storytelling was *Lady in the Dark* (1941), where three dream ballets give the audience insight into the leading character's psychological being.

---

[26]Don McDonagh, *George Balanchine* (Boston: Twayne, 1983), 85.
[27]McDonagh, 85.
[28]Citron, *The Wordsmiths*, 203.

Lady in the Dark

There was a great deal of buzz in anticipation of the 1941 opening of *Lady in the Dark* at the Alvin Theatre: librettist Moss Hart was writing without his customary co-author (George S. Kaufman), this was Ira Gershwin's first foray back to Broadway following the tragic death of his brother, and the great star Gertrude Lawrence was to essay the leading role of Liza Elliott. With other luminaries such as producer Sam H. Harris, composer Kurt Weill, and choreographer Albertina Rasch on the production team, expectations were high. The hype was not misplaced as the reviews were unanimous in their praise for Lawrence, whom the *New York Herald Tribune* simply called "the greatest female performer in the theatre."[29]

In *Lady in the Dark*, Liza is seeking the help of a psychoanalyst as her love life is not in concert with her success as the editor of a highly acclaimed magazine. Her longtime affair with married man Kendall Nesbitt is thrown when he gets a divorce and asks Liza to marry him. Simultaneously, she is chased by the dashing movie star Randy Curtis, and she comes to realize that she is actually attracted to a coworker, Charley Johnson, who is also a rival for her position at the magazine. In the course of the narrative, Dr. Brooks unpacks three of Liza's dreams: in "Glamour Dream" she is a glamorous socialite, in "Wedding Dream" she is a bride, and in "Circus Dream" she is a circus performer. Liza tells Dr. Brooks that she is haunted by a children's song that invades her dreams and her waking life, yet she only hears a portion of the melody and cannot remember or hear the words. The melody is heard in all three dream sequences, but it is not until "My Ship" that Liza realizes the song was one her father often enjoined her to sing, the same man who called her his "ugly duckling" and "plain." This abuse, coupled with taunting from other children for her looks, convinced young Liza that she would never be seen as beautiful. As she is able to complete "My Ship" only after she admits that she loves Charley Johnson, Liza agrees to step aside from the magazine so that Charley can become both boss and husband. This outcome would strike most of us today as sexist, but in prewar America, an unmarried career woman still drew raised eyebrows. 1940s Liza sets aside her successful career in order to get married.

Hart sought to write a serious play about psychoanalysis, dubbing the work "a musical play." Indeed, only the dream sequences contain the songs of the score. While some reviewers were not sure what Hart meant by a musical play, *New York Journal*'s John Anderson skirted the issue by classifying *Lady in the Dark* as "Broadway's most spectacular whatyoumaycallit."[30] As Lawrence was uniformly praised for her work, most reviews were about her prowess. Of the eight reviewers who covered the New York opening, only three mention the choreography, with the *World-Telegram* noting, "The dancing by a group of the Albertina Rasch girls was exquisite," and the *New York Times* describing Rasch's contributions as "vivid."[31] Writing later, Brooks Atkinson returned to *Lady in the Dark*, stating, "in the design of the dancing, Albertina Rasch has captured the phantomlike rush of dream disorder."[32] With three dream ballets to choreograph, Rasch pulled from her encyclopedic

[29]*Critics' Theatre Reviews*, reviews of *Lady in the Dark*, week of January 27, 1941, 400.
[30]Quoted in Naomi Graber, *Kurt Weill's America* (New York: Oxford University Press, 2021), 171.
[31]*Critics' Theatre Reviews*, reviews of *Lady in the Dark*, week of January 27, 1941, 401, 403.
[32]Quoted in Raphael Francis Miller, "The Contribution of Selected Broadway Musical Theatre Choreographers: Connolly, Rasch, Balanchine, Holm, and Alton" (PhD diss., University of Oregon, 1984), 133.

knowledge of dance forms (classical ballet, jazz, tap, eccentric dancing, social dance, and acrobatics) to provide movement variety to the evening. For example, she used tango as the unifying movement style for the final dream ballet, treating it as a metaphor for the tensions between Liza and the men in her life.[33] Another signature aesthetic of a Rasch routine was "uniformity, speed, precision, and repetition for effect,"[34] a trait that Atkinson labeled the "rush" of her kinesthetic approach. Dance critic Walter Terry was one of the few contemporary writers to devote much ink to describing her choreography:

> Albertina Rasch devised the dances for the ensembles in *Lady in the Dark* and did a bang-up job of them. The choreography as such is not epoch-making, but Mme. Rasch had made the dance episodes an integral part of the whole scheme of the production. Dance of the Tumblers in the circus scene provides a moment of real dancing that recalls, perhaps, a vivid sequence from some glittering Russian ballet.[35]

Using a large palette of dance styles, Rasch was committed to advancing the story with movement. The resulting dream sequences were successful in illuminating character and clear in their narrative arc as they supplied material for Dr. Brooks to analyze, thus helping Liza align her goals with her values. *Lady in the Dark* was a hit with audiences, running for 467 performances.

Shuffle Along and the Popularization of Jazz Dance

As various forms such as melodrama, extravaganza, operetta, vaudeville, and minstrelsy were laying the groundwork for the creation of the American musical, this last genre morphed directly into the Black musicals that proliferated 1890–1910. Artists such as Bob Cole, Billy Johnson, Will Marion Cook, James Weldon Johnson, and Paul Laurence Dunbar broke from the conventions of minstrelsy to create original works featuring African American characters played by African American actors, with many of the plots set in Africa. Since the librettos of many of these musicals are no longer extant, it is not possible to ascertain whether any contained a dream ballet. Even so, dreams and dreaming were sometimes the focus of songs in these musicals. For example, the *Rufus Rastus* (1906) song "Say, Wouldn't It Be a Dream?," sung by Ernest Hogan (playing the title role), tells the story of Rufus falling asleep dreaming he is the barber called to shave the president. The *fin de siècle* flourishing of Black-authored musicals took a hiatus until the 1921 arrival of *Shuffle Along*.

Not only did *Shuffle Along* make stars out of many of the performers in its cast—Florence Mills, Josephine Baker, Flournoy Miller, Noble Sissle, Aubrey Lyles, and Charlie Davis—the show was the first Black musical to play white theatres in New York and on the road. While the musical included several male dancers (either solo or in duets), the focus of the production was the sixteen-girl chorus line. Like *The Black Crook*, scantily clad young women were front and center, but whereas *The Black Crook*'s chorus helped popularize ballet as a "high art" form, *Shuffle Along* made a persuasive case for the new genre of jazz dance. Jazz might be

---

[33]Bruce D. McClung, *Lady in the Dark: Biography of a Musical* (New York: Oxford University Press, 2007), 61.
[34]Casey, "The Ballet Corporealities of Anna Pavlova and Albertina Rasch," 19.
[35]Quoted in Ries, "Albertina Rasch, The Broadway Career," 129.

"low art," but its energetic abandon, rhythmic complexity, and sex appeal meant that it was a lot of fun, and audiences lined up to experience this novelty.

Alas, *Shuffle Along* engaged in a racist practice that would happen all too often in twentieth century American musical theatre. African American director Lawrence Deas had helped shape the production in rehearsal and during its pre-Broadway tryouts. Nervous producers brought in white director Walter Brooks, before the show arrived in Boston, "to give the show 'that Broadway touch,'" remembered composer Eubie Blake. Deas was paid a flat fee for his work and let go, while Brooks got 2 percent even though he contributed little to the final product.[36] Marshall Winslow Stearns and Jean Stearns's *Jazz Dance: The Story of American Vernacular Dance*, chronicles the appropriation of the work of Black dancers and choreographers of the period by white directors, choreographers, and producers. Even though some of the artists who helped create *Shuffle Along* were not acknowledged or compensated for their work, the musical helped win over reviewers and white audiences to embrace jazz music and jazz dance. The popularity of this new dance form would soon find its way into dream sequences in musicals, even though they were still often referred to as dream ballets.

As jazz dance moved from the juke joints and speakeasys to the stage and film musical, it underwent a myriad of changes. The Nicholas Brothers took tap dance to an unparalleled level of technical virtuosity, smooth jazz, and sophistication. Balanchine would do his own experiments with classical ballet and jazz, inserting both into *On Your Toes* (1936), and other musicals. In *Cabin in the Sky* (1940), Balanchine collaborated with Katherine Dunham who brought her own style, incorporating modern dance, ballet, jazz, Caribbean social dance. Robbins took jazz dance, classical ballet, vernacular dance, and everyday gesture to create a vocabulary to convey character with rhythmic variety and dynamic complexity. Agnes de Mille had this to say about Robbins' choreography for *On the Town* (1945), which includes the dream ballet "Subway Ride/The Great Lover Displays Himself/The Imaginary Coney Island":

> The comment is truthful and poignant, the humor superb, and the style altogether fresh. It is in the vernacular, the contemporary jazz idiom, but superimposed on the discipline and cleanliness of classic technique and it has inaugurated a new choreographic style.[37]

A discussion of the development of the jazz dream ballet in musical theatre would not be complete without a mention of Robert Alton's work in *Pal Joey* (1940). While trained in ballet, Alton was more schooled in the Broadway choreography of the 1920s.[38] Like Seymour Felix,

---

[36]Marshall Winslow Stearns and Jean Stearns, *Jazz Dance: The Story of American Vernacular Dance* (New York: Macmillan, 1968), 137.

[37]Agnes de Mille, *And Promenade Home* (Hamish Hamilton, 1956), 177.

[38]Robert Alton was a well-regarded dancer and choreographer for both the stage and film. His dance training included studying with Mikhail Mordkin (Bolshoi Ballet and Serge Diaghilev's Ballets Russes), with whose company he performed on Broadway starting in 1919. With his wife, Marjorie Fielding, Alton created a vaudeville dance act, and he started taking on freelance choreography gigs. A choreography job at New York's Paramount Theatre in 1933 led to a Broadway career working on some of the major hits of the 1930s and 1940s: *The Ziegfeld Follies* (1934, 1936, 1942), *Anything Goes* (1934), *Du Barry Was a Lady* (1939), *Panama Hattie* (1940), and *Hazel Flagg* (1953). Alton's first Hollywood film was *Strike Me Pink* (1936), after which he served as dance director for MGM, 1944–51. For more on Robert Alton see chapter 2.

Alton became devoted to creating choreography that was tailored to the story and characters of the musical. With a book by John O'Hara and score by Rodgers and Hart, *Pal Joey* is one of the first musicals to feature an antihero, a womanizer who neither learns a lesson nor is redeemed at the end. *Pal Joey's* first act closes with Joey dreaming of the nightclub he wants create, Chez Joey. Working with Gene Kelly in the title role, Alton worked in ballet, tap, and jazz to create Joey's dream. *New York Times* dance critic John Martin celebrated Alton's choreography as "an integral part of the proceedings." "Indeed, the whole production is so unified that the dance routines are virtually inseparable from the dramatic action."[39]

Looking at Alton's work in Hollywood can give us a glimpse of his Broadway oeuvre. His chorines-with-attitude in "Oh You Kid" (*The Harvey Girls*, 1946) give us a taste of the non-MGM-type show girls who might be in Chez Joey. Ditto for the sweaty club scene in "Stepping Out With My Baby" (*Easter Baby*, 1948). It is worth celebrating that Alton choreographed tap routines for some of the biggest stars – the muscular Gene Kelly, the suave Fred Astaire, the rubber-legged Ray Bolger – helping to define and reinforce their individual, unique signature styles. Alton is also one of a select group of musical choreographers who excelled in visual humor. Just a peak at "A Couple of Swells" (*Easter Parade*) or Marge and Gower Champion's duet as Frank and Ellie Schultz in *Showboat* (1951) are ample evidence that he was able to create humorous physical sequences where the audience is not intended to laugh at the characters, but rather to admire their skill as virtuosic performers.

Alton directed and choreographed *Pal Joey's* wildly successful Broadway revival in 1952, paving the way for the director-choreographers who came after him: Jerome Robbins, Michael Bennett, Tommy Tune, Susan Stroman, Kathleen Marshall, etc.

Oklahoma! and the Maturation of the Dream Ballet

As Hammerstein and Rodgers both had prior experience experimenting with the dream ballet, it should hardly be surprising that they decided to include one in their first collaboration together.[40] Working with choreographer Agnes de Mille, they created *Oklahoma!* (1943), denoted as a landmark musical for the integration of all its elements. Bringing her expertise in concert dance (ballet and modern) to the project, de Mille reasoned that "the dances would have to suit the book; they would have to build the author's line and develop his action." De Mille recognized the challenge of introducing a new narrative form late in the musical, stating, "If the audience could not be swung from dramatic dialogue through song into dance and back again without a hitch, the dance would be destroyed. The choreographer was going to have to learn surgery, to graft and splice."[41] The success of the dream ballet in *Oklahoma!* was due not only to de Mille's talents as a choreographer, but also to her collaboration with Rodgers and Hammerstein, who set up the context for "Laurey Makes Up Her Mind." The song before this scene is Laurey's song "Out of My Dreams," which gives

---

[39]Dame, "The Integration of Dance as a Dramatic Element," 35.
[40]Richard Rodgers had written dream ballets for *Peggy-Ann* (1926), *Babes in Arms* (1937), *I Married an Angel* (1938), and *Pal Joey* (1940), while Hammerstein had experimented with the form in *Three Sisters* (1934), *Gentleman Unafraid* (1938), and *Very Warm for May* (1939).
[41]Agnes de Mille, *Dance to the Piper* (New York: Columbus Books, 1987), 242.

voice to her belief that her dreams will come true. Laurey also has faith that Ali Hakim's sleeping potion, the Elixir of Egypt, will help "make up my mind fer me."

While dream scenes in early films were a mainstay, it is rare for a stage character to be seen falling asleep prior to a dream sequence. With a "dream" Laurey waiting in the wings to enter, *Oklahoma!* could show one Laurey falling asleep while the dream Laurey encounters her fears in the seventeen-minute dance sequence. Part of the genius of *Oklahoma!* is that its dream ballet is not a happy fantasy of a typical 1940s Broadway ingenue, but rather a sexually violent nightmare of a young woman who has conflicted feelings about Jud and Curly. In a standard pre-1940 musical, Laurey's choice of Curly as a love object would not be questioned, but *Oklahoma!* gives Laurey psychological depth as she confronts her emotions and urges. Hammerstein originally conceived of the dream as "bizarre, imaginative and amusing, and never heavy," but de Mille had other ideas: "Girls don't dream about the circus. They dream about horrors. And they dream dirty dreams."[42] Laurey's Dream Curly seems to be a virgin, while the Dream Jud clearly has intercourse on his mind. When he symbolically tears a bit of Laurey's dress in de Mille's choreography, Jud might as well have ripped off her clothes. Laurey knows what she doesn't know, and therefore is intimidated by the sexually experienced Postcard Girls. The horror of this nightmare is that even though Laurey marries Curly in her dream, she is intimidated by Jud and goes off with him.

But what does the dream ballet in *Oklahoma!* mean? While the libretto is explicit concerning the action and plot of this scene, seventeen minutes is a long time onstage, so the show's choreographer has a great deal of sway in how audiences might interrupt this narrative. Psychologist Kelly Bulkeley poses several interpretations: "Has Laurey unknowingly performed a ritual of dream incubation? She drinks the 'Elixir of Egypt,' sleeps in a special place, focuses her mind on a particular question as she drifts off, and then has a dream relating to her question.[43] That's pretty much the definition of a dream incubation ritual (as per Kimberley Patton)." Bulkeley asks whether Laurey's dream is a "threat simulation," as she had a dream of Jud strangling Curly, arguably a reasonable assessment of what could happen on her farm. Freud might see her dream as "sexual wish-fulfillment" since Laurey has a more physically sensual relationship with Dream Curly than she does with his real-life counterpart, and that the Postcard Girls inhabit a carnal world, not a romantic one. Carl Jung, on the other hand, might see Jud as a shadow symbol for the community. Is Jud all the darkness that is not permitted to be part of the community, the light of conscious awareness, and so in need of driving out? Bulkeley goes on to ask:

> Does Laurey misinterpret her dream? How exactly is her action upon awakening (choosing Jud over Curly) justified by what she has dreamed? In both fiction and real life, people who instantly interpret their dreams usually get it wrong. The quick response often overlooks deeper, more important meanings that the conscious mind may be all too ready to move past.[44]

---

[42]Quoted in Kelly Bulkeley, "The Horrors of the Dream Ballet in *Oklahoma!*," *Psychology Today* (blog), February 21, 2018, https://www.psychologytoday.com/us/blog/dreaming-in-the-digital-age/201802/the-horrors-the-dream-ballet-in-oklahoma.
[43]Bulkeley.
[44]Bulkeley.

Image 6.1 Dream Ballet, *Oklahoma!* Dancers, (not in order): Joan McCracken, Kate Friedlich, Margit DeKova, Bobby Barrentine, and Vivian Smith (Jud's Postcards) in *Oklahoma!* (1943). Photo by Vandamn. Billy Rose Theatre Collection, New York Public Library Digital Collections.

Regardless of which message the choreographer purports to stage, audience members are free to make up their own minds as to what they just witnessed. With the dream ballet coming at the end of act 1, the authors give the audience an entire intermission to contemplate Laurey's dilemma. They might remember a scene before the ballet in which Jud rejects the "pornographic" postcards on his walls, but then blurts out "I ain't gonna dream 'bout her arms no more!" Even though Jud does not mention Laurey's name in "Lonely Room," we know he is dreaming about her. There is a lot of dreaming going on in this territory.

Dreams were definitely on Daniel Fish's mind when he directed the first professional production of his radically reconceptualized *Oklahoma!* in 2015. Pruning away decades of expectations about the musical, Fish staged a production with an orchestra of seven, new orchestrations, a cast of twelve, and no overture, chorus, or elaborate scene changes. When this revised version opened at Bard College, even the dream ballet had been excised. Before the production moved to St. Ann's Warehouse in 2017, Fish and choreographer John Heginbotham agreed that the larger space would allow for more dance in the production, but what to do about the dream ballet? After workshopping several ideas, Heginbotham came up with a thirteen-minute, barefoot, modern dance solo for one woman: Gabrielle Hamilton. The dream ballet now opens act 2. As a Black, bald dancer wearing a brilliant white T-shirt emblazoned with "Dream Baby Dream" in large block letters, Hamilton not only portrays Laurey's attraction to these two men, but also grapples with the reckoning that some choices can change the rest of our life. Fish's production boldly embraces Curly's vision of his future, "Country-a-changin', got to change with it!"

Conclusion

Of course, the world of musical theatre contains many more examples of dream ballets as creative teams continue to experiment with the form. The dream ballet in *Carousel* (1945) takes place fifteen years after the events of the storyline and serves the double function of telling the audience something they did not know (Billy's daughter, Louise, is an outcast) and forcing Billy to confront the consequences of his actions.[45] *Fiddler on the Roof* (1964) contains a traditional dream ballet where Teyve dreams of his daughter who has eloped, "Chavaleh (Little Bird)." What is more interesting is "Tevye's Dream," where he pretends to wake from a nightmare and proceeds to lie to his wife that he had a dream where he was visited by Lazar Wolf's first wife, who vows vengeance if Tzeitel marries Lazar. In *Follies* (1971), "Who's That Woman" starts off in reality as former Weismann girls try to remember an old dance routine, when their younger selves appear and mirror the older dancers. The characters Tony and Maria share the same dream fantasy in *West Side Story* (1957). A similar case can be made for the duet at the end of *Billy Elliot* (2005), where young Billy dances with his older self. Is this Billy's dream of his future as a professional dancer, or is this the combined dream of Billy and his father? Embracing many musical theatre tropes, *The Book of Mormon* (2011) contains Elder Price's dream where he abandons his mission, thus triggering the nightmares he had as a child ("Spooky Mormon Hell Dream").

Not only has the dream sequence continued to be employed in musical theatre, it also endures in other mediums. The dream that is danced has appeared in television shows *Smash* (2012–13) and *Crazy Ex-Girlfriend* (2015–19), and in the films *La La Land* (2016) and *The Greatest Showman* (2018). In Benj Pasek and Justin Paul's "A Million Dreams," P. T. Barnum could be speaking for all of us:

'Cause every night I lie in bed
The brightest colours fill my head
A million dreams are keeping me awake
I think of what the world could be
A vision of the one I see
A million dreams is all it's gonna take

Schmigadoon's Melissa rejects the dream ballet, but this dramatic convention shows no signs of disappearing from the musical stories we tell.

---

[45]Agnes de Mille's 1945 choreography hews to the libretto, where a young carnival barker flirts with Louise in a voluptuous duet that climaxes in a kiss. The barker leaves her "abruptly," and Louise is left with feelings "overwhelmingly beautiful, painful, and passionate." On the other hand, Kenneth MacMillan's rigorously athletic choreography, created for the Nicholas Hytner-directed 1992 revival of *Carousel*, shows Louise as sexual victim, harassed by the local boys. When she attempts to stop the barker's advances, he physically overpowers her. Louise consents to cooperate in a lush pas de deux ("If I Loved You"), but after the barker kisses her and lies on top of her, he too leaves "abruptly." Oscar Hammerstein II and Richard Rodgers, *Carousel* (New York: Williamson Music, 1945), 169.

Bibliography

Atkinson, Brooks. Review of *Babes in Arms*, Schubert Theatre, New York. *New York Times*, April 15, 1937.

Atkinson, Brooks. Review of *Very Warm for May*, Alvin Theatre, New York. *New York Times*, November 18, 1939.

Banfield, Stephen. *Jerome Kern*. New Haven, CT: Yale University Press, 2006.

Brantley, Ben. Review of *Babes in Arms* revival at City Center, directed by Kathleen Marshall. *New York Times*, February 13, 1999.

Bulkeley, Kelly. "The Horrors of the Dream Ballet in *Oklahoma!*" *Psychology Today* (blog), February 21, 2018. https://www.psychologytoday.com/us/blog/dreaming-in-the-digital-age/201802/the-horrors-the-dream-ballet-in-oklahoma.

Casey, Carrie Gaiser. "The Ballet Corporealities of Anna Pavlova and Albertina Rasch." *Dance Chronicle* 35, no. 1 (2012): 8–29.

Citron, Stephen. *The Wordsmiths: Oscar Hammerstein 2nd and Alan Jay Lerner*. New York: Oxford University Press, 1995.

Critics' Theatre Reviews. Reviews of *Lady in the Dark*. Week of January 27, 1941, 400–4.

Critics' Theatre Reviews. Reviews of *Pal Joey*. Week of December 31, 1940, 172–4.

Dame, Robert G. "The Integration of Dance as a Dramatic Element in Broadway Musical Theatre." Master's thesis, University of Nevada, Las Vegas, 1995.

De Mille, Agnes, *And Promenade Home*. Boston: Little, Brown, and Co., 1956.

De Mille, Agnes. *Dance to the Piper*. New York: Columbus Books, 1987.

Gänzl, Kurt. "Double-Treat: 'The Black Crook' from New York to London." *Encyclopedia of the Musical Theatre*, Operetta Research Center, last updated October 4, 2001. http://operetta-research-center.org/double-treat-black-crook-new-york-london/.

Gennaro, Liza. *Making Broadway Dance*. New York: Oxford University Press, 2022.

George Balanchine Foundation (website). Accessed May 2, 2022. https://www.balanchine.org/.

Graber, Naomi. *Kurt Weill's America*. New York: Oxford University Press, 2021.

Hammerstein, Oscar, II, and Richard Rodgers. *Carousel*. New York: Williamson Music, 1945.

Hart, Moss, Ira Gershwin, and Kurt Weill. *Lady in the Dark*. In *Great Musicals of the American Theatre*, edited by Stanley Richards, vol. 2, 55–123. Randor, PA: Chilton Book, 1976.

Knapp, Raymond. *The American Musical and the Formation of National Identity*. Princeton, NJ: Princeton University Press, 2005.

Leve, James. *American Musical Theatre*. New York: Oxford University Press, 2016.

Lodge, Mary Jo. "Dance Breaks and Dream Ballets: Transitional Moments in Musical Theatre." In *Gestures of Music Theater: The Performativity of Song and Dance*, edited by Dominic Symonds and Millie Taylor, 75–90. New York: Oxford University Press, 2014.

MacDonald, Laura. Review of *Lady in the Dark*, Hannover Staatsoper, Hannover, Germany. *Theatre Journal* 64, no. 3 (2012): 417–22.

Marinelli, Lydia. "Screening Wish Theories: Dream Psychologies and Early Cinema." *Science in Context* 19, no. 1 (2006): 87–110.

Martin, John. "The Dance: Number for Our Revues." *New York Times*, October 18, 1931.

McClung, Bruce D. *Lady in the Dark: Biography of a Musical*. New York: Oxford University Press, 2007.

McDonagh, Don. *George Balanchine*. Boston: Twayne, 1983.

Miller, Raphael Francis. "The Contribution of Selected Broadway Musical Theatre Choreographers: Connolly, Rasch, Balanchine, Holm, and Alton." PhD diss., University of Oregon, 1984.

Nolan, Frederick. *Lorenz Hart: A Poet on Broadway*. New York: Oxford University Press, 1994.

Paul, Cinco, Ken Daurio, and Allison Silverman, writers. *Schmigadoon*. Season 1, episode 5, "Tribulation." Released August 6, 2021, on Apple+ TV.

Perez, Natalia Alexis. "'It's Like I've Walked Right Out of My Dreams': Dream Ballets in the Broadway Musical." Master's thesis, Florida State University, 2017.

Plotkin, Fred. "When Dreams and Dreamers Inhabit Opera." *Operavore*, November 2, 2015. https://www.wqxr.org/story/when-dreams-and-dreamers-inhabit-opera/.

Postlewait, Thomas. "The Hieroglyphic Stage: American Theatre and Society, Post–Civil War to 1945." In *The Cambridge History of American Theatre*, edited by Don B. Wilmeth and Christopher Bigsby, vol. 2, 107–95. Cambridge: Cambridge University Press, 1999.

Ries, Frank W. D. "Albertina Rasch: The Broadway Career." *Dance Chronicle* 6, no. 2 (1983): 95–137.

Ries, Frank W. D. "Albertina Rasch: The Hollywood Career," *Dance Chronicle* 6, No. 4 (1983), 281–362.

Rousseau, G. S. "Dream and Vision in Aeschylus' 'Oresteia.'" *Arion: A Journal of Humanities and the Classics* 2, no. 3 (Autumn 1963): 101–36.

Sievers, W. David. *Freud on Broadway: A History of Psychoanalysis and the American Drama*. New York: Hermitage House, 1955.

Smith, Cecil. *Musical Comedy in America*. New York: Theatre Arts Books, 1950.

Stearns, Marshall Winslow, and Jean Stearns. *Jazz Dance: The Story of American Vernacular Dance*. New York: Macmillan, 1968.

Stiehl, Pamyla. "The Dansical: American Musical Theatre Reconfigured as a Choreographer's Expression and Domain." PhD diss., University of Colorado, Boulder, 2008.

Ziegfeld, Richard and Paulette. *The Ziegfeld Touch: The Life and Times of Florenz Ziegfeld, Jr*. New York: Harry N. Abrams, 1993.

7 Making Space, Keeping Time: Musical Theatre Dance and Temporality in the United States

JOANNA DEE DAS

When you walk into a theatre and the lights dim, you begin to experience two senses of time simultaneously: the one your physical body undergoes as it sits in the seat, the minutes and seconds passing as you normally experience it, and the time of the world on the stage. The show may be set in the past, present, or future; regardless, time passes differently, as characters often skip over days, weeks, months, or years as they tell a story in two hours. Sometimes the characters remember past worlds or dream of future ones, adding further layers of temporal experience. Musical theatre offers an even more complex experience of time because of how song-and-dance numbers interrupt the plot. Scholar Scott McMillin calls such moments "lyric time," in which the narrative logic of cause and effect (or "progressive time") is displaced by music's logic of repetition. This displacement is what creates a musical's "crackle of difference," a pleasure that audiences receive when they experience the irreconcilability of two temporal modes, one seemingly moving forward from beginning to end and another circling back.[1] McMillin's definition of lyric time, however, is based on the structures of music, not movement. While production numbers in musicals often combine song and dance, the two forms of expression do not have entirely the same temporal effects.

This chapter argues that dance uniquely contributes to temporality in musical theatre by making vivid the kinesthetic and spatial metaphor of time as motion. Bodies moving through *space* signal visually to an audience that bodies are moving through *time*. This movement can be in the progressive mode of book time (ie. the timeline of the plot, moving from a beginning to a middle to an end) or in the lyric mode of repetition; it does not belong solely to the latter. Dance in musical theatre can also suspend, rewind, and blur time, breaking open the concept of time as motion by expanding in a multitude of directions. Dance's multidimensional expansion fosters contemplation of new modes of being. Its ability to keep time returns that expansion to the physical self, making the imagined seem possible through the irreducible materiality of the body. For instance, in *On the Town* (1944), the character Gabey falls asleep on the subway as he journeys to Coney Island in pursuit of Ivy, his love interest. The "Coney Island Dream" dance number occurs in his subconscious. He and Ivy engage in a seductive duet before two men lift her up and take her away, leaving Gabey humiliated. The conductor then wakes him up. The dance takes the audience out of "real"

---

[1]Scott McMillin, *The Musical as Drama* (Princeton, NJ: Princeton University Press, 2006), 9, 2.

time for a suspended dreamworld, and yet, they also see Gabey dancing in "real" time with Ivy. Dance allows for a simultaneity of distinct temporal worlds—the fantastical and the real—which facilitates deeper contemplation of Gabey's emotional state as well as an opportunity to see how such a dream might materialize.[2]

The following case studies highlight how dance offers a multilayered sense of time and thus acts as a mediating force between the real and the unreal of musical theatre. All are from musicals that were created in the United States and that take place in the United States. This cultural specificity informs how danced temporalities manifest meaning in the examples provided. What Ariel Nereson calls America's "racial past," its legacy of slavery, continues to inform the relation between aesthetics and politics on Broadway to this day.[3] Temporality is not a universal, neutral experience. Instead, how a person senses time depends on their context. For some people, reckoning with slavery feels not like ancient history, but rather a part of their everyday present. For others, it feels distant, or like someone else's story. How different musicals grapple with the multitude of perspectives on the mingling of past, present, and future timescapes is a focus of this chapter.

Suspending Time: The Showstopper

The clearest example of musical theatre dance operating in lyric time is the showstopper. This type of dance number interrupts a narrative flow and breaks the fourth wall. Well-regarded examples include the "Civil War Ballet" from *Bloomer Girl* (1944), Gwen Verdon's star turn in the "Quadrille" number from *Can-Can* (1953), "One" from *A Chorus Line* (1975), and "Springtime for Hitler" from *The Producers* (2001). If a showstopper is effective at getting an audience onto its feet to clap and cheer, the performers extend the hold of their final poses. In their smiling faces, one can sometimes detect acknowledgment of the audience's praise, a slight break in character. They send gratitude and awareness energetically back to the audience, creating a reciprocal moment of shared joy. The audience, after all, is clapping not for the characters, but rather for the virtuosity of the performers as their "real" selves. Showstopping dances wow audiences with the spectacularity of unified rhythmic precision, complex floor patterns, and thrill of bodies in motion. The extended applause suspends book time, as the show's action cannot continue until the audience quiets down.

With the rise of the so-called integrated musical in the mid-twentieth century, such numbers were often looked down on for appealing to sensory pleasure over the supposedly more sophisticated artistry of weaving dance into the narrative. Critics and tastemakers commended choreography that drove the plot forward, explored a character's psyche, or served one of the other seven primary functions of musical theatre dance as identified by Liza Gennaro and Stacy Wolf.[4] Yet spectacular pleasure also carries meaning. Showstopping dance numbers that on the surface seem to keep swirling in the same place allow us to plumb down.

---

[2] See Bud Coleman's chapter 6 in this volume for more on dream ballets in musical theatre productions.
[3] Ariel Nereson, *Democracy Moving: Bill T. Jones, Contemporary American Performance, and the Racial Past* (Ann Arbor: University of Michigan Press, 2022).
[4] Liza Gennaro and Stacy Wolf, "Dance in Musical Theater," in *Oxford Handbook of Dance and Theater*, ed. Nadine George-Graves (New York: Oxford University Press, 2015), 148–68.

One example is "Steam Heat" from *The Pajama Game* (1954). The dance, staged as an amateur production number at a rally of pajama factory union members, has ostensibly nothing to do with the plot or the characters' emotional lives. Instead, "Steam Heat" is famous for its introduction of Bob Fosse's signature choreographic style to the musical theatre world. Fosse combined the cool jazz of Jack Cole (sharp isolations, virtuosic lunges) with the shuffling and slouching of vaudevillians Jimmy Durante and Joe Frisco. All three of these white men had, in turn, drawn upon Black dance aesthetics of the 1920s and 1930s, namely eccentric dancing (as exemplified in the work of Earl "Snakehips" Tucker) and Lindy Hop.[5] In the film version, which stayed fairly true to Fosse's stage choreography, the three dancers draw the audience's attention immediately with the opening pose—heads down, eyes covered by bowler hats, pelvises slouched, one leg straight and the other knee bent, arms dangling. Suspense builds as Carol Haney, center stage, raises her head sharply on the beat. The other two dancers look up on the next beat, silently communicating the start of the dance. With pulses of the knees, chugs of the feet, clicks of the tongue, and savvy manipulation of the bowler hats, the precision of the movement wows in its simplicity and attention to detail. Audience members can delight in catching a subtle turn of the head; their bodies can vibrate with kinesthetic empathy when all three dancers pivot on a dime. Seeing performers move in harmony creates a sense of *entrainment*: the pleasure of synchronization, which neuroscientists have shown is felt on the bodily level.[6] Quick turns and slides on knees flash out of nowhere, arms reaching and bodies whirling, before returning to the controlled, cool state of "staccato" rhythmic pulsing of limbs.[7] In previews in New Haven, Connecticut, "Steam Heat" stopped the show. Instead of appreciating the audience's pleasure, director George Abbott decided that such disruption to narrative time was a problem and tried to cut the number. Luckily, Jerome Robbins, who was involved in staging *Pajama Game*, lobbied successfully to keep it.[8]

While considered unessential to the plot, "Steam Heat" serves an important function in its stoppage of time, both for the audience within the show (the members of the pajama factory union) and for the audience of *Pajama Game*. For factory workers, a chance to be off the clock provides a moment of relief and restorative community-building, which allows their union movement to grow. Forward momentum paradoxically requires strategic pause. For the *Pajama Game* audience, the affective joy created by "Steam Heat" increases empathy. The positive emotions generated by rhythmic entrainment are felt in the body and connect

---

[5]On the influence of Cole, Durante, and Frisco, see Kevin Winkler, *Big Deal: Bob Fosse and Dance in the American Musical* (New York: Oxford University Press, 2018), 40–1; for Black influences on Cole, see Constance Valis Hill, "From Bharata Natyam to Bop: Jack Cole's 'Modern' Jazz Dance," *Dance Research Journal* 33, no. 2 (2001): 29–39; on eccentric dancing, see "Earl 'Snake Hips,' Tucker," ca. 1930, YouTube, posted January 18, 2008, accessed March 12, 2023, https://www.youtube.com/watch?v=7U4ww-MmAY4.
[6]W. J. Trost, C. Labbé, D. Grandjean, "Rhythmic Entrainment as a Musical Affect Induction Mechanism," *Neuropsychologia* 96 (2017): 96–110.
[7]Choreographic analysis from my viewing of "Steam Heat" from the film version of *Pajama Game* (1957), "The Pajama Game—Steam Heat," uploaded by MarcosCohen, May 15, 2008, YouTube video, 4:33, https://www.youtube.com/watch?v=0szHqlXQ2R8. The labeling of Fosse's choreography as "staccato" comes from Kevin Winkler, *Big Deal: Bob Fosse and Dance in the American Musical* (New York: Oxford University Press, 2018), 40–1.
[8]Winkler, *Big Deal*, 41.

Image 7.1 "Steam Heat," *The Pajama Game* (1955). Photo by Roger Wood, Jerome Robbins Dance Division, The New York Public Library Digital Collections.

audience to performer.[9] We may not learn more about the characters' psyches, but we connect to them as vibrant, living beings by not merely watching, but also *experiencing* them dance.

While the Black aesthetic influences in "Steam Heat" are layered, woven deeply into Fosse's signature style, "Blow, Gabriel, Blow" from the musical *Anything Goes* (1934) more explicitly draws on spectacular Black aesthetics to stop the show. Because of the history of chattel slavery in the United States, embodied spectacularity is often racialized. From the minstrel show of the nineteenth century, in which white men applied burnt cork to their faces and moved in exaggerated fashion, to the white celebrity appropriation of Black social dances such as twerking in the twenty-first, white Americans have framed Black dance aesthetics as over-the-top, sensuous, primitive, and, as Martha Graham wrote in 1930, "dangerous."[10] Such spectacularity, as noted above, is also temporalized: Black dance,

[9]Trost, Labbé, and Grandjean, "Rhythmic Entrainment."

[10]Martha Graham, "Seeking an American Art of the Dance," in *Revolt in the Arts: A Survey of the Creation, Distribution and Appreciation of Art in America*, ed. Oliver M. Sayler (New York: Brentano's, 1930), 254. For more on the framing of Black dance by white Americans, see Jasmine Johnson, "Black Laws of Dance," *Conversations across the Field of Dance Studies: Decolonizing Dance Discourses* 40 (2020): 25–7; Nadine George-Graves, "'Just Like Being at the Zoo': Primitivity and Ragtime Performance," in *Ballroom, Boogie, Shimmy Sham, Shake: A Social and Popular Dance Reader*, ed. Julie Malnig (Urbana: University of Illinois Press, 2009), 55–71.

viewed as always-already spectacular, prevents the ordinary march of linear time. In a modern capitalist society, disrupting this march signals unproductivity. Ideas of productivity and efficiency became dominant in the late nineteenth century with Frederick Winslow Taylor's theory of scientific management. Taylor argued that efficiency was the key to making greater profits. Efficiency meant reducing extraneous movements; therefore, workers were put on assembly lines, where they would do the same task over and over. Bodily efficiency applied to workers' lives outside the factory floor as well. Workers were meant to save their energy for labor, not exhaust it through dancing. Tired bodies would work more slowly and prevent the machine of capitalism from moving forward.[11] Spectacular dance that works against the efficiency of moving the plot along opens up space for imagining a world dominated not by the punch clock (which had been invented in 1888), but by dreams of a better world.

The creators of *Anything Goes* set the show on a ship, the *SS American*, bound for England from New York. Already the setting takes us out of "regular" time. Life on the ocean exists apart from daily routines and standard communication devices; the characters get to step out of time, allowing for "subjective reflection" before being thrust back in the real world of crashing stock market prices, job insecurity, rising fascism, and everyday problems.[12] "Blow, Gabriel, Blow"—headlined by character Reno Sweeney, a nightclub singer— complements this dream space of the ship. In the 1934 version Sweeney decides to burst into song to cheer up her fellow passengers, accompanied by her backup dancers. In the 1987 and 2011 versions, the song exists as part of Sweeney's planned performance for ship passengers. While Kathleen Marshall's 2011 Broadway revival did not reproduce Robert Alton's original 1934 choreography, she stuck with the ethos and impulse of the "real showmen" of that era just as did Alton, who "knew they were creating popular entertainment."[13]

In the song, Sweeney narrates a story of religious revelation. While she and her fellow characters are almost all white (save two Chinese men, Ching/Luke and Ling/John), the vocal and embodied aesthetics draw from Black Pentecostal traditions. When the number begins, Sweeney wears a long white robe and is flanked by four dancers in long red robes. They stand with their hands clasped in prayer position. Their opening movements are simple arm gestures, changing every four or eight counts as Sweeney sings that she was "headed for hell" but then heard the Angel Gabriel "blowin." The angel "purged my soul/And my heart too," and thus she is now "all ready to fly" and "climb up the mountaintop." This scene is a restrained church service as one would see in a white Protestant congregation.[14]

A dance break interrupts the lyrical arc of a journey from sin to sanctity. Sweeney stops singing, struts back onto the upstage platform, and disrobes to reveal a sparkly, short

[11]Kélina Gotman, *Choreomania: Dance and Disorder* (New York: Oxford University Press, 2018), 225; Alan Trachtenberg, *The Incorporation of America: Culture and Society in the Gilded Age* (New York: Hill and Wang, 1982).

[12]George Burrows, "*Anything Goes* on an Ocean Liner: Musical Comedy as a Carnivalistic Heterotopia," *Studies in Musical Theatre* 7, no. 3 (2013): 341.

[13]Nelson Pressley, "Kathleen Marshall, Broadway's 'Vintage Girl,'" *Washington Post*, June 7, 2013.

[14]Movement analysis in this discussion taken from the April 3, 2011, Broadway performance of *Anything Goes* at the Stephen Sondheim Theatre, "Sutton Foster—Blow, Gabriel, Blow (Anything Goes)," uploaded by BroadwayDVDs, May 17, 2021, YouTube video, 8:20, https://www.youtube.com/watch?v= EGVMJuE9QA0.

showgirl outfit. Her "Angels" follow suit. As a trumpet wails, the dancers descend from the platform to approach seated passengers on the ship. They kick their legs to the ceiling, revealing both extreme flexibility and a flash of crotch. The seductive, confident struts continue as they crisscross the stage to entice new tuxedoed passengers with an arm draped around the neck or a slow layout on a table, accented by a sharp kick. The song has stopped "progressing": Sweeney's sung narration has ended, an arrest of time within a number that is already a narrative pause within the show. The music switches to pulsing tom-tom drumbeats, calling to mind Benny Goodman's "Sing, Sing, Sing," which he recorded in 1937, three years after the original production of Anything Goes. The bespectacled Goodman, son of Jewish immigrants, became known as the King of Swing after the success of this song; similarly, dancing to "Sing, Sing, Sing" became an entry point for white performers to access Black aesthetics, whether through Jack Cole's famed nightclub number in 1947, the big "Sing, Sing, Sing" dance number in the Broadway musicals Dancin' (1978) and Fosse (1999), or the swing social dance revival of the 1990s.[15]

In the 2011 version of "Blow, Gabriel, Blow," the tom-tom drumbeats call the male dancers out of their seats. Possessed by the music, they chug their way to center stage, where they roll on the floor, hands thrusting up on the brass accents. The women start circling their hips and accentuating their buttocks as the men draw closer. In the 1920s, white supremacists denounced such pelvic movement as a distressing sign that Black aesthetics were taking over white civilization.[16] Shoulder shimmies, kicks, thrusts all build until the entire ensemble is dancing. In what George Burrows has identified as the "carnivalistic heterotopia" of Anything Goes, this final dance break of "Blow, Gabriel, Blow" doubles down on the class-crossing, jumbled vision of a topsy-turvy world in which we cannot distinguish saint from sinner, British nobility from American gangster.[17] The diegesis also breaks down, as characters who are supposedly everyday passengers dance with technical skill. Over twenty people gather in a clump together, gyrating their torsos, throwing back their heads on the drum's insistent downbeat. The dance increases in speed and intensity, with sharp, accented kicks, swinging arm movements to mimic trumpet playing, quick spins, and jazz runs across the stage. The stage is full of kinesthetic motion and intensity that envelop the audience.

Marshall's choreography, in its fully embodied embrace of the music and pleasure of movement, suggests that perhaps this is what heaven looks like: a stoppage of time in which social class, nationality, and other distinctions do not matter. This utopic reading has a racial subtext in a US context: the long history of white performers accessing Black aesthetics in order to release themselves from social constraints. Audiences vicariously receive a cathartic reprieve as well. The liberatory potential thus opened up by the lyric time operates on multiple registers, offering different types of liberation for different constituents.

---

[15]For more on the relationship between Jewish performers and Black aesthetics, see Michael Rogin, Blackface, White Noise: Jewish Immigrants in the Hollywood Melting Pot (Berkeley: University of California Press, 1996).
[16]Isadora Duncan, "I See America Dancing," 1927, in The Art of the Dance, ed. Sheldon Cheney, 47–50 (New York: Theatre Arts Books, 1977). See also David Savran, Highbrow/Lowdown: Theater, Jazz, and the Making of the New Middle Class (Ann Arbor: University of Michigan Press, 2009).
[17]Burrows, "Anything Goes on an Ocean Liner."

Transporting the Audience to the Past

In many other musicals, dance places an audience in a specific historical moment rather than taking them out of that moment. Elissa Harbert makes a distinction between history musicals, such as *1776* (1969), and fictional period musicals, such as *Ragtime* (1998). The former, which take real historical characters and situations as their foundation, "are promoted and received as more or less true stories," whereas the latter imagine the lives of fictive persons living in a particular historical moment.[18] While the stakes are indeed higher for the history musicals in terms of the significance of their impact on cultural memory, fictional period musicals share the desire to transport audiences to the past in a way that audiences accept as believable on some kind of level. One strategy has been an attempt at realism, which is never fully complete in the theatre, let alone musical theatre. Several choreographers have made the choice to research dance styles of the time and place of the musical's setting to offer something deemed authentic. Jerome Robbins, active on Broadway from the 1940s through the 1960s, championed this approach of maintaining "adherence to the given conditions of time, place, and character" and using what loosely might be considered ethnographic research to do so.[19] The famed "Bottle Dance" from *Fiddler on the Roof* (1964), a musical about Eastern European Jewish life in the early twentieth century, is a case in point. Robbins attended Hasidic weddings in New York City as background research for *Fiddler*. At one of them, at the Riverside Plaza Hotel, a man "wove through a partying crowd" with a bottle balanced on his head.[20] More importantly, Robbins was impressed by the "virile ferocity" of the men dancing at the wedding—their improvised stomps, kicks, and gripped hands, in "a dedication to a rite, claiming survival & joy, procreation & celebration."[21] Robbins wanted the audience's world to meld with the world onstage, and so he sought to re-create that "virile" energy in his production of *Fiddler*.

The "Bottle Dance" happens in the wedding scene. The audience is an extension of the cast onstage, who watch as a heavily bearded man, dressed in a black suit with a black hat, emerges from the crowd as a clarinet solo begins. He places a bottle on his head and slowly lets go, the bottle balancing on the hat. He raises his arms up and down in the air as he walks slowly in a circle, the crowd murmuring its appreciation of his feat. Another man joins him; they face each other with right palms touching, executing deep knee bends. Eventually two other men join. They line up, four men in a row, dressed identically in all black with black beards, hands raised and clasped, rarely letting go as they walk, stamp, and touch heel-toe side to side, eventually lowering to their knees and virtuosically lunging forward on the diagonal, pulling themselves as a unit downstage left and right. The crowd then breaks out into a frenzy of joyous dancing.[22]

[18]Elissa Harbert, "Embodying History: Casting and Cultural Memory in *1776* and *Hamilton*," *Studies in Musical Theatre* 13, no. 3 (2019): 253.

[19]Liza Gennaro, *Making Broadway Dance* (New York: Oxford University Press, 2021), 77.

[20]Alisa Solomon, "Balancing Act: *Fiddler*'s Bottle Dance and the Transformation of 'Tradition,'" *TDR: The Drama Review* 55, no. 3 (2011): 26.

[21]Robbins, quoted in Solomon, 27.

[22]Analysis gathered from Robbins's choreography in the 1971 *Fiddler on the Roof* film, "Fiddler on the Roof—Bottle Dance from Wedding Scene," uploaded by Tomáš Pumprla, July 31, 2010, YouTube video, 3:57, https://www.youtube.com/watch?v=yGBG8mCt59s; and Steppin' Out Theatrical Productions,

But both *research* and *authenticity* are fraught terms in relationship to live performance, particularly in musical theatre dance. How does one capture the improvised innovations of social dances of the pre–recorded era? Even formal, staged dance steps, for which both written notation and embodied, person-to-person transmission exist, have their notorious gaps. "The Bottle Dance" requires a leap of faith. Was what Robbins observed at a 1960s wedding in Manhattan in any way similar to what Jewish communities were doing at the dawn of the twentieth century in Eastern Europe? Even if research—whether that means observing a wedding, studying archival photographs, or learning from an octogenarian dancer who recalls steps taught to her as a teenager—produces something akin to *what was done in the past*, it might not register as "authentic" to audiences if it does not coincide with the various mediated images or personal experiences that have shaped their cultural memory. Lyricist Oscar Hammerstein II warned about "research poison," the idea that adhering too closely to historical fact ruined the creative process.[23] If the show does not captivate an audience, no matter its accuracy, that audience will not feel transported to another temporal world. A dress made with appropriate eighteenth-century materials makes no difference if the dancing lacks ingenuity. Audience members will feel their seat itching uncomfortably, hear a cough behind them, or think about a work deadline coming up rather than immerse themselves in the colonial era.

Sometimes, deference to an audience's expectation of what the past looked or felt like slips into nostalgia, commonly understood as a longing for a mythical past or home that has been "irretrievably lost."[24] Nostalgia, in this characterization, imagines the past as a better world from which the present is in irreversible decline. Dance scholar Phoebe Rumsey takes a different approach, drawing on Svetlana Boym's concept of "reflective nostalgia" to suggest that the emotion can be a vehicle for "a compassionate and critical rethinking of our contemporary moment."[25] Sergio Trujillo's choreography for *Memphis* (2009) is open to two potential readings, one more critical of its nostalgic impulses and another that recognizes a more positive potential in its temporal permeability. *Memphis* is loosely inspired by the true story of a white radio disc jockey in the 1950s who introduced his listeners to what were then "race records"—what became rock 'n' roll. It was a success, enjoying a three-year run of over a thousand performances and winning four Tony Awards, including Best Musical. The music numbers are all original compositions. *Memphis* takes a highly contentious moment in US history—the early civil rights movement in the South—and softens it by refracting the structural social issues through a personal love story between a white disc jockey and a Black singer.

By the time he began work on *Memphis*, Trujillo was already a seasoned expert in rock 'n' roll dances of the 1950s and 1960s. His Broadway debut as a dancer came in *Jerome*

Richmond Hill Centre for the Performing Arts, Ontario, Canada, November 21–5, 2012, "Fiddler on the Roof—Bottle Dance—Steppin' Out Theatrical Productions," uploaded by the5shermans, November 26, 2012, YouTube video, 3:39, https://www.youtube.com/watch?v=hKvvEo9P15c. Most regional productions have to use Robbins's choreography.

[23]Richard Rodgers, *Musical Stages: An Autobiography* (New York: Random House, 1975), 274.

[24]See, for example, Christopher Lasch, "The Politics of Nostalgia: Losing History in the Mists of Ideology," *Harper's*, November 1984, 65–70.

[25]Phoebe Rumsey, "Embodied Nostalgia: Early Twentieth Century Social Dance and U.S. Musical Theatre" (PhD diss., City University of New York, 2019), 9.

Robbins' Broadway in 1989, where he met choreographer Jerry Mitchell, who became one of his mentors. Mitchell is known for researching the time period of the shows he works on and is particularly known for his social dance choreography. One of Trujillo's first major gigs as a choreographer was for the West End musical *Peggy Sue Got Married* (2001), for which he consulted Hollywood films, television programs like *American Bandstand*, and photographs. *Peggy Sue* established his reputation as an expert in mid-twentieth century social dance, and Broadway producers hired him to rework the choreography for *All Shook Up,* the short-lived 2005 musical about Elvis Presley. He then choreographed *Jersey Boys*, a jukebox musical based on the career of the Four Seasons. *Jersey Boys* enjoyed a tremendous twelve-year run (2005–17) on Broadway and continues to appear on stages around the globe in regional, touring, and school productions. Trujillo became known as a choreographer not wedded to a personal "Sergio" style, but rather someone who was interested in "servicing the material," much like Robbins before him.[26]

But Trujillo chose not to replicate any iconic dances such as the twist or the mashed potato in *Memphis*. Instead, he mixed in highly virtuosic ballet and theatrical jazz steps. His reasoning was based, in part, on the music. Because the show had an original score written by David Bryan, former keyboardist for the rock band Bon Jovi, Trujillo wanted to match what he called the "fresh, hip quality" of Bryan's twenty-first-century take on a 1950s sound.[27] It was also a white rock musician's take on a Black sound, an ironic replication

Image 7.2 Rehearsal for *Memphis* (2009). Photo by Helen Maybanks.

---

[26]Lyn Cramer, *Creating Musical Theatre: Conversations with Broadway Directors and Choreographers* (London: Bloomsbury, 2013), 231.
[27]Quoted in Sagolla, "Capturing the Feel of 1950s Memphis."

of the historical circumstances of the musical, in which white Memphis deejays were instrumental in bringing Elvis Presley to national fame. A criticism levied at *Memphis* was its centering of a white male savior (a deejay, Huey Calhoun, who defies social norms to play Black music on the radio) in a story ostensibly about Black music and the coming civil rights movement.[28] The musical trades on white fantasy: one major plot development is that Calhoun's racist mother is transformed by hearing Black gospel music. Another is that Calhoun can win over suspicious Black folks by simply showing how much he loves their culture, as he does with the song "The Music of My Soul." Cultural love transcends cultural theft or structural racism.

The choreography colludes in this fantasy by depicting white and Black dancers coming together. In the show, dance represents the first "breach" of the walls of segregation, as Black teenagers from Beale Street mingle with white kids from Main Street.[29] The embodiment of cultural borrowing helps literalize the phenomenon of Black musical aesthetics becoming "mainstream" (i.e., accepted by white America). The number "Radio" is a case in point. As lead Calhoun sings about how he bucks social norms to play Black music on the radio, a group of Black women (playing teenagers) double Dutch center stage. A group of white teens enter and gesture that they would like to be included. At first regarding the interlopers with suspicion, the Black teens relent, and a white chorus dancer jumps into the ropes, showing prowess and skill. A reluctant Black dancer joins her, and they hold hands, a symbol of racial reconciliation. The racial groups merge to do ballet-inflected choreography, performing *panchés* (reaching one's torso down to the ground, one leg up in the air behind), *tours* (turns in the air), and *jetés* (leaps) in between jazzier shimmies and sanding (sliding heel-toe across the stage). The male dance choruses racially merge as well, doing acrobatic split jumps, barrel turns, and cartwheel roundoffs. The message is clear: in 1950s Memphis, popular music brought Black and white youth together. The white kids, once graciously invited in, hold their own. This version of history perhaps satiates white audiences' desires to imagine themselves in the past as well-intentioned people ruined by a few rotten racist apples, but clashes against what we know about southern white youth of the 1950s and early 1960s, of whom only a "tiny minority" were involved in the civil rights movement.[30] In photographs of Ruby Bridges, the Little Rock Nine, and Black college students integrating schools and department stores, the white youth clustered around them are shouting hateful messages, spitting, and demonstrating physically hostile body positions, poised to attack rather than to dance.

Rather than simplistically condemning Trujillo's work to the dustbin of nostalgic misfires, however, we can read the choreography more optimistically as operating on a second temporal register. Trujillo gave a second reason for jettisoning original social dances: audience appeal. He stated, "I felt it was important for me to consider a younger audience

---

[28]See, for example, Michelle Dvoskin, "Embracing Excess: The Queer Feminist Power of Musical Theatre Diva Roles," *Studies in Musical Theatre* 10, no. 1 (2016): 93–103.
[29]Sylviane Gold, "When Rock Took Off," *Dance Magazine*, November 2009, 64.
[30]David L. Chappell, *Inside Agitators: White Southerners in the Civil Rights Movement* (Baltimore, MD: Johns Hopkins University Press, 1994), xxi.

and to make the choreography cool and hip and interesting and fresh for them."[31] In other words, younger audiences might be more willing to immerse themselves in the show's temporal moment if the dancing resonated with their contemporary experience. Trujillo's goal was to give the audience the feel of a new aesthetic being born, the characters' excitement of rock 'n' roll being birthed, a temporality of *now* that felt emergent. On that level, the choreography succeeds: the energy that bursts forth when the dancers come together, barrel leaping across the stage, transports audiences to a threshold of the future in the past. Trujillo admits that anyone who grew up in 1950s Memphis would not recognize the dances, but as Jake Johnson persuasively argues, musical theatre's "lies" are part of its power.[32] Untethered from historical truths, musical theatre can imagine new ways forward. Perhaps rather than sanitizing the past, Trujillo's re-visioning worked against nostalgia to galvanize audiences to make that emergent sense of possibility, especially around race, manifest in their own lives.

Dance *as* Time

A clear example of a musical that works against sanitized nostalgia is the Broadway hit *Bring in 'da Noise, Bring in 'da Funk* (1996), choreographed by tap phenom Savion Glover at a mere twenty-one years of age. The musical tells the history of the Black experience in the United States through tap dance, offering both the spectacularity of lyric time and the progressive motion of linear time. The show has a clear historical arc, proceeding from the Middle Passage, when Africans were brought to the Americas in slave ships, to life on southern plantations, to work in industrial northern cities in the early twentieth century, to the civil rights movement, through to the show's present (1990s), when Black men attempt to hail taxicabs in New York City and get passed by. This arc is danced rather than spoken, and thus dance does not disrupt the narrative: it *is* the narrative. When the lighting and set designers arrived at rehearsals only weeks before opening night, they discovered there was no script to work with. Instead, they watched the dance and music rehearsals, making "piles of notes."[33] In each segment of the show, "'da beat," as represented by tapping feet, showcases continuity from "'da beat" from before, signifying the persistence of Black life and joy despite oppressive circumstances. Whether in a ring shout circle in the nineteenth century or a Hollywood sound stage in the twentieth, tap dance persists. Glover, however, also created new riffs and rhythms in each segment, such as "clickety-clack" train sounds

---

[31]Quoted in Sagolla, "Capturing the Feel of 1950s Memphis." Despite Trujillo's desire to appeal to younger audiences, it is likely that the audience was not that young. The average age of a Broadway theatregoer in *Memphis*'s opening season of 2009–10 was forty-seven, and the average stayed in the mid-forties throughout the show's run. Audiences were also 75 percent white and had an average income of $200,000, compared to the US national average income of $54,283. See Ken Davenport, "Broadway Audience Demographics for 2009–10 Released!," *Ken Davenport* (website), accessed October 10, 2022, https://kendavenport.com/broadway-audience-demographics-for-2009-10-released/ (this site also has demographic reports for subsequent years); *Reuters*, "U.S. Incomes Fell Sharply in 2009: IRS Data," August 3, 2011, https://www.reuters.com/article/us-usa-economy-incomes/idUSTRE77302W20110804.

[32]Quoted in Sagolla, "Capturing the Feel of 1950s Memphis"; and see Jake Johnson, *Lying in the Middle: Musical Theater and Belief at the Heart of America* (Urbana: University of Illinois Press, 2021), 1–2.

[33]Elizabeth Kendall, "'Bring in 'da Noise' Steps Uptown, Feet First," *New York Times*, April 21, 1996.

for the Great Migration northward to cities such as Chicago starting in the 1910s.[34] *Noise/Funk* covered greater temporal ground than almost any other musical—hundreds of years. To take audiences on such a long journey, tap was perhaps the perfect medium. Its constant rhythmic pulse gave audiences a kinesthetic sense of constant temporal motion, while its dynamism reminded them to keep shifting gears.[35] Cultural critic Margo Jefferson mused in her review of *Noise/Funk* that Black history is "a series of experiments (driven, desperate, crafty, witty, ebullient) in style and esthetics."[36] There was perhaps no better way to have an audience experience a broad arc of Black history, therefore, than through tap.[37]

Where *Noise/Funk* utilized dance as the primary mechanism for showing the passage of time, *Hamilton: An American Musical* (2015) utilized it for considering the nature of time itself. In this story of US Revolutionary-era political figure Alexander Hamilton, choreographer Andy Blankenbuehler rejected Robbins's dictum to place the dance historically in time, place, and space; the characters do not perform social dances popular in eighteenth-century New York. Neither did he create showstoppers. Instead, Blankenbeuhler spatialized time, using movement as a meditation on temporality: how the past, present, and future are related. His choreography integrates various forms of hip-hop (popping, locking, etc.) with theatrical jazz, social dances, and contemporary commercial dance, which combines acrobatic athleticism and expressiveness of emotional states.[38] Like the musical's casting choices and deployment of hip-hop music, the present-day choreographic aesthetic invites audiences to reconsider their received notions of American history and even their relationship to history. The musical reframes Alexander Hamilton not as a crusty old white founding father, but as a young Caribbean immigrant who "get[s] the job done."[39] Dancers who use movement vocabulary born from the African diasporic experience, including jazz and hip-hop, help convey that reframing. The presentist nature of the dancing encourages the audience to see themselves and their present world as capable of producing the same revolutionary, dynamic change.

When and why choreography happens also shape the temporal experience of *Hamilton*. Rather than have set-apart "dance numbers," the ensemble moves continuously. Scholar Anne Searcy calls it a "danced-through" musical, and head creator Lin-Manuel Miranda called the choreography a "parallel physical score."[40] Sometimes the choreography provides visual cues to reinforce the meaning of the rapped lyrics, which are faster paced than Broadway audiences are used to, and at other times the choreography works obliquely, providing an alternative interpretation of the situation as spoken. Either way, the kinesthetic commentary is continuous. Theatre critics have disagreed about whether the choreography

---

[34]Kendall.

[35]I thank Phoebe Rumsey for pushing me to think further about this.

[36]Margo Jefferson, "'Noise' Taps a Historic Route to Joy," *New York Times*, November 26, 1995.

[37]See Benae Beamon's chapter in this volume for more on tap and musical theatre, particularly the musical *Black and Blue* (1989), which saw Glover nominated for a Tony Award at fifteen years old.

[38]For more on the aesthetic variety of the choreography, see Phoebe Rumsey, "The Convergence of Dance Styles in *Hamilton: An American Musical*," in *The Routledge Companion to the Contemporary Musical*, ed. Jessica Sternfeld and Elizabeth L. Wollman (New York: Routledge, 2020), 255–62.

[39]Lin-Manuel Miranda, "The Complete Libretto of the Broadway Musical," in *Hamilton: The* Revolution, by Lin-Manuel Miranda and Jeremy McCarter (New York: Hachette Book Group, 2016).

[40]Anne Searcy, "Bringing Dance Back to the Center in *Hamilton*," *American Music* 36, no. 4 (2018): 448, 449.

"overwhelm[s] the narrative," but implicitly seem to agree that if so, that would be a mark against the musical.[41] But "overwhelming the narrative" has a temporal effect: it throws linear time into chaos, which arguably gives the audience an affective experience of what *that moment in history might have been like*. What does it *feel* like, in your body, to be on the eve of a revolution? To be in the middle of a war? The perpetual-motion-machine choreography helps one gain a kinesthetic sense of chaos: a temporality in which motion keeps happening, but not in a clear forward path.

Blankenbuehler's choreography extends beyond human bodies to set pieces. The stage floor has two giant rotating discs, one moving clockwise and the other counterclockwise. One represents the forward motion of time, the future of the historical past, whose ending the audience already knows. The other turntable features characters who want to disrupt that linear momentum. Blankenbuehler points to the duel between Hamilton and Aaron Burr as a case in point. Hamilton "rotates the way of resisting fate" and ends up shot.[42] Even when the stage turntables don't rotate, the choreography offers a "what if" sense of the contingency of historical time. Earlier in the show, for example, a dancer depicts a bullet going in slow motion over Hamilton's head as he bows to write. Though not a showstopper moment, it brings the audience into a suspended temporal state to consider the possibility of a different world: what if Hamilton had raised his head? All of this chapter's examples, in some sense, imagine a different future for the past. In musical theatre dance, history is not a fixed temporal moment, but dynamic.

* * *

Dance in musical theatre gives audiences the gift of temporal flexibility. Because of its material grounding in bodies that move through space, audiences have a kinesthetically felt sense of time passing. At the same time, dance's spectacularity can rupture linear time to imagine other ways of being in the world. Such opportunities are fraught with questions about how to transport audiences to another time ethically. Are the methods used in musical theatre dance to make an audience feel they are living in a previous era justified if such methods distort histories of America's racial past? When is accuracy about specific movement vocabularies needed to make a temporal moment resonate, and when can such fidelity in fact inhibit the kinesthetic sense of time travel? When is it better to employ contemporary movement to make the world onstage feel alive, in the temporal present, even if depicting a previous era? Such rich questions arise when analyzing musical theatre dance with the concept of temporality in mind.

Bibliography

Burrows, George. "*Anything Goes* on an Ocean Liner: Musical Comedy as a Carnivalistic Heterotopia." *Studies in Musical Theatre* 7, no. 3 (2013): 327–45.

Chappell, David L. *Inside Agitators: White Southerners in the Civil Rights Movement*. Baltimore, MD: Johns Hopkins University Press, 1994.

---

[41]Rumsey, "The Convergence of Dance Styles in *Hamilton*," 255, 260.
[42]Andy Blankenbuehler, quoted in Ruthie Fierberg, "Andy Blankenbuehler on Making History with *Hamilton*," *Playbill*, June 3, 2016.

Cramer, Lyn. *Creating Musical Theatre: Conversations with Broadway Directors and Choreographers.* London: Bloomsbury, 2013.

Davenport, Ken. "Broadway Audience Demographics for 2009–10 Released!" *Ken Davenport* (website). Accessed October 10, 2022. https://kendavenport.com/broadway-audience-demographics-for-2009-10-released/.

Duncan, Isadora. "I See America Dancing." 1927. In *The Art of the Dance*, edited by Sheldon Cheney, 47–50. New York: Theatre Arts Books, 1977.

Dvoskin, Michelle. "Embracing Excess: The Queer Feminist Power of Musical Theatre Diva Roles." *Studies in Musical Theatre* 10, no. 1 (2016): 93–103.

"Fiddler on the Roof—Bottle Dance from Wedding Scene." Uploaded by Tomáš Pumprla, July 31, 2010. YouTube video, 3:57. https://www.youtube.com/watch?v=yGBG8mCt59s.

"Fiddler on the Roof—Bottle Dance—Steppin' Out Theatrical Productions." Uploaded by the5shermans, November 26, 2012. YouTube video, 3:39. https://www.youtube.com/watch?v=hKvvEo9P15c.

Fierberg, Ruthie. "Andy Blankenbuehler on Making History with *Hamilton*." *Playbill*, June 3, 2016.

Gennaro, Liza. *Making Broadway Dance.* New York: Oxford University Press, 2021.

Gennaro, Liza, and Stacy Wolf. "Dance in Musical Theater." In *Oxford Handbook of Dance and Theater*, edited by Nadine George-Graves, 148–68. New York: Oxford University Press, 2015.

George-Graves, Nadine. "'Just Like Being at the Zoo': Primitivity and Ragtime Performance." In *Ballroom, Boogie, Shimmy Sham, Shake: A Social and Popular Dance Reader*, edited by Julie Malnig, 55–71. Urbana: University of Illinois Press, 2009.

Gold, Sylviane. "When Rock Took Off." *Dance Magazine*, November 2009.

Gotman, Kélina. *Choreomania: Dance and Disorder.* New York: Oxford University Press, 2018.

Graham, Martha. "Seeking an American Art of the Dance." In *Revolt in the Arts: A Survey of the Creation, Distribution and Appreciation of Art in America*, edited by Oliver M. Sayler, 249–51. New York: Brentano's, 1930.

Harbert, Elissa. "Embodying History: Casting and Cultural Memory in *1776* and *Hamilton*." *Studies in Musical Theatre* 13, no. 3 (2019): 251–67.

Hill, Constance Valis. "From Bharata Natyam to Bop: Jack Cole's 'Modern' Jazz Dance." *Dance Research Journal* 33, no. 2 (2001): 29–39.

Jefferson, Margo. "'Noise' Taps a Historic Route to Joy." *New York Times*, November 26, 1995.

Johnson, Jake. *Lying in the Middle: Musical Theater and Belief at the Heart of America.* Urbana: University of Illinois Press, 2021.

Johnson, Jasmine. "Black Laws of Dance." *Conversations across the Field of Dance Studies: Decolonizing Dance Discourses* 40 (2020): 25–7.

Kendall, Elizabeth. "'Bring in 'da Noise' Steps Uptown, Feet First." *New York Times*, April 21, 1996.

Lasch, Christopher. "The Politics of Nostalgia: Losing History in the Mists of Ideology." *Harper's*, November 1984, 65–70.

McMillin, Scott. *The Musical as Drama.* Princeton, NJ: Princeton University Press, 2006.

Nereson, Ariel. *Democracy Moving: Bill T. Jones, Contemporary American Performance, and the Racial Past.* Ann Arbor: University of Michigan Press, 2022.

"The Pajama Game—Steam Heat." Uploaded by MarcosCohen, May 15, 2008. YouTube video, 4:33. https://www.youtube.com/watch?v=0szHqlXQ2R8.

Pressley, Nelson. "Kathleen Marshall, Broadway's 'Vintage Girl.'" *Washington Post*, June 7, 2013.

Reuters. "U.S. Incomes Fell Sharply in 2009: IRS Data." August 3, 2011. https://www.reuters.com/article/us-usa-economy-incomes/idUSTRE77302W20110804.

Rodgers, Richard. *Musical Stages: An Autobiography.* New York: Random House, 1975.

Rumsey, Phoebe. "Embodied Nostalgia: Early Twentieth Century Social Dance and U.S. Musical Theatre." PhD diss., City University of New York, 2019.

Rumsey, Phoebe. "The Convergence of Dance Styles in *Hamilton: An American Musical*." In *The Routledge Companion to the Contemporary Musical*, edited by Jessica Sternfeld and Elizabeth L. Wollman, 255–62. New York: Routledge, 2020.

Sagolla, Lisa Jo. "Capturing the Feel of 1950s Memphis." *Back Stage*, November 19–25, 2009.

Savran, David. *Highbrow/Lowdown: Theater, Jazz, and the Making of the New Middle Class.* Ann Arbor: University of Michigan Press, 2009.

Searcy, Anne. "Bringing Dance Back to the Center in *Hamilton*." *American Music* 36, no. 4 (2018): 448–66.

Solomon, Alisa. "Balancing Act: *Fiddler*'s Bottle Dance and the Transformation of 'Tradition.'" *TDR: The Drama Review* 55, no. 3 (2011): 21–30.

"Sutton Foster—Blow, Gabriel, Blow (Anything Goes)." Uploaded by BroadwayDVDs, May 17, 2021. YouTube video, 8:20. https://www.youtube.com/watch?v=EGVMJuE9QA0.

Trachtenberg, Alan. *The Incorporation of America: Culture and Society in the Gilded Age.* New York: Hill and Wang, 1982.

Trost, W. J., C. Labbé, and D. Grandjean. "Rhythmic Entrainment as a Musical Affect Induction Mechanism." *Neurosychologia* 96 (2017): 96–110.

Winkler, Kevin. *Big Deal: Bob Fosse and Dance in the American Musical.* New York: Oxford University Press, 2018.

Section II Approaches to Choreography and the Body

8   Take Off with Us: Expressing Gender and Sexuality in Golden Age Broadway Choreography

KEVIN WINKLER

While doing promotional talks in conjunction with the publication of my 2018 book *Big Deal: Bob Fosse and Dance in the American Musical*, I was asked more than once whether I thought Fosse's work had particular appeal to LGBTQ+ audiences. These questions led to further discussions of the queer elements of Fosse's style. In truth, it was a topic I had only tangentially engaged with in the book. But it offered an intriguing new avenue of inquiry into the art of a choreographer about whom I thought I knew a great deal.

This line of questioning got me thinking about how Fosse's work, perhaps more than that of other choreographers, celebrates the individual body, including the queer body. His fondness for diegetic, performative numbers and penchant for trio formations push his work beyond the conventional heterosexual couplings in many musicals. The instantly recognizable Fosse silhouette—with its hunched shoulders, turned-in feet, and ever-present hat tipped over the eyes—grew out of Fosse's own physicality (rounded shoulders, lack of a ballet turnout, and premature hair loss) and became a universal totem of his style, easily adopted by anybody regardless of race, gender, or sexual orientation.

Through a series of case studies from *Oklahoma!*, *West Side Story*, *Applause*, and select Fosse shows, this chapter examines the evolving expression of gender and sexuality through dance by Golden Age choreographers. The Golden Age of the musical is often designated as beginning with the Broadway opening of *Oklahoma!* in 1943 and running through *Fiddler on the Roof*'s arrival in 1964, a two-decade span when the musical enjoyed particular cultural currency and a remarkable consistency of achievement. For this essay, I extend this "golden" era into the 1970s, the period of Bob Fosse's greatest successes.

These contrasting case studies begin with an examination of the choreography of Agnes de Mille in *Oklahoma!*, with its rigidly defined roles and movement specifications for men and women. But even within these restrictions, de Mille's women were allowed alternative means of expressing themselves. Jerome Robbins's *West Side Story* (1957) was an equally codified world that hewed closely to prescribed gender roles, but with space for nonconforming bodies like that of Anybodys, the tomboy hanger-on to the Jets, and the aggressive dance styles of the Shark women. *Applause* (1970) with Ron Field's staging and choreography in support of the text, explicitly heralded gay male bodies and spaces and allowed for the acknowledgment of the sexual identity of its characters, making it the first post-Stonewall Broadway musical.

In looking at Bob Fosse's body of work, the chapter focuses on staging that leaned away from conventional romantic dance pairings, including face-front, performative numbers like

"Steam Heat" (1954's *The Pajama Game*) and "Who's Got the Pain?" from *Damn Yankees* (1955), both choreographed with gender neutral vocabulary specific to Fosse's style. Additionally, works like the alluring "Magic to Do" in *Pippin*, feature the dancers' erotic energy—the throbbing hip isolations and insinuating shoulder rolls performed with lavalike fluidity—which is directed at the audience rather than an opposite-sex target. In these case studies, Fosse's noirish cynicism leaves little room for romance but plenty of opportunity for celebrating the self, of any gender or orientation. Fosse wasn't alone in challenging male/female binaries, nor was he the first. Even in the 1940s and 1950s, choreographers were making inroads in establishing character in terms of gender expression and sexuality.

Girls Falling Down

In *Rodeo*, Agnes de Mille's 1942 ballet set on a Colorado ranch at the turn of the century, a tough, plucky young cowgirl dresses in buckskins, boots, and cowboy hat and tries to ingratiate herself with the ranch hands. Nursing a crush on the Head Wrangler, she tries to emulate the cowboys' roping and riding maneuvers but falls short. Her failures don't discourage her, and she always tries again, but when she's thrown from a bucking bronco, the Wrangler impatiently turns her out of the corral. Later the Cowgirl is crushed to see him escorting one of the pretty visiting city girls, with her frilly dress and hair bows. Still later, at a square dance, the Cowgirl is without a partner, and forlornly watches the Wrangler dance with the same pretty girl. With big brotherly concern, the ranch's Champion Roper offers to teach her to dance. But the Cowgirl can only think of her unrequited love for the Wrangler. Finally, she runs off and returns in a dress and with a ribbon in her hair, looking more like the other girls, but exhibiting the same fearless energy. The Roper's dance lessons pay off as the Cowgirl proceeds to outdance everyone, and her excitement and high spirits pique the interests of the Wrangler. He and the Roper compete to dance with her, and in the end, the Cowgirl realizes it is the Roper, not the Wrangler, she truly loves.

Rodeo, with its score by Aaron Copland, was one of several narrative ballets created by de Mille and set in the American West. That the Cowgirl and the other hoydenish, independent-minded young women in these ballets didn't always conform to standard feminine codes of behavior and dress made them no less desirous of romance with the men in their frontier communities. *Rodeo*'s happy ending arrives when the Cowgirl dons a dress and joins the ranks of female dance partners to the ranch hands. Her dress may be less frilly and feminine than the other girls', but it still serves as the cost of entry to the world of romance. The Cowgirl isn't a rebel who questions or rejects gender conventions. Quite the opposite: she's an awkward tomboy who finally learns the "proper" feminine attributes in order to acquire that which is most essential to a frontier woman, as de Mille herself noted: "Without a man [the Cowgirl] can have no love, no children, no land, no home, no occupation, no reason for being. She will be wasted."[1]

Rodeo debuted at the Metropolitan Opera House on October 16, 1942, with de Mille dancing the role of the Cowgirl. In the audience that evening, at de Mille's invitation, were

---

[1] Agnes de Mille's program notes for the October 28, 1976, Joffrey Ballet production, quoted in Carol Easton, *No Intermissions: The Life of Agnes de Mille* (Boston: Little, Brown, 1996), 188.

composer Richard Rodgers and lyricist-librettist Oscar Hammerstein II, who were preparing a new musical, their first as a team. Lynn Riggs's *Green Grow the Lilacs* (1930), a play set in the Oklahoma Territory in the early 1900s just before it became America's forty-sixth state, was the source material. When de Mille learned of the new musical's setting, she immediately proposed herself as its choreographer. *Oklahoma!*, as the show was eventually titled, spoke directly to the themes de Mille had been developing in her frontier ballets—those of independence and self-sufficiency, but also the sustenance that came from being part of a larger, American community, something that resonated deeply with World War II audiences.

As a dancer, de Mille made up for spotty technique with crackerjack comic timing and the gestural flair of a dramatic actress. As a choreographer, she built many of her ballets around a female character like the Cowgirl, who pushed at, but never really challenged, conventional notions of femininity. Though grounded in classical ballet, de Mille's work combined elements of modern and American folk dance and emphasized honest, realistic gesture and characterization. Her demands on dancers were as much dramatic as technical, and to help them develop those skills de Mille developed a class she called Acting for Dancers. "Until Agnes, dancers were fairies and dolls," observed one of her students. "Agnes asked us to be *people*."[2]

De Mille clashed almost immediately with Rodgers, Hammerstein, and *Oklahoma!*'s director, Rouben Mamoulian, in her insistence on hiring dancers with strong acting and comedic skills regardless of their looks. For Broadway chorus lines of the time, physical beauty was more highly prized than dancing or acting ability. Two dancers de Mille fought to cast were Bambi Linn, then sixteen years old with remarkable, gazellelike leaps, and Joan McCracken. McCracken, a Philadelphia native, had trained at Catherine Littlefield's ballet school and later danced with the company.[3]

Linn and McCracken had what de Mille called "piano legs"—thick and muscular, not the long, slim legs favored by the other creative staff. "They're certainly not pretty," Mamoulian declared when he saw them. "They can't act. Possibly, they can dance. That's your department. They're useless to me." But de Mille knew better. When she called his bluff and threatened to quit if she didn't get her choices, Mamoulian waved her off: "Then just keep them out of my way."[4] As she shaped the dances for *Oklahoma!*, de Mille took full advantage of Linn and McCracken's unique personalities and abilities.

Linn was costumed as a youngster, with pigtails and a broad-brimmed schoolgirl hat, and de Mille spotlighted her in key bits of dance staging. In the show's first act ballet, "Laurey Makes Up Her Mind," Linn displays her youthful excitement at Laurey and Curly's wedding with spirited "bell kicks" (a click of the heels together in the air while the legs are out to the side), then offers Laurey a bridal bouquet before bursting into tears.[5]

More noteworthy, de Mille featured McCracken in the dance that accompanies "Many a New Day." Laurey is in love with cowboy Curly, but also fascinated by her earthy and sinister

---

[2]Bambi Linn, quoted in Easton, 179.
[3]Like de Mille, the Littlefield Ballet took an interest in ballets that focused on Americana themes and incorporated vernacular dance styles. McCracken had lately danced with Eugene Loring's Dance Players and distinguished herself as a sparkling presence in his dramatic story ballets.
[4]Agnes de Mille, *Dance to the Piper* (New York: New York Review Books Classics, 2015), 319.
[5]See Easton, *No Intermissions*, 204; and Max Wilk, *OK! The Story of Oklahoma!* (New York: Grove Press, 1993), 132.

farmhand Jud. She impulsively agrees to go with Jud to the evening's box social, thereby spurning Curly's offer. Curly gives her some of her own back by promptly arranging to escort another girl. In "Many a New Day," Laurey covers up her heartbreak by asserting her independent spirit.

Laurey's friends perform a series of maidenly movements conveying their excitement at the upcoming party. But their airy leg lifts and gentle petticoat rustling are interrupted by another rambunctious young friend of Laurey's. De Mille expected each dancer to come up with her own distinctive character, and McCracken stood out as a young girl, perhaps on her way to her first social, who cannot hew to the others' feminine standards of behavior. Excited and awkward, she dances along with the other girls, sometimes in sync but more often falling short of their gracefulness. "Falling" is the operative word, as she falls to the ground not once but twice while attempting what the others do so nimbly. But she is undeterred, pulling herself up each time and rejoining the others. She tries to tamp down her natural high spirits but always gets impatient, sometimes pushing out her hip in a childlike manner, other times launching into a spontaneous knock-kneed tap dance. At last, Laurey gives her a sharp look to pull her back in line. But the girl has the final say when, as everyone exits the stage, she gives one final jump, flinging her head back in youthful triumph.[6]

McCracken's performance as the Girl Who Falls Down long ago became part of Broadway lore, and others involved in *Oklahoma!* have taken at least some credit for the idea behind it. But the character is a close relation to *Rodeo*'s Cowgirl. Just as dance historian Megan Pugh observed that "*Rodeo*, with its don-a-dress, find-a-man love plot, takes place within a heteronormative world,"[7] the Girl Who Falls Down, like all of de Mille's dancers, is part of "a coherent community in which gender roles are clear," according to theatre historian John M. Clum.[8] There was no space in de Mille's (or Rodgers's or Hammerstein's or Mamoulian's) *Oklahoma!* for a cowboy attracted to other cowboys, or a farm girl uninterested in acquiring a male date for the box social. The Cowgirl and the Girl Who Falls Down gently challenge but never threaten the prevailing social-sexual hegemony of their frontier settings.

De Mille utilized the particular dance and dramatic skills of Linn and McCracken in later musicals. As two of the notable dancers to emerge from her shows, they came to represent de Mille's favorite female prototypes: the comic soubrette and the tortured tomboy. In *Bloomer Girl* (1944), a musical set during the Civil War that engaged with issues of female emancipation, McCracken played Daisy, a hoydenish young housemaid bemused by the earnest suffragettes who long to trade their hoop skirts for the then-new, and scandalous, bloomers. Her rowdy and unladylike dancing disturbs their orderliness with an impetuousness that calls to mind the Girl Who Falls Down.[9]

---

[6]For a detailed description of McCracken in the "Many a New Day" dance, see Lisa Jo Sagolla, *The Girl Who Fell Down: A Biography of Joan McCracken* (Boston: Northeastern University Press, 2003), 1–4. On the significance of the Girl Who Falls Down as a secondary character created entirely in dance, see Kara Ann Gardner, *Agnes de Mille: Telling Stories in Broadway Dance* (New York: Oxford University Press, 2016), 40–3.

[7]Megan Pugh, *America Dancing: From the Cakewalk to the Moonwalk* (New Haven, CT: Yale University Press, 2015), 149.

[8]John M. Clum, *Something for the Boys: Musical Theater and Gay Culture* (New York: St. Martin's Press, 1999), 30.

[9]See Sagolla, *The Girl Who Fell Down*, 100–102, for a detailed discussion of Joan McCracken's performance in her *Bloomer Girl* numbers. See also Gardner, *Agnes de Mille*, 71–2.

In Rodgers and Hammerstein's *Carousel* (1945), adapted from Ferenc Molnár's play *Liliom* (1909), Linn played Louise, the daughter of carnival barker Billy Bigelow and his wife, Julie. When Billy learns Julie is pregnant, he attempts a robbery in order to get money to support the child. Instead, he is killed, and his spirit is sent to a kind of spiritual waiting room. When Louise, the child born after his death, turns fifteen, God sends Billy to visit her. But he finds her to be just as troubled as he was, and during a lengthy ballet sequence, de Mille dramatizes key moments in the unhappy girl's life. Linn, a standout in de Mille's Acting for Dancers class, conveyed through movement and pantomime the anger and hurt of this lonely child born to poverty without a father. The ballet took Louise over a rough terrain of emotions, much as *Oklahoma!*'s "Laurey Makes Up Her Mind" explored Laurey's intense psychosexual conflict over two men. Louise begins as a roughhousing tomboy but soon experiences a sexual attraction to an older boy. When the boy realizes just how young she is, he roughly rejects her, leaving her in tears. Later she is ostracized by the other children in her community, and she ends the ballet utterly alone and dejected. Linn's transparency as an actress powerfully registered each step of the passage.[10]

"In Agnes's shows, it's almost always the woman who's the top dancer, never the man," Linn later reflected.[11] Through her Broadway ballets, de Mille was a pioneer in investigating the rich emotional lives of women. Working within strictly coded gender roles, her choreography for *Oklahoma!* and other musicals brought a new sophistication and complexity to the portrayal of women through dance.

Any Bodies

During Ballet Theatre's 1941 season, de Mille selected a young male ensemble dancer for a brief, thirty-two-bar crossover in her ballet *Three Virgins and a Devil*. "This Boy Robbins," as de Mille described him, "was greeted with cheers and shrieks" and "stopped the show."[12] Robbins's breakthrough as a choreographer was the 1944 ballet *Fancy Free*, with a score by Leonard Bernstein. Its story of three sailors on leave in New York City was the jumping-off point for the musical *On the Town*, also with music by Bernstein (and book and lyrics by Betty Comden and Adolph Green), which opened just months after *Fancy Free*'s debut. Robbins's choreography, his first for a Broadway musical, along with Bernstein's symphonic jazz score, drove the musical with fresh, kinetic energy.

Robbins, who was only twenty-five when he created *Fancy Free*, nursed lifelong conflicts about his homosexuality and his Jewish roots (his birth name, Rabinowitz, was quickly changed), feeling that both were hindrances to success. In a senior essay titled "My Selves," the seventeen-year-old wrote of the various masks he donned to present himself to the world.[13] It is no stretch to imagine that at least one of those masks hid the homosexuality that was so vexing to him.

---

[10]*Carousel*'s ballet was filmed in its entirety during the show's Broadway run; see "Carousel Ballet — Original Broadway Cast, with Orchestra Added," uploaded by Broadway Classics, January 26, 2016, YouTube video, 12:36, https://www.youtube.com/watch?v—P7oatLydC0.
[11]Bambi Linn, quoted in Easton, *No Intermissions*, 249.
[12]Agnes de Mille, untitled article in *Dance Magazine*, March 1958, 69, in Agnes de Mille clipping file, Jerome Robbins Dance Division, New York Public Library for the Performing Arts; and de Mille, *Dance to the Piper*, 200.
[13]See Amanda Vail, *Somewhere: The Life of Jerome Robbins* (New York: Broadway Books, 2006), 26–7.

Robbins had justification for skittishness surrounding his homosexuality. He had been a member of the Communist Party for a brief time in the 1940s, as had many in the performing arts. He knew as early as 1950 that the House Un-American Activities Committee (HUAC) would call him to testify. That it wasn't until 1953 that he was finally subpoenaed to appear meant three years of panicked anticipation of the dread event. Communists and homosexuals were held in equal scorn by HUAC. Robbins was so fearful of being revealed as a homosexual that while he was living with dancer Buzz Miller during this time, he suffered disturbing visions of them being surveilled in their apartment. During rehearsals for the revue *Two's Company* in 1952, Robbins insisted that Miller, who was a cast member, move out of their apartment for fear of the two being seen coming and going together.[14] It was another example of the masks Robbins donned to hide his homosexuality.[15]

West Side Story, one of Robbins's most enduring works for the stage, was driven by men dancing. The prominent muscularity of male dancing is a recurring motif in Robbins's work. From the showboating sailors in *Fancy Free* through the ecstatic Jewish revelers in *Fiddler on the Roof*, Robbins subtly upended the tradition of ballet-trained male dancers as noble princes and courtly supporters to lissome ballerinas.

In this resetting of Shakespeare's *Romeo and Juliet* amid the gang rivalry between young Puerto Rican immigrants (the Sharks) and a mongrel mix of Irish-Italian-Polish teenagers (the Jets) in New York City, gender roles were strictly codified in the show's male-dominated landscape. Yet Robbins found subtle ways to push against those boundaries through the use of dance movement and body language.

The Jet girls are passive and clinging, their status conferred only by their association with individual gang members. The Shark girls are bolder, more outspoken, and Robbins gave them greater opportunities to assert their points of view. Co-choreographer Peter Gennaro created a dance to accompany a song for the Sharks and their girls in which they debate the merits of Puerto Rico against those of their adopted country. But as Robbins biographer Deborah Jowitt later wrote, "Robbins took the men out of the number, thus giving the show a women's group to balance the dominant warring males and turning 'America' into a dazzle of swishing skirts, rapidly flicking feet, and scornful female tongues."[16]

The Jet girls are almost as tagalong as Anybodys, the young tomboy who dolefully follows the boys, angling for a change to prove her gangworthiness. Anybodys, played in the original Broadway production by Lee Becker, is a 1950s descendant of de Mille's Cowgirl in *Rodeo*. She is spunky and resourceful but refuses to present as a conventional girl. There is no final donning of a dress for this troubled urban teen who seeks to occupy the same space as her male counterparts. While the de Mille character comes up short in standard feminine decorum, she eventually arrives at the cherished realization of her womanliness. In contrast, Becker's Anybodys is a small, feral 'tween who stays low to the ground and darts in and out

---

[14]See Deborah Jowitt, *Jerome Robbins: His Life, His Theater, His Dance* (New York: Simon and Schuster, 2004), 210–11.
[15]It was never entirely clear whether HUAC pursued information about Robbins's sexuality, but his testimony before the committee, in which he named names of others he had known during his Communist Party days, was a stain on his character he never entirely erased.
[16]Jowitt, *Jerome Robbins*, 277.

Image 8.1 Jerome Robbins and Lee Theodore (a.k.a. Lee Becker) rehearsing for the stage production of *West Side Story* (1957). Photo by Martha Swope. Billy Rose Theatre Collection, New York Public Library Digital Collections.

of shadows and crowded gatherings. She identifies with the boys and is dismissed by their girls for her complete lack of feminine signifiers. ("An American tragedy," one of them witheringly refers to her.)[17] Anybodys stays separate from the Jet girls. She insists on dancing alongside the Jet boys in "Dance at the Gym" and "Cool." In the former, she's gangly and pretend suave, in the latter she matches the boy's coiled athleticism. She actively coordinates gang maneuvers with the boys, and eagerly participates in the harassment and near rape of Anita.

But in the end, just like de Mille's Cowgirl, Anybodys reveals herself to be a regular girl after all. Late in the second act, when Action, one of the Jets, compliments her strategy skills, she dreamily thanks him: as the stage directions state, "she has fallen in love." *West Side Story* further defines her role within the gang in its listing of characters in programs and scripts. The cast is strictly segregated by sex, with the Jets and Sharks listed separately from "their girls." Anybodys is placed in the latter group and relegated to the very end of the list, though she has more stage time than the other girls.

During workshop rehearsals for *Jerome Robbins' Broadway*, the 1989 anthology of musical sequences from Robbins's Broadway shows, dancer Mary Ann Lamb was performing the role of Anybodys when Robbins made a startling admission. "He turned to me and goes, 'And Anybodys is me. That young gay boy in New Jersey.' . . . And he said,

---

[17]All dialogue and lyrics from William Shakespeare and Arthur Laurents, *Romeo and Juliet/West Side Story*, music by Leonard Bernstein, lyrics by Stephen Sondheim (New York: Dell, 1965).

'In the 1950s we couldn't cast a young feminine boy.' So they cast a girl in that part. 'But that's me.'"[18] Robbins's comments add a further layer of ambiguity to the character. Anybodys occupies an in-between space, both a part of and separate from the gang. Her apparent crush on Action might be that of a hero-worshipping young gay boy. Her attempts to match the performative macho swagger of the Jets, both on the dance floor and in their turf wars with the Sharks, carry an air of desperate striving by an outsider to fit in with the cool kids.

Anybodys can be seen as a stand-in for queer kids of the conservative 1950s who could never quite conform to prescribed gender norms. And she is not the only character of questionable gender conformity in *West Side Story*. When the excessively cheerful Glad Hand, a young man from the neighborhood who could be a teacher or social worker, attempts to get the rival gangs to mingle during the "Dance at the Gym" sequence by forming two circles with "boys on the outside, girls on the inside," he is instantly met with a mocking "Where are you?" and derisive laughter. Baby John, the youngest Jet, is nearly as big a hanger-on as Anybodys (who is the keener fighter). He can only approximate the other Jets' strutting toughness and seemingly has no interest in girls. It is Baby John who the others force to carry out the attempted rape of Anita, as if rape by this boy would be the ultimate degradation. While the two gangs demand allegiance and conformity from their members, not everyone in *West Side Story* can meet all the requirements.

It is interesting to note that when Robbins grouped the show's dances into an extended concert dance piece titled *West Side Story Suite* (1995), Anybodys was erased from the cast. (She was similarly jettisoned from *Jerome Robbins' Broadway*, despite Mary Ann Lamb's workshop experience.) The violent tension of the Jets and Sharks conflict, the flamboyant aggression of the dancing Shark girls, and the star-crossed romance of Tony and Maria were easier to re-create in the ballet world of *West Side Story Suite* than were the musical's characters who are from marginalized gender and sexual identities.

Lee Becker's embodiment of the untamed little tomboy who finally shows that she's like other girls served as the template for several generations of Anybodys. But in director Ivo van Hove's 2020 Broadway revival of *West Side Story*, he and choreographer Anne Teresa De Keersmaeker created a tougher, present-day urban landscape that included a new take on Anybodys. Zuri Noelle Ford was a solidly built Black Anybodys with a shaved head and brash manner. She danced with bravado alongside the Jets and, despite dialogue to the contrary, looked less like a hanger-on than a mostly active member of the Jets.

Van Hove and De Keersmaeker also expanded the membership of the Sharks to include a gender nonconforming person who dressed in slacks and flowing blouses and danced with the girls in the "America" number. (The production adopted the 1961 film version of "America," which returned the Shark boys to the number.) This tall, willowy character may have been non-binary or transgender. They appeared to have a relationship with one of the Shark boys, though it was not clearly defined. They executed the curving, preening dance moves of the Shark girls, but in a brief lift section they supported the boy rather than vice versa. And in the spirit of further inclusivity, this production did away with separate

---

[18]"Fan Fare: Jerome Robbins' Broadway—Part 2," uploaded by Stage17.tv, February 5, 2015, YouTube video, 9:36, https://www.youtube.com/watch?v=Q-UM14-IDh0.

designations for boy and girl members of each gang, instead listing everyone as either a Jet or a Shark.

Following two gang deaths, West Side Story's "Somewhere" ballet imagines a utopian space in which, their conflicts forgotten, Jets and Sharks dance and live together peacefully, with the dance partnering strictly male-female. In the most overt sign of inclusion in their West Side Story, Van Hove and De Keersmaeker created a new "Somewhere" sequence—less a ballet than a weary meditation on the spiritual havoc wrecked by violence. The bodies of Jets and Sharks rise from a foggy, rain-soaked terrain and entwine themselves around each other, in comfort, in succor, in love, regardless of their gang affiliation. Notably, a few of the couples are same sex, some embracing in friendship and support, others in romantic intimacy.

In Steven Spielberg's 2021 film of West Side Story, he and screenwriter Tony Kushner take Anybodys from tomboy to trans man. Played by transmasculine nonbinary actor Iris Menas, Anybodys is a barely tolerated "dickless wonder" as he is called by one of the Jets. "I ain't no goddamned girl!" he asserts, but when he tries to dance with the men in "Dance at the Gym," executing Justin Peck's street swaggering moves with as much authority as the other Jets, he is violently shoved aside. In Kushner's screenplay, Anybodys is given a deeper character arc. For instance, when his successful strategizing against the Sharks is recognized by Action with "You done good, buddy boy," it is both a compliment and an acknowledgment of Anybodys's correct gender. But where De Keersmaeker blurred binary movement in the "Somewhere" ballet and along with Van Hove sought to subvert gender in some of her casting, in the new film version, Peck reverts back to rigidly gendered choreography for the gangs.

In the sixty-plus years between West Side Story's original production and the Van Hove–De Keersmaeker and Spielberg-Kushner-Peck reimaginings of the classic musical, major shifts in perceptions of gender and sexuality have occurred. These new, twenty-first-century interpretations at last acknowledged some of these changes. It is impossible to imagine that future productions of the show will not take note of these changes, and possibly further expand on them.

"Varied Flamboyant Attire"

There had been musicals set in the world of the theatre before Applause, and all of them—from Babes in Arms (1937) to Kiss Me, Kate (1948), from Me and Juliet (1953) to Funny Girl (1964)—took place in a theatre entirely devoid of any self-disclosed LGBTQ+ characters. So did All about Eve, the classic 1950 comedy-drama that was the basis for Applause.[19] While librettists Betty Comden and Adolph Green, composer Charles Strouse, and lyricist Lee Adams timidly tiptoed into recognition that yes, there actually were LGBTQ+ persons working in the theatre, it was director-choreographer Ron Field who turned Applause into the gayest Broadway musical produced up to that time.

Field is an often overlooked figure now, but in 1970 he was one of the busiest choreographers working in theatre, television, and nightclubs. A New York City native, Field

---

[19]Due to rights issues with the film's producer, Twentieth Century Fox, the musical was based both on the screenplay by Joseph L. Mankiewicz and on Mary Orr's 1946 short story "The Wisdom of Eve."

lived a life virtually defined by show business, beginning with an appearance at the age of eight in the children's ensemble of *Lady in the Dark* (1941) on Broadway. He was the first male dance student to enroll in New York's legendary High School of the Performing Arts. Field danced on Broadway in *Carnival in Flanders* (1953) and *Kismet* (1954), beginning an association with choreographer Jack Cole. He toured with Cole's dance troupe and danced on television variety shows before striking out on his own as a choreographer. His breakthrough came with *Cabaret* (1966), in which his dances and cabaret numbers projected the ambivalent sexuality and decadent atmosphere of the musical's Weimar-era setting, and won him the Tony Award for Best Choreography.

The plot of *All about Eve* long ago passed into legend: a young fan named Eve Harrington meets and ingratiates herself into the life of Margo Channing, an older, insecure stage star played by Bette Davis at the peak of her stardom. Before Margo knows it, Eve has become a threat to both her career and her personal life. Eventually, Margo chooses to step away from her career and concentrate on married life, while Eve achieves the stardom she so avidly pursued. In the final scene, Eve meets another ambitious young fan, and the same pattern looks to play out all over again, with Eve now in a position of vulnerability.

In the twenty years that separated *All about Eve* from its musical adaptation, the culture had changed to the extent that it would have been ludicrous to portray its backstage world without at least some recognition of the queer lives of many who work in the theatre. After all, *Applause* opened less than a year after the Stonewall Riots kicked off the contemporary gay rights movement.[20]

Margo Channing's loyal maid-companion in *All about Eve* was Birdie Coonan, a plainspoken former vaudevillian played by flinty character actress Thelma Ritter. *Applause* transformed Birdie into Duane Fox, Margo's hairdresser and confidante, always ready with a sharp quip. While the creators assigned him the easiest, most clichéd profession, for once a gay character was not sad and lonely, nor a focus for easy laughs. Duane was an integral, comfortable-in-his-own-skin member of Margo's community of friends and associates. The matter-of-factness of his sexuality was conveyed early on in this exchange with Margo:

Margo   Duane, how'd you like to escort two lonely ladies out on the town?

Duane   I've got a date.

Margo   Bring him along.[21]

Fifty years on, it's no more than a throwaway line, but in 1970 Margo's breezy suggestion spoke volumes about her nonchalant acceptance of Duane—and indicated that he enjoyed a functioning romantic life. (It was light years removed from the marginal, barely tolerated space occupied by Anybodys.)

---

[20]The Stonewall Inn, a mob-controlled bar in New York City's Greenwich Village, was frequented by marginalized members of the LGBTQ+ community: homeless youths and drag queens of various races and ethnicities. As with most gay bars of the time, patrons were used to periodic raids and arrests by the police. But one night in June 1969, in response to yet another raid, they fought back, and over the next few nights their actions sparked a series of demonstrations that came to be known as the Stonewall Riots. The riots galvanized the community and gave birth to a new wave of gay activism.
[21]All dialogue, lyrics, and stage directions are from Betty Comden and Adolph Green, *Applause*, music by Charles Strouse, lyrics by Lee Adams (New York: Random House, 1971).

Referring to Duane, Field said, "I don't want him to come across as a gay stereotype. For once, if there's a homosexual onstage, I'd like him *not* to be effeminate."[22] Tall and good-looking, with a strong singing voice and just a touch of camp about him, Lee Roy Reams originated the role to Field's specification. Reams, in fact, had made numerous television and nightclub appearances as a dancer, including for Field. His handsome, non-threatening presence was seen as the perfect complement to female stars.

"But Alive" is Margo's first musical statement in *Applause*. No sooner does she insist she feels "twitchy and bitchy and manic" than she and Duane and Eve arrive at a Greenwich Village establishment peopled exclusively by men "dressed in varied flamboyant attire," according to the stage directions, and decorated with posters of gay icons like Marlon Brando in *The Wild One* (1953), Mae West, and assorted beefcake images. For the first time, a Broadway dance ensemble was dressed not as Jets or Sharks, not as farmers or cowmen, but as young New York City gay men of every stripe. And they were dancing not in a dank watering hole, but in a well-appointed and welcoming neighborhood establishment.

Field based the number's movement on the kind of uninhibited, ass-shaking social dancing done in gay clubs, with no straights watching. Margo, the center of attention, giddily joins in all the head-swinging variations on the frug, the jerk, and the pony. She even leads the crowd in a line dance that looks directly transferred from the scene in the play (and film) *The Boys in the Band* where characters perform a flamboyant step-touch, back-and-forth line dance they associate with their vacations on Fire Island. Midway through the number, the smallest, most elfin dancer (originally played by Sammy Williams, who would later originate the role of Paul, the gay dancer who tells of working in a drag show, in the 1975 *A Chorus Line*) challenges Margo to a dance-off. The two shimmy and shake and booty bump, and it's a clear case of hero(ine) worship for Sammy.

By the time he directed and choreographed *Applause*, Field had proven himself a master stager of television and nightclub routines for female stars like Liza Minnelli, Chita Rivera, Angela Lansbury, and Ann-Margret, surrounding them with an ensemble of male dancers to support and glorify them. With dozens of such numbers to his credit, Field was a principal architect of the diva-worshipping dance number in which slim young men appear to be in romantic thrall to the various deities they lift and carry and dance behind in styles ranging from jazz to tap to ballroom.

These performances carried whiffs of the kind of idolatry gay men have traditionally displayed toward larger-than-life female stars, but they rested uneasily within a "we're all straight" narrative. "But Alive" bore some resemblance to the diva-adoring title numbers in *Mame* (1966) or *Hello, Dolly!* (1964), in which the female star is the intense focus of attention as a phalanx of men perform unison movements, often in deliberate, cakewalk rhythms around her. She is paid the ultimate respect by not being required to dance or exert herself to any significant degree. Instead, the men strut, high kick, jump, and *jeté* themselves into

---

[22]Garrett Lewis quoting Ron Field in Sam Staggs, *All about "All about Eve": The Complete Behind-the-Scenes Story of the Bitchiest Film Ever Made* (New York: St. Martin's Press, 2000), 295. Lewis's emphasis. Lewis was originally cast as Duane, but replaced early in rehearsals by Lee Roy Reams.

exhaustion in her honor—presumably because she's just so fabulous. In "But Alive," the men's glorification of, and identification with, Margo feels authentic rather than contrived for story purposes.

Elsewhere, Field stages brief opportunities for movement between same-sex partners, including in full-cast numbers, like the opening "Backstage Babble," featuring New York first-nighters or a gala party at Margo's apartment. In "Fasten Your Seat Belts," the show's musicalization of Margo's defiant, martini-fueled breakdown, she performs a pseudo-striptease with two women dressed in outlandish getups that could easily lead them to be mistaken for drag queens.

Scenes set in Joe Allen's, the theatre district hangout, are populated by those who used to be called "gypsies," chorus dancers who go from show to show. The tone of these scenes is not dissimilar from the gay bar sequence, nor do the male dancers here display a different body language. When nudity is presented, as in an *Oh! Calcutta!* spoof, the focus is on male flesh (a flash of bare buttocks) in a brief bump-and-grind routine.[23]

Along with Sammy Williams, *Applause*'s male dance ensemble featured Nicholas Dante, who would go on to co-write the libretto for *A Chorus Line* and, in fact, based the role of Paul on himself. Dante, Williams, and the others danced with lissome, youthful grace and a bursting, childlike energy. Their vitality and attractiveness were different from the strapping Reams, but no less appealing, both to the audience and to Field. Gene Foote, another dancer in the show, commented later on Field's casting approach, noting, "if you see someone who turns you on, you'll probably want to work with him. A lot depends on the choreographer. For instance, in *Applause*, the majority of the dancers were good-looking and gay."[24]

In 1973, the year after *Applause* finished its two-year Broadway run, Field took diva-worshipping musical staging further out of the closet when he directed and choreographed a musical revue at New York's infamous Continental Baths. The Continental gained notoriety with the breakthrough performances of Bette Midler a few years earlier. Midler's phenomenal success singing for the towel-clad, men-only bathhouse audience made the Continental a thriving performance venue that welcomed a wildly diverse roster of artists, including Sarah Vaughan, Peter Allen, Melba Moore, and Julie Wilson. Field built *Pazazz '73* around Laura Kenyon, a young singer with a powerful voice. But the male and female dance ensemble disrupted the construct of male-female pairings in numbers that displayed a variety of sexualities. For instance, in a *pas de trois* (a dance for three people), a man cruises a woman, whom he dances with in a representation of sex. Another man enters and the woman and the first man then cruise him, and each dances with him to represent both a homo- and heterosexual encounter. Finally, the three perform a danced *ménage à trois*.

Applause was of its time, gently pushing the musical forward in acknowledging gay men both in the theatre's ranks and in the audience. The 1970s saw many gay, dancing characters: Tommy Tune played an out gay choreographer in the musical *Seesaw*. Two years later, *A Chorus Line* matter-of-factly featured two gay characters among its cast of

---

[23]*Oh! Calcutta!* was the "shocking" theatre sensation of the time, a musical revue in which the cast frequently disrobed, including a fully nude male-female pas de deux choreographed by Margo Sappington.
[24]Arthur Bell, "Homosexuality: A Gay Activist Looks at Broadway," *Playbill*, January 1973, 10.

hopeful dancers. In 1983, a fully realized relationship between two men operating a drag nightclub was the basis of the popular and much revived *La Cage aux Folles*. Into the twenty-first century, a wider range of sexualities has come to be represented onstage in musicals—whether about the theatre or not. *Applause*, driven by Ron Field's choreography and staging, deserves credit for getting there first, and if its steps were small, they led to bigger strides by others. Many of those strides were made eagerly and with characteristic flair by Bob Fosse.

Erotic Ambiguity

The list of artists that influenced Bob Fosse's singular dance style and theatrical aesthetic is well documented in books, interviews, documentaries, and television shows: eccentric vaudeville dancers like Joe Frisco and Harland Dixon; Charlie Chaplin, whose balletic grace and incongruous dignity Fosse channeled in several dances; Fred Astaire and Paul Draper, with their sleek tap stylings; and, above all, the strippers and burlesque dancers with whom he shared stages as one half of the teenaged tap-dancing Riff Brothers. All these dance influencers shared one thing in common: they generally performed solo, with little or no romantic connection to another person, thereby detaching them from presumed heterosexuality and allowing audiences to read the performance through their own orientation. For instance, Fred Astaire danced many romantic duets throughout his long career, but in his tap numbers, he most often danced alone.

Fosse absorbed not just the dance moves but the ambiance of the nightclubs, burlesque theatres, and strip joints that were a formative part of his early performing career. His view of sex was informed by his youthful affairs and backstage assignations with the women who worked in these venues. It was a world of little romance or tenderness, and it's likely that these experiences influenced Fosse's approach to portraying love and sexuality in his dances.

It's noteworthy how few numbers Fosse created in which opposite-sex couples dance together. Even in his early partnership with Mary Ann Niles, his first wife, the two danced in tandem but seldom in each other's arms during their nightclub and television appearances. It was quite the opposite approach from that of Marge and Gower Champion, contemporaries of Fosse and Niles, who excelled at narrative dances that revolved around courtship and romantic sparring.

Fosse's early choreography for theatre and film featured dances that challenged traditional romantic pairings. His film choreography is more readily accessible than his stage work. In the film *Kiss Me, Kate* (1953), Fosse choreographed a brief portion of the group number "From This Moment On," and danced it with Carol Haney. In their one-minute duet, Fosse appeared to be creating a new dance style—impudent, with jagged starts and stops, louche and low to the ground. But Haney's screams and burlesque bumps, Fosse's playfully domineering attitude, and the Apache references in which Haney crawls on the floor following Fosse come across as playacting.[25] Their ardor is smart aleck and sexy but hardly romantic.

---

[25]Apache dancing originated in the early twentieth-century Parisian underworld and portrayed a brutish dynamic between men and their female partners.

Much later, in "Take Off with Us" from his film *All That Jazz* (1979), Fosse created three nearly naked pas de deux for one heterosexual couple, one female couple, and one male couple that presented the body as an erotic delivery mechanism, regardless of who was dancing with whom. The stripped-down dancers mime passionate embraces and explicit sexual acts (a man takes a woman from behind, another moves her legs into a spread-eagle position) with cold, robotic efficiency. Despite the hard-bodied perfection of the dancers and the general libidinous atmosphere, an air of ironic detachment pervades the number.

When Fosse staged large ensemble numbers like "Hernando's Hideaway" in *The Pajama Game* (1954) or "Two Lost Souls" in 1955's *Damn Yankees*, the same-sex partnering has a detached, performative feel, with the dancers at their most animated when dancing separately within a group. His choreography, which frequently isolated body parts and moved them in different directions, looks cleaner and more precise when danced solo. "He's very sensual and he thinks movement is the same for men and women, the only difference is that women wear high heels," Gwen Verdon, his wife and collaborator, once observed about Fosse.[26] When he began developing his own stage productions, starting with *Sweet Charity* (1966) and continuing through *Pippin* (1972), *Chicago* (1975), *Dancin'* (1978), and *Big Deal* (1986), Fosse frequently eschewed opposite-sex couple dancing and instead foregrounded the individual body, giving space to envision a stage full of diverse genders and orientations.

These later Fosse musicals were drenched in eroticism, with his well-established appetite for women on full display. They often featured statuesque, provocatively clad women whose images were often used to advertise and promote the shows. Yet inside *Chicago*'s hedonistic 1920s Windy City or the medieval kingdom conjured by a traveling theatrical troupe in *Pippin*, and even as he showcased stars like Verdon, his most celebrated interpreter, and Ann Reinking, who emerged in the 1970s as a new dance inspiration for Fosse, this most heterosexual of choreographers created communities that welcomed an array of sexualities and allowed the individual to flourish.

Sweet Charity's protagonist, Charity Hope Valentine, searches for love and dreams of escaping the dance hall world she lives in. For a musical that's all about finding love, it's noticeably absent much heterosexual romance, and leaves room to imagine other options in its crowded New York City. The dead-eyed discotheque habitués in *Sweet Charity*'s "Rich Man's Frug" never touch as they execute Fosse's satire on then-current social dances. Ostensibly dancing in pairs, they barely pay attention to their partners. Much of the choreography consists of unison variations on the frug, the monkey, the jerk, and other 1960s popular dance moves performed in lines and other formations, with little of it differentiated by gender.

In "Big Spender," *Sweet Charity*'s most famous number, the dance hall hostesses greet an unseen customer with well-practiced come-ons. But their desultory enticements leave little doubt that they're only there for whatever money can be extracted from the men. In the rousing polka "I Love to Cry at Weddings," the dance hall hostesses and their regular customers share a good-natured camaraderie but little sexual tension. Charity's happiest moments are not with Oscar, her romantic interest (who ends the show by pushing her into

---

[26]Quoted in Jay Scott, "Fosse's Legacy Nears Perfection," *Globe and Mail*, September 25, 1987.

a lake), but in her own company. In "If My Friends Could See Me Now," she basks in the good fortune of being in a famous movie star's luxurious apartment (while the movie star is out of the room), strutting and mugging like a vaudeville clown. She's a brash drum majorette in "I'm a Brass Band," a private reverie in which she rejoices in being in love, but never mentioning with whom. "There's Gotta Be Something Better Than This" allows Charity and two of her dance hall colleagues to imagine better lives and careers, with no mention of men. They appear to be declaring their independence of the opposite sex as they traverse the stage in some of Fosse's rangiest and most muscular movement.

Fosse introduced a new, more erotic style of movement during the 1970s. It was a style his regular dancers like Candy Brown, Christopher Chadman, Cheryl Clark, Gene Foote, Richard Korthaze, Ann Reinking, Paul Solen, and Pamela Sousa, understanding its dramatic underpinnings, became adept at performing. As Foote later explained, "Bob said, 'When you move, I want you to move as though you're moving against water.' It does something to your body . . . it's sexy to resist movement."[27] At the same time, Fosse brought a new, expanded attitude toward sexual expression to these shows, as he discussed in an interview after *Pippin* opened, acknowledging the gay male dancers in its cast. This time, I used the kind of people they were to give the show a kind of individuality, and they were so happy about it I think it helped the show."[28]

Both *Pippin*'s traveling players and the denizens of *Chicago* move with erotic ambiguity, their liquid movements performed in Fosse's new moving-against-water style and driven by pulsating pelvises. They slither across the stage in costumes that blur the lines between the sexes, with the men showing as much flesh as the women. By now Fosse had moved away from unison dancing for large ensembles. Instead, in their opening numbers—*Pippin*'s "Magic to Do" and *Chicago*'s "All That Jazz"—each dancer moves to their own unheard rhythm, allowing Fosse to create an atmosphere of individual expression within a larger, teeming community.

"Steam Heat" was Fosse's first trio number, and he worked new variations on it in nearly every show that followed. These tight trio formations allowed Fosse to magnify the simplest movement by three, thus giving it greater impact. *Pippin* and *Chicago* contained two especially potent trios. "The Manson Trio" was named for its sinister allusions to the charismatic but disturbed Charles Manson, who, with his followers, committed a series of grisly Hollywood murders in 1969. *Pippin*'s Leading Player dances this macabre yet sprightly vaudeville soft shoe with two of his female players. To a percolating calliope beat, the three swivel and glide in perfect, menacing symmetry across the stage. In *Chicago*'s "Me and My Baby," Roxie revels in her new role of celebrity murderess, strutting to a Dixieland fanfare along with two men who match her every finger flick and shoulder roll.

In these and other trios, Fosse refused to gender the body in terms of movement, though they were often gendered in costume. Gestures and movements that might elsewhere be labeled "male" or "female" are performed by each dancer, allowing everyone to see themselves in his provocative dance vocabulary. Ben Vereen, the original Leading Player, executed the burlesque bump and grinds with bravado. Gwen Verdon as Roxie brought her

---

[27] Gene Foote, telephone interview by the author, June 6, 2010.
[28] Chris Chase, "Fosse, from Tony to Oscar to Emmy?," *New York Times*, April 29, 1973.

powerful physical attack to the runs and leaps that carried her across the stage. Performers could be substituted without any change to the choreography. For instance, in the 2013 Broadway revival of *Pippin*, Patina Miller was a female Leading Player. Her "Manson Trio" partners were two men, but they could just as easily have been two women. Similarly, when "Nowadays/Hot Honey Rag" from *Chicago*, originally a duo number for two women, was performed at a fundraiser by two men, it became a dashing Fred Astaire–Gene Kelly–style showstopper—all without changing a step.[29]

The sense of sexual fluidity and matter-of-fact same-gendered groupings in Fosse's choreography is as casual as Margo's "Bring him along" remark. Moreover, his insistence that dancers could perform choreography regardless of gender identity brought a unique sexual *frisson* to his shows. These themes continue to resonate in striking new ways. A 2023 Broadway revival of *Dancin'* featured gender non-binary Kolton Krouse, dancing's Ann Reinking's iconic "Trumpet Solo" during the ensemble number "Sing Sing Sing," matching the original interpreter's every slashing kick and elongated extension. And in this case, they wore heels while doing so. The relentlessly heterosexual Fosse welcomed LGBTQ+ audiences by offering them space to see themselves in his sexually charged musicals. By celebrating the individual body, musical theatre's great sensualist continues to expand the expression of sexuality and desire.

Today, when musical theatre characters display greater diversity in gender and sexual identity expression than ever, choreography is sometimes only one marker of that expression. In *Kimberly Akimbo* (2022) the queer members of a high school show choir perform choreographer Danny Mefford's gangly dances with the same awkward energy as the straight kids. *& Juliet* (2022), a new jukebox reimagining of *Romeo and Juliet*, features a prominent non-binary character who dances Jennifer Weber's dense, hip-hop derived choreography no differently than the rest of the cast, which includes several other queer and gender non-conforming performers. In the musical re-envisioning of the classic film comedy *Some Like it Hot* (2022), Jerry and Joe, two dancer-musicians, disguise themselves and join an all-girl band in order to escape a mob hit. But one of them experiences a sexual identity reawakening when dressed as a female. Director-choreographer Casey Nicholaw creates rough, hard-edged tap routines for the two men, but when Jerry finds that he's happier as Daphne, Nicholaw cannily showcases the character in movement that conveys both Daphne's femininity and Jerry's masculinity. Nicholaw and the gender non-binary J. Harrison Ghee as Joe/Daphne create an all-inclusive dance vocabulary that runs from athletic to dainty, muscular to delicate. Choreographic representation of gender and sexuality continues to evolve to match the expansion of visibility in culture and society.

Challenging the heterosexual, male/female binary in Broadway choreography didn't just start in recent years. There has always been at least some space for diverse bodies and sexualities. De Mille, Robbins, and Field challenged norms of representation within the strict boundaries of the eras in which they worked. An iconoclast like Fosse pushed these efforts

---

29 "Nowadays/Hot Honey Rag" was performed By Tony Yazbeck and Michael Berresse at the 2014 Broadway Backwards fundraiser for Broadway Cares/Equity Fights AIDS; see "Tony Yazbeck, Michael Berresse—Chicago's 'Nowadays/Hot Honey Rag' 2014 Broadway Backwards," uploaded by Broadway Cares/Equity Fights AIDS, December 3, 2014, YouTube video, 6:45, https://www.youtube.com/watch?v=Z1OYgF-kFfg.

further in ways both stimulating and subversive. Their efforts may look timid by twenty-first-century standards, but they signify incremental, and important, steps on the road to a more expansive representation of bodies and sexualities in Broadway dance, both today and in the future.

Bibliography

Bell, Arthur. "Homosexuality: A Gay Activist Looks at Broadway." *Playbill*, January 1973.

"Carousel Ballet—Original Broadway Cast, with Orchestra Added." Uploaded by Broadway Classics, January 26, 2016. YouTube video, 12:36. https://www.youtube.com/watch?v—P7oatLydC0.

Chase, Chris. "Fosse, from Tony to Oscar to Emmy?" *New York Times*, April 29, 1973.

Clum, John M. *Something for the Boys: Musical Theater and Gay Culture*. New York: St. Martin's Press, 1999.

Comden, Betty, and Adolph Green. *Applause*. Music by Charles Strouse. Lyrics by Lee Adams. New York: Random House, 1971.

De Mille, Agnes. Clipping file. Jerome Robbins Dance Division, New York Public Library for the Performing Arts, New York Public Library.

De Mille, Agnes. *Dance to the Piper*. New York: New York Review Books Classics, 2015.

Easton, Carol. *No Intermissions: The Life of Agnes de Mille*. Boston: Little, Brown, 1996.

"Fan Fare: Jerome Robbins' Broadway—Part 2." Uploaded by Stage17.tv, February 5, 2015. YouTube video, 9:36. https://www.youtube.com/watch?v=Q-UM14-IDh0.

Gardner, Kara Ann. *Agnes de Mille: Telling Stories in Broadway Dance*. New York: Oxford University Press, 2016.

Jowitt, Deborah. *Jerome Robbins: His Life, His Theater, His Dance*. New York: Simon and Schuster, 2004.

Kaiser, Charles. *The Gay Metropolis: The Landmark History of Gay Life in America*. New York: Grove Press, 2019.

Pugh, Megan. *America Dancing: From the Cakewalk to the Moonwalk*. New Haven, CT: Yale University Press, 2015.

Sagolla, Lisa Jo. *The Girl Who Fell Down: A Biography of Joan McCracken*. Boston: Northeastern University Press, 2003.

Scott, Jay. "Fosse's Legacy Nears Perfection." *Globe and Mail*, September 25, 1987.

Shakespeare, William, and Arthur Laurents. *Romeo and Juliet/West Side Story*. Music by Leonard Bernstein. Lyrics by Stephen Sondheim. New York: Dell, 1965.

Staggs, Sam. *All about "All about Eve": The Complete Behind-the-Scenes Story of the Bitchiest Film Ever Made*. New York: St. Martin's Press, 2000.

"Tony Yazbeck, Michael Berresse—Chicago's 'Nowadays/Hot Honey Rag' 2014 Broadway Backwards." Uploaded by Broadway Cares/Equity Fights AIDS, December 3, 2014. YouTube video, 6:45. https://www.youtube.com/watch?v=Z1OYgF-kFfg.

Vail, Amanda. *Somewhere: The Life of Jerome Robbins*. New York: Broadway Books, 2006.

Wilk, Max. *OK! The Story of Oklahoma!* New York: Grove Press, 1993.

9 Asian Faces, American Bodies: Reading Asian/American Movement on the Broadway Stage

KIM VARHOLA

In 2002, a highly acclaimed Japanese production of Stephen Sondheim and John Weidman's musical *Pacific Overtures* was invited from Tokyo to appear at both Lincoln Center in New York City and the Kennedy Center in Washington, DC. Two years later, the Roundabout Theatre Company revived the production on Broadway, inviting the original Japanese director-choreographer, Amon Miyamoto, to pilot the show, only this time with an Asian American cast instead of Miyamoto's Japanese team. For the Roundabout production, Miyamoto created a near replica of his Japanese production, leading critics to quickly make comparisons. Where the Lincoln Center and Kennedy Center productions overwhelmingly won praise, the Roundabout production was met with less enthusiasm; and yet, apart from the cast, very little had changed. Critical response to the two casts was disparate: American reviewers found the Japanese cast "fiercely funny," "particularly moving," and "committed to the task of adding vibrant levels of feeling" to the show, but found the Asian American cast "more nimble than impressive," with "the aura of a crisis of confidence."[1] The critics' preference for the (Asian) Japanese cast over the Asian American cast in otherwise identical productions suggests that artists of Asian heritage answer to specific standards in the West: the quality of their performance in an Asian story may be measured by how "Asian" their performance is. But what does it mean to perform "Asian," and how is it applicable to an *Asian American* cast reclaiming an *Asian American* musical for the Broadway stage?

These critical responses are examples of a broader phenomenon that bring to the surface the often subliminal expectations that audiences (and critics) place on Asian American bodies in American musical theatre. This chapter digs into these expectations of Asianness, examining how Asianness is embodied and authenticated within the choreography of Asian American Broadway musicals. By pointing to critical reviews and considering firsthand accounts from Broadway performers who identify as Asian American, the chapter looks at choreography and movement from different productions of *Flower Drum Song* and *Pacific Overtures* in an attempt to define what Asian American movement looks like, or what it is expected to look like, in a Western space. The chapter considers a query posited by pioneering Asian American scholar David Palumbo-Liu: "How does the history of Asian

---

[1] Charles Isherwood, "Pacific Overtures," *Variety*, July 14, 2002; Peter Marks, "Sondheim, Gaining Much in Translation," *Washington Post*, September 5, 2002; Clive Barnes, "Unspecific 'Overtures' — Japanese Staging Misfires in Latest Sondheim Revival," *New York Post*, December 3, 2004; Ben Brantley, "Repatriating the Japanese Sondheim," *New York Times*, December 3, 2004.

America demonstrate the centrality of Asia in the imagination of modern America?"[2] His question suggests that in the West, it is the "Asian" that is assumed, and therefore expected, of the "Asian American" within American culture. Taking into consideration how the concept of "moving Asian" on the Broadway stage is a construct of the West, this chapter invites a reconsideration of the examined choreography as neither "Asian" nor "American," but culturally hybridized.

To begin, it is important to address the terminology used to mark cultural identity in this chapter in order to understand the specific applications implied in terms like "Asian" and "Asian American." For instance, the term "Asian" has commonly been adopted to include a body or story attached to Asian heritage, and it continues to be ubiquitously used in the United States to explain this hereditary status. But its use when discussing American musicals and Asian American musical artists is not entirely accurate, and can be limiting. The term "Asian American," which defines US American nationals of Asian heritage, along with the specific hybrid cultural space they occupy, is also insufficient for the whole of artists and musicals from the Asian diaspora; artists like Miyamoto, for example, do not fall into this particular category. In his book *Asian/American: Historical Crossings of a Racial Frontier*, Palumbo-Liu asserts another term, "Asian/American," whereby the slash (or solidus) represents at once a "choice between two terms, their simultaneous and equal status, and an element of indecidability."[3] Thus, for the purposes of this essay, I regularly use Palumbo-Liu's "Asian/American" as a singularly inclusive term to suggest all Broadway artists and Broadway musicals that exist along the Asian diasporic spectrum as well as the mutability of Asian, American, and Asian American identity in Western spaces.

Despite an extremely limited canon of Asian/American Broadway musicals from which to choose, *Flower Drum Song* and *Pacific Overtures* do provide solid case studies for comprehensive investigation. Not only do both shows feature stories comprising Asian/American characters, but they both overtly contain modes of assumed Asian/American authenticity in their movement.[4] Both are also critical to the history of Asian/American musical theatre. With *Flower Drum Song*, Rodgers and Hammerstein's original 1958 production holds historical merit for being the first Broadway musical set inside Asian America, and for striving to cast Asian/American actors in a time when racist practices like yellowface were still common in American media. The 1961 film version (based largely on the Broadway original) and the 2002 Broadway revival offer disparate tactics for presenting Asian/Americanness through choreography. The film, starring Hollywood darling Nancy Kwan, resists Asian tropes throughout most of the dance numbers. But the Broadway revival embraces these tropes for the purposes of social commentary. For *Pacific Overtures*, the chapter considers both the original 1976 Broadway production and the 2004 Broadway revival. Directed by Harold Prince, the 1976 production infused the Japanese dramatic conventions of kabuki theatre into its overall artistic construction. Miyamoto's 2004 vision,

---

[2]David Palumbo-Liu, *Asian/American: Historical Crossings of a Racial Frontier* (Stanford, CA: Stanford University Press, 1999), 1–2.
[3]Palumbo-Liu, 1.
[4]*Pacific Overtures* does include the American figure Commodore Matthew C. Perry as well as several nameless American and European characters, but they are all intended to be played by the Asian/American members of the company.

by contrast, dispensed with kabuki traditions of movement, opting instead for a more general movement vocabulary not uncommon to American musical stages. Both *Flower Drum Song* and *Pacific Overtures* provide cases for reading how Asianness is expected, presented, and understood via Asian/American bodies on Broadway.

As a former practitioner, I derive my perspective on "moving Asian" from a lived experience of performing in Asian/American Broadway musical spaces, and the unique pressures that go along with it. As a cast member in both the 2002 production of *Flower Drum Song* and the 2004 production of *Pacific Overtures*, I was granted access to the power dynamics between white creatives and Asian/American actors and insight into the power white critics had on our success. I was usually willing to perform whatever mode of "Asianness" was asked of me, because doing so could make the show "better." Asian/American identity in Broadway spaces is a complex balancing act that deserves an examination of the expectations historically placed on our community.

Assimilating the Asian/American Body: *Flower Drum Song* (1958)

What mid-century Chinese American artists were doing in these San Francisco nightclubs was trying to appeal to a white audience, and that meant playing on Asian stereotypes that the white audiences would expect. So, when we started building the nightclub numbers for *Flower Drum Song*, we said, "we're going to really exaggerate this, make this movement as weird as possible." And in doing so, we were in actuality placing the joke on them.

—Marc Oka, dance captain and assistant choreographer, 2002
Broadway revival of *Flower Drum Song*

By the time that *Flower Drum Song* premiered in 1958, mid-twentieth century New York audiences had already seen two Broadway hits by the pioneering team of Richard Rodgers and Oscar Hammerstein II set in Asian locales: *South Pacific* (1949) and *The King and I* (1951). In 1957, the duo teamed up with playwright Joseph Fields, who was optioning the rights to create a show based on a novel by Chinese American writer C. Y. Lee. Set in San Francisco's Chinatown, *Flower Drum Song* tells the story of Chinese immigrant Mei Li, a picture bride brought over by a traditional Chinese American matron to marry her Americanized son, nightclub owner Sammy Fong. Sammy carries a torch for his club's starring act, the sexy chanteuse Linda Low, and thus passes Mei Li on to a Chinatown elder, Master Wang, as a match for his eldest son, Wang Ta. Generational conflict and Old World/New World culture clash humorously ensue within the Chinatown community in this lighthearted musical romance set firmly within the spirit of Broadway's Golden Age.

Lee's story was based on the people and places found in Chinese America during the first half of the twentieth century. In the years leading up to and including World War II, San Francisco's Chinatown was an intersection of modern energy and traditional values, of the old and the new, and acts of assimilation into American culture materialized in places like the many local nightclubs intent on attracting white audiences with disposable income. San Francisco establishments such as the Forbidden City, Kubla Khan, and the Chinese Sky Room modeled themselves after popular American supper clubs of the day, and were part of the Chop Suey Circuit, a larger national network of nightclubs featuring Chinese American talent. Chinese American acts billed under such titles as the "Chinese Fred Astaire" or the "Chinese Sophie Tucker" dressed in Western formal wear and performed in popular styles, catering to a white clientele that enjoyed the novelty of Asian faces delivering American mannerisms. As Asian American scholar SanSan Kwan states, the result was a successful meeting of the "exotic and accessible."[5] San Francisco's Forbidden City served as inspiration for C. Y. Lee's novel, and the Broadway show set much of the nightclub action inside the fictitious club the Celestial Gardens.

Although *Flower Drum Song* is definitively set within a US city's Asian American community, its 1958 Broadway script (along with its 1961 film version) takes Asian/ Americanness and exaggerates it in binary terms. The older characters represent the Asian "Old World" in their speech and everyday mannerisms; although they don't speak in broken English, their English dialogue is awkwardly stilted to mimic Chinese grammar and, as such, makes them sound "Oriental."[6] By contrast, the younger characters of the American "New World" use a speech pattern that is packed with mid-twentieth-century American slang. Historically, a Western perspective of Asian/Americans as Other has led to a host of distorted, caricatured gestures—the bow, the hands in prayer position, the covering of the mouth with the open palm—to indicate the Asian in Western storytelling. These gestures often appear in scenes involving the elder characters as well as Mei Li and her father, who have just arrived from China. But for the younger players, who perform much of the choreography, Oriental tropes are absent from gesture and dance vocabulary.

Footage from the original Broadway production of *Flower Drum Song* is difficult to locate, but an extended promo featuring several numbers did appear on the *Ed Sullivan Show* on December 14, 1958, and suggests that the 1961 film also preserved the original production's intention to present choreography that resisted stereotyped Oriental posturing. The 1958 stage production was directed by Gene Kelly (in his Broadway directorial debut) and choreographed by Carol Haney, and the 1961 film was choreographed by famed Hollywood dance director Hermes Pan. Kelly, Haney, and Pan reject Oriental caricature in the dance numbers and opt instead for a vocabulary of Western, jazz dance and a musical theatre aesthetic reminiscent of some of their more famous works. For instance, in the dance break of the song "Sunday," we see the same rhythmically swung grapevines and traveling shuffle steps that Kelly utilized in the iconic "Singin' in the Rain" (1952). A dance trio sporting bowler hats is modeled after Haney and her appearance in *The Pajama Game*'s "Steam Heat" (1954). And the extensive dance number "Grant Avenue" in the 1961 film, with its jazz runs, slides, and pirouettes, harks back to Pan's choreography for "Tom, Dick or Harry" from the film *Kiss Me Kate* (1953).

The group number "Chop Suey" likewise avoids Oriental posturing, and instead features a variety of popular Western social dances, from do-si-do, to Charleston, to swing. But while the movement maintains a definitive all-American quality, the unfortunate lyrics of the song remind us that Asians are still "foreigners." Chop suey, a Chinese American dish that

---

[5]SanSan Kwan, "Performing a Geography of Asian America: The Chop Suey Circuit." *TDR: The Drama Review* 55, no. 1 (2011): 121.
[6]For further reading on the designation of "Oriental" and its use when describing Asian cultures in the West, see Edward W. Said, *Orientalism* (New York: Pantheon Books, 1978).

combines a variety of vegetables, meats, and other ingredients, serves here as a metaphor for America, and the oddly random list of "American" items in the lyrics (hula hoops, Maidenform bra, Perry Como, Wichita) juxtaposed against a repetitive melody makes the song come off as an oversimplified nursery rhyme.[7] The "Chop Suey" scene is Wang Ta's graduation celebration, yet it's hard to imagine this same sort of sophomoric chorus being sung by white American adult characters at a grown-up dinner party. However, the over-simplistic lyrics followed by standard American social dancing do signify the creative team's attempt to integrate "East" with "West" in Broadway's first bona fide musical about Asian America.

David Henry Hwang's Revisionist Revival: *Flower Drum Song* (2002)

As a Rodgers and Hammerstein product that didn't uncomfortably venture outside mid-twentieth century Western expectations of Asianness, the 1958 production was embraced by Broadway audiences, running for a total of six hundred performances in New York, followed by a national tour. Then the show sat in the Rodgers and Hammerstein vaults for the next four decades; despite initial success, *Flower Drum Song* quickly lost its appeal. Viewed as an offensive, stereotyped expression of Asian America, and considered by musical theatre scholars as second-rate Rodgers and Hammerstein material, *Flower Drum Song* didn't seem destined for a life beyond its initial offering. But in the mid-1990s, Tony Award–winning playwright David Henry Hwang, who was intent on reclaiming the piece for the Asian/American community, proposed a reexamination of the show. While keeping some basic plot points intact, Hwang wrote an entirely new script around a rearranged order of the original songs, and in the fall of 2002, a new-and-improved *Flower Drum Song* opened on Broadway at the Virginia Theatre.

The revised script still finds Chinese immigrant Mei Li landing in San Francisco's Chinatown, only this time she is a political refugee running from events that will lead to the Cultural Revolution. Master Wang owns a Chinatown theatre that offers traditional (and unpopular) Chinese opera fare, and he begrudgingly allows his son, Wang Ta, to use the theatre once a week as a nightclub. Ta finds himself romantically torn between Mei Li and his nightclub's starring act, the Americanized playgirl Linda Low. Ta's nightclub show catches the eye of savvy theatrical agent Madame Liang, and she pushes Master Wang to permanently turn his run-down theatre into a Western-style nightclub that caters to white audiences. "Club Chop Suey" opens to surprising success, and Master Wang, caught up in the popular energy and booming box office receipts, takes center stage as the club's MC, adopting the name Sammy Fong.

Unlike the 1958 text, which flipped back and forth between a formalized mode of awkwardly stereotyped speech for the elders and an overabundance of silly slang for the youth, Hwang's script employed natural American English speech patterns for all, thus removing Asianness from the dialogue. The Asianness indicators that were removed from the dialogue, however, were in turn transferred into the choreography, and to excessive effect. SanSan Kwan addresses the act of "playing Oriental" when Chinese American

---

[7]Richard Rodgers and Oscar Hammerstein II, *Flower Drum Song* (New York: Williamson Music, 1958).

Image 9.1 Pat Suzuki and dancers in the stage production of *Flower Drum Song* (1958). Photo by Friedman-Abeles (Firm). Billy Rose Theatre Division, The New York Public Library Digital Collections.

nightclub artists would play to Western expectations by performing dances like the "Fan Dance," the "Chinese Sleeve Dance," and the "Coolie Dance."[8] The items used in these dances—the fan, the long sleeves extending beyond the hands, the conical hat—are signifiers not only of Chinese culture, but of Asian culture, and the presence of these signifiers in Western spaces suggests Asianness. So when an Asian signifier such as a conical "coolie hat" is added to a dance number, the dance number then registers as Asian, regardless of the actual movement.

Director-choreographer Robert Longbottom, along with associate choreographer Darlene Wilson and assistant choreographer Marc Oka, incorporated fans, Chinese sleeves (also known as "water sleeves") and coolie hats into several nightclub numbers, with the explicit purpose of using the items to heighten the effect of Asianness. The choreography was then distorted to further amplify a sense of foreignness that could be read as more "exotic" or "Oriental." Oka explains, "Because we were making the choice to use stereotyped movement, since that's what was historically done in these nightclubs, as an Asian American I felt I could be generous with exaggerating these moments. That was built into the point of our story."[9] The conscientious choice to incorporate exaggerated movement that registered

[8]Kwan, "Performing a Geography of Asian America," 122.
[9]Marc Oka, pers. comm., January 2022.

as "Oriental" placed the power to "play Oriental" directly in the hands of the Asian/American performers. This movement was then coupled with Asian-signified items; thus, the use of fans in the number "Fan Tan Fannie," water sleeves in the opening sequence "Warrior Dance," and coolie hats along with water sleeves in "I Enjoy Being a Girl" render these moments as a fan dance, a Chinese sleeve dance, and a coolie dance, respectively.

The "Fan Tan Fannie" number is one of the highlights of act 1, serving as the feature floor show number to open Ta's new nightclub, Club Chop Suey. In the 1961 film version, "Fan Tan Fannie" is a nightclub number performed by Linda and the ladies' ensemble. For the film, Hollywood starlet Nancy Kwan adorably struts across the dance floor, beveling now and then while fluttering a modest little fan, and flirting with Sammy as he watches from the side. But the 2002 Broadway version takes the number and turns it on its head. The cutesy flirtations of Kwan and her ladies are replaced by a tough, seductive Linda, played to fearless effect by Sandra Allen. Outfitted in a red-and-black bustier, crisscross leggings, and a skeletal coolie hat, this Linda takes one expected stereotype of the Asian female, a playfully adorable "China doll," and trades her in for the other expected stereotype, the "dragon lady," and she does so to the extreme. She carries two red fans, each longer than her forearm, made of a hard plastic that emits a loud whacking noise when she throws them open. Linda sings the first verse of the number with a quiet, confident purr. She utilizes a standard, era-appropriate jazz sound when she sings, but in the middle of the verse, she punctuates the lyric, "bye bye!" with a biting nasal quality, altering the pronunciation such that it sounds like "bay-ee bay-ee!" As she sings, she displays her fans, sometimes open, sometimes closed, moving them up and down slowly and deliberately. At the end of the verse, Linda is joined by two male dancers in red-and-black double-breasted suits and fedoras, and the trio goes into a dance break.

The "Fan Tan Fannie" dance trio aggressively begins the dance break, matching jumps, pelvic bumps, and contractions with the whacking sound of fans, which they throw open to the beat. The fans seem to operate like weapons, and one fears that, at any point, a fan could shoot across the stage without warning. The trio is eventually joined by the entire dancing ensemble, who continue to punctuate deliberate body isolations and back arches with the whacking open of fans. The orchestrated dance arrangement has a driving, suspenseful beat that sounds inspired by the likes of 1960s TV spy shows such as *Secret Agent Man*. The dancing ensemble's movement is both lithe and unbalanced as they alternate between fully extended, open-arm positions and extreme, bent-over stances where they look as though they may fall over.

A fan dance in traditional Chinese performance often connotes delicacy, beauty, and balance, but its excessive, superfluous use within Western expressions of Asian performance has turned the fan dance into a cliché.[10] It has come to be expected when Asianness is performed in America, and Chinese American artists from the Chop Suey Circuit found it necessary to oblige their white clientele with the dance. The revival "Fan Tan Fannie" also

---

[10]See "Chinese Fan Dance," Chinese Cultural Dances, CCCH9051 Group 31, Hong Kong University Online Learning, accessed December 10, 2022, https://learning.hku.hk/ccch9051/group-31/items/show/7. Practically every American Broadway musical to date set within communities of East Asian heritage contains a dance number where fans play a central role: *The King and I* (1951), *Flower Drum Song* (1958), *Pacific Overtures* (1976), *Shogun: The Musical* (1990), and *Allegiance* (2015).

Image 9.2 *Flower Drum Song* (2002 revival). Photo by Joan Marcus.

obliges the audience by giving it the expected fan dance. But this fan dance is forceful, aggressive, unsteady, and dangerous.

In addition to the many elaborate nightclub numbers, the 2002 revival also employed authentic movement from the Chinese opera tradition by bringing in specialist Jamie Guan to teach and advise on technique. Guan created choreography based on Chinese opera sequences and taught several actors how to properly dance with water sleeves, which are the elongated sleeves used by female characters. In the show's opening scene, the "Warrior Dance," Master Wang and his son, Ta, are performing a traditional Chinese opera dance, with Master Wang playing the male warrior, and Ta playing the "girl." Ta's costume is an elaborate headdress and robe, with long sleeves that reach to the ground. He takes on a series of poses, flipping the sleeves, sometimes right over left, sometimes left over right. He flicks the sleeves up in the air, then shuffles around in a circle, the sleeves trailing behind in a wavelike manner.

The use of water sleeves in the "Warrior Dance" sequence is not the stereotypical Chinese sleeve dance to which SanSan Kwan refers, given that the "Warrior Dance" is grounded in authentic Chinese movement. The water sleeves' presence in the show as an expression of Chinese heritage symbolizes how cultural traditions are passed along in order to connect generations, despite the passage of time or changes in geographic location. Both the 1958 and 2002 productions of *Flower Drum Song* aimed to present San Francisco's Chinatown as just like any other American community, albeit one that still had ties to the "old country." The traditional values of Master Wang are set against Ta's Americanization, and the conflict is addressed through dance: the Chinese opera versus the nightclub numbers. But despite Ta's American ambitions he is still tied to his Chinese roots. Thus is the Asian American condition, and David Henry Hwang's rewrite specifically addresses this internal struggle through Ta's character. Ta negotiates the challenges of his Asian American identity through dance, taking the traditional water sleeves vocabulary and later applying it to the choreography of a nightclub number. But when Ta takes the water sleeves and places them in the number "I Enjoy Being a Girl," their use as an Asian signifier turns the moment into a Chinese sleeve dance.

"I Enjoy Being a Girl" is the most recognizable tune from the *Flower Drum Song* score, and the original 1958 version was belted with loads of Broadway brass by the incomparable Pat Suzuki. It was a solo moment, a consummate "I Am" song for the Linda Low character. But the song as an ode to the joys of simplified maidenhood has received much criticism over the years for its overtly antifeminist messaging, and thus posed a challenge for the 2002 revival. The team's solution was to expand it with dance and make it into a floor show number. Chinese opera, theatrical jazz dance, and striptease are all utilized to create a moment that comments on Asian/American identity.

In the 2002 revival, Linda begins "I Enjoy Being a Girl" inside her dressing room as she prepares for the show. By verse's end, Linda is dressed in a traditional Chinese opera costume and heads out to the stage for her entrance. We then see Ta, acting as MC, onstage about to introduce Linda and her dancers. Ta is flanked by two men tugging on rickshaws, heads enthusiastically bobbing left and right. They sport coolie hats and suits infused with Chinese elements, and are soon joined by several others wearing the same. Linda takes center stage, moving her water sleeves in the same manner that Ta did when we saw him rehearsing Chinese opera choreography with his father; her movement is supported by orchestral underscoring that uses the "Oriental riff," a stereotyped open-fourth chord progression that is heard throughout Western media to connote Asianness. The underscoring then suddenly changes to a horn-infused, swinging, bump-and-grind rhythm, and Linda in turn does an about-face with her movement, exposing legs and heels from beneath the Chinese skirt. This back-and-forth between Chinese opera and burlesque continues until Linda begins singing again. As she starts a second refrain, the coolie dancers help Linda systematically strip off her Chinese garb, revealing a bedazzled white bikini underneath. The group then launches into a dance break infused with coolie dance elements.

Unlike the fan dance and the Chinese sleeve dance, which have roots in actual Chinese tradition, the coolie dance is a product of caricature, an act that Kwan estimates to be a "self-parodying Western style of dance where the dancers wear coolie hats."[11] One of the most famous examples of the coolie dance comes from the ballet world, distinctly expressed in *The Nutcracker*'s Chinese Dance. Although the specific dance steps of the Chinese Dance change with every choreographer's vision, certain physical postures persist, most notably the upward pointing of two index fingers held more than a shoulder width apart. The exact origin of the two index fingers pointing up remains unknown, but the gesture has come to symbolize Chineseness and Asianness in Western dance expressions, despite its lack of authentic Chinese extraction.[12] In the dance break of "I Enjoy Being a Girl," Linda and the coolie dancers use the pointing index finger position excessively, holding the pose with the upper body while employing Western theatrical steps like arabesque jumps with the lower

---

[11]Kwan, "Performing a Geography of Asian America," 123.
[12]Doug Fullington and Phil Chan, "Choreography," *Final Bow for Yellowface* (website), accessed January 20, 2022, https://www.yellowface.org/nutchoreography; Jennifer Fisher, "'Yellowface' in 'The Nutcracker' Isn't a Benign Ballet Tradition, It's Racist Stereotyping," *Los Angeles Times*, December 12, 2018.

body. But unlike *The Nutcracker*'s Chinese Dance, which similarly merges the finger points with Western dance vocabulary, "I Enjoy Being a Girl" has a self-reflexive humor, with wide cheesy grins emanating from the dancers as they knowingly move in a self-parodying fashion. The self-reflexive commentary continues into the latter portion of the dance break, when the male dancers leave and are replaced by female dancers in white bikinis. The coolie dance, with its self-referential wink, gives way to a grandiose burlesque bump-and-grind finish.

The movement in Ta's floor show numbers draws its inspiration from the extravagant material seen in movie musicals of the mid-twentieth century. Longbottom and Wilson's choreography references movement found in the likes of "Diamonds Are a Girl's Best Friend" from the movie *Gentlemen Prefer Blondes* (1953), "Heat Wave" from *There's No Business Like Show Business* (1954), and "I Don't Care" from *The I Don't Care Girl* (1953). "Unlike other American communities who have Broadway movement that they are culturally connected to—tap and the African American community, tango and salsa and the Latinx community—our community isn't culturally connected to any Broadway dance vocabulary," says cast member Robert Tatad. "So Bobby and Darlene looked to some of the silhouettes of Jack Cole, with the hinges and angles."[13] Keeping in mind Western expectations of Asian/American bodies, Longbottom and Wilson created a vocabulary of physicalized foreignness built on angular shapes, punctuated motions, and imbalance. This movement, however, was not meant to represent Asian/American identity; it was meant to comment on it. The exaggerated movements, coupled with the Asian signifiers, were used purposefully to express how awkward Western stereotypes of otherness have been used to define Asian/Americans in Western spaces. The choreography is American, but the signifiers are Asian. The result is a hybridized combination of both.

Pacific Overtures: Asian/American Integration, Intercultural Movement

> The original *Pacific Overtures* creative team was borrowing from Japanese theatre forms in order to tell what they thought was a musical from a Japanese point of view.
> —Francis Jue, Broadway actor and American director-choreographer

The Asian/American hybridization that began with *Flower Drum Song* evolved further with *Pacific Overtures*, as another American creative team took unorthodox steps toward a cultural integration of performance forms. And just as the 2002 Broadway revival of *Flower Drum Song* prompts a review of the original 1958 production's use of movement, so too does the 2004 Broadway revival of *Pacific Overtures* prompt a reassessment of the original 1976 production's creative intent and subsequent response. In 1976, the all-white American creative team of Sondheim, Weidman, and Prince looked to the Japanese theatrical tradition

---

[13]Robert Tatad, pers. comm., January 2022. For more on Jack Cole's dance background and style, including his study of the East Indian classical dance Bharata Natyam, see Constance Valis Hill, "From Bharata Natyam to Bop: Jack Cole's 'Modern' Jazz Dance," *Dance Research Journal* 33, no. 2 (2001): 29–39; Bob Boross, "The Jack Cole Notebooks," *Dance Chronicle* 27, no. 3 (2004): 409–13.

of kabuki for aesthetic inspiration. Conversely, the 2004 Broadway revival production, with its Japanese director-choreographer, rejected the kabuki aesthetic entirely; as associate choreographer Darren Lee recalls, "I think Amon Miyamoto's approach with the 2004 Broadway revival of *Pacific Overtures* was, 'I have an American cast. And this is an American musical.'"[14] Through an examination of the choreography, we see how both productions defy Western expectations of being either Asian or American, and instead create an overall integrated aesthetic of both.

In an effort to better illuminate how Asian/Americanness is hybridized in *Pacific Overtures* through movement, it is first useful to explain the framework of this musical, which remains one of Sondheim's lesser-studied pieces. *Pacific Overtures* is a story about the westernization of modern Japan as told from the perspective of its Japanese characters, exploring the complexities of an isolated nation's collective existential crisis with the arrival of forced American diplomacy. The narrative begins with the landing of an American expedition led by Commodore Matthew C. Perry off the coast of Japan in 1853, and extends into the present day. The show is a series of episodic scenes of Japanese citizens, some historical, some inconsequentially nameless, reacting to (and resisting as best they can) the Americans' entrée. Despite an omniscient narrator character known as the Reciter, the show lacks a traditional protagonist; Japan itself serves as the main character, with the show taking on an empathetic perspective of the country at the hands of Western cultural imperialism.

Pacific Overtures (1976)

Librettist John Weidman initially conceived *Pacific Overtures* as a political play, but director Hal Prince believed the piece needed more grandeur, an element that music could easily provide. Prince also thought that adding the theatrical conventions of kabuki, a dramatic form largely unknown in the United States, would help center the show's proposed Japanese perspective. Kabuki had been introduced to New York audiences by way of an international touring company from Tokyo, which presented key works from the tradition at New York City Center in 1960. A hallmark of traditional Japanese dramatic expression that traces its roots to the sixteenth century, kabuki has many similarities to what Western audiences understand and expect from musical theatre: the art form brings together song, dance, and drama into a cohesive performance, and actors must be trained in the art of all three. But while many Broadway musical stories are built on American concepts of dramatic realism, the kabuki aesthetic is presentational. In kabuki, a company of entirely male actors don elaborate makeup design, colorful costumes, and grand wigs, performing dynamic physical gestures on a *hanamichi*, or runway that extends out into the audience. Additionally, where American musical theatre advances the emotional development of character by integrating the internal and the external through text, song, and dance, kabuki theatre places importance on the external, whereby, "every aspect of performance strives for physical beauty."[15] Kabuki movement presents a visual ideal through the precise gestures of the kabuki performer. And

---

[14]Darren Lee, pers. comm., January 2022.
[15]Paul Griffith and Okada Mariko, "Nihonbuyo: Classical Dance," in *A History of Japanese Theatre*, ed. Jonah Salz (Cambridge: Cambridge University Press, 2016), 146.

as Japanese traditional dance scholar and ethnomusicologist Tomie Hahn further explains, "Though dance movements vary according to which genre they stem from, choreography is tied to narrative, however abstract."[16]

Japanese scholar Kawatake Toshio traveled with the 1960 touring company, and in his reflections of the experience at New York City Center, he makes special note of the differences between Western expectations of theatrical performance and the principles of kabuki, citing that "Western theatre gives priority to dramatic complication and conflict," which contrasts with Japanese forms like kabuki, whereby "the dramatic element travels incognito, as it were, hidden below the surface of the stage's colorful opulence."[17] In an effort to prepare the Broadway audience, the 1976 *Pacific Overtures* playbill included an extensive set of notes about the dramatic conventions of kabuki. This artistically bold new musical was about to defy American theatrical expectation by presenting a piece that, in every aspect of its production and performance, "borrows liberally from the techniques of the Japanese kabuki theater."[18]

The 1976 creative team attempted to construct a libretto and score that reflected the "presentational" notion of kabuki theatre rather than the American conventions of dramatic realism and linear storylines. Choreographer Patricia Birch, with the help of kabuki consultant and cast member Haruki Fujimoto, connected kabuki steps with Weidman's text and Sondheim's songs, taking the Japanese dance approach of "choreography is tied to narrative, however abstract" and applying it literally to the show's second number, "There Is No Other Way." With the arrival of the Americans, minor samurai Kayama Yosaemon is tasked with the impossible mission of telling the Americans to leave. Kayama, along with his wife, Tamate, knows full well that his assignment is a suicide mission; he prepares for the meeting nonetheless. Although "There Is No Other Way" is thematically Kayama and Tamate's song, neither of them sing any of it. The number instead separates the internal from the external: two ensemble singers vocalize the character narrative through song while Kayama and Tamate go through the physical motions of preparation.

The 1976 production used male actors for the female roles, a kabuki tradition known as *onnagata*, with Korean American actor Soon Teck Oh delivering the role of Tamate. Using male bodies to present the visual ideal of the feminine form in kabuki dance places even more emphasis on the external, and *onnagata* are thus reliant on choreographed gesture to communicate character emotion. Tamate's choreography matches literal movement to lyric. While the two ensemble singers sing the line "the word falls, the heart cries, the heart knows, the words disguise," Tamate dances to each short phrase by lowering both hands from her mouth toward the ground, covering her heart with both hands, covering her heart again with one hand while the other hand pushes forward with a raised index finger, and covering her

---

[16]Tomie Hahn, *Sensational Knowledge: Embodying Culture through Japanese Dance* (Middletown, CT: Wesleyan University Press, 2007), 46–7.

[17]Kawatake Toshio, *Kabuki: Baroque Fusion of the Arts*, trans. Frank and Jean Connell Hoff (Tokyo: International House of Japan, 2003), 13. The touring company was led by a young theatre producer and kabuki enthusiast named Nagayama Takeomi. Nagayama would later become chairman of the Shochiku Company, one of Japan's leading film production companies.

[18]"Pacific Overtures," Playbill: Broadway Database, accessed January 12, 2022, https://playbill.com/production/pacific-overtures-winter-garden-theatre-vault-0000011540.

mouth with her hand.[19] Tamate's movements are slow, deliberate, and delicate, and the face avoids emotional expression. As Tamate dances, Kayama changes out of his simple kimono into samurai uniform. He too lacks emotional expression, although we catch him glance at Tamate every now and then. The couple's outward emotional restraint actually renders the number more heartbreaking. In American musicals, characters almost always voice their own internal emotional state during a song. Here, Tamate's emotional somberness is thoroughly presentational; her sorrow is externally voiced by other singers, while her body movement externalizes her internal thoughts.

Birch was tasked with constructing another conceptually presentational musical moment for a different non-singing character, this time for the formidable Commodore Perry. Perry's act 1 finale, "Lion Dance," remains the most recognizable moment from the 1976 production, given that the Perry figure within the "Lion Dance" scene served as branding for the show. The lion character in the kabuki tradition is a dynamically recognizable figure, as there are several lion dances that are considered staples within the kabuki repertoire. At the end of act 1, the American and Japanese leadership are parting ways after what appears to have been a successful meeting to discuss the terms of their trade relationship. The Americans wish for Japan to open its doors to trade with the West. Japan wishes to be left alone. Upon the Americans' departure from the meeting the Reciter joyfully proclaims: "The barbarian threat had forever been removed! Ha!"[20] One might think this would signify a Japanese negotiation victory. What immediately follows however, is a re-entrance by Commodore Perry into the "Lion Dance" sequence.[21] Perry's costume juxtaposes kabuki with the image of Uncle Sam; he wears top hat, tie, and tails, all in a flashy red, white, and blue, but no shoes. His kabuki makeup gives the suggestion of the *aragoto*, male kabuki characters of a bold, dynamic nature. Perry dons a long white wig that extends almost to the floor, with two thick strands framing his face at the front that he often grabs. This wig invokes the lion character from the kabuki tradition, but it is smaller, narrower, and less bushy.

Perry starts the dance with a series of high kicks, timed to the beat of a drum. He clutches the two long strands of hair that frame his face, a position that is taken directly from the kabuki lion dance repertoire, known as *shakkyô mono*. A series of quick, emphatic head nods is then followed by a modified version of the signature move of the kabuki lion dance: the tossing of the great, long hair around and around in a circular motion. Perry once again returns to high kicks as the music starts to pick up speed. Perry continues this back-and-forth between kabuki and Western dance vocabulary: chassé gallops followed by exaggerated, frozen facial expressions called "mie," soft shoe leading into more hair tossing and a dragging step on one knee, and then the cakewalk, which comes off as particularly grotesque with Perry's mugging smile made all the more frightening through the kabuki makeup.

Historian Carol Ilson cites Birch's recollections of creating the "Lion Dance" as "half Americanized, half Lion Dance . . . half bravura and half cocky American," and of taking "the

---

[19]Stephen Sondheim, *Finishing the Hat: Collected Lyrics (1954–1981)* (New York: Alfred A. Knopf, 2010), 306.
[20]John Weidman et. al., *Pacific Overtures* (New York: Dodd, Mead, 1976), 80.
[21]The role of Commodore Perry was played by Patricia Birch's kabuki consultant, Japanese American actor Haruki Fujimoto.

Image 9.3 A scene from the Broadway production of *Pacific Overtures*, original Lion Dance (1975). Photo by Martha Swope. Billy Rose Theatre Division, New York Public Library Digital Collections.

vernacular of the Japanese dance and turn[ing] it in my [Birch's] own direction."[22] What Birch indicates is that the "Lion Dance" was purposefully built with the intention of hybridizing Asian and American movement. But what Birch doesn't offer up is a clearly defined point to the "Lion Dance." When reading the "Lion Dance" from the perspective of the Japanese councillors, one could say it serves as an artful symbol, with the American Perry represented as a prominent character from the Japanese tradition. However, history tells us that the Americans were going to return in greater numbers and with more demands. Thus, it seems more apt to read this character's dance as an American "win"; the immediate entrance of Perry as the lion could be viewed as a fierce, wild, American victory dance. The use of modified kabuki movements infused with Western steps, eventually culminating in a triumphant cakewalk, could serve as an affront to Japan's desires for continued global isolation; the imperialistic Americans have arrived by way of the powerful lion.

The addition of the cakewalk in the "Lion Dance" adds another layer of complexity to our understanding of this dance, and hardly seems coincidental in a scene that could be read as satirical. As Ashley M. Pribyl suggests in her historical research of *Pacific Overtures*, the inclusion of the cakewalk in the "Lion Dance" may be a remnant from an earlier version of Weidman's play, which includes a scene where the Americans traveling with Commodore

---

[22]Carol Ilson, *Harold Prince: A Director's Journey* (New York: Limelight Editions, 2000), 235–6.

Perry perform a minstrel show for the Japanese.[23] As a dance created by the oppressed to mock the oppressor, with the oppressor obtusely adopting the dance as their own mode of modern social expression, the cakewalk—in essence what scholar Jayna Brown aptly defines as "black people's manipulation of masks, a particular form of complex, multi-layered racial mimesis"—thematically aligns here with its use in the "Lion Dance."[24] The Asian/American dancer in "whiteface" (someone who is playing the white Perry and using white kabuki makeup) can be read as a direct jab at white America's historical use of blackface and yellowface, where Asian/American Perry mocks the haughty white "Americans" and their assumed victory. The chain of appropriation—American, Broadway creatives appropriating the Asian kabuki aesthetic for a white character (Perry) who is appropriating an African American dance form of the cakewalk to indicate American imperialistic victory—could be understood as expressing patterns of injustice. In its intention and implication, the "Lion Dance" remains abstract, and therefore thematically kabuki-like.

The "Lion Dance" is a complex example of how multiple nonwhite historical, cultural, and physical signifiers are adopted in order to convey not only meaning, but spectacle. Additionally, the appearance of a lion dance signature move in the final number, "Next," brings to light the inequity of gender in kabuki. In "Next" we see women populate the stage for the first time. The number, set in present-day Japan, expresses hybridity by showing a Western-attired cross-section of Japanese society moving with a contemporary Western groove. Yet, in the middle of their dance, the ladies begin swinging their upper bodies around and around, their long hair flowing freely in a circular motion. Thus, from within a stage of current American movement comes the signature step of the kabuki lion, only this time placed on female bodies, which have been historically banned from the kabuki stage. Before "Next," the stage was reserved for male players. But with the contemporary setting of "Next," women are free to move, and even mock, masculinized characters.

Putting forth direct dance references from both Japanese and American aesthetics, the 1976 production exemplifies how kabuki and Broadway dramatic expression, decorative symbolism and direct narrative, and the Asian and the American can intertwine in choreographed moments to express hybridity. And with examples like the "Lion Dance," the Asian/American body used to express the sociopolitical views of a white American creative team (which has chosen a traditional Japanese figure to comment on race in America) reflects the team's intention to render the show both Asian *and* American in meaning. But the effort to create a Broadway production of hybrid purpose was lost on most critics of the time, with Walter Kerr from the *New York Times* posing the following question to the American creative team: "Why tell their [the Japanese] story when they can do it better?"[25] Thirty years later, Amon Miyamoto would respond to Kerr's figurative challenge with a production vastly different from the original aesthetic of the show, yet equally potent in its Asian/American hybrid presentation.

---

[23]Ashley M. Pribyl, "Politics, Representation, and Collaboration in *Pacific Overtures* (1976)," in *Sondheim in Our Time and His*, ed. W. Anthony Sheppard (New York: Oxford University Press, 2022), 165.
[24]Jayna Brown, *Babylon Girls: Black Women Performers and the Shaping of the Modern*. (Durham, NC: Duke University Press, 2008), 128.
[25]Walter Kerr, "'Pacific Overtures' Is Neither East nor West," *New York Times*, January 18, 1976.

Pacific Overtures (2004)

The "Lion Dance" was an important scene for the 1976 production, positioned not only as a concise, physicalized expression on the theme of American hegemony, but also as a prominent marketing tool used on posters, playbills, and the 1976 cast album. Yet, despite its significance, Japanese director-choreographer Amon Miyamoto decided to remove the "Lion Dance" entirely from the 2004 Broadway revival. In an interview Miyamoto talked about seeing the 1976 production on TV in Japan, and described his reaction to the original production's use of the kabuki aesthetic: "It looked a little bit weird, because it was kabuki style. It was kabuki style and a musical mixed together. But . . . that was a little bit strange for the Japanese."[26] Perhaps Miyamoto refrained from including the "Lion Dance" in the revival because of the lion figure's inaccurate depiction as a villain in the 1976 production. "The lion of the 'Lion Dance' is not what a lion is in Asian cultures," states cast member Francis Jue. "I assume it was just unfathomable to Amon, because his associations with the lion and lion dances is not what Perry was doing in that moment."[27] Although the "Lion Dance" included steps from actual kabuki lion dances, the kabuki lion's signified meaning as a courageous, mystical character doesn't align with the antagonistic purpose it was given in the Pacific Overtures story. Cutting the "Lion Dance" and deviating from the original creative team's vision, Miyamoto dropped all indicators of the kabuki aesthetic and opted instead for a more narratively realistic and Western-influenced style.

As one of the most celebrated musical theatre directors in Japan, Miyamoto has shared stories about his love for Broadway musicals and his rigorous self-study of the American art form from an early age. Interviewing Miyamoto for the New York Times, Jesse Green discusses Miyamoto's unique contribution to the 2004 revival, making the following observation on how Miyamoto's involvement adds yet another unusual vine into the already complexly tangled use of the Asian and the American in Pacific Overtures: "Japanese history written by American artists using Japanese techniques as revisited by an American cast overseen by a Japanese director who is a devotee of American theater."[28] Further along in the interview, Green shares a moment inside the rehearsal room, where Miyamoto is telling the cast, "Like in Chicago . . . with the feathers!" Miyamoto's allusion to a well-known choreographed moment in the iconic 1975 Bob Fosse musical is an indication of how he approached the revival's movement, and what his own expectations were from the Broadway cast. Throughout the show, Miyamoto replaces the abstract presentational style of kabuki with a form of movement that is more story driven, and analogous to standard Broadway fare.

Miyamoto's reference to the musical Chicago is played out in the song "Welcome to Kanagawa," a bawdy number straight out of the vaudeville playbook. As Commodore Perry and the Americans are about to enter Japan by way of the port city Kanagawa, an older courtesan Madam proceeds with schooling her young brothel brood on how best to entertain this fresh "clientele" of American sailors. The Madam, using comic innuendo as her main

---

[26]"Pacific Overtures—2004," uploaded by You'reGonnaLoveTomorrow, April 17, 2020, YouTube video, 13:27, https://www.youtube.com/watch?v=XPTd6F0r_2c.
[27]Francis Jue, pers. comm., January 2022.
[28]Jesse Green, "Broadway's Fondest, Furthest Fan Comes Home," New York Times, November 28, 2004.

mode of communication, sings the entire song directly to the audience. Sondheim utilizes the five-seven-five syllabic pattern of Japanese haiku poetry twice in the song, but to humorous effect. The haikus, though Japanese in rhythmic structure, are comedically American in their euphemistically sexual content. The Reciter recites each poem in the manner of a vaudevillian "setup" to a joke, and the Madam responds to each with a precisely timed punch line.

The "Welcome to Kanagawa" movement in the original 1976 production utilized the fan dance as its concept, with the Madam and the courtesans waving around large fans with semipornographic Japanese imagery. The 2004 revival, however, chose a very different approach. Apart from the Madam, who carries a small fan that she instructively indicates with like a graceful schoolmarm, Miyamoto removes the fans and trades them in temporarily for bits of rope that the courtesans use as suggestive sight gags. The Madam wears a tight kimono that hugs her figure, forcing her hips to wiggle as she walks, her stance maintaining a constant bevel as though she's on fashionable display at a department store. When the chorus of the song ends and the orchestration swells, Miyamoto gives us an assortment of more traditional Broadway dance vocabulary; the ladies descend toward the audience from behind a set of upstage screens, arms stretched out to the side like showgirls. *Balancés* are followed by an arrangement of pivots, elongated *tendues*, and cutesy leg flicks. Then comes the homage Fosse's choreography in *Chicago*: the ladies create a pinwheel with the trains of their robes, framing the Madam as they rotate around her, much like the *Chicago* ladies do with their feathers around Billy Flynn in the number "All I Care About." The vaudeville concept that structures *Chicago* thematically aligns with how Sondheim built "Welcome to Kanagawa." Miyamoto taps into this alignment, bringing the Broadway showgirl movement quality of *Chicago* and placing it onto a group of Japanese courtesans.

Counter to the 1976 production's interpretation of "Welcome to Kanagawa," where the Oriental-stereotyped fan dance structured the movement, Miyamoto opts to activate the American mode of vaudeville, pointing to the original context of what this number's position is within an American-built Broadway musical. Despite Miyamoto's use of Western, American dance vocabulary, his refusal to use Western stereotypes of Asian movement makes his perspective on the piece ostensibly *less Western*, and thus more Asian.

It is unclear whether Miyamoto's rejection of physicalizing racial stereotypes through movement in "Welcome to Kanagawa" was intentional. The omission of the "Lion Dance" also flags questions about how race factors into the 2004 production. But cast member Francis Jue points to Miyamoto's cultural origins as influencing his choices, saying, "the 1976 production of *Pacific Overtures* purposefully had Asian Americans playing white characters. And there was an irony to that. But I don't think Japanese people have to deal with race in the same way we have to deal with it."[29] Although race in and of itself may not be symbolically addressed in the 2004 production, Miyamoto addresses how the greed of one culture has the potential to be absorbed by another, only to be counter-actively weaponized.

Miyamoto takes the *Pacific Overtures* theme of American military "might is right" and applies it as a movement concept for the show's final number, "Next." "Next" gives a condensed, accelerated account of how Japan westernizes from the end of the nineteenth

---

[29]Francis Jue, pers. comm., January 2022.

century into the present day. The concise lyrics set against a rhythmically driving melody speak of only looking forward, but every so often a line grabs our attention and makes us wonder: is "old is boring" really true?[30] Sondheim messes with our sense of the importance of progress no matter the cost with a handful of phrases that demand pause. As such, "Next" as a whole remains twofold in meaning, whereby the virtues of cultural tradition and global advancement are cynically weighed against one another.

Unlike the 1976 production's version of "Next," which visualizes the thematically presentational aspect of kabuki with a contemporary display of colorful, frenetic spectacle, Miyamoto's 2004 concept grounds the movement in linear narrative, with twentieth century Japanese history serving as the source. The top of the number starts with just a few ensemble members with rifles, dressed in dark, Western military–style attire. As the number progresses, more identically outfitted ensemble members join one by one, until finally, the stage is filled with soldiers. Their stance is strong and rigid, but as the song continues their movement becomes actively aggressive, punctuated with forward-moving foot stomps. They aim their rifles toward the audience on the final note, and then suddenly, the stage flashes brightly with an explosive sound, and we are plunged into darkness. The atomic bomb has been dropped. As the music starts up again, the ensemble members, who "died" onstage during the bomb, rise one by one. They have stripped off their military jackets, revealing black shirts. They dance with an emphatic grabbing motion, grasping with arms outstretched to the sides and toward the audience. Once again they strip off their shirts, exposing uniform black tank tops underneath. The next dance break is a more frenzied variation of grabbing: they jump and grab, jump and grab, reaching for something, wanting for something, clutching feverishly at air. This sequence of movement sections, marked by the removal of costume pieces, alluded to a post-war Japan, where the US demanded for the disbandment of Japanese military forces. After Japan had rebuilt from the ashes of near nuclear annihilation, the postwar era gave rise to a different sort of Japanese power, one of economic ambition and financial dominance.

Miyamoto's "Next" is in direct opposition to aesthetic devices used in traditional kabuki theatre: rather than visually opulent, the costumes are stark; rather than narratively symbolic, the story here is linear and clear. Miyamoto is using American dramatic structures as his artistic compass for this story set in Japan, reconfiguring this Asian/American musical into an entirely new beast: an Asian production of an American show about Asian history, a production that refuses American clichés about Asia and instead embraces the "traditional" conventions of the American stage.

Acceptance of Asian/American hybridization as a viable aesthetic remained lost on many viewers. Although Ben Brantley's 2004 *New York Times* review title, "Repatriating the Japanese Sondheim," could have been meant to infer the cultural mélange of an Asian production of an American show about Asia, the prominence of the label "Japanese" still implies that "Asian" is the central adjective in the Asian/American musical.[31] What's more, labels like these are never equitably appointed to musicals with overwhelmingly white players that take place in foreign locales. When was the last time *A Little Night Music* (1973) was referred to as the "Swedish Sondheim," or *Passion* (1994) as the "Italian Sondheim"?

---

[30]Sondheim, *Finishing the Hat*, 329.
[31]Brantley, "Repatriating the Japanese Sondheim."

Image 9.4 "Welcome To Kanagawa," *Pacific Overtures* (2004). Francis Jue, as Madam. Photo by Sara Krulwich, Courtesy of Eyevine.

Assigning the term "Japanese" to *Pacific Overtures* from the onset establishes an expectation of Asianness, a belief that the show should prominently present Japanese despite its American aesthetic and English linguistic foundations. As a result, there is an ongoing pressure felt by Asian/American artists to try to meet these unrealistic expectations. *Pacific Overtures* cast member Yuka Takara recalls a conversation with the late Alvin Ing, a pioneer of the Asian/American musical community who appeared in both the 1976 original and 2004 revival productions: "Alvin was stressed that we weren't going to be Japanese enough, and I think that translated into an underlying fear for him that we weren't going to be good enough. This fear is felt very strongly by older members of our community who had to fight so hard for a place in this business."[32] Unfounded expectations of Asianness placed on Asian/American musical artists have created a community who demand of themselves a mastery of every type of aesthetic that fits under the heading of Asian/American. But why is this pursuit necessary?

Making Room for an Asian/American Aesthetic

There is a desire, a need even, to fit into "white" Broadway standards. And we learn the standards, we learn the technique. I myself didn't grow up with Japanese influence; my influence and training was here. And the goals are to be better than the standard in order to just fit in.

—Alan Muraoka, Broadway actor and American director

---

[32]Yuka Takara, pers. comm., January 2022. Takara was also in the *Flower Drum Song* 2002 Broadway revival company.

On Broadway, Asian/American bodies have historically been denied generically American, ethnically unspecified roles, and have instead been assigned parts that are explicitly of Asian heritage. But there have been times when Asian/Americans have created ethnically unspecified roles simply based on their ability and talent. In 1944, highly accomplished Japanese American ballerina Sono Osato originated the role of Ivy Smith in Leonard Bernstein and Jerome Robbins's collaborative dance musical *On the Town*, a role that would later be portrayed by Vera Ellen in the 1949 film version. Osato's Japanese heritage was used to help characterize the role of Ivy in the story in a nonverbalized, indirect manner. With Ivy the newly anointed "Miss Turnstiles" of the New York City subway system, her (and thus, Osato's) face appears onstage in a sizable poster in the middle of act 1, featuring the phrase "Exotic Ivy Smith."[33] Beyond this visual marker, Osato's Asian/Americanness had no bearing on her portrayal of the part. In 1975, Asian American Broadway veteran Baayork Lee created the role of Connie Wong for *A Chorus Line*, making Connie the first Asian American principal character to exist in a musical story set outside of the Asian diaspora. Unlike Ivy Smith, whose ethnicity is determined by the actor playing the role, Connie Wong is Asian American because she was built from Lee's existing Asian Americanness. But despite Connie's Asian Americanness, she is not expected to "move Asian" in the story; she is expected to move exactly like her non-Asian/American dancer colleagues.

These two casting examples, however, are exceptions: Asian/American musical artists continue to encounter Western creatives who question their fitness. Although "looking Asian" does not necessarily correlate with "moving Asian," Western observers conflate the Asian/American body with the Asian face, and the resulting expectation inevitably leans toward the nonwhite American Other. American theatre choreographer and 2002 *Flower Drum Song* alum Lainie Sakakura illustrates this phenomenon as she recalls an episode when she was denied a part: "The choreographer cast me in the lead dance role, but the celebrated Tony Award–winning director wouldn't allow it. They said, 'Her face would be distracting and confusing to the audience.'"[34] Michael K. Lee, 2004 *Pacific Overtures* cast member, also reflects on the ongoing struggle of the "foreign versus the endemic on American stages," whereby "we as Asian/Americans identify as American. But the view from the outside is that we are still foreign."[35]

Who gets to determine what "moving Asian" should look like on the Broadway stage? "We have grown accustomed to listening to these so-called voices of authority in musical theatre," muses Robert Tatad. "But when, say, a white man is critically commenting on how actors of Asian heritage are telling a story about Asia . . . by what criteria is he basing his opinions on?"[36] White American individuals who have set the standards of Broadway performance have yet to demonstrate how they can comprehensively assess material that does not center their perspectives, even if that material was created by white American artists. Assumptions of Asianness that manifest as either the stereotyped "Oriental" or the

---

[33]Florence Vandamm, "Sono Osato, Lyle Clark, Don Weismuller, Richard D'Arcy, Frank Westbrook, John Butler, and Duncan Noble in a Scene from the Stage Production of *On the Town*," photograph, 1944, Billy Rose Theatre Division, New York Public Library Digital Collections, Catalog ID b21360730.
[34]Lainie Sakakura, pers. comm., October 2021.
[35]Michael K. Lee, pers. comm., January 2022.
[36]Robert Tatad, pers. comm., January 2022.

"authentic Asian foreigner" remain creations of the Western imagination, and do not reflect the reality of how Asian/Americans exist within and express from their Asian/American bodies. From the Asian/American artist's perspective, Darren Lee comments, "We shouldn't have to spend time worrying about being, say, Japanese. We should be thinking about how we can be great musical theatre performers."[37] The Asian/American musical body holds cultural duality. And when Asian/American musicals use Asian/American bodies to tell a given story, the cultural duality of the Asian/American artist leads to artistic output that is naturally hybridized.

Despite critical opinions to the contrary, the Asian/American artists who appeared in the 2004 revival of *Pacific Overtures* are authentically Asian, because Asianness is embodied in every Asian/American artist. And, as studied practitioners of American musical theatre, Asian/American artists are, likewise, authentically American. Asian/Americanness may lack the measures to be codified in a way typical to or desired by current Broadway authorities, however, we can recognize that Asian/Americanness has the potential as its own cultural aesthetic, one that has yet to set any standards of definition. As Asian/American musical artists are being given the chance to take more ownership of work that directly reflects them, it will become necessary to embrace new positions of reception, ones that actively recognize innate and intentional Asian/American hybridity.

Bibliography

Barnes, Clive. "Unspecific 'Overtures'—Japanese Staging Misfires in Latest Sondheim Revival." *New York Post*, December 3, 2004.

Boross, Bob. "The Jack Cole Notebooks." *Dance Chronicle* 27, no. 3 (2004): 409–13.

Brantley, Ben. "Repatriating the Japanese Sondheim." *New York Times*, December 3, 2004.

Brown, Jayna. *Babylon Girls: Black Women Performers and the Shaping of the Modern*. Durham, NC: Duke University Press, 2008.

"Chinese Fan Dance." Chinese Cultural Dances, CCCH9051 Group 31. Hong Kong University Online Learning. Accessed December 10, 2022. https://learning.hku.hk/ccch9051/group-31/items/show/7.

Fisher, Jennifer. "'Yellowface' in 'The Nutcracker' Isn't a Benign Ballet Tradition, It's Racist Stereotyping." *Los Angeles Times*, December 12, 2018.

Fullington, Doug, and Phil Chan. "Choreography." *Final Bow for Yellowface* (website). Accessed January 20, 2022. https://www.yellowface.org/nutchoreography.

Green, Jesse. "Broadway's Fondest, Furthest Fan Comes Home." *New York Times*, November 28, 2004.

Griffith, Paul, and Okada Mariko. "Nihonbuyo: Classical Dance." In *A History of Japanese Theatre*, edited by Jonah Salz, 141–9. Cambridge: Cambridge University Press, 2016.

Hahn, Tomie. *Sensational Knowledge: Embodying Culture through Japanese Dance*. Middletown, CT: Wesleyan University Press, 2007.

Hill, Constance Valis. "From Bharata Natyam to Bop: Jack Cole's 'Modern' Jazz Dance." *Dance Research Journal* 33, no. 2 (2001): 29–39.

Ilson, Carol. *Harold Prince: A Director's Journey*. New York: Limelight Editions, 2000.

Isherwood, Charles. "Pacific Overtures." *Variety*, July 14, 2002.

---

[37]Darren Lee, pers. comm., January 2022.

Kawatake Toshio. *Kabuki: Baroque Fusion of the Arts*. Translated by Frank and Jean Connell Hoff. Tokyo: International House of Japan, 2003.

Kerr, Walter. "'Pacific Overtures' Is Neither East nor West." *New York Times*, January 18, 1976.

Kwan, SanSan. "Performing a Geography of Asian America: The Chop Suey Circuit." *TDR: The Drama Review* 55, no. 1 (2011): 120–36.

Marks, Peter. "Sondheim, Gaining Much in Translation." *Washington Post*, September 5, 2002.

"Pacific Overtures." *Playbill*: Broadway Database. Accessed January 12, 2022. https://playbill. com/production/pacific-overtures-winter-garden-theatre-vault-0000011540.

"Pacific Overtures—2004." Uploaded by You'reGonnaLoveTomorrow, April 17, 2020. YouTube video, 13:27. https://www.youtube.com/watch?v=XPTd6F0r_2c.

Palumbo-Liu, David. *Asian/American: Historical Crossings of a Racial Frontier*. Stanford, CA: Stanford University Press, 1999.

Pribyl, Ashley M. "Politics, Representation, and Collaboration in *Pacific Overtures* (1976)." In *Sondheim in Our Time and His*, edited by W. Anthony Sheppard, 160–84. New York: Oxford University Press, 2022.

Rodgers, Richard, and Oscar Hammerstein II. *Flower Drum Song*. New York: Williamson Music, 1958.

Said, Edward W. *Orientalism*. New York: Pantheon Books, 1978.

Sondheim, Stephen. *Finishing the Hat: Collected Lyrics (1954–1981)*. New York: Alfred A. Knopf, 2010.

Vandamm, Florence. "Sono Osato, Lyle Clark, Don Weismuller, Richard D'Arcy, Frank Westbrook, John Butler, and Duncan Noble in a Scene from the Stage Production of *On the Town*." Photograph, 1944. Billy Rose Theatre Division, New York Public Library Digital Collections. Catalog ID b21360730.

Weidman, John, Stephen Sondheim, Harold S. Prince, and Hugh Wheeler. *Pacific Overtures*. New York: Dodd, Mead, 1976.

10 Tap and the Broadway Musical: Subversion and Subjectivity through Historical Consciousness

BENAE BEAMON

Few understand them, study them like they are worth something, realize their inherent value. If you listen closely, you can hear the whole world in a bent note, a throwaway lyric, a singular thread of the collective utterance.

—Saidiya Hartman

In Saidiya Hartman's *Wayward Lives, Beautiful Experiments*, she explores the lives of women of color subjugated because of their unwillingness to acquiesce to or approximate the norm. In unearthing this radical subaltern, she notes the fragility of normativity and the uncompromising orientation of women of color who refuse the circumstances to which society desires to relegate them. The radical journey of the wayward parallels, or perhaps offers a frame, for us to understand the investments of black women in the chorus (i.e., the ensemble of Broadway casts historically comprised of black women as chorus girls).[1] This chapter explores the representation of tap dance in revue formats as reverberations of classist and racist perceptions. This representation foregrounds the subversive work of the chorus, focusing on black women, and their ability to produce an *otherwise* through an engagement of subjectivity via historical consciousness. To highlight the chorus and its work, this chapter prioritizes the voices of women in the chorus based on interviews with black women that were part of the ensemble in relevant Broadway shows, and centralizes embodiment through discussions of their experiences.[2] I will first discuss the difference between Broadway revues and musicals, since revues are a notably common format in which tap dance is presented. I will then explore the differences in the performative capacity for tap dance in those revues and musicals and the more generative possibilities of the musical, noting that the musical allows for a more robust expression of agency.

To understand the chorus and the value of historical consciousness, we must understand the work of the griot – the poet and storyteller – that brings history forward, that preserves

---

[1] I am very intentional about the way that I use black and the choice to make it lower case. I use black when talking about black people and white when talking about white people, only capitalizing if I am talking about Whiteness or Blackness as a concept.

[2] It is important to note that because we are talking about embodiment through the experiences of individuals it means that their conversation takes on a more phenomenological tone, focusing on the experience of embodiment more than embodiment or performance itself.

the memory, the link that undoes our linear expectations of time.[3] The chorus enacts some of this work. They stand in not as background but as evocations of the past meeting present and embodied griots, navigating their own subjectivity and the social and historical consciousness. They are the "collective utterance" that "envision[s] things otherwise."[4] With that in mind, this paper is a dedication to the chorus and the historical consciousness that informs their presence and physicality within musical theater. The nuanced subjectivity of the contemporary chorus elides the limitations of time, and thereby white patriarchal and capitalist structures in ways that subvert historical narratives. In order to fully discuss such nuanced subjectivity, we must consider the spaces and storytelling realities to which tap dance is relegated.

Blackness in Performance: Tap Dance in Revues

In 1937, in the midst of a complicated political landscape and growing contributions to what would become part of the musical theater canon, Ted Shawn, the founder of Jacob's Pillow (a prominent dance center in the Northeast US) known as a pioneer of modern dance in the US, wrote and published *Fundamentals of Dance Education*. In the text, Shawn addresses the growing popularity of tap dance in cinema and states that "[i]f tap dancing has any legitimate place at all it is in vaudeville and the revue as a cheap form of entertainment."[5] Shawn's statement makes a declaration about the cultural value of tap dance as an art form. Revues were "theatrical production[s] consisting of several loosely connected performances," often a compilation of dancers, singers, comics, sketches, etc.[6] The revue as a structure, or a kind of "variety show," is unintentionally classed and proves reminiscent of vaudeville shows which held the same basic format as foundational to the form of entertainment. This classed understanding of revues, noted in Shawn's claim that they are "cheap entertainment," mirrors perceptions of vaudeville. This is in part because vaudeville stages were tied to race and helped to codify pernicious understandings of race. The cultural value of tap dance is inextricably linked to discourse about class, and thereby race in ways that underscore an extension of vaudeville, or spaces in which minstrelsy and the capitalist exploitation of black life and black cultural expression flourished.

Tap dance became a staple in US entertainment during the late nineteenth and early twentieth century. Just as Ted Shawn notes the popularity of tap dance in early twentieth century film, so too the vaudeville stage found this art form foundational. Much like the minstrelsy from which it evolved, vaudeville was rooted in "the increasing influence of the [black] style of song and dance in American life" that seemed to primarily populate "low-class dives."[7] As vaudeville emerged (geared towards white audiences), the value of black

---

[3]I am capitalizing chorus here in order to belabor the importance and power of this collective. Rather than attempting to offer a monolithic notion of the chorus this choice to capitalize accounts for the individual subjectivities that constitute the collective, noting that without the parts there is no whole.
[4]Ibid., 345, 347.
[5]Ted Shawn, *Fundamentals of Dance Education* (Haldeman-Julius Publications, 1937), 23.
[6]*Merriam-Webster.com Dictionary*, s.v. "revue," accessed October 2, 2022, https://www.merriam-webster.com/dictionary/revue.
[7]Marshall Stearns and Jean Stearns, *Jazz Dance: The Story of American Vernacular Dance* (New York: The Macmillan Company, 1968), 43, 44.

entertainment was understood as an asset, especially at the beginning of the twentieth century, as it was understood that the addition of a "Negro act" would improve the overall show.[8] It is important to consider both the lower class functions of black minstrel shows alongside the use of black artists as commodities in white vaudeville. Both white and black vaudeville participated in the cultivation of tap dance as an art form and even "desirable."[9] Vaudeville as "'fast-moving entertainment'" that "demanded freshness," or original perspectives and acts that typically translated to innovation and, at times, camp-y gimmick.[10] What I am drawing out about vaudeville, especially white vaudeville, is its investment in "blacking up," as Tina Post connotes, in a way that makes "*darkness* visible."[11] While Post is discussing the use of blackface by black artists in minstrelsy, her basic idea about the ways that we obfuscate black subjectivity through the mapping of black commodified value helps us consider the implications of the revue as an extension of vaudevillian interests. The gimmicks encouraged and thereby employed, obscure the subjectivity and the unique rhythmic contributions, particularly for black artists in white vaudeville. "Rather than pointing to blackness as an embodiment, blacking on a black body reveals 'blackness' as an idea."[12] The gimmicks, while at times innovative, ultimately serve hegemony, by hiding black subjectivity and emphasizing the ideas and the constructed notions of blackness as "Truth." While vaudeville thrived on this model, which reproduced Blackness as Other (i.e., the dark, or oppositional), it is informed by cultural understandings that invest in blackness as spectacle to be exploited rather than subjects to be understood and engaged. As the popularity of vaudeville stages were replaced by film, the popularity of tap dance transferred to the screen, inciting frustration from some, like Ted Shawn.[13] This transition though is not to be understood as a fading of this tradition and investment in black subjectivity. Hegemonic efforts to obscure black subjectivity took on a new form through this new media and reach that invested still in "'blackness' as an idea."[14]

White vaudeville, then, assumed the fungibility of Blackness; meaning that it assumed that black people were interchangeable in ways that assume black people are units of commerce.[15] The revue, then, marks tap dance for relegation as tap dance is bound to its raced and classed vaudevillian roots and limited by the popular frame. Revues stand in contrast to shows like *Jelly's Last Jam* (1992) and *Bring in 'da Noise Bring in 'da Funk* (1996)

---

[8]Ibid., 80.

[9]Constance Valis Hill, *Tap Dancing America: A Cultural History* (New York: Oxford University Press, 2010), 54. During the late nineteenth and early twentieth centuries there was a black and white vaudeville in large part due to the ongoing function of black codes (the progenitor to Jim Crow laws). White vaudeville included primarily white artists, though the occasional black artist was able to contribute, and leaned heavily on minstrelsy. Black vaudeville still abided some notions of minstrelsy that degraded black existence in its early years.

[10]Ibid., 61, 62.

[11]Tina Post, "Williams, Walker, and Shine: Blackbody, Blackface, or the Importance of Being Surface," *The Drama Review* 59, no. 4 (2015): 87. Emphasis by the author.

[12]Ibid., 94.

[13]Hill, *Tap Dancing America*, 147.

[14]Post, "Williams, Walker, and Shine," 94. Post and *Jazz Dance* by Marshall and Jean Stearns does a great job of describing that the way that vaudeville profited off of minstrelsy and its use of black stereotypes (like the "coon"), or creating caricatures of black people, rather than actual black experiences.

[15]C. Riley Snorton, *Black on Both Sides: A Racial History of Trans Identity* (Minneapolis: University of Minnesota Press, 2017).

that use tap dance as a tool to speak about evolving music and legacy as well as black experience; speak to social and historical realities *through* the use of tap dance; and understand tap dance as a storytelling medium in itself. This is to say that in contrast to the revue structure, which is able to stay silent on the experiential realities of black life and black history. In order to consider, the ramifications and the way that the revue might be limiting, it is important to speak to the realities of vaudeville culture and the function of tap dance within such spaces.

As a reverberation of vaudevillian structures, revues understandably hold some of the ideological remnants as well.[16] This is to say that revues often reproduce ideas that were at the center of vaudeville culture, and in doing so, end up reproducing the same pernicious ideas about black people and Blackness. While this is not meant to undermine the value of a revue, I am noting that revues cannot be divorced from the historical and cultural context, which bears with it an objectifying and limiting understanding of blackness and its capacities. Such limitations translate, too, to tap dance as an artistic expression impacted by the classist and racist assumptions fundamental to vaudeville and minstrel spaces. There are exceptions to the use of revues as propagations of classist and racist investments. *Black and Blue* (1989) and *Black Broadway* (1979), an "all-black musical review," are examples of such exceptions.[17] These exceptions happen through recognition of the historical and social context, and while they don't negate a clear systemic interest in avoiding the use of tap dance as a storytelling technique, these exceptions, namely *Black and Blue*, help us take seriously the possibility of the revue in engaging tap dance in generative ways despite the structure and format.

Black and Blue: A Revue All Its Own

Black and Blue stands out as an example of the generative way that revues can be structured such that it centers black life and black subjectivity. *Black and Blue* was a revue that premiered in Paris in 1985 at the Theatre Musical de Paris Chatelet Theatre and in the US, at the Minkoff Theatre, in 1989.[18] This production featured some of the most notable tap dancers, e.g., Bunny Briggs, James "Jimmy Slyde" Godbolt, Lon Chaney, Dianne Walker, and more along with a young Ted Levy and Savion Glover.[19] The production garnered several Tony nominations and was a microcosm of the generational exchange at the core of tap dance and showcased the varied styles and approaches within the art form. The show engaged tap dance tradition in ways that subverted the typical revue structure. While understood, as a harkening back to vaudeville, it's structure recognizes, and thereby reflects, black subjectivity in part by engaging some of tap dance's more satirical and subversive qualities.[20] For example, *Black and Blue* includes a piece titled "Hoofers A Capella," aspects

---

[16]Ethan Mordden, *Beautiful Mornin': The Broadway Musical in the 1940s* (New York: Oxford University Press, 1999), 176, 177.

[17]Hill, *Tap Dancing America*, 247.

[18]Ibid. 285.

[19]Ibid.

[20]Tony Awards. "1989 Tony Awards 'Black and Blue' Revue." Published 2017. Video, 7:18. https://www.youtube.com/watch?v=UelL8kK1sSE

of which are more traditionally referred to as a hoofer's line.[21] The dancers do a step called a paddle and roll (or paddle), four per bar, starting the step on every whole note. All the while the line of dancers offer a guttural sound marking the start of each bar and, in unison, draw their arms up in the air to parallel the floor. Each dancer on line takes a turn improvising with the collective as the sonic backdrop. The paddles keep time and the movement and vocal aspects add a sense of unison and connection where there is an engagement of breath emphasized through movement. Such that, the hoofer's line and its embodiment highlights "breathing itself, as performative act, as performative gesture."[22] I want to focus on the breath as a kind of gesture that is tied to agency – just as the improvised spotlight on each individual artist within the hoofer's line, focuses on their individual voice, contribution, and thereby value, so too does the breath. This choice, the inclusion of the hoofer's line, functions as a nod to black subjectivity, integrating the play and satire of tap dance with the proclamation of individuality and innovation in each dancer's unencumbered voice. Rather than the vaudevillian structure that relies on "freshness" as a code for constant innovation, camp, and gimmick, *Black and Blue* offers black subjectivity and black voices in community in ways that mirror ancestral realities and prioritize longstanding tap dance traditions. Undoing the classic revue structure, i.e., the standard song and dance variety show featuring acts loosely tied together, or at least some of the ways in which it attempts to reconstruct vaudevillian investments of black fungibility, *Black and Blue* asserts black subjectivity as self-determined in ways that rend it from an emphasis on commerce and exploitation.

Tap dance becomes a storytelling device that allows for the introduction of black subjectivity in a way that speaks to the historical and cultural context of blackness in the United States, through ancestral reference. The first number in the musical extends into a series of solo performances from tap dance legends, such as Briggs, Slyde, Chaney, Walker, etc., and performances by Ruth Brown and Linda Hopkins, grounded by an ensemble that brings its own energy and vibrance. As the ensemble performers are the primary iteration of fast-paced, high-energy hoofing tied to precise formations and configurations on stage, they draw a kind of formality through their unison movement, their dress in tuxedos and top hats, and their upright posture. These performances are acts of self-determination as their improvisational elements allow for self-expression and highlight the individual and distinctive voice of the performer. By disavowing the common notions and limiting factors of revues, *Black and Blue* speaks to the possibilities within this format, though, pointedly, does not redeem the revue altogether or tap dance's relegation to it.

The costumes, too, contribute to this more intentional investment in, or the alternate and nuanced approach employed by *Black and Blue* that prioritizes black subjectivity. While the costumes harken back to a vaudevillian era, even those became objects that participated in the determined subjectivity of the performers. From Bunny Briggs' multicolored patchwork velvet suit and Jimmy Slyde's light blue checkered suit to Ruth Brown and Dianne Walker's elegant, sequined dresses, there is a way in which the costumes contribute to the subjectivity

---

[21]Hill, *Tap Dancing America*, 286.
[22]Ashon Crawley, *Blackpentecostal Breath: The Aesthetics of Possibility* (New York City: Fordham University Press, 2017), 33, 36. This thought is tied to Crawley's claim that breath is a fugitive (read: resistant) act in an antiblack world that understands black life as disposable.

Image 10.1 Tap dancers performing in a scene from the Broadway production of the musical *Black and Blue* (1988). Photo by Martha Swope. Billy Rose Theatre Division, New York Public Library Digital Collections.

of the performers.[23] These outfits contribute to the audience's understanding of the subject, highlighting the figure in a way that prioritizes the black body and thereby movement. In a white supremacist society, these costumes are elegant adornments that resist ideas about black people as valueless. These outfits are tied to societal perceptions of the assumptions of glitz, glamour, and adorning and thereby "elevate" the black body and attest to its value in ways that align with bourgeois respectability. In a seemingly paradoxical matter, these outfits do that profound work despite the possibility that the same clothing could be perceived as of ostentatious. The costume "outlines the impressionable skin" as it shows us the form of the subject which is enhanced and underscored through agential and gestural performance.[24] While this costume can be used to "both ass[ert] an essential value within a representation economy" it can also "be blinding or dis[tort]."[25] There is a potential contradiction because the costumes function as bling, inferring the commodification of blackness, yet when engaged in conjunction with the use of dance, in this case hoofing, agential expression, etc., prioritizes individuality. This is to say, individuality through

[23]Jiri Veltruvsky, "Man and Object in the Theater," in *A Prague School Reader on Esthetics, Literary, Structure, and Style*, trans. Paul L Garvin (Washington, DC: Georgetown University Press, 1964), 82.As referenced in Tina Post's "Williams, Walker, and Shine."

[24]Benae Beamon, "Fashioning the Subject: Black Queerness, Identity, and an Ethic of Honor," in *Silhouettes of the Soul: Meditations on Fashion, Religion, and Subjectivity* (London: Bloomsbury Publishing, 2022), 108.

[25]Post, "Williams, Walker, and Shine," 94.

costuming arises through the connection of the clothing with the embodied act of movement/performance.

Furthermore, this individuality shines through in the movement and style showcased by each artist; Slyde with his gentle yet intentional glides around the floor and open swung movement or Briggs with his fast paced footwork that plays with small, almost directional gestures that guide the gaze. The costumes "mark the contours of the self-determined body" in ways that enhance our ability to bear witness to the gestures and styles central to personhood as demonstrated within Slyde and Briggs's performances. The costumes support and serve possibilities of black subjectivity, and yet the delicate balance within a revue structure can quickly tip towards the hegemonically palatable. This possibility of being sucked into larger systemic and oppressive narratives is enhanced though in part through structures and paradigms associated with the revue structure, and vaudeville as its historical referent. With that in mind, *Black and Blue*, showcases the possibilities through which tap dance as a story telling technique as well as an expression of identity and culture can work in tandem to shift the function of some previously managed notions of black existence, namely subverting understandings of blackness as fungible.

While *Black and Blue* speaks to the potential within the revue structure, it is understandably the exception rather than the rule. This is underscored by the complex navigation of black subjectivity over and against black objectification described in the discussion of costume. This intricate navigation belies the complicated structure that is the revue. The musical, though, is a structure comprised in ways that mimic cinematic productions of the early twentieth century with the potential to utilize tap dance within its lexicon of thoughtful storytelling modalities. Within the musical, some musical theatre tap dancing focuses more on large motions and steps that prioritize movement and aesthetic over rhythmic complexity in ways that differ from rhythm tap dancing. This chapter references rhythmic tap dance as coterminous with tap dance because it is built into the evolution of the art form. Its communicative function and its use in storytelling in ways that are referential to its West African roots, make it part of a broader historical and cultural context that is central to the art form in itself. Therefore, the use of tap dance within the musical beyond the musical theatre tap dance, which has value and its own unique function, can ultimately be tied to the encouragement of black subjectivity within the field of musical theater. Musical theater tap dancing is, at times, less interested in the rhythmic contributions of the art form and more in the use of space and stage. Though, this description prioritizes the traditional use of tap dance within the "Great White Way" and undermines the contributions of others that challenge this use, such as Glover, or more recently Ayodele Casel. My focus here is on the use of tap dance as a storytelling medium, which requires its attention to, and even prioritization of, rhythmic complexity in addition to physical dynamism.

New Consciousness: Historical Awareness and Mediums in Musical Theater

To consider the ways that tap dance can contribute rhythmically to musical theater storytelling, a case study is particularly helpful. While there are several examples, as listed above, I will focus on *Shuffle Along, or, the Making of the Musical Sensation of 1921 and All That Followed* (or *Shuffle Along*), as conceptualized and produced in 2016. This show explored the making of *Shuffle Along*, the first all-black hit Broadway musical from the early twentieth century, and its consequent legacy. In the 2016 show, the Jazz Jasmines were a robust cast of black women that acted as part of the ensemble for the overall production. While they were not themselves chorus girls, their roles within the production were in part inspired by the chorus women, and the immense background research described by cast members considered the social circumstances of the chorus. As Lisa La Touche, notes, her experience as a Jazz Jasmine was like "going to get a PhD, an education."[26] La Touche noted that there was a standing research station available that culminated in a different kind of experiential reality: a merging of the past and the present, like "living inside of the history." This merging of time defies the limiting ways in which we understand time as strictly linear in an effort to construct new possibilities. This perception of time is one that mimics Afrofuturist principles, which seek to "reenvi[sion] the past" and speculate as to the future. This reenvisioning of the past occurs *in an effort to* speculate towards a future that disavows antiblackness.[27] This idea also coincides with a queer theoretical frame presented by Lee Edelman that notes that particular futures are cultivated through a reproduction of the past; meaning that, the reconstruction, or the retelling, of the past can mean a new consciousness in the future.[28]

The creative exploration fostered for the cast, including the Jazz Jasmines, during the 2016 reimagining seems to have been pivotal to realizing new possibilities. For La Touche, she found her commitment was cultivated in a way that oriented her towards activism through the recognition of her own agency. Through this study and embodiment of the realities and stories of the Chorus, La Touche found this welcome creative exploration contributed to the production of *Shuffle Along* and the projects with which she would participate. La Touche found that the experience fundamentally transformed her investments saying that "after I had to really embody and learn what my ancestors d[id] for all of us . . . I don't feel like I'm willing to tell just any story anymore." These sentiments are echoed by Karissa Royster, another Jazz Jasmine, as she felt "there was a kinship to those people that [they] d[id]'t even know."[29] Both La Touche and Royster described a sense of an altered consciousness in the wake of *Shuffle Along*, not just the work but the experience it engendered. La Touche speaks to an expanded sense of her own agency, shaping the way she understands the world and empowering her to be intentional about the ways that she uses her voice. And for Royster, there is a new sense of identity and its consequent possibilities. Royster found that there was a sense of "safety and comfort and home" cultivated by the elders in the space. This mutuality and space while rooted in legacy deeply informed "what our purpose was in that space together."

---

[26]Lisa La Touche was a Jazz Jasmine in the 2016 production and a participant in the show from development through the entirety of its run. All quotations attributed to La Touche are drawn from a brief interview conducted with her for the purposes of this chapter.

[27]Ytasha L. Womack, *Afrofuturism: The World of Black Sci-Fi and Fantasy Culture* (Chicago: Lawrence Hill Books, 2013), 9.

[28]Ytasha L. Womack, *Afrofuturism: The World of Black Sci-Fi and Fantasy Culture* (Chicago: Lawrence Hill Books, 2013); Lee Edelman, *No Future: Queer Theory and the Death Drive* (Durham: Duke University Press, 2004).

[29]Karissa Royster was the Dance Captain and member of the ensemble. Similarly, all quotations attributed to Royster are drawn from an interview conducted with her, specifically for the purposes of this chapter.

There is a way in which this experience described by La Touche and Royster is addressed by Daphne Brook's work on "unruly black cultural performance."[30] Brook notes that "the resistant excesses of black women's cultural identity formation [is] made visible [through] performance," and these excesses seem to push back against the limitations to which black women have been relegated, and the subsequent monolithic notions and stereotypical depictions.[31] By exploring and acknowledging the subjectivity of the Jazz Jasmines in the original production, the fictive kinship established supports the realization of black femininity and its complexities.[32] "She uses that excess to emancipate herself;" such that, it is through the excess, through the resistance of hegemonic constraints, more possibilities are reached.[33] My argument, here, is that the education mentioned simultaneously undoes hegemonic investments in assigning expectations to black femininity and challenges the linear function of time (by collapsing the past and the present), and thereby offers the capacity for new possibilities and futures.

While Brooks is discussing black women's creative production on Broadway in the early twentieth century, specifically that of Pauline Hopkins as she worked on her first musical *Peculiar Sam; or, The Underground Railroad* (1879), her investment in "encourag[ing] her people to embrace the nurturing sustenance of autonomous cultural production" clearly parallels the interests of *Shuffle Along* (2016) director George C. Wolfe and choreographer Savion Glover, who created an atmosphere that was both educational, creative, and generative.[34] This educational process though is not separate and apart from the medium through which it is told. The process recognizes the medium in itself is infused with hegemonic notions that seek to limit its use. If revues harken back to vaudevillian depictions of tap dance, undermining their subversive origins and the unique style, then shows that engage tap dance as a significant part of the storytelling practice reinscribe tap dance in its rarely discussed historical and cultural lineage. Royster reflects this claim as her time in *Shuffle Along* made her "feel like [she] was able to tap into another level of what tap dancing can be, outside of its aesthetics, and the fancy steps, and people dancing for their lives." Royster was able to access new understandings of tap dance as an art form through the revival of these stories *and* individuals. It is through this "revisionary black female iconography [that] the African American female performer [becomes] a medium and narrative agent of Pan-Africanist desire."[35] The function of the Jazz Jasmines as mediums and narrative agents supports and enacts their investment in expressing and owning their own agency. Furthermore, this function is informed by a revival that realizes black femininity as whole rather than fragmented, thereby exceeding white heteropatriarchal interests. This notion of the excess as uncovering possibility and futures is enhanced by the way that it extends beyond the social and cultural into the spiritual. The knowledge that was foundational to the

---

[30] Daphne A. Brooks, *Bodies in Dissent: Spectacular Performances of Race and Freedom, 1850–1910* (Durham: Duke University Press, 2006), 9.
[31] Ibid., 319.
[32] Thelathia Nikki Young, *Black Queer Ethics, Family, and Philosophical Imagination* (New York: Palgrave Macmillan, 2016), 164.
[33] Brooks, *Bodies in Dissent*, 319.
[34] Ibid., 283.
[35] Ibid., 293.

creative production and embodiment within *Shuffle Along* (2016) created a sense of responsibility. For instance, Royster felt the need to "gift [others] with this knowledge and inform [others] as to the sacredness of it." This sense of duty is inspired by the fictive kinship as well as the sense of legacy that tap dance has as the art form is engaged through the medium itself.

Both Royster and La Touche describe their experiences engaging tap dance in this capacity as something that defied their notions of Broadway, subverting common iterations of tap dance in those spaces. Beyond that, they both describe the profound impact of the historical investment in the space as something that reinforced new capacities in their own embodiment and new ways of engaging the world in their own lives. The new agential capacities that La Touche describes and Royster's description of the sacrality of the space as informing her sense of comfort and belonging are examples of shifting ethical understandings of the world and black feminine capacities therein. This comes through even in the use of tap dance in the "Act One Finale." In this instance, there is a stark shift from the traditional engagement of chorus girls, replete with leg extensions and a showy demeanor; instead, the Jazz Jasmines abandon this for a hard-hitting interjection that takes on a more grounded posture hitting sharp whole notes followed by a more nuanced double time with just the balls of their feet. This posture is one that holds together what would feel like a contradiction: stunning "feminine" and dressy costumes with a more grounded, perhaps read as "masculine" stance that allows for intentional rhythmic engagement. La Touche describes an unwillingness to compromise and Royster describes a new understanding of how space *can* function *for blackness*. These are new ethical orientations enacted through the construction of new presents *because of* nuanced engagements of the past.

In discussing the impact of the show on their lives, La Touche describes her participation in *Shuffle Along* as "life changing," noting that it shifted her understanding of her own body as well as her positionality within an intersectional reality. La Touche recognized that despite the opportunities and vast education to which she had access during the development of the show that she would "never know what these women experienced." In many ways, the notion of kinship undergirds this statement. The language itself alludes to a connection *despite* the significant difference in historical and cultural context. That distinction is built into the complex matrices of power by which the original Jazz Jasmines were impacted but does not undo the sense of connection in ways that seem to mimic the notion of fictive kinship that Royster describes. Furthermore, this sense of gratitude that acknowledges some sense of privilege in a different historical context is echoed in La Touche's understanding of how this show also changed her sense of her own body. La Touche describes a body consciousness in ways that were clearly tied to societal beauty standards, i.e. rooted in Eurocentric and imperialist ideas, many of which are propagated through the "Great White Way" that is Broadway. La Touche references the ways in which *Shuffle Along* broadly was subverting this hegemonic interest as it showcased the diversity of black women's body's, rewriting both the white supremacist nature that pervades Broadway as well as the "classical" image of the chorus in which many of the women look the same. Touche mentioned that her time in *Shuffle Along* "taught her how much [her body] could carry." La Touche clearly outlines a kind of gratitude for her body *through* a recognition of a new capacity, one previously untapped.

These new embodied capacities parallel the subjective and agential realizations mentioned earlier. Again, La Touche found that in the wake of the show she was no longer "willing to tell just any story anymore." La Touche describes an altered orientation to professional work in ways that express both a sense of agency and a sense of responsibility and duty that is connected to this notion of kinship. This exploration of agency is one that speaks directly to subjectivity. Given the function of forces like hegemony, patriarchy, and white supremacy, which have an aim in dehumanizing and undermining the value, agency, and freedom of marginalized populations, an investment that many social and cultural theorists like Audre Lorde and Paulo Freire have noted, the recognition of agency, moreover the practice of such, is itself subversive.[36] The experience of engaging tap dance as an art form in this nuanced capacity creates the opportunity for fictive kinship, for the connection to the original 1921 Jazz Jasmines. This fictive kinship, which is enacted by acknowledging the subjectivity of the Chorus, incites an altered understanding of the body's capacity and a new moral posture.

In some ways, this recognition of the new and altered realities uncovered through fictive kinship parallels Royster's experience. Royster notes a profound sense of belonging, describing the experience as "spiritual." Moreover, this sense of belonging is inextricably linked to several ethical values; a sense of responsibility driven by connection and the sacrality of such a duty. Royster found that not only was there a "general sense of 'we are a family'" among the cast and crew, but there was also a sense of kinship across time as the readily available research made their predecessors seem "so human. . .[as if] this was us." The sense of belonging, connected to this notion of kinship, bred a new sense of subjectivity in the present that translated to the connection to the past and the subjectivity within these two temporal realms co-constituted one another. As noted before, Royster understood the sense of legacy and responsibility espoused through the passing on of a story that honors the subjectivity of the Chorus rather than omitting it.

The legacy and responsibility acts as a gift, and it is through the story and its embodiment that the gift is exchanged, the duty completed. I argue that this notion of the sacred Royster identifies, one that is tied to subjectivity and found in community, is a manifestation of Audre Lorde's discussion of the erotic. Lorde illuminates the ways in which embodiment intersects with moral value systems in ways that address the sacred. The erotic connotes a "creative energy. . .now reclaim[ed] in our language, our history, our dancing, [etc.,]."[37] This sense of the erotic uncovers an altered sense of one's own capacity and calls the individual to engage in the world with an affirmed sense of one's value. This parallels La Touche and Royster's description of their experience in *Shuffle Along*. This intimacy, as Lorde highlights, is cultivated through connection that does not prioritize exploitation or self-interest and instead focuses on understanding the individual, and in turn allows for an investing in the individual's subjectivity.[38]

Stallings builds on Lorde's work and notes that intimacy is engaged through community and through dance, drawing this specific embodied manifestation into the conversation. Furthermore, Stallings recognizes that in so doing this engagement of the erotic uncovers

---

[36]Audre Lorde, *Sister Outsider: Essays and Speeches* (Tucson: Kore Press, 1984), 38.
[37]Ibid., 8.
[38]Ibid., 59.

the sacrality of such spaces. Stallings astutely finds that "the collaboration between the. . .dancers in such spaces potentially allows for sacredly profane communal erotics that employ rhythm as an inhuman force that sweeps away time's barrier between the living and the dead."[39] While Stallings focuses on different forms and settings in which dance dictates, the point is that communal intimacy lends itself to a kind of eroticism that is literally transformative, socially and ethically. Furthermore, communal intimacy rewrites constructions of time all of which seem to uncover a kind of sacred subjectivity and capacity often denied marginalized populations in a hegemonic constitution. The fictive kinship that is crafted through embodied engagement and dancing together in ways that are tied to black historical and cultural traditions, reproduces the transformative possibility that Stallings notes. With that in mind, I end with Stallings work because it recognizes the centrality of embodiment, namely dance, in establishing the community as well as the traversing of time. Dance as a "black cultural practice" honors a black aesthetic and 'provoke[s] the will to remember."[40] Tap dance very clearly fits into this category as both black cultural practice, and as an art form that has always prioritized black and anti-captialist interest. Stallings highlights the ways in which dance, specifically as a form that is bound to a particular cultural and historical lineage, does work in rewriting white supremacist narratives of beauty and sites of memory. The Chorus, the original Jazz Jasmines, were understood as parts of a whole rarely considered to be subjects, or whole persons, in their own right. Through the restructuring of time and the undoing of constraints often placed on black femininity through the investment in community, the dance itself becomes an avenue through which "new" Jazz Jasmines like Royster and La Touche, become mediums recognizing the subjectivity of their predecessors and untapped elements of their own subjectivity.

The power of dancing as black cultural practice, particularly tap dance, when used in ways that capture the historical and cultural lineage of the dance, allow for the creation of environments that cultivate subjects and new modes of storytelling. The essential discursive claim here is how a black cultural practice and art form's use in telling and recounting black experiences can push us to hear and see differently. La Touche and Royster are impacted distinctly by the embodied function of this reality, and many of their comments about the shift in their worldview (as well as the subversive function of highlighting black stories in a white supremacist context) might also be the function of exploring and engaging stories through black cultural practice for viewers as well. To see tap dance used in ways that extend beyond the aesthetic function of the dance is to attune oneself to new ways of hearing and engaging the world, one that encourages an anti-black approach and tap dance as word and language in itself. This pushes the audience (as well as the performer) in ways that the revue structure rarely does. With the revue structure, we leave behind the unique capacities of Broadway shows that prioritizes black voices and historical lineages in multiples ways. Through the exploration of stories like 2016's *Shuffle Along* (and *Jelly's Last Jam* and others) we engage new possibilities in storytelling and possibilities towards black subjectivity.

---

[39]L.H. Stallings, *Funk the Erotic: Transaesthetics and Black Sexual Cultures* (Urbana: University of Illinois Press, 2015), 204.
[40]Ibid., 192.

Conclusion

For over a century, Broadway has proven an essential form of entertainment that like many others adapts with the times, offering commentaries on social and political climates or new imaginative takes on classic stories. Despite the innovation and intentionality that exists in Broadway, it has also been influenced by the hegemonic realities in which it has long thrived, informed by the white supremacist and imperialist interests. The way that tap dance has been included on Broadway speaks to this broader hegemonic influence. The relegation of tap dance as an art form to revues rather than exploring its use as a storytelling vehicle within shows is a holdover from a time in which tap dance as an art form was understood as low-brow, or unrefined, in ways that were tied to race. Through the exploration and analysis of *Black and Blue* and *Shuffle Along*, this chapter has explored the uses of tap dance that defy this relegation by ways that reference it as historical and cultural tradition. The racist and classist perspectives regarding tap dance fit the political and cultural ideas that have long controlled the social discourse about tap dance. Like vaudeville, and its roots in minstrelsy, Broadway seems to have inherited some of the more limiting notions of tap dance. These sentiments are reflected in the use of tap dance to produce a kind of aesthetic that separate it from its historical and cultural lineage. Meaning that, by disconnecting tap dance from the ways in which it manifests black cultural production, tap dance still functions in a "readable" and commodifiable way, i.e., in a way that makes it feed white expectations of blackness. This relegation, or limitation, is dangerous in that it reinforces ideas about tap dance that fuels hegemonic notions of classism, imperialism, gender, and racism.

Through the use of tap dance in a way that allows it to function as a storytelling device, to be seen and heard as an added voice, making it an integral component to share the "burden" of the storytelling/communication, we tie tap dance back to its communicative and intentionally subversive historical and social lineage. Furthermore, this action invests necessarily in the subjectivity of those within the narrative and those embodying said roles. Through discussions with Lisa La Touche and Karissa Royster, we can see the way that engaging tap dance enhances notions of subjectivity, self-empowerment, and individual capacity through ideas of kinship and embodiment. La Touche and Royster through commitment to education gained a new sense of the subjectivity of the "original" Jazz Jasmines, producing a sense of kinship that erased temporal boundaries. The engagement and recognition of the Chorus from the original production of *Shuffle Along* and their experiences produces a sense of connection that merges past and present, rewriting traditional temporal and anti-black scripts that seek to reduce blackness (particularly black femininity) to commodities.

The acknowledgement of black subjectivity in ways that affirm and invest in fictive kinship rewrite hegemonic patterns that obfuscate and reduce blackness and black femininity. The power of fictive kinship is that it taps into the erotic possibilities, pushing audience members to bear witness to the cast as whole subjects, and perhaps even to bear the weight of the responsibility and the significance of the noted histories. For the cast, though, the experience lent itself to a shift in embodiment and ethical perspective as happening *only* through community. It enhanced the possibility for noting and recognizing the sacrality and intimacy of the experience; moreover, it encouraged them to shift their perspective of what is possible in the world in ways that are embodied with ethical reverberations. The limiting ways in which we constitute chorus girls is subverted through their individual subjectivity and communing with the Chorus in ways that uncover "hidden" futures. The Chorus becomes a medium, a central point of passage for the enacting of kinship and the subversion of hegemonic narratives. The Chorus uncovers the otherwise, even "as exhausted as they [may be], they don't relent, they try to make a way out of no way, to not be defeated by defeat."[41] Through the subversion and denial of the narratives meant to relegate and dehumanize, the Chorus imagines new possibilities and new futures therein. In so doing, the Chorus becomes "the vehicle for another kind of story;" one that "incites change" and "propels transformation."[42] The Chorus is rooted in collective action in the engagement and construction of community through which subjectivity and hope is accessed; it is the "collective movement [that] pointes toward what awaits us, what has yet to come into view, what they anticipate—the time and place better than here; a glimpse of the earth not owned by anyone."[43] Saidiya Hartman reminds us about the world-shifting power and possibilities when the Chorus is actually at the center of the story and allowed the space to engage subjectivity through the collective. If the Chorus, in their dancing and embrace of black femininity, irrupt our ideas of what is possible, then new storytelling modalities, like tap dance, that lift black stories *and* black subjectivity might not be an inevitability but an empowering and world-making necessity.

Bibliography

"1989 Tony Awards 'Black on Blue' Revue (68)." Uploaded by Gladstone Girl4, June 27, 2016. YouTube video, 7:17. https://www.youtube.com/watch?v=UelL8kK1sSE.

Brooks, Daphne A. *Bodies in Dissent: Spectacular Performances of Race and Freedom, 1850–1910*. Durham, NC: Duke University Press, 2006.

Edelman, Lee. *No Future: Queer Theory and the Death Drive*. Durham, NC: Duke University Press, 2004.

Hartman, Saidiya. *Wayward Lives, Beautiful Experiments: Intimate Histories of Social Upheaval*. New York: W. W. Norton, 2019.

Hill, Constance Valis. *Tap Dancing America: A Cultural History*. New York: Oxford University Press, 2010.

Lorde, Audre. *Sister Outsider: Essays and Speeches*. Tucson, AZ: Kore Press, 1984.

Mordden, Ethan. *Beautiful Mornin': The Broadway Musical in the 1940s*. New York: Oxford University Press, 1999.

Post, Tina. "Williams, Walker, and Shine: Blackbody, Blackface, or the Importance of Being Surface." *TDR: The Drama Review* 59, no. 4 (2015): 83–100.

Shawn, Ted. *Fundamentals of Dance Education*. Girard, KS: Haldeman-Julius, 1937.

Snorton, C. Riley. *Black on Both Sides: A Racial History of Trans Identity*. Minneapolis: University of Minnesota Press, 2017.

Stallings, L. H. *Funk the Erotic: Transaesthetics and Black Sexual Cultures*. Urbana: University of Illinois Press, 2015.

Stearns, Marshall Winslow, and Jean Stearns. *Jazz Dance: The Story of American Vernacular Dance*. New York: Macmillan, 1968.

---

[41] Hartman, *Wayward Lives, Beautiful Experiments*, 347.
[42] Ibid., 348.
[43] Ibid., 349.

Veltruský, Jiří. "Man and Object in the Theater." In *A Prague School Reader on Esthetics, Literary Structure, and Style*, translated by Paul L. Garvin, 83–91. Washington, DC: Georgetown University Press, 1964.

Womack, Ytasha L. *Afrofuturism: The World of Black Sci-Fi and Fantasy Culture*. Chicago: Lawrence Hill Books, 2013.

Young, Thelathia Nikki. *Black Queer Ethics, Family, and Philosophical Imagination*. New York: Palgrave Macmillan, 2016.

11 Ballet, Race, and the Great White Way

RAMÓN FLOWERS

Sometimes people hold a core belief that is very strong. When they are presented with evidence that works against that belief, the new evidence cannot be accepted. It would create a feeling that is extremely uncomfortable, called cognitive dissonance. And because it is so important to protect the core belief, they will rationalize, ignore and even deny anything that doesn't fit in with the core belief.

—Frantz Fanon (1952)

Even though great progress has been made in recent years, how is it that Broadway musicals and classical ballet remained exclusively for the white elite for so long? What systems were put into place, and what of those systems remains, to help facilitate such exclusivity? How much of the United States' institutionalized racism remains operative in these two grand and storied genres of theatrical performance? And finally, what lenses, prescriptions, and mental frameworks are available and necessary as we work to move beyond the past and into a new, more equitable and sustainable dance performance paradigm?

A clear-eyed examination of actual practices over the last hundred years reveals a history of racism in both classical ballet and Broadway musicals. Over the course of many decades, performers of color have been required to play racialized characters, to be segregated onstage, and to promulgate stereotypes inherited from blackface minstrelsy, all the while performing alongside white cast members who dominate the production. These actions are not only limited to what happens onstage. Behind the curtain, in the casting, hiring, and management of ballet and Broadway shows, the bona fide racism that for so long coursed through the very marrow of the Great White Way and elsewhere has compromised performing artists of all races as they have attempted to work within their respective crafts to both create art and achieve successful and durable performance careers.[1] George Balanchine, one of the most prominent American ballet choreographers of the twentieth century, would eventually hire a Black male dancer, Arthur Mitchell, in 1955. However, at times he struggled with the idea of tainting the European art form with dancers of another race. He stated: "I don't want to see two Japanese girls in my Swan Lake. It's just not right. It's not done for them. It's like making an American blonde into a geisha. It's a question of certain arts being things unto themselves."[2]

---

[1] For more on working relationships with Black artists, see Ruthie Fierberg, "Broadway's Mykal Kilgore Calls Out Racism in the Theatre on Facebook," *Playbill*, June 3, 2020.

[2] Richard A. Long, *The Black Tradition in American Dance* (New York: Rizzoli, 1989), 119.

In *Black Skin, White Masks*, Frantz Fanon, the psychiatrist and political philosopher from the French colony of Martinique, wrote: "The fact of the juxtaposition of the white and black races has created a massive psycho-existential complex."[3] What I deduce from this quote is that Black performers working in a predominantly white production would no longer question their existence within that production if they not only were included in that production but were made to feel a true sense of belonging. In classical ballet and musical theatre, Black people who are included in predominantly white productions often are asked to change an aspect of who they are in order to "fit in."

Through a phenomenological approach—that is, speaking from my own lived and embodied experiences as a ballet and musical theatre dancer working in the highest echelons of performance in companies, Broadway shows, and venues across the United States, Europe, and Asia—I explore the real-world manifestations of this psycho-existential complex. The aim of this chapter is to interrogate systemic racism within the performing arts with the hope to open up a space that allows for newly enlightened productions, casting, and performance paradigms to grow. This is not just a theoretical discussion. My direct experience in this high-profile and high-pressure field of theatrical dance performance here serves as a lens with which to view the issues at hand. This chapter unfolds these concepts by way of discussions on racialized casting practices, tokenism, and the managing of expectations, and concludes with reflections on a path toward a more equitable and inclusive future. I review informative examples and controversies from within the art, ranging from star ballerina Misty Copeland's comments on blackface in the Bolshoi Theatre's production of *La Bayadère* to problematic typecasting and tokenism on Broadway, but I also include hopeful examples of enlightened practices in casting, direction, and production in the modern era.

Casting, Typecasting, and Stereotypes

Nontraditional casting, or "blind" casting, is becoming increasingly prevalent in the Broadway musical. In the last ten years, since the early 2010s, shows like *Les Misérables* and *Phantom of the Opera* have opted for blind casting, which in the case of *Phantom*, allowed the first Asian American and African American actors to be cast in the principal roles of the Broadway production.[4] Markedly, Lin-Manuel Miranda's *Hamilton* (2015) has helped reinforce Broadway's steady gravitation toward diverse casting, and the musical's continued success has brought a resurgence to the idea of blind casting. This new trend of inclusive or blind casting—choosing an actor regardless of their race, gender, or ethnicity—stands athwart the decades-long practice of casting principal roles in Golden Age musicals on Broadway. Certain roles, however, fall more easily into a category that can facilitate blind casting. For example, the role of Mr. Mistoffelees in the original Broadway production of *Cats* (1981) was played by Timothy Scott, who was a white American ballet dancer. This role is known as one of the most technically difficult dance roles in Broadway history. Dame Gillian Barbara Lynne, choreographer of *Cats*, was an English ballerina who pulled from her experiences in classical

---

[3]Frantz Fanon, *Black Skin, White Masks* (New York: Grove Press, 1952), 14.
[4]On January 26, 2022, Emilie Kouatchou was cast as the first Black Christine in the musical's thirty-four-year run on Broadway.

ballet when she choreographed the solo for the role of Mr. Mistoffelees. She added all the most difficult male bravura technical tricks normally found in a classical male variation. (An example of a classical male variation is the solo performed after the duet with the ballerina, which is usually two jumping passes, followed by two pirouette combinations, executed by double tours [turns in the air] or entrechat sixes [beating the legs together in the air]. Some variations have a quality manège added in [jumping in a circle going around the stage]). As a result, when this role is cast, the primary focus is on which man attending the audition will be able to pull off all the technical requirements eight times a week. With the focus less on race, Mr. Mistoffelees has been played by male ballet dancers of all races.

Typecasting during the casting process—replacing a dancer with another of the same race or similar features and qualities—is a widespread practice in the Broadway musical and historically can often be race related (though not always the case, as body types and physical abilities come into play, as with Mr. Mistoffelees in *Cats*). Another example of where typecasting is less about race and more about body types and physical abilities is in casting the role of Miss Turnstiles in *On the Town*, who should be a triple threat, but most importantly, she must be an accomplished ballet dancer. In the original Broadway production of *On the Town* (1944), Sono Osato, a Japanese American ballet dancer (whose own father was being held in an internment camp at the time), created the role of "Miss Turnstiles," an American beauty queen of the subway. Following Broadway's tradition of typecasting, revival productions of *On the Town* also cast experienced ballerinas from diverse backgrounds as their stars. The first Broadway revival of *On the Town* opened in 1971, with Donna McKechnie, a white American who has major ballet training, in the role of Ivy Smith (Miss Turnstiles); the second revival, which opened in 1998, starred Tai Jimenez, Boston Ballet, African Latina principal ballerina; and the third revival, which opened in 2014, starring Megan Fairchild, white American principal ballerina of New York City Ballet, who was replaced by Misty Copeland, first African American female principal dancer of the American Ballet Theatre, and Georgina Pazcoguin, New York City Ballet's first female Asian American soloist. Like Mr. Mistoffelees in *Cats*, Miss Turnstiles, has also been played by female ballet dancers of all races.

Typecasting has the potential to be problematic because it can normalize and perpetuate stereotypes in society. For instance, in the second act divertissement of the ballet *The Nutcracker*, dancers are exoticized in the misrepresentation of Asian culture in the section called Chinese. Phil Chan, co-founder of Final Bow for Yellowface, sat motionless with his father after watching a traditional performance of *The Nutcracker* with Asian caricatures. Chan always expressed himself through dance; however, after seeing that performance with his father he had this to say: "It reminded me that I didn't belong. He goes, 'Do you really want to devote your life to this? This is how they see you, this offensive portrayal of Chinese people.'"[5]

Typecasting can also involve the misrepresentation of a culture or group of people. This broad typecasting finds its roots in the stereotypes that have been perpetuated since the nascent years of the American musical. Before *In Dahomey* (1903), the first Broadway

---

[5]Nancy Chen, "Dancers seek to rid ballet performances of Asian stereotypes," *CBS Evening News*, May 19, 2021.

musical that was written and performed by African Americans, it was assumed that white people would rather see plays that showed stereotypes that did not truly depict what an African American embodied and encompassed. The popularity of minstrel shows reinforced this attraction to stereotypical Black characters and types.[6] Eventually, the racist aspects of blackface in Broadway productions were seen as disrespectful of social norms and were discontinued. However, though Broadway productions no longer used blackface makeup after the civil rights movement (culminating with the Civil Rights Act of 1964 and the Voting Rights Act of 1965),[7] the formula of creating characters from a combination of negative, stereotype-based depictions of nonwhite people continued.

Furthermore, in terms of character development, complex roles and revolutionary depictions of three-dimensional characters in musical theatre come from collaboration in the creative voices, whether it be the book writer, librettist, director, or choreographer, all of whom come together to find truth in character interpretation. Pointedly, there exists a high possibility of missing the depth and complexity of character when the dominant creative voice is always white. Diversity behind the scenes, both in the developmental process and in the staging, is as important (if not more so) as it is onstage. White directors and choreographers are limited when directing a Black actor or dancer who has lived the experiences they are being asked to interpret in a scene or in a ballet. White directors and choreographers often give Black actors and dancers the impression they think they know more about the lived experiences of a person from a marginalized community than does the person who has been directly affected by systemic racism.

I have had conversations with numerous Black Broadway actors, and each one has had an experience with a director who wanted them to play their roles "more Black." Directors and choreographers often try to find a clever way of asking a Black performer to engage with spoken or embodied characteristics from a minstrel show—broken English or stereotypical gestures, say—while interpreting their characters. While such practices might not be directly asked for, those of us who have been in the room on such occasions know exactly what is being asked of us.

Is there a way to remain true to the time period of a production without using such negative and ill-informed interpretations? Yes. In the 2015 revival of *The Color Purple*, for instance, director John Doyle decided not to have the actors speak in the dialect as it was originally written. Nothing was lost in the translation.

Generally speaking, in the past three decades, since roughly the 1990s, Broadway and classical ballet have come a long way with their hiring and casting policies as they relate to race. However, there remain double standards regarding which shows receive the financial

---

[6]Detailed discussions of minstrelsy can be found in Marshall Winslow Stearns and Jean Stearns, *Jazz Dance: The Story of American Vernacular Dance* (New York: Macmillan, 1968); Megan Pugh, *America Dancing: From the Cakewalk to the Moonwalk* (New Haven, CT: Yale University Press, 2015); William J. Mahar, *Behind the Burnt Cork Mask: Early Blackface Minstrelsy and Antebellum American Popular Culture* (Urbana: University of Illinois Press, 1999); and Samantha Kubota, "How Minstrel Shows Led Us to Racist Stereotypes in Culture Today," *Today*, NBC, June 26, 2020, https://www.today.com/tmrw/how-minstrel-shows-1800s-led-us-racist-stereotypes-culture-today-t185341. See also chapter 10 in this collection.
[7]For a useful overview of these acts, see "The Civil Rights Act of 1964 and the Voting Rights Act of 1965," Khan Academy, https://www.khanacademy.org/humanities/us-history/postwarera/civil-rights-movement/a/the-civil-rights-act-of-1964-and-the-voting-rights-act-of-1965.

backing needed for a successful run. Many amazing shows never make it to Broadway because producers do not think the content will sell if it is not "whitewashed." Some shows that do get picked up are asked to change aspects of the show that the producers feel are less of a selling point. I will elaborate more on this topic later in the chapter when I reflect on my experience as a cast member of the Broadway production *Hot Feet* (2009). Prior to that elaboration, in an effort to bring the impact of racial stereotyping to the forefront of art making and the performative experience, an interrogation of the black dancing body onstage sheds light on how racism plays out in the identity crisis of the African American, or any member of a marginalized group who has to wear the "white masks" of assimilation into a white power structure.[8] From a performance perspective, this analysis informs an understanding of some of the mythologies that surround the question of who can play what role onstage in a ballet or musical.

The Black Dancing Body

During chattel slavery, and for many years after enslaved people were set free, Black men were, and still are, thought of as being brutes and overly sexual creatures. These stereotypes have long contributed to accusations of rape in consensual—or nonexistent—sexual encounters with white women. Black women as well have been overly sexualized and often are seen as "Jezebels," too strong, too muscular, or too aggressive. If these constructions of identity are thought about in the context of classical ballet, it can be understood why a Black man dancing with a white woman could seem problematic in the United States during every era in American history except the last two decades or so. Likewise, these ingrained interpretations can support why a director of a mainstream classical ballet company might find it difficult to see a Black ballerina in the role of a virtuous princess, or a "fragile" sylph.

Is it not ironic that dancers in classical ballets often are asked to live in a fantasy world, portraying mythical, fictitious characters, but casting directors and choreographers cannot use their imaginations during the casting process to contemplate casting a Black body in a role (and in fact find it detrimental to the overall unity of a production to do so)? According to Brenda Dixon Gottschild, as evidenced in her book, *The Black Dancing Body: A Geography from Coon to Cool*, there is a "love-hate" paradox with the Black body in America.[9] Historically, the same qualities that are characterized as repulsive in the Black body are also desired by the white hierarchy. African American culture is both distinct and enormously influential on American and global culture as a whole. So why is it that white directors and choreographers love Black culture but disdain the people who create it? Why would Elvis Presley imitate Big Mama Thornton, an African American blues singer, and gyrate his hips as if he were the white version of Jackie Wilson? Why did George Balanchine use significant markers of African American culture when creating some of his most iconic ballets, such as *The Four Temperaments* (1946), *Agon* (1957), or *Jewels* (1967)?

---

[8]For more on the broader power structures that surround dance, see K. Sue Jewell, *From Mammy to Miss America and Beyond: Cultural Images and the Shaping of US Social Policy* (New York: Routledge, 1993).
[9] Brenda Dixon Gottschild, *The Black Dancing Body*. New York: Palgrave Macmillan, 2005, 199.

Ballet and Broadway have to adapt to the times and changing culture if they are to survive. Traditionalists may ask: how can classical ballet modernize and survive while remaining true to classicism and tradition? Examples that can answer this question, however, are readily found.

Classical ballet has been deeply affected by cultural changes in the past. After the social revolution of the 1960s, British choreographer Sir Frederick Ashton added a solo to *Swan Lake* that was based on the social dance the twist. Maurice Béjart, internationally renowned French choreographer, revolutionized ballet when he cast a male dancer, Jorge Donn, in a role that was originally created for Yugoslav ballerina Duška Sifnios in the ballet that put Béjart on the map, *Boléro* (1960). Also challenging the heteronormative ballet spectrum is Matthew Bourne's version of *Swan Lake* (1995), in which men danced as the swans.

In December 2019, American ballerina Misty Copeland posted a photo to her Instagram of two ballerinas posing in blackface for a performance of *La Bayadère* at Moscow's Bolshoi Theatre. "This is the reality of the ballet world," she captioned the post, kicking off an international debate about racism in ballet. The Bolshoi Theatre responded to the backlash spurred by Copeland's post by saying it has no plans to change the ballet, which has featured performers in blackface since its premiere in 1877. Moreover, Bolshoi director Vladimir Urin told Russia's RIA Novosti news agency: "The ballet *La Bayadère* has been performed thousands of times in this production in Russia and abroad, and the Bolshoi Theatre will not get involved in such a discussion."[10] A commenter on Russian state television asked, further, "In what way is it racist to portray a culture's most recognizable attributes? In 2021, not even ballet is safe from the P.C. police."[11] Regardless of these perhaps inevitable reactions, a sea change in the art of ballet is inexorably underway in today's productions. With the rise of antiracism movements and people of the global majority taking a stand, Broadway and ballet are slowly making changes to keep up to date and to remain relevant.

As an illustration of this gradual shift, Chan changed the course of how we approach *The Nutcracker*, America's favorite holiday ballet, which has been under fire for several years for its misrepresentation of cultures. Meeting with then ballet master-in-chief of the New York City Ballet Peter Martins in 2017, Chan highlighted the offensive misrepresentation of Chinese culture in Balanchine's *The Nutcracker* and encouraged changes. That conversation led to more than an updated production at the New York City Ballet: it started an international movement for change and catalyzed changes in how we talk about race in America. In 2021, the Berlin State Ballet announced that it would skip *The Nutcracker* entirely that year, a decision that angered some cultural critics, who cited concerns about freedom of expression. "People are not stupid," Roger Köppel, a former editor of *Die Welt*, a German newspaper, said in an email. "They can think for themselves and do not have to be shielded and protected from art that is declared politically incorrect by people who want to force their worldview on all of us."[12] The stakes are high; for many ballet companies, *The Nutcracker* is

---

[10]Quoted in Todd Prince, "Bolshoi to Continue Using Blackface Makeup, Despite Criticism," *Radio Free Europe/Radio Liberty*, December 15, 2019.
[11]Javier C. Hernández, "As 'Nutcracker' Returns, Companies Rethink Depictions of Asians," *New York Times*, November 19, 2021.
[12]Quoted in Hernandez.

the biggest show of the year, a financial lifeline that generates a large percentage of annual ticket sales. Dancers and artistic leaders have said that reimagining *The Nutcracker* is essential to attracting diverse audiences. Nonetheless, others stated there is still room for improvement.[13]

Broadway has also made an attempt at diversifying its productions, making sure to be inclusive during its casting process. What that has traditionally looked like, however, is a few token Black performers mixed in with the otherwise all-white cast. For example, the Broadway musical *A Chorus Line* (1975) had one African American man, one Asian American woman, one Puerto Rican woman, one Puerto Rican man who self-identified as Italian, and one Jewish American man. Another show that illustrates the usage of tokenism is the 1994 revival of the Broadway production *Carousel*, which featured six-time Tony Award–winner Audra McDonald. McDonald was the first African American to be cast in the role of Carrie Pipperidge, and it happened during Broadway's foray into nontraditional casting. McDonald's undeniable talent and accomplishments, however, deflated the idea that she was hired as just a token attempt at diversification, paving the way for additional talented people of color to be considered for their abilities first in the hiring process. In the 1980s, both ballet and Broadway always seemed to have only one "token" Black person represented on the stage, and their white colleagues seemed to think of that "token" as just that, completely overlooking the possibility of their presence having anything to do with their qualifications for being there.

One example from my personal experience helps illustrate tokenism in the hiring practices of the Broadway musical. I was invited to audition for the ensemble of the 2002 revival of *Oklahoma!*, directed by Trevor Nunn and choreographed by Susan Stroman. To my surprise, when I arrived at the audition, the holding room was full of only Black men. We were considered the crème de la crème of Black Broadway dancers of that time, and we all knew one another. The competition was stiff, and the sad reality was that we all also knew that they would be hiring only one of us. This was made clear to us in the holding room for the audition when a white dancer showed up who was not invited to the private audition, and that dancer was informed that all spots for the ensemble had been filled except for the track they were casting at that audition. Looking around the room at who was invited, we could see that the production was looking for a Black male dancer to complete the cast.

At one moment during the audition, Stroman asked us all to go one at a time, showing off our most impressive skills. One dancer, after seeing how proficient we all were, said he might as well just pack up his things and leave, because he felt like he could not hold a candle to the rest of us. Given his execution of earlier steps during his solo, it was clearly evident that he was the weakest of the bunch; however, he was the one who ended up getting the job. My theory is that as dark-skinned Black dancers, we naturally stand out in a crowd of all-white dancers like a raisin in a bowl of milk, so in this case they went with the weakest dancer, assuming he wouldn't pull too much focus from the white male lead dancer. In fact, the director ended up placing him in the last row onstage. Notably, this trend of diversification does not discriminate; it affects otherwise all-Black musicals as well. An examination of the 2009 musical *Hot Feet* draws attention to this effect.

---

[13]Hernandez.

Hot Feet and Commercial Visibility

The Broadway production of *Hot Feet* (2009) was conceived by Maurice Hines to be an all-Black urban retelling of the all-white movie *The Red Shoes* (1948). When Transamerica agreed to produce the show, it came with the caveat that the show would be produced only if half of the cast were white. Although the show had already been cast with Black performers, Hines was required to hold an audition. In this case instead of there being an audition to hire one Black man to complete the all-white production, it was to hire several white people to assuage the demands of the producers. As a cast member of *Hot Feet*, I experienced firsthand the racial dynamics at play in the production of a Broadway musical, during the filming of the commercial for the production.

To ensure a long run for the show, the producers had us film a television commercial. During the filming of the commercial, directed by internationally renowned dance photographer Lois Greenfield, Hines informed the dancers that he was instructed to put the "lighter" dancers in the front. Hines wanted the dancers to know that the decision was not his, and he went on to say that as the commercial's target audience is middle America, apparently it would be more appealing to have white dancers in the front because "Black doesn't sell tickets." The assumed fear was that by having the Black dancers in the front, America would get the impression that the cast of *Hot Feet* was all Black, which supposedly has less appeal. Once Broadway shows are up and running, they depend on an out-of-town audience for box-office support to guarantee their longevity. The circulation of this commercial would attract the attention of potential ticket buyers.

I asked a few former cast members of *Hot Feet* to reflect on the commercial shoot for the Broadway production. Ensemble member Felicity Stiverson Mrnak said:

> It was so incredibly uncomfortable. I was already in the front. That's how the staging was. It was the end of the production number "September," when we were doing that rhythm foot section, and the photographer started adjusting the dancers' positions for the videos/photos. And then it became obvious that she was moving white dancers to the front of the formation and Black dancers to the back. Maurice put a stop to it, but it was super uncomfortable and felt terrible all around. I don't remember exactly who was moved, but it did seem like there was an obvious racial bias with the photographer's choices of who she moved.[14]

For his part, ensemble member Steve Konopelski said:

> I do remember the incident you are speaking of. . . . I do remember being placed in the second row for the commercial rehearsal and then being moved to the front in the final rehearsal. I then remember being moved back to the second row just before filming, when Maurice made his speech about not "tolerating that racism" by the producers. I feel for anyone who has ever been made to feel like they don't belong because of the color of their skin. Each performer has earned their right to be part of a show, a cast, a performing family . . . and I do think it a shame that on so many levels there is someone who is made to feel or told they don't belong. What you might not know is how incredibly embarrassing it was to be moved by Maurice that day.[15]

---

[14]Felicity Stiverson Mrnak, interview with the author, August 10, 2021.
[15]Steve Konopelski, interview with the author, August 8, 2021.

Ensemble member Monique Smith responded more briefly, stating, "Maurice said, 'They just asked if we could put more white faces in the front.' They said it to him privately, but he called it out in front of all of us. I'll never forget it."[16]

Finally, ensemble member Hollie Wright stated, "I remember it happening in rehearsal. And the director wanted to move one of the Black male dancers to the back, and one of the white female dancers to the front. And in front of us Mr. Maurice called her on it. He said, 'Oh you want the Black guy in the back and the white girl in the front?' The director was really embarrassed, and she said she was trying to make it look multicultural."[17]

I reached out to Hines and Greenfield to find out what they remembered from the commercial shoot for *Hot Feet*. Although Hines was not available for comment, here is what Greenfield remembered from her work as director/photographer:

> Working on a TV commercial for the Broadway show *Hot Feet* in 2006 was my first experience being involved in directing a commercial video for a major Broadway show. It was actually intimidating for me, as I was used to photographing dance companies either live onstage or in my studio. In one of the scenes, we filmed on the set of *Hot Feet*, there were a few lines of orchestrated dancers.
>
> At some point, the producers of the show came over to me and my assistant, asking me to talk to Maurice Hines, who was the choreographer and director of the show, and to ask him about rearranging the dancers in their lineup, so that the darker-skinned dancers were upstage and the lighter-skinned dancers were in front. No one asked my opinion, as my job was just to shoot film, and it was very awkward for me, and certainly for Maurice, and the dancers.[18]

Based on my personal experience during the commercial shoot for *Hot Feet*, I conclude that Broadway producers are more concerned about their return on investment in a production than the impact their casting decisions may have on the performers of that production. Such decisions are exemplary of the direct and indirect message of racial socialization and internalized racism, which are known to be contributing factors to post-traumatic slave syndrome, discussed later in this chapter. Moving forward, I put forth structural instances of racism within ballet training and hierarchal structures in ballet companies to offer another entry into problematizing ballet and to shed light on the systems in place that facilitate the exclusivity of the white elite.

A Tyranny of Certain Expectations

When I was in ballet school and had gotten to the point where I was ready to audition for placement in professional companies, one of my teachers asked everyone in the class their goals for desired ballet companies. When he got to me, he didn't really ask; instead, he told me that my choices were either the Dance Theatre of Harlem or Alvin Ailey, the modern dance oasis for people of color. I was the only Black person in my class, and it was at that moment that I felt my Blackness for the first time. In order to understand the path I pursued,

---

[16]Monique Smith, interview with the author, August 8, 2021.
[17]Hollie Wright, interview with the author, August 10, 2021.
[18]Lois Greenfield, interview with the author, May 9, 2022.

a brief historical contextualization of these companies and the development of opportunities for Black dancers is useful. The Dance Theatre of Harlem was founded in 1969 by Arthur Mitchell, who in 1955 became the first African American to join the New York City Ballet. Mitchell's company created opportunities at a time when there were even fewer possibilities for Black ballet dancers to gain professional employment. Through the Dance Theatre of Harlem, many Black ballet dancers got to perform roles they probably never would have had the opportunity to dance, if they were lucky enough to be one of the only Black dancers in a white company. The female lead in *Giselle*, for example (a ballet staged in 1984 for the Dance Theatre of Harlem by Frederic Franklin), is a role that normally requires the idea of pure and virtuous weightlessness, as this is considered a romantic ballet. Given the stereotypes that surround the Black dancer's body, a Black ballerina in a white ballet company would normally never have the opportunity to dance such a role. Likewise, Black male ballet dancers have their own hurdle to jump over when it comes to the roles they would be considered for as a principal dancer in a mainstream classical ballet company.

As a principal dancer, one is required to dance what is called a *pas de deux*, which is French for "a step for two people." In the 1950s, when Mitchell joined the New York City Ballet, America was not prepared to see a Black man dance a sensual *pas de deux* with a white woman. As the Black man still was stereotyped as being a sexual brute, and the white woman was considered pure, virtuous, and innocent, especially in ballet roles during this period of time, it was not easy for mainstream America to move past the images of lynchings and the unjustifiable reasons that such atrocities occurred.[19]

Thanks to pioneers like Alvin Ailey, who founded the Alvin Ailey American Dance Theater in 1958, I had the audacity to dream of becoming a dancer in America. Ailey's company represented something larger than itself for little Black and brown children who didn't see themselves represented on most of the predominantly white concert dance stages in the United States. At the time of its founding, there was no other concert dance company for dancers of color to dream of joining (the Dance Theatre of Harlem would not be founded until eleven years later). Ailey made his presence known in disadvantaged communities of color by touring around the New York City area and neighboring cities and doing lecture-demonstration performances, where he would give children who might not ever have been able to afford it the opportunity to see a world-class dance performance for the first time in their lives—for free. After such performances, Ailey would hold a question-and-answer session to pique the interest of potential future dancers.

Though I loved the works of and had the utmost respect for both Ailey and Mitchell, I made a conscious decision to never dance for either of their companies, right there on the spot. I was defiant about not being put in a Black box. I made it my goal to prove to that teacher that he could not define me. I would go on to become the first African American male dancer of the Pennsylvania Ballet, as well as a principal dancer with several mainstream ballet companies around the world, and often the only Black person in a Broadway production.

---

[19] During the Jim Crow era (1896–1954), white mobs often used lynchings to keep Black people "in their place." Black men could fall victim to being lynched if they owned a business that was seen as competition to white businesses, were caught having a consensual sexual encounter with, startling, or (in the case of Emmett Till) whistling at a white woman, or were simply trying to register to vote.

As a result of being the first Black dancer in the Pennsylvania Ballet company since its formation in 1963, I was interviewed by many local newspapers, TV shows, and magazines. Though my accomplishments, as far as I was concerned, were a result of my hard work and talent, the question on everybody's mind was: what is it like to be the first African American dancer in the company? Until I was asked that question in those interviews, I was not treated any differently than any other dancer in the school for the Pennsylvania Ballet, and for that I am thankful. In many of my classes at the school, not only was I the only Black dancer, I also was the only male dancer. The classes ranged from level 1 up to the most advanced, level 6. There were approximately two hundred students in the school.

It was not until I was interviewed for being the first Black male dancer to join the company that I was made to feel like a "Black dancer," and from that moment on I began to notice and think about race differently. I started to notice in other mainstream ballet companies in the United States that there seemed to be only one Black dancer, if any. This trend also seemed to be consistent on Broadway, on television, and in film. A perfect example of this is in the cast of the Broadway musical *A Chorus Line* (1975), where the only Black character in the show points out the obvious when he's asked to tell a little bit about himself to the director of the show within the show: "My name is Richie Walters. I'm from Herculaneum, Missouri, I was born on a full moon on June 13, 1948. And I'm black."[20] I also noticed that it was even more rare for there to be a Black female dancer in these companies.

Ballet Companies and Structuralized Colorism

To return to Misty Copeland, the first female African American to be promoted to the prestigious rank of principal dancer with the American Ballet Theater in its eighty-four-year history: Copeland, who is very fair skinned, is a talented dancer who worked hard and deserves everything she has earned throughout her career. One cannot help but wonder, though, whether she would have had the same amount of success and recognition were she a dark-skinned ballerina. Though Copeland is seen in the ballet world as Black, one gets the impression that mainstream ballet is far more accepting of her because she blends in a little better with the white ballerinas once the lights are on her, which might be considered more of a problem if she had darker skin that really stood out.

Copeland, like Janet Collins and Raven Wilkinson, light-skinned African American ballerinas who came before her, could put on makeup to look white under the lights (something that has been suggested to all three of these ballerinas). Others would not be as successful at hiding their Blackness with makeup because lighter makeup on darker skin tones makes the person wearing it look like they have xeroderma, dry ashy skin. Given that directors of mainstream classical ballet companies have asked light-skinned ballerinas to lighten their skin, it is safe to assume that dark-skinned ballerinas do indeed still remain at a disadvantage at mainstream ballet companies in the United States.

Ben Stevenson, former director of the Houston Ballet company and school, initially told dancer Lauren Anderson's father that she did not have the body for classical ballet and that

---

[20] Michael Bennett, *A Chorus Line: The Book of the Musical*, book by James Kirkwood and Nicholas Dante, music by Marvin Hamlisch, lyrics by Edward Kleban (New York: Applause, 1995).

she might be better suited for musical theatre. Anderson changed her diet and worked hard to prove him wrong. Stevenson rewarded her with the lead role in the school's production of *Alice in Wonderland* (1978). Confused by Stevenson's casting decision, Anderson remarked that Alice was "white." Stevenson replied, "The only color in art is on a canvas."[21] In 1990, Anderson became the first African American principal dancer of the Houston Ballet. Unfortunately, Stevenson is a rarity in classical ballet, and he was not able to shield Anderson from the racial discrimination and hatred she endured from the outside world and at times from her peers and visiting artists.

Ballerina Michaela DePrince, at age eight, was told that she could not dance the role of Marie in *The Nutcracker* because, sadly, "America's not ready for a black girl ballerina." A year later, a teacher told her adoptive white mother that Black dancers weren't worth investing money in.[22] Despite encountering instances of racial discrimination, DePrince was one of the stars of the 2011 documentary film *First Position* (on the Youth American Grand Prix ballet competition), and she went on to become a member of the Dance Theatre of Harlem, a soloist with the Dutch National Ballet, and, in 2021, a soloist with the Boston Ballet.[23]

Returning to the notion of casting and the complexities I have previously established, I turn now to the cattle call experience to shed new light on auditions for the Broadway musical and round out the discussion of the myriad of systems that must be negotiated or worked around as a Black dancer.

Adventures in the Cattle Call

I have been "typed out" during many of my Broadway auditions. This was back when Broadway productions were still using typecasting practices as a matter of course. Being typed out often had more to do with my skin color and body type than my talent. The first time I auditioned for *Cats*, in 1981, I was typed out after the classical ballet pirouette combination. In the 1980s, when there were lots of dancers showing up to what was called a "cattle call" audition, choreographers often started with a combination that had a lot of ballet technique in it to narrow down their search, since it was understood that many Broadway dancers did not take ballet on a regular basis, if at all, once they became professional dancers. As previously described, I am a well-trained ballet dancer who has been a principal dancer in internationally renowned ballet companies. After I did the pirouettes flawlessly, I was asked my height, which I lied about because I thought they wanted me to be taller than I actually am. Depending on the show, height matters, especially if you are auditioning for the ensemble. Ensemble men are normally expected to be at least five feet nine, and women should not be taller than five feet eight. This of course varies from show to show. I said I was five feet ten because I'm long-limbed and give the impression that

---

[21]Quoted in Stav Ziv, "As an African American Ballet Star, Lauren Anderson Inspired the Next Generation," *Muse*, June 19, 2020, https://www.themuse.com/advice/lauren-anderson-trailblazer-first-african-american-principal-dancer-houston-ballet.

[22]Carley Petesch, "Star Dancer Born into War Grows Up to Inspire," *Associated Press*, July 11, 2012.

[23]An interesting exploration of these themes can be found in Jessica Jacolbe, "The History of African-American Casting in Ballet," *JSTOR Daily*, February 20, 2019.

I am taller than I really am, which is five feet nine. I was cut from the audition after that. I called my best friend, Phineas Newborn III, who was a cast member of the Los Angeles Company of *Cats* at the time, and explained what had just happened. He let me know that they were looking for Coricopat, who is an on-stage cover for Mr. Mistoffelees, who are both kittens and should be no taller than five feet eight, and that if I were going to lie, I should have gone down in size, not up.

I was invited back to audition six months later. This time I lied about my height, taking my size down an inch, and I got the job of portraying Coricopat. It was rewarding for me to go to the *Cats* audition the second time with more information about how typecasting works and to be hired based on my abilities and not my color or my actual height. *Cats* is a sung-through musical, unusual in its construction, with music and dance the main focus of the production. Notably, the necessity of a casting height requirement is not clear to the audience while watching the show. It was not until I was doing the show that I understood that the differences in height determined the age of the cat, or that kittens were often on all fours, adolescent cats were upright, and the older cats were hunched over. It was from this experience that I also realized casting directors had imaginations, and that they could use their imaginations—with a little persuasion. I persuaded them into thinking that I was the height they were looking for, and it landed me the job.

Another notable experience at this audition was that we were asked to do typical male techniques such as turns in second position or double tours in the air on a raked stage. In my experience dancing in Europe, I was accustomed to raked stages. Thus, I felt right at home at this audition, where most dancers around me struggled. I happened to be the only African American man at my audition, and I got the job. I was hired as Coricopat and an onstage cover for the role of Mr. Mistoffelees. This was one example where typecasting worked in my favor. I was the right physical and technical type for the role they were trying to replace at that audition. In this particular case, the color of my skin was not a factor that weighed in on the outcome of my audition, I assume because all the performers in *Cats* wear heavy cat makeup and wigs, rendering the cast members unrecognizable. It is important to understand that not all typecasting has a negative impact on the person being cast. As the next example shows, a person's type might be determined by their skill set rather than their physical attributes.

Another opportunity I had to be seen for my talents and not the color of my skin was during the audition for Matthew Bourne's Broadway production of *Swan Lake* (1995). Sir Matthew Bourne is a British choreographer and dancer noted for his uniquely updated interpretations of traditional ballet repertoire. He is also known for his choreography for popular revivals of classic musicals. I was familiar with the classical ballet version of *Swan Lake*, so I had my reservations about going to the audition, assuming that there would be very few positions for a person of color in this production, if any. However, Bourne was practicing nontraditional casting in every sense of the word. The swans, traditionally danced by pale and fragile-looking ballerinas, were cast using men of all shapes, sizes, and colors, based on their ballet technique and dance abilities. In this audition, a strong ballet background and one's own abilities took precedence over the color of one's skin. I did not feel like a "Black dancer" at that audition; I felt like an accomplished ballet dancer who was at home doing the movements that were asked of me with the greatest of ease. I was one of seven Black dancers who were hired in the original Broadway production of *Swan Lake*.

Image 11.1 Mathew Bourne's *Swan Lake* (1995). Photo by Joan Marcus.

A counterpoint to Broadway dance was an experience I underwent in 1985 when I was approached to join Balanchine's New York City Ballet. Peter Martins, at the time the ballet master-in-chief of the New York City Ballet, expressed his interest in hiring me for the company, letting me know that he was looking for a replacement for Mel Tomlinson, the second African American, after Arthur Mitchell, to join the company. He added that as Tomlinson was leaving the company, he would need someone who had a funky, jazzy approach to ballet movements with the classical ballet aesthetic and lines. This was for the upcoming American Music Festival, where I would have been cast to dance in the new William Forsythe and Paul Taylor creations. Before Martins brought it to my attention, I never saw myself as a funky, jazzy dancer with a classical ballet dancer's aesthetic; I only saw myself as a dancer. I assume that Martins knew the history of Balanchine's influences and wanted to continue the legacy by having me replace the token of the times. Today, in New York City Ballet's commitment to antiracism, the company acknowledges that it has existed within a larger system in the ballet field that has historically marginalized people of color and has not recognized the value of diversity and inclusion to the art form.[24] The landscape of the company looks very different than it did in 1985. Martins's decision to take me into the company when Tomlinson was on his way out is an example of the tokenism that people of African descent experience on a regular basis when dancing in a mainstream ballet company,

---

[24]"Our Commitment to Anti-Racism," New York City Ballet (website), accessed October 10, 2022, https://www.nycballet.com/about-us/commitment-to-diversity-equity-and-inclusion/a-message-from-new-york-city-ballet/.

and often on Broadway as well. This approach to typecasting based on race has become so normalized that Martins did not think twice about his actions, or how they might affect me. Coming from his position of privilege, he had likely never had to empathize with the Other in the predicament in which he placed me. Out of curiosity, I asked what my role in the company would be after the American Music Festival. I was told I would eventually be dancing most of Tomlinson's repertoire, which he had inherited from Arthur Mitchell. I declined the offer to be placed in an even smaller "Black box."

Toward a More Equitable and Inclusive Future

Mainstream ballet companies have only just started to rethink their approach to doing racial, ethnic, and national stereotyping in story ballet. The ranks of ballet companies contain dancers of varied backgrounds; race-blind casting and interracial partnerships have been widespread for decades. Yet clichéd and sometimes offensive views of race continue to permeate American culture across the art form. Several traditional classical ballets still feature stereotypical caricatures, like the depictions of national dances in the second act of *The Nutcracker*, or of people from the Middle East in *Raymonda* and *Le Corsaire* (the title heroine of *Raymonda* has two suitors, and the unsuccessful one is Abderakhman, a Saracen). And yet these ballets draw audiences. As previously mentioned, the Bolshoi Theatre continues using racially insensitive blackface, despite criticism, in its production of *La Bayadère*. These are just a few examples of art imitating life, where people of color living in a white power structure are often vilified, creating negative stereotypes that have a strong impact on their everyday lives—as well as on their casting on Broadway and in classical ballet productions.

Broadway's nickname, the Great White Way, was inspired by all the electric white lights on the theatre marquees, as well as the many billboard signs that illuminate the area. However, as a child growing up near New York City, seeing only white performers on the stages of Broadway and listening to the record albums that featured photos of the casts, I assumed the "Great White Way" meant that it was only for white people. I also assumed that classical ballet was only for white people, because that was the only representation I saw on the stage.[25] My hope is that this discussion of racial discrimination in American ballet and the Broadway musical might, through analysis, help diminish future fears and misunderstandings. More conversations need to be had about race in America if we are ever going to be able to truly reconcile our differences and realize that we actually are more alike than we are different.

It is my aim that by pulling back the curtain and openly describing these historical and continuing issues of biased casting, stereotyping, and typecasting in classical ballet and Broadway productions by way of my experiential knowledge, I can disrupt these practices where and when they still may be occurring. The goal is to level the playing field for all comers. I hope my stories and analysis might help lay a foundation for change in the next generation, through the lens of my own embodiment of a double consciousness. May these elucidations serve as useful examples and case studies to counter the inevitable excuses

---

[25]For an extended discussion, see Warren Hoffman, *The Great White Way: Race and the Broadway Musical* (New Brunswick, NJ: Rutgers University Press, 2020).

from traditionalists who would rather that things always remain the same. Here is fodder, kindling, and ammunition that I hope will engender and support vigorous advocacy for new and better ways of doing our art.

Bibliography

"The Civil Rights Act of 1964 and the Voting Rights Act of 1965." Khan Academy. Accessed October 10, 2022. https://www.khanacademy.org/humanities/us-history/postwarera/civil-rights-movement/a/the-civil-rights-act-of-1964-and-the-voting-rights-act-of-1965.

Bennett, Michael. A Chorus Line: *A Chorus Line: The Book of the Musical*, book by James Kirkwood and Nicholas Dante. Music by Marvin Hamlisch, lyrics by Edward Kleban (New York: Applause, 1995)

Du Bois, W. E. B. *The Souls of Black Folk*. Mineola, NY: Dover, 1994.

Fanon, Frantz. *Black Skin, White Masks*. New York: Grove Press, 1952.

Fierberg, Ruthie. "Broadway's Mykal Kilgore Calls Out Racism in the Theatre on Facebook." *Playbill*, June 3, 2020.

Foster, Susan Leigh. *Choreographing Empathy: Kinesthesia in Performance*. New York: Routledge, 2011.

Foucault, Michel. *Discipline and Punish*. New York: Pantheon Book, 1977.

Gardner, Sebastian. *Sartre's Being and Nothingness*. London: Continuum, 2009.

Gottschild, Brenda Dixon. *The Black Dancing Body*. New York: Palgrave Macmillan, 2005.

Gottschild, Brenda Dixon. *Digging the Africanist Presence in American Culture: Dance and Other Contexts*. Westport, CT: Greenwood Press, 1996.

Hernández, Javier C. "As 'Nutcracker' Returns, Companies Rethink Depictions of Asians." *New York Times*, November 19, 2021.

Hoffman, Warren. *The Great White Way: Race and the Broadway Musical*. New Brunswick, NJ: Rutgers University Press, 2020.

Jablonski, Nina G. *Living Color: The Biological and Social Meaning of Skin Color*. Berkeley: University of California Press, 2012.

Jacolbe, Jessica. "The History of African-American Casting in Ballet." *JSTOR Daily*, February 20, 2019.

Jewell, K. Sue. *From Mammy to Miss America and Beyond: Cultural Images and the Shaping of US Social Policy*. New York: Routledge, 1992.

Kubota, Samantha. "How Minstrel Shows Led Us to Racist Stereotypes in Culture Today." *Today*, NBC, June 26, 2020. https://www.today.com/tmrw/how-minstrel-shows-1800s-led-us-racist-stereotypes-culture-today-t185341.

Leary, Joy Degruy. *Post Traumatic Slave Syndrome*. Milwaukie, OR: Uptone Press, 2005.

Long, Richard A. *The Black Tradition in American Dance*. New York: Rizzoli, 1989.

Mahar, William J. *Behind the Burnt Cork Mask: Early Blackface Minstrelsy and Antebellum American Popular Culture*. Urbana: University of Illinois Press, 1999.

"Our Commitment to Anti-Racism." New York City Ballet (website). Accessed October 10, 2022. https://www.nycballet.com/about-us/commitment-to-diversity-equity-and-inclusion/a-message-from-new-york-city-ballet/.

Petesch, Carley. "Star Dancer Born into War Grows Up to Inspire." *Associated Press*, July 11, 2012.

Prince, Todd. "Bolshoi to Continue Using Blackface Makeup, Despite Criticism." *Radio Free Europe/Radio Liberty*, December 15, 2019.

Pugh, Megan. *America Dancing: From the Cakewalk to the Moonwalk*. New Haven, CT: Yale University Press, 2015.

Stearns, Marshall Winslow, and Jean Stearns. *Jazz Dance: The Story of American Vernacular Dance*. New York: Macmillan, 1968.

Tolle, Eckharte. *The Power of Now*. Vancouver: Namaste, 1997.

White, Deborah Gray. *Ar'n't I a Woman?* New York: W. W. Norton, 1999.

Wood, Amy Louise. *Lynching and Spectacle: Witnessing Racial Violence in America, 1890–1940*. Chapel Hill: University of North Carolina Press, 2009.

Ziv, Stav. "As an African American Ballet Star, Lauren Anderson Inspired the Next Generation." *Muse*, June 19, 2020. https://www.themuse.com/advice/lauren-anderson-trailblazer-first-african-american-principal-dancer-houston-ballet.

12 Conversations, Creators, and Storytellers in *Contact*: An Interview with Tomé Cousin

PHOEBE RUMSEY

Contact is a physical acting piece that has undercurrent to it. You have to have that experience as well to be able to bring that joy into your body and the explosiveness of it, you have to have that to understand it.

—**Tomé Cousin**

This chapter follows an interview that Dustyn Martincich conducted with dancer, choreographer, director, and interdisciplinary artist Tomé Cousin on June 20, 2022.[1] The interview spans Cousin's career from his early training to his work in concert dance and Broadway shows, then hones in on his role in the original production of *Contact* (2000), which was conceived, directed, and choreographed by Susan Stroman. The dance-based Tony Award–winning musical is discussed at length, from the early auditions and devising process to the eventual Broadway and international success. The interview also explores Cousin's staging and directing of the musical around the world and his current involvement in the upcoming 2023 revival of *Contact*.

Throughout, Cousin emphasizes the importance of physicality for identity formation and the necessity of following what he terms the *movement text* when devising character in performance. He describes his experience of training to become a professional dancer through the college system and the way the narrative potential of the body in motion has been threaded throughout his career. As he has moved toward studying professionally, he has engaged with the theatrical nature of a variety of techniques, including Graham Technique. Cousin explains how his personal methodology of working has served him as a dancer in concert dance, the New York downtown contemporary world, and musical theatre, particularly amid the multiple casts, revivals, and tours of Broadway musicals.

The conversation between Cousin and Martincich helps convey the deeper dimensions of how movement informs the genres of musical theatre. Further, through its focus on *Contact*, the discussion details the complexities that surround multiple dance forms and the synergy of the creative process. For Cousin, this process offers up a still-nascent method of "moving" musical theatre. For the reader, the real-time conversation offers a sense of how dance is talked about and problematized and allows for an understanding of narrative

---

[1] For full biography, see *Tomé Cousin* (website), "Biography," accessed October 21, 2022, https://www.tomecousin.com/biography.

movement and the development process behind it. The interview mode of research and dissemination of knowledge salutes the importance of embodied knowledge. Cousin generously offers a glimpse into the conversations, creators, and stories that are woven together to create the intricate choreography of a pioneering and exceptional musical.

The interview delves into the following overarching questions: What makes Stroman's body of work significant in the musical theatre dance canon? How does it communicate values of its time? How does it connect to history, both social history and the history of musical theatre? What has been the impact of *Contact* on musical theatre dance, both at its premiere and now? This frank discussion centers the personal experience of someone on the ground floor, a dancer who went on to become integral in the circulation of a musical that traveled from body to body, as opposed to via a libretto or score. *Contact* places dance first and explores the nature of human connection from there. Cousin explains how that innovation came to be, and in so doing demonstrates the fruits of labor of experimenting with the musical theatre form. Uniquely, the lasting impact of his experience is felt in Cousin's lived contact with others (whether with fellow performers, teachers, choreographers, or Stroman herself) and in the grace and generosity of the communal experience of dance.

Background

Dustyn Martincich (DM): When talking about embodied history in musical theatre, where do you see yourself fitting in terms of your biography and embodied experiences?

Tomé Cousin (TC): When living in Baltimore, Maryland, in 1968, at seven years old, I was fortunate to be enrolled in a summer camp that had dance every day. And that dance was Dunham Technique. One of the masters who came in to teach was Geoffrey Holder. On the final day, Geoffrey said, "this young man's got something," and it just kind of pulled me into affirmative action you know—it was the first time a mentor/mentee kind of thing was happening. I realized I could *do* something and it wasn't a dyslexic handicap. And so I started to learn through movement, picking up things really quickly, and that became a skill set.

Fast-forwarding very quickly from theatre to dance, I ended up in a children's musical, *The Me Nobody Knows*. There wasn't the term *workshop* yet, it was just kind of like kids running around and experimenting with these poems. That was my introduction to text and movement combined. Even though it was a musical, it was more movement oriented, and so that approach has always been in my DNA.

Later, when I trained to become a professional dancer, I was always given these acting parts to interpret. Luckily, the time period was quite ripe—we're talking the seventies—and I was working with a lot of Graham dancers who had worked with Graham herself, as it was that last generation when Graham was still dancing. Graham Technique has drama built in, so it just kind of fit. So, for a great deal of my time it was about the drama of the dance, in a time when the dance world had kind of taken over in the seventies. I graduated from Point Park University with a degree in dance, dance theatre, and dance notation, and all that stuff. I ultimately ended up working with Bill T. Jones. Again, it was about gesture—movement and gesture—so it's always been in my head and to me that's what performance is. Then I had a career in musicals. And you know the ways of performance, in *A Chorus Line*, for example—for me, it was always the acting parts I got. I was always given that particular kind of track. The track had character work, as opposed to technically tricky kind of stuff, and it appealed to me.

I basically retired in my thirties and came back to Pittsburgh to teach at Point Park. Due to weird circumstances, I had a dance theatre company and we were doing a work about dance marathons. This was around the same time Stroman had *Steel Pier* on Broadway. Someone said, "Come up to New York to see what this is because you've kind of got this thing." I had never heard of Stroman, maybe in the back of my head, likely because I was really heavily into concert dance at this time and I had kind of left musicals.

So, I came back to New York, and while I was there, I went to an audition for the national tour of *Dreamgirls* and got the job. So that pulled me back into theatre. I did the tour of that for two years, and then everyone said, you know mature dancers are back in vogue.

So, I moved back to New York and I landed the audition for *Contact*.

The Audition

DM: Let's start with *Contact*: where do you begin in the history of *Contact*, and can you talk me through the trajectory before it got to Lincoln Center, specifically from your experience?

TC: Sure, I was back in New York, and I was doing an off-Broadway play, *The Bingo Long Traveling All-Stars and Motor Kings*—a very long title. It was a Motown property all about baseball. At the time Vinnie Liff (he had his casting agency and Tara Rubin was his assistant) sent out a call for dancers who could act for a workshop for Susan Stroman. This is the funniest and most bizarre story of it all, as a friend of mine was called, then he got his boyfriend invited, and then I came over and they said to me, you should call and see if you can get to this. I said wait a minute, this is an invited call, you just can't keep calling. Then he said what can they say besides no? So, I called and they said okay come in, here's your time.

It was for a totally new show called *Contact*, and I just assumed it was for contact improvisation so that's why I went. And I knew Stroman was a choreographer.

I went to the audition, and everyone was given a two-hour block as they wanted to know specifically how many men and women and would we'd go in together. I figured that made sense as I thought it was a contact improv partner kind of thing.

It was at City Center, and my call was at twelve noon, and so, then, I understood, she was seeing people in two-hour blocks. I knew there was no chance in hell of me getting the job because I had never met her, did not know her, and I fought my way in. Also, I didn't have an agent pushing me, etc. When my group went in, she was great. Still, to this day, I think it was the best audition atmosphere I have ever been in. I always try to recapture that in the auditions for the show. This same feeling of a positive atmosphere was [felt] in the recent New York City 2022 auditions for the revival of *Contact*. I'm very proud of that.

DM: Yes, that would be great.

TC: It was like a dance class. It really was like having fun with no pressure that you should not be yourself. She wanted you to be yourself and bring your best in this relaxed energy. It was very supportive in everything everyone did. She just called out names and partnered people up and started teaching this swing dance movement, which shocked me—I thought, "Okay, a swing jazz dancing kind of day." It was very period oriented, and I ended up with a very tall woman.

We did the combinations, and then she came by and asked everyone their name. That's the other thing she still does, which makes you feel seen, which is very rare. She specifically goes and greets every single performer that is in the room, so you know—eye to eye—you feel validated that you were there. And that was it.

The Workshop

TC: About two weeks later, there was a call—would I like to do the workshop? There was no callback. That's the important thing, there were no callbacks. That was in October of 1998, and the workshop was to start in January of 1999.

We showed up at Lincoln Center, and when we walked into the space, I knew two other performers. There were nineteen of us, Stroman, and her assistants. She explained what the piece was—it was going to be this one work about this ad executive. We were going to play around and create these characters that are going to inhabit this bar in his subconscious, and that was it. So, we just started partnering back and forth, switching partners constantly, while all this dance vocabulary was being taught.

And then one day she just came in and said, this is what it's going to be—you're going to be with you, etc. I ended up with a French dancer, Pascale Faye, who had done nine Broadway shows, and she had danced with the Paris Opera Ballet. She was an exquisite ballerina. Our energies were completely opposite: I'm all fire, and she was the coolest thing in the world!

We just didn't get it, you know we weren't kind of jiving, we weren't getting it together. And then one day, and I found this so funny, I found out who she was. I was complaining to my friend—here's this woman, she's great, but we're just not jiving and I don't know.

And they said what's the name, and I said Pascal, and they were like literally—Pascal who? And then they said "Pascale Faye is your partner?" and I said yeah, and they showed me a clip of her. And I went "Okay, I get it!" So the next day, I came in and I explained her, "Pascal, I'm from concert dance and even though we don't know each other, I know how to partner really well, and I get it, I get who you are and everything." From that moment on she trusted me, and we clicked in all the lifts and everything was fine, but it took a little bit of meshing.

And it was like that, with everyone I eventually found out, because there were people from New York City Ballet and there were people from modern dance companies.

What all of us had in common, however, was that we had acted heavily in whatever genre we were coming from, so if they came from American Ballet Theatre they had done a lot of acting, I mean they were like the "acting-ballerina." So, everybody had that germ of creating a character and not necessarily having to be told everything we had to do. It was like a perfect storm of artists that came together. Even Robert Wersinger from City Ballet was always the character-dancer-actor.

And so it was in this company that we eventually started to see it was made up of dancers who had strong acting or actors who could move really well. The story just developed as it went along, and we just kept with storytelling. We were rarely, very rarely, told, "no, that's not following the story." Everything [Stroman] was seeing, everything in the background, it's a large picture and then it just came about.

Fast-forwarding, we took a three-month break, and everybody started auditioning again because we didn't know what was going to happen. Then we got a phone call saying they're going to pick it up and they want to add two more stories to complete it, to make it a full evening. Then the day after we said yes, the very next day, they called to say not only is it going to go into workshop but it's also going to open off-Broadway here in September. All this happened within six months, it was bizarre how quick.

DM: One section was built with some time and workshops, and the other two portions had nothing?

TC: Yes.

Character Building

TC: Yes, and so for my character in part 2, "Did You Move," I gave my scene partner, Stephanie Michels, this engagement ring, and that became my entire story from that moment on, then we developed this relationship that the whole scene was about me trying to propose to her—the whole time. And because we were considered the new young love couple, I said, well, I'm just going to make him this nerd. I mean, I felt awkward, I'm the only Black guy out here, and I'm playing this Black Italian dude so I'm going to make my character a nerd. So, he was a combination of my father, Don Knotts, and Milton Berle.

DM: Amazing.

TC: And so, with everything he did he was just a nervous wreck. He had a list of things his brother had told him he was supposed to do: you get her flowers, you get her to do this, you pull out her chair, everything I tried to do was on that list. Everything fell apart because the lead couple, Jason and Karen, interrupted, so it was a mess. He was always a nervous mess and so that became the character, and that ended up being Biagio Villanova, because she, Bella, was the beauty and I the beast.

DM: I see.

TC: Then there was the pregnant couple. So, we all had these three distinct stories going on, but everything related to the things that Karen Ziemba as the Wife had to have done and we worked backwards from there. And so, with the three couples, there's a little bit of all these character roles in the section as well as the glasses of drinks and things we ate—in fact we ate food before we even did a step. And that became the style of the piece. That was my character in that piece, and that informed how drastically different my character BooBoo (in part 3, "Contact") had to be.

The wig came off. [Stroman] said, "wear what you would normally wear, you know the skullcap you wear? Yes!" And so I wore suspenders to keep my pants up—so that was my look, and I became the instigator, if you will, of the seven men.

Now here's the other thing in "Contact": there are seven men and they form the bar, and Boyd Gaines's character is a neurotic. The whole concept is that if he does not make contact tonight, he's going to end his life—he's at that point. In his subconscious, if you took all seven men and smashed us together, you made the perfect person, who he thought he wanted to be. Each of us had an aspect of a personality that he wanted, and each of the women had an aspect of the perfect woman, and you smash them all together you got the Girl in the Yellow Dress. That's who we were psychologically in the piece. It's very deep psychologically. However, that is all internal, or inner things, and the audience may not know that's going on.

DM: Indeed, that's the key to any really good character. Your actor or characterization "points" in your head and gives you direction, so the audience is able to put together a bigger picture. They may not know nuances or all of the minutiae of details, but as an actor the motivation absolutely gives you something to contribute to the picture.

So, when you are creating from the workshop, in that very quick moment that the show expanded to having two other pieces in the overall production, were you working with all the materials? For instance, did you know what set pieces were going to be there?

TC: Yes.

DM: Did you know what music was going to be on? From my understanding, Stroman is an incredibly musical choreographer, she hears and sees story within these sorts of pieces of music and so she selected all three of those pieces of music ahead of time?

TC: Yes, everything was selected, and we just worked inside of it; however, the development of the actual story of how things came about was created in the space. Along with what props were needed. For example, there is this whole funny part with a three-card monte kind of thing, with the gangster, who can't find his gun.

That happened simply as the gun fell out of Karen Ziemba's hand and fell on the floor. Everyone stood there, and no one knew what to do. Nina Goldman ran over and grabbed one of the waiter's pans and slammed it on top of the gun, and then the other two waiters did the same, and then it became a three-card monte. It became one of the funniest moments. You know just little things like that were added. Stroman was very encouraging to just kind of play around and see what happens.

Process

DM: Would you say that the choreography or the structure of the set moves were the foundation and then there was an added improvisation as part of the choreographic tool kit, or would you say it was more improvisation, structure, and then more improvisation, on top of that?

TC: Improvisation first and then structure, and then more improvisation on top of that because things happened by accident and then I think that inspired her—once things got cooking. This method ended up in particular with "Contact," and the finale of that section, "Sing, Sing, Sing."

There were three versions of "Sing, Sing, Sing" on Broadway that same year, *Fosse* had it, *Swing* had it, and us. There were three versions, but ours was the only version of it where there was actually swing dancing and we touched. They don't touch in *Fosse* or *Swing* (of all things), so we had this thing going on, and she knew she wanted the climax of the story to spin, if you will. (Because there was a pinball machine in it, and we're inside the pinball machine and all the choreography was spinning around and all the girls are like bumpers, etc.) So, we knew somehow that everything was going to move, and then she asked us to make the bar and everything in the room revolve around with us as if you were on a turntable. We just went "bizarre!" and okay let's give it a try, but you know, it still had to be in character.

The other thing I'm going to say in relationship to *Contact* and another famous dance theatre piece [is about] *A Chorus Line*, [which I consider] to be a dance theatre piece at its core. The difference between the two for me is that when you are in *A Chorus Line* you are acting to be these iconic characters that were established and you are forced in these roles. Whereas in *Contact*, they are real people in the moment of it, so you're in a bubble, and those three stories, when performing it, you're not really aware of the audience at all, I mean unless there's jokes and laughing. But when it's cooking you are so in the environment, in particular—that bar is real, it's like a bubble and the characters are there—I've never experienced anything like that physically as an actor, as a dancing actor. I have never experienced not seeing the other person for who they really are. I see that character, because you don't have time to think, you just don't have time to be out of it, you really have to be involved. So that's a different way of performing.

Ensembles

DM: That style of thinking about *Contact* makes me think about shows like *Hamilton*, for instance, where the ensemble is literally so interconnected—if you don't have the person who is moving the chair at the right time, the rest of the piece is going to fall apart. Those tracks are so specific and necessary in order for everything else to keep going.

I'm also thinking about who might be cast in *Contact*, as all need to also be actors that can both intensely listen to the others onstage and adapt instantly if someone laughs or drops something.

TC: Yes, absolutely. Each section of the musical—"The Swing," "Did You Move?" and "Contact"—has so many little internal things that had to happen, like pool balls for example. One pool ball had to move, when it needed to move. There was a water bottle and a dinner menu that were thrown and had to be caught. There were so many little things with the food as well. There was a moment when I had to cut a piece of ziti and spear it and then start lifting it to my mouth, then the wife grabbed a fork at it and put it back. It was absurd, it was absolutely absurd, and we would rehearse it like hours. It was just me cutting food—I mean I had not danced one step!

But cutting and eating and drinking and all this stuff with glasses going up and down and napkins, it was insane. But, once it fit, you asked, "Why am I doing this?" It was always about why, and then it became the action that needed to been done and the character just took over. It was very crucial timing for so many movements and moments.

DM: *Contact* is one of the shows that I remember seeing when I got to go to New York from Chicago with my dance community. And we were thinking, okay we are going to go see this show and it's a brand-new concept, it's really out there and are we ready? And it really spoke to me. I remember those moments and the nuances you mentioned. I was so captivated by everyone onstage and that sense of urgency imbued within the piece. To ask everybody to be really attentive the entire time, to the magnificent details, it doesn't feel like they're just playing, it's actually happening. The performance is synchronous, calculated, and defined — it was different than any other musical theatre.

TC: Are you familiar with the filmmaker Jacques Tati? He was a French filmmaker, and his films are about movement, there's very little text, there's a lot of sound but the movement told the story. And so, in the first section of *Contact*, it's a monologue. Basically, the character is accepting the award, and then it transitions to his apartment, and I think he says two words (Good Luck) in the entire scene. Everything comes from an answering machine, and the rest is all physical movement. It's all just him moving props, moving chairs and windows. It's all physical movement that's movement text. Even before we started doing *Contact*, I knew where Stroman was going, so I could adapt right away to the language she was speaking and the questions she was asking for me to work out personally. I knew right away the world I was in, so I could release the musical theatre aspect of it. I knew it was going to be a very high level of art.

DM: Yes.

TC: There is a whole transition from [the character] Michael Wiley's apartment to the bar. We called this "Limbo," and it's just walking in a circle in the dark, and he's being paranoid. It's all done to the sound of pool balls clinking together. It's very haunting and frightening, you know how New York can be when you are walking down a street by yourself, it can be very intimidating. So in interpreting, I went again to that connection. There's that level of art and physicality and movement. I keep calling it *movement text*. It was very intimidating to watch, and then it flowed into this movement thing. The more I think about the piece and the more I go back to it, and in relation to everything I've seen since, . . . *Contact* [is] the ultimate actor-dancer piece. It is an actor-dancer piece in a completely different way than *A Chorus Line*. *Contact* is a physical acting piece that has undercurrent to it. You have to have that experience as well to be able to bring that joy into your body and the explosiveness of it, you have to have that to understand it.

DM: I love that you equate musical theatre with joy, as that is at the essence of the engagement, and if you don't have joy in the process in the genre it's not the space for you. To the next question: Why Broadway? Why did Stroman want Broadway, and why did it feel like the right fit for it?

TC: It wasn't her first choice. At first it was in the downstairs studio at Lincoln Center, and then they picked it up and it stayed there. I believe we opened in October, and it was supposed to run until December. After the opening and all the positive reviews that it received, they called us the next day. It was explosive, everything happened so quickly. They said here's the scenario, we love the show, the public loves the show, so we will see about requesting a venue when something opens (*Marie Christine* would be playing upstairs). They were prepared to keep us under contract until a house opened. They said, here's your projected future, etc. And so that's what happened, the show upstairs was not a success, and they said we're going to bump you upstairs. And so we ran into the New Year (it was 2000), and then we came back two and a half months later and opened on Broadway.

The cast was the same, I think there were two swings added. This was the time when Stroman also had the film *Center Stage* opening. So, she was really cooking. Unfortunately, during the same period that's when her husband, director Mike Ockrent, became very ill. *Contact* is one of the only pieces that was truly hers, and so she is very protective with it, and as a cast we were very tight because of that situation where she was with her husband. Everybody was embracing her at that time. I think that's why it's such a tight unit.

DM: If you hadn't all been together at that time it would not have been the piece that it was.

TC: Yes, and here's the other beauty part of this. There was no callback for any of us. Like there was no callback so all that time from when we were put together in January, up until the opening, I had no idea of the why and how we were all there. We were there with a zoo of people at the audition and workshops, you know, different looks and everything. She told us opening night, "I guess you're wondering how you got here?" Yes, and we were like, "Tonight? You tell us now?!" She said (I'm paraphrasing here), "you came in, you put what I wanted forward, I saw what I wanted, and each of you had a career trajectory that got you here and I didn't want to insult you, so I just made phone calls, as opposed to bringing you back in over and over. I just talked to people you worked with and asked: do they play well in the room, etc? And so you earned [your spot] here." No one had ever said anything like that to us dancers, that all that work and all that stuff, all your hard work paid off. It was one of those golden moments—she said if one of you was not here it wouldn't work. It really validated the ballet dancers particularly—Nina Goldman, Dana Stackpole—as they had been in the corps de ballet forever and they were validated for being acting dancers, both were acting geniuses, very funny women. So, it just made everybody relax and have a nice time. I think that's why we all gelled so well.

DM: What do you think makes Stroman's body of work significant in the musical theatre canon? It's unusual, as the body of her work is vast, between activating social dance and activating people in ensembles as actors. She also creates full scenic pictures, by the use of props, the use of set pieces, and other visual storytelling elements in order to create a cohesive world.

TC: I think she sees people moving in everything, people moving and using their bodies physically to tell a story. I think that's at the core of all her works. I've staged *The Producers*, *Thou Shalt Not*, *The Scottsboro Boys*, and *Big Fish* for her, and there's always this traffic of human emotions moving, with a lot of people moving. I think that's combined with considering that we as people use our hands a lot, and that we use things and objects. Stroman's a prop woman, and so that is integrated into her love of storytelling. From my understanding of her past, her father was very musical. She's very musical herself—sings, writes music, and plays instruments, and so on. She likes Fred Astaire and the Nicholas Brothers, not so much

Ginger Rogers, but the men, the male jumping, leaping around; things women could do, but we never got to see that.

She likes the big musicals a lot, and she loves dance, she LOVES to dance. Combine that with her love of theatre and respect for artists. She has a really deep respect for everyone's art and what they can bring uniquely, so I think that is pushing it way forward. Also, she's a tapper. I think one of her best pieces of choreography is in *The Scottsboro Boys*. I think there's some extraordinary work in that piece. Deep emotions, really raw emotions, that have to be polished, but it still has to have a rawness to it, because they should always appear like young men that are under extreme stress, constantly moving. I think that's really completely opposite of the show girls in like *The Producers*.

DM: Yes, those are complete opposites.

TC: I think her productions are very representative of her thought process and her vocabulary. I'm waiting for the Stroman retrospective, like the Robbins or Fosse retrospectives. There was one gala performance and we did excerpts from each of her shows, so I think that's going to happen, eventually. And once you see them stacked up side by side, then you go—wait, that's a lot. Even the new play she has, *POTUS*. I'm going, it's just so smart and humorous—there's her brilliant slapstick stuff, but she's also very concerned with the audience being invested in physically moving. As opposed to sitting there and the piece coming to them, I think she's really about them coming forward, and back and forth. She wants you to leave the theatre with this energy in your body, and that's an ongoing concern and one of mine as well.

Tours and Translation

DM: In terms of training folks and producing *Contact* in translation and working with the tour and other companies, can you talk a bit about that process?

TC: I think the value of a person who is originally in the room when something is being created and has the answers to everything is key. They know the reason *why* the person is doing this, or that move, or what this step is called and why it has to be done and the drama behind it and the intent. Once that is passed on to the next person, it gets looser and looser and looser. With a piece like *Contact*, it's crucial that somebody was in it from the beginning because there is so much going on, and so many prop things. Otherwise, it becomes robotic and there is no motivation.

For me, the second tour was not as successful because there was no one connected with it from the original version, and it was taught by someone from the British company. So, when I watched it, I specifically watched my role and was like, "What?" It just didn't make sense, you know, because it's so detailed oriented. I think the reason Stroman likes what I do with it is because I figured out a way to make it very personable even when it's in a big arena. Because I knew all the little nuances and I knew how to make an ending to each bit. These nuances and such matter, they show up and make a difference. They help make the audience come into the piece, as opposed to trying to push it on them. I think that's what's really important about the process in any show. However, in particular with this one, too, because of the many details, it's crucial. I think that's why some tours don't work when they ship out. They were made or designed for larger houses, for one, and often they lose its nuances. Or, someone is a third someone, teaching someone, and then teaching another.

DM: Like telephone.

TC: Yes, and then unfortunately you lose everything.

DM: I wanted to talk about translation. What are some of the things that are really crucial in terms of the way that you translate work to a new company that's going out there? Particularly in regard to how it's going to be settling with a particular audience. You mentioned a little bit about finding recognizable cultural touch points, something to put people's finger on. Is that for the performers, or is that also for the audience? Can you talk a little bit more about that?

TC: I would say, first the challenge is for the performers, because it's a lot of style and you have to do a lot of particular styles. This is particularly for the international companies. For example, the Asian companies have a very different movement style. There were a couple of former Eastern Bloc companies as well. For example, there was a Polish company, and everything they process is different in how they see the detail, so you have to drill and drill them in the details—the minute detail—and then you explain the *why*. Addressing *why* we are doing something is because it has to be so drastically different from this other story, and from what you've done before, and it's not like the mega mixes in big musicals.

DM: Can you say more about that?

TC: Let's see, I'll relate to a show that everybody knows.

In *Cats* or *Joseph* there is a big flashy performance style, for example. As a performer in *Contact* you have to go completely opposite to that and strip away all of that, everything. *Contact* is just about people, it's about people moving and the urgency of contact in particular in the story with these people here, and you can go only so far. It's a small little club—it's not even a club, it's a bar—a small dingy bar where they push the pool tables back and it's a Tuesday night at three o'clock in the morning.

These people are desperate, they have to dance, they are there because they want to do it. They're not there because they want to go out; it's a Tuesday night, not even like a Thursday. They have a need, they have to move, that's the urgency of it. Everyone is at a high level. They're thinking, "I'm here because I want that and I love to dance and I gotta dance," and that's it, period.

That's the motivation. And then in the middle, this girl walks in. Then, this guy in a tuxedo comes in. We're all in our normal stuff, and a tuxedo walks in—what's going on? That's the urgency of it. And for the audience, what's interesting is there's three different time periods, and you have to get that across, particularly in terms of behavior. So, in the first story there's no problem with people making contact at all. In the second one they bump heads badly, and in the third one it is a desperation, so those emotions have to hit people universally across the countries. That message has to get across, those three stories, those three different emotions and desperate need of making contact—why do you think it's called *Contact*?

DM: Yes, I was wanting to mention that.

TC: Why is it called *Contact*? Because people have to make contact. There is easy contact, there's contact that doesn't work, and then there's desperation. All three of those things, overall, Stroman said that it's a New Yorker thing, you know, that's how New Yorkers live: it's the easy contact, or they don't make it big time, or they're desperate to make contact. That's the energy of the piece, that's the whole thing, and that has got to be translated, like, New York is coming at you! From wherever it goes that's the understanding of it.

So, in a new company there's a lot of talking, before you start getting the steps together, about who the characters are. And then personal stories. I mean, I come loaded with who these people are and who the actor was that created this part. Then with knowing that personality, find who you are—do you have a little bit of that personality? The alpha male? You may not be the biggest guy or a most feminine or aggressive person, and now's your chance to take on this alpha male dominant guy.

There's a lot of trust that goes along with it as well, because everything is seen. You are exposed, so exposed, they see everything. When *Contact* starts really cleanly you can follow any of the performers and see a different story.

DM: Yes, that openness to be okay with allowing these other threads to happen is unique. Again, I think of that in concert dance and dance theatre. However, for some folks they may think it's quite chaotic and are looking for some unison. But this is what the world looks like. In fact, that's what makes it feel so delicious when people actually come together for that double pirouette.

TC: Yes.

DM: That in life feels so magical when it happens.

TC: Yes, when I am trying to get people who have been trained through musicals or films we know such as *Gypsy* or *Hello Dolly*, we then have to untrain ourselves to see what is natural. As opposed to watching the big stuff. Which is great, but musical theatre is a large umbrella. It's like this year at the Tonys you have *MJ* and then right behind it you have *A Strange Loop*, and those two performances are like night and day. When people say, "what's *Strange Loop* about?" and I say, "a whole lot, you just really have to see it." We didn't get that big flash-bang form of performance, but that's okay too, you know.

DM: But there are plenty of flash-bangs, and it can't just be about that. It is not about kicks and jumps, it's about other things that are happening internally that need to be looked at.

TC: The whole collective is a dance theatre movement, and that's the difference. It's about what we talked about earlier, bringing the audience forward instead of sitting back and coming to them. It's like with "Do Me Theatre" everything is worked out for you. I also really don't care for preshow announcements asking the audience to *Sit back, relax, and enjoy _____*. Why not say something like, *We invite you, or we welcome you, to join us in the world of _____*? Make the audience sit forward and invest.

DM: I wanted to return for a minute to the kind of prompts that you would use when starting the process.

TC: Well, Stroman and I both teach about the same way, we do a whole series of combinations of steps, or something like that, and then have them done in a couple of different ways. For example, do the entire combination as if you were happy, like you were deliriously happy, or you were like really sad, or you were pissed off, or really angry, like really, really, angry—because in the song we used, "Simply Irresistible," even though it comes across as a big energy thing it's really about excitable danger.

Those are the prompts to take on. For "Did You Move?" every single person had to become the prima or primo dancer in the company. Everyone had to take on the combination as if the entire world paid like $1,000 to see us just do this one step, and with all of us combined, the attitude is beyond pulled up, I mean we had to pull up, up, up!

So, there were prompts like that, general big scales, and then sometimes Stroman would mix them. So that's how my character and Pascale's came together. I would be doing mine as angry, and she would be doing hers as happy. They were polar opposites of each other, so then we were put together as a couple.

DM: I see.

TC: For Rocker Verastique, his character was a lonely guy in the bar, so everything he did related to that. He has multiple partners all evening, like the quirky girl (Nina Goldman), or the "sex bomb" Shannon Hammonds as we called her, so how did he react to them? They had all these polar opposites going on.

DM: In that interaction of what to do when your partner offers you something, and considering you are all generally "Yes, *and*" types, you are listening to your partner. Then you have your objective and your partner has their objective, and we see that back and forth play out all the time.

TC: Absolutely, all the time.

DM: It sounds like it's a lot about energy and quality.

TC: Yes, and what happened when the Girl in the Yellow Dress said, finally, yes to you. After you're offering a hand to dance with her all night, and she finally says yes. Or there were times where we worked, and sometimes even though it was choreographed or directed for her to dance with me, Stroman would tell her say no and see what happens. Then I would have to do a whole other lap, because now, I have all these counts of eight and I've got to do something, so then that became something.

DM: I mean that really is directing, right? That's what you're trying to do all the time, and dancers just have a bigger arsenal of movement. Meaning, in terms of expression we have so much more to offer.

TC: Exactly.

DM: Thank you so much for everything, Tomé, this has been an invaluable dive into the world of *Contact*.

TC: You're welcome.

Conclusion

Cousin's generous account of his personal and embodied experience with *Contact* brings us that much closer to understanding what dance scholar Joanna Dee Das calls the "kinetic vibrancy" within the show.[2] Uniquely, this exploration comes from a dancer in the show looking outward, as opposed to that of Stroman looking in. The point of view of an original ensemble dancer is often unknown as they navigate the varied demands of the choreographer and director. Having these conversations and sharing stories is key to comprehending the many possibilities offered by the body in motion in musical theatre. As Cousin explains, the process of creating *Contact* was very much about their own previously established approaches as actor-dancers. Importantly, Stroman allowed the space and creative generosity for the cast members to develop their own characters' truths. In sharing the unique happenings alongside the nuts and bolts of the show, Cousin articulates what so many dancers and ensemblists work toward across their careers, but are often unable to put their finger on. His detailing of how one can learn through movement about the world around them and communicate that experience in a visceral manner to an audience, both locally and internationally, underpins how dance, particularly the dance in *Contact*, "provides a lifeline" to finding meaning in the world around us.[3]

By opening a window into the audition process, and the respect for the dancer put forth by Stroman, Cousin reveals the sense of openness needed to help make a show—hinged on bodies in constant motion, risk-taking, boundary-pushing, and timing—flourish. The emphasis that Stroman placed on celebrating the self and working in a manner that came from oneself, allowed everyone to be seen onstage and heard in rehearsal. This model stands in stark contrast to the aggrandizing and often bullying behavior of choreographers of the past, people like Jerome Robbins who ran a completely different kind of rehearsal and character-building concept.[4]

As this interview demonstrates, the way Cousin learned about life and character through movement from an early age became a valuable skill set that has carried him through a multifaceted career. Specifically, a movement text–based approach to character illuminates how these essential levels of subtlety are achieved in performance. The concept of a movement text underpins much of the discussion surrounding what dance can *do*. For Cousin, discovering and embracing the concept has proved to be productive in his development and success as an artist.

On the whole, the concept of the acting dancer is becoming more firmly rooted in the landscape of contemporary musical theatre and in the skill sets of musical theatre performers. This is particularly key with regard to theatricality in musical theatre, where one's bodily interpretation is integral in bringing the essence of a piece, particularly one as layered as *Contact*, to life. *Contact* has long since staked a claim for the acting dancer, the actor-ballerina, and those that delve into creative endeavors not from a place of virtuosity but from

---

[2]Joanna Dee Das, "What Makes a Musical? *Contact* (2000) and Debates about Genre at the Dawn of the Twenty-First Century," in *The Routledge Companion to the Contemporary Musical*, ed. Jessica Sternfeld and Elizabeth L. Wollman (London: Routledge, 2019), 240.
[3]Das, 240.
[4]For more on Robbins's rehearsal process, see Deborah Jowitt, *Jerome Robbins: His Life, His Theater, His Dance* (New York: Simon and Schuster, 2005).

a sense of self, nuance, and curiosity as a way to put forth a captivating, truthful, and visceral performance style. Cousin's contributions to dance in musical theatre and beyond are vast and ongoing. Keeping his work and methods (along with Stroman's) at the forefront when considering one's approach to musical theatre reveals how movement can offer so much more than it is so often given credit for.

Bibliography

Das, Joanna Dee. "What Makes a Musical? *Contact* (2000) and Debates about Genre at the Dawn of the Twenty-First Century." In *The Routledge Companion to the Contemporary Musical*, edited by Jessica Sternfeld and Elizabeth L. Wollman, 236–45. London: Routledge, 2019.

Jowitt, Deborah. *Jerome Robbins: His Life, His Theater, His Dance*. New York: Simon and Schuster, 2005.

Tomé Cousin (website). "Biography." Accessed October 21, 2022. https://www.tomecousin.com/biography.

13 Postmodern Dance's Legacies on the Contemporary Musical Theatre Stage

ARIEL NERESON

On the morning of December 11, 2006, the day after the original Broadway production of *Spring Awakening* premiered, the cast, crew, producers, critics, and potential spectators saw the kind of review every new musical hopes for, but that few ever receive: Charles Isherwood of the *New York Times* breathlessly exhorted his readers, "A straight shot of eroticism steamed open last night . . . and Broadway . . . may never be the same."[1] Widely praised by Isherwood and others, *Spring Awakening* enjoyed meteoric success for a new musical, and many cultural critics observed that its achievements were even more notable given that several elements of the production seemed stacked against it in terms of its chances for popularity and longevity on Broadway. Of all the musical's dramaturgical elements—including its music, lyrics, spoken text, and design choices, which structure the production's storytelling—Bill T. Jones's choreography has been most routinely singled out as unprecedented for the musical theatre stage, contributing to a broader sense of "the new" that *Spring Awakening* delivered to Broadway. Writing in 2006 for *Dance Magazine*, Sylviane Gold claimed that while the production was replete with several surprises, "The most unlikely thing about the whole project could well be the presence of Bill T. Jones."[2] In Liza Gennaro's historical survey of musical theatre dance, she uses similar language as she notes that in the 2000s, "innovation in musical theater choreography emerged from an unlikely individual."[3] The widely shared sense of the unlikeliness of Jones, a celebrated contemporary concert dance choreographer, creating dance for the Broadway stage, largely came from Jones's aesthetic values. Honed over forty years of professional work across concert dance, community-based performance, opera, and dramatic theatre, Jones's choreographic approach values abstraction, both pedestrian and virtuosic movement, juxtaposition and counterpoint, politically charged and even confrontational content, and fragmented, multiple narratives—values located in a postmodern dance lineage that has historically positioned itself as oppositional to the commercial theatre (that is, theatre that seeks to turn a profit) in general and Broadway specifically. The production team's unconventional approach to developing *Spring Awakening* created an opening for Jones's postmodern aesthetic.

[1]Charles Isherwood, "Sex and Rock? What Would the Kaiser Think?" *New York Times*, December 11, 2006.
[2]Sylviane Gold, "On Broadway," *Dance Magazine*, November 2006, 82–3.
[3]Liza Gennaro, *Making Broadway Dance* (New York: Oxford University Press, 2022), 188.

This chapter documents Jones's use of postmodern movement values in both process and product in his work for *Spring Awakening*, and it contextualizes this creative labor against the art/entertainment dichotomy that characterizes artistic production in the United States. The production is often touted in musical theatre history as infusing Broadway with new aesthetics. These aesthetics, so this narrative goes, did not originate in the commercial performing arts context and yet were successful in a highly conservative producing environment where artistic risk-taking was (and remains) disincentivized to a heightened degree because of the escalating costs of production that have accompanied the corporatization of Broadway. As Elizabeth Wollman argues, "The history of Broadway can be brought more sharply into focus with closer attention to the ways its machinery influences its artistic output. After all, musicals reflect our changing cultural obsessions, but they also reveal our cultural limitations."[4] *Spring Awakening* and Jones's choreography are particularly worth our attention precisely because postmodern dance has been positioned as antithetical to the "machinery" to which Wollman refers—that is, late capitalism and its exigencies. I'm interested in the extent to which Gennaro and Stacy Wolf's claim that Jones's *Spring Awakening* choreography "ushered in a postmodern contemporary dance aesthetic" on Broadway holds when we look at the means of production—the machinery—as well as the movement vocabulary itself.[5]

I first consider what is meant by *postmodern* in reference to dance, a medium with a historiographically distinct relationship to the term in comparison to other art forms. I introduce readers to signature aesthetics of postmodernism in both the creation and the performance of "downtown dance," a label that has endured in identifying dance that challenges the spectator's perception by seeking some level of illegibility. I contrast these aesthetics with the Broadway environment Jones entered in 2006, in many ways a producing climate wherein, as Wollman writes, "The lure of familiarity cannot be underestimated."[6] Into this climate came the unfamiliar nineteenth-century German drama, which, when partnered with avant-garde dramaturgies of sound, text, and movement, fairly exploded theatregoers' assumptions about the Broadway musical form. Isherwood's review, while a bit hyperbolic, is also sincerely hopeful, a tone that was foreshadowed in his review of the preceding off-Broadway run at the Atlantic Theater Company: "When was the last time you felt a frisson of surprise and excitement at something that happened in a new musical? For that matter, when was the last time something new happened in a musical?"[7] In this chapter, I analyze how and why *Spring Awakening*'s "newness" is attributed, at least in part, to the postmodernism of Bill T. Jones's choreography, and how Jones's contributions changed choreography for the Broadway stage, as seen in subsequent work from Spencer Liff, John Heginbotham, and Raja Feather Kelly.

[4]Elizabeth Wollman, "How to Dismantle a [Theatric] Bomb: Broadway Flops, Broadway Money, and Musical Theater Historiography," *Arts* 9, no. 2 (2020): article 66, p. 12, https://doi.org/10.3390/arts9020066.

[5]Liza Gennaro and Stacy Wolf, "Dance in Musical Theater," in *The Oxford Handbook of Dance and Theater*, ed. Nadine George-Graves (New York: Oxford University Press, 2015), 163.

[6]Elizabeth Wollman, *The Theater Will Rock: A History of the Rock Musical, from "Hair" to "Hedwig"* (Ann Arbor: University of Michigan Press, 2006), 145.

[7]Charles Isherwood, "In 'Spring Awakening,' a Rock 'n' Roll Heartbeat for 19th-Century German Schoolboys," *New York Times*, June 16, 2006.

Postmodern Dance's Challenges to and on Broadway

Defining postmodernism in dance is not straightforward, in part because the broader movements of modernism and postmodernism across music, visual art, architecture, and theatre do not chronologically or aesthetically align with modern and postmodern dance. Modernist approaches of these other fields that favor minimalism and austerity have much more in common with early postmodern dance than they do with the expressive, narrative-driven modern dances of Martha Graham, José Limon, and Hanya Holm, among others. In other words, what we commonly historicize as modern dance is not, in fact, *modernist* dance, despite sharing a chronology with several modernist movements in other art forms. Rather, *postmodern* dance partakes of these approaches much more deliberately.[8] For dance critic Marcia Siegel, whose criticism largely chronicles the development of postmodern dance in New York City, "the meaning of 'postmodern' . . . varies profoundly between and even within disciplines. . . . In dance studies, the term 'postmodern' originated as an historical category." Dance historian and postmodern dancer Sally Banes agrees, writing, "the term 'postmodern' is not an evaluative one, but a descriptive, historical one."[9] Siegel and Banes remind us that *postmodern* is a historical descriptor grounded in contexts of time and place that influenced a set of artists' aesthetic values toward what became known as postmodern dance—this reminder is important because of how regularly the term *postmodern* is taken as an evaluative descriptor of a given artist or artwork's aesthetic, a usage wherein the term is often interchangeable with *experimental* or *avant-garde*.

Most historians point to Judson Dance Theater and its collective of artists as the progenitors of a set of approaches to organizing movement in space and time now understood as postmodern dance (the term *postmodern* was seldom used by the artists themselves during the time when they were developing it).[10] Judson Dance Theater was a group of artists who were interested in modern dance abandoning its concert, elite presentation, as well as its valorization of emotional expressivity and truth, technical virtuosity,

---

[8]Distinctions between modern and postmodern aesthetics in dance as an art form are often murky and contested. I point the reader to the debates between Sally Banes and Susan Manning as an example of why we might hold these definitions more loosely; see Banes and Manning, "Terpsichore in Combat Boots," *TDR: The Drama Review* 33, no. 1 (1989): 13–16. In terms of dance's departures from shared aesthetic timelines with other art forms, Roger Copeland reminds us that "to an architect, the term postmodern connotes a rejection of the very austerity and reductivism that characterized so many early postmodern dances," while "modernism in dance meant the 'hot,' expressive, deeply personal work of choreographers like Graham, not the icy, impersonal, geometric purity that one associates with a modernist architect." Banes further explains, "Since the modern dance of the historical era was never modernist . . . to incorporate modernist notions in dance was actually to rebel against historical modern dance." Copeland and Banes are both quoted from Ann Daly, ed., "What Has Become of Postmodern Dance? Answers and Other Questions by Marcia B. Siegel, Anna Halprin, Janice Ross, Cynthia J. Novack, Deborah Hay, Sally Banes, Senta Driver, Roger Copeland, and Susan L. Foster," *TDR: The Drama Review* 26, no. 1 (1992): 65, 66, 59–60.

[9]Siegel and Banes are quoted from Daly, "What Has Become of Postmodern Dance?," 48, 58.

[10]In general, the dance historical position can be summarized by Maiya Murphy: "I will mark postmodern dance as the work that was generated by Judson Dance Theater through the present. I take the Judson work as a point of departure, but recognize that the exact definitions of modern and postmodern dance are complicated." Murphy, "Fleshing Out: Physical Theater, Postmodern Dance, and Som[e]agency," in *The Oxford Handbook of Dance and Theater*, ed. Nadine George-Graves (New York: Oxford University Press, 2015), 128.

and narrative form. The impacts of Judson Dance Theater are remarkable given its brief duration: the group met from only 1962 to 1964, holding weekly workshops in the Judson Memorial Church in Greenwich Village, where they could get free space. Artists who contributed to Judson are a who's who of choreographers now considered postmodern, including Yvonne Rainer, Trisha Brown, Douglas Dunn, Simone Forti, David Gordon, Lucinda Childs, Steve Paxton, and Deborah Hay. Banes describes the set of postmodern creative processes the Judson Dance Theater advanced: "from chance procedures to improvisation to picture-scores to rule-game and tasks," their processes produced enduring movement vocabularies that included "democratic pluralism, [an embrace of] unstylized ordinary activities . . . as well as the more specialized actions of athletics, ballet, and modern dance techniques."[11] Shared aesthetic values of "openness, indeterminacy, and inclusiveness" produced a point of view wherein, as Jose L. Reynoso describes, "anything could be dance and looked at as dance."[12] This approach affected who could be considered a dancer as well: postmodern choreography tends to reject aesthetics that value uniformity among dancers, including strong, contemporaneous traditions of the corps de ballet and the musical theatre dance chorus. The incorporation of pedestrian movement into postmodern choreography further suggests a rejection of what had been traditionally understood as technical virtuosity in dance performance, and thus dance training and education became more than simply mechanisms through which dancers developed their technique. For postmodern choreographers, dancers were explicitly cocreators, bringing ways of thinking to the choreographic process, not only skills of technical execution.[13]

Often taken as emblematic of the Judson era, Yvonne Rainer's *Trio A* (1966) provides a useful capsule of postmodern movement values. In describing this work, I aim to highlight how the aesthetic qualities and commitments of *Trio A* might be understood as oppositional to commercial theatre's priorities, thus framing how Jones's "postmodern" Broadway choreography exists in a popular imaginary wherein postmodern dance and Broadway dance are not only opposites, but antagonists. What we now know as *Trio A* was first performed as *The Mind Is a Muscle, Part I* by Rainer, David Gordon, and Steve Paxton as a set of three simultaneous, not unison, solos. While the choreography does not explicitly require more traditional modes of technical virtuosity, it does ask performers to cultivate a highly specific movement quality and sustain it throughout the solo's duration. *Trio A* is task-based and performers apply the same quality of equanimity to the series of gestures, many of them pedestrian. Gestures happen sequentially without phrasing—maintaining a single effort quality effectively strips the dance of a narrative that depends on dynamic shifts. In a 1978 filming of *Trio A*, Rainer stands in profile to the camera in a tight parallel, arms at her sides. Her knees bend, her head turns to the left, facing upstage, and her arms flap around her torso right left right left. She takes two steps over her left shoulder, pauses midwalk, and

---

[11]Quoted from Daly, "What Has Become of Postmodern Dance?,"59.

[12]Jose L. Reynoso, "Democracy's Body, Neoliberalism's Body: The Ambivalent Search for Egalitarianism within the Contemporary Post/Modern Dance Tradition." *Dance Research Journal* 51, no 1 (2019): 50.

[13]As Maiya Murphy writes, "before and after Judson Dance Theater there were very different assumptions about what dancers needed to be able to do and how training should prepare them. In this way, postmodern dance training was in many ways defined by what Judson suggested dance could be." Murphy, "Fleshing Out," 129.

circles her arms in tight circles initiated from the shoulder. The work continues largely in this fashion and is a feat of memorization. No movements are repeated, and no movement is given any more emphasis than any other. The effect of Rainer's choices is to create a gestural landscape where each gesture is of equal value, regardless of its inspiration from everyday life or from technical movement practices. In this way, as Maiya Murphy describes, postmodern dance "carve[s] out the path to creative agency as a two-pronged approach of cultivating creative empowerment while removing restrictions on output."[14] This removal of restrictions and the weighing of all movement allegedly equally are part of postmodern dance's reputation as an egalitarian form.

In 1965 Rainer shared her "No Manifesto," now taken as a clarion call of postmodern dance (though treated with irreverence by Rainer herself), in which she declared, "NO to spectacle no to virtuosity no to transformations and magic and make-believe. . . . no to seduction of spectator by the wiles of the performer."[15] We can see much of this ethos in *Trio A*, as well as the way these statements might obviously conflict with the values of the commercial musical theatre stage. For example, the idea that performers play to the spectator is largely absent from *Trio A*—performers rarely face front, and when they do their focus is directed elsewhere—and explicitly rejected in the "No Manifesto." As Banes wrote of postmodern dance, it consists of "action undistorted for theatrical effectiveness, drained of emotional overlay, literary reference, or manipulated timing."[16] These are opposite priorities to much of musical theatre choreography, particularly following Agnes de Mille, which is focused nearly entirely on theatrical effectiveness—on the effects of the choreography on the spectator, with the most highly valued effects being those of narrative clarity, legibility, and characterization.

Very few early postmodern choreographers had any interest in commercial work, and this was a significant break with tradition, particularly in New York City. Many ballet and modern dance choreographers moved easily between concert and commercial stages prior to the 1960s: de Mille, Jerome Robbins, George Balanchine, Hanya Holm, and Katherine Dunham, among others. However, as Liza Gennaro recounts, "This fluid transfer of ballet and modern dance choreographers to Broadway diminished throughout the twentieth century as a post-modern dance focused on the abstract dancing body separated from narrative, and young post-modern choreographers were no longer trained in, or interested in, legible dance storytelling."[17] In this context, legibility refers to choreography that tells a story through tone, characterization, or plot development, and in all cases relates to the entire production (rather than discrete numbers). Jones entered the postmodern scene via his partner, Arnie Zane, in the 1970s, and the early works the duo made were indeed less concerned with legibility and more concerned with experimentation, though they were less invested in eschewing technique than were early postmodern dancemakers. As Jones remembers, "We were rule breakers. . . . That other world—Broadway, the commercial theater—was one that I didn't

---

[14]Murphy, 133.

[15]Yvonne Rainer, "Retrospective," *The Tulane Drama Review* 10, no 5 (1965): 178.

[16]Sally Banes, *Terpsichore in Sneakers: Post-Modern Dance* (Middletown, CT: Wesleyan University Press, 1987), 17.

[17]Gennaro, *Making Broadway Dance*, 190.

have to aspire to."[18] In this formula, postmodern dance opposes commercial dance (the "other" world) primarily through its commitments to maintaining total creative freedom, to questioning all rules. These commitments are difficult to uphold in the commercial musical theatre, which, by its very designation, is concerned with breaking even and ideally turning a profit.

How, then, did Jones enter—and conquer—"the ultra-legible world of Broadway"?[19] By the time Jones started collaborating on *Spring Awakening* in 2006, he was one of the best-known contemporary choreographers in the world and had directed the Bill T. Jones/Arnie Zane Company for over twenty years. At the time, securing a spot in his company was as unlikely as a spot in a Broadway show; CNN reported in 2006 that "a recent audition call drew 421 women and 70 men for two company openings."[20] Unlike first-generation postmodern choreographers, Jones maintains an interest in technical virtuosity: his choreography is technically demanding and complex, and it incorporates several trained movement practices including ballet, modern, and vernacular forms. His prestigious reputation for experimentation but also virtuosity appealed to the *Spring Awakening* creative team, which was interested in rock rebellion and avant-garde aesthetics. When Jones began working on *Spring Awakening*, the Broadway scene was dominated by white choreographers like Susan Stroman (*The Producers*), Kathleen Marshall (*Wonderful Town* and *The Pajama Game*), and Jerry Mitchell (*La Cage aux Folles*), who regularly choreographed more than one Tony-nominated production each season. A decade prior to Jones's own Tony nomination for *Spring Awakening*, Black choreographers Savion Glover and Garth Fagan received this honor (for *Bring in 'da Noise, Bring in 'da Funk* and *The Lion King*, respectively), however the list of Tony winners for Best Choreography remains overwhelmingly white and is just one indicator of the racism faced by Black artists (including Jones) working in commercial theatre.

The primary friction point for Jones as he encountered the Broadway stage was its commitment to legibility, to movement that clearly served story and characterization, when Jones's modern dance career had thus far favored abstraction, juxtaposition, and confrontation in a series of movement experiments rather than narratives. Jones understood the challenge to his aesthetic posed by working on Broadway, describing how, with his company, "I don't try to calculate what the effect will be on the public. In the theater . . . they're making entertainment. I mean that in no patronizing way. In theater it's 'We need this, we need that.' The abstract must be kept at a minimum—all the things I have relied on in my work."[21] Because the commercial theatre as a business model centers on its effects on the public—as evidenced by its success in selling tickets—the audience member is prioritized in production dramaturgy, even if ideas about who the general audience member is may depend on class and race bias. It is this kind of calculation that the early postmodern choreographers were, in part, rebelling against.

---

[18]Quoted in Roslyn Sulcas, "It Takes a Rule Breaker to Create Dance for Rebels," *New York Times*, June 7, 2007.
[19]Gennaro, *Making Broadway Dance*, 192.
[20]Porter Anderson, "Bill T. Jones: Narrative of Trauma," *CNN*, May 22, 2007, https://www.cnn.com/2007/US/02/20/bhm.billtjones/index.html.
[21]Quoted in Gold, "On Broadway," 83.

Importantly, if Jones's choreography was the most unprecedented element of *Spring Awakening*, it was hardly alone in pushing the boundaries of musical theatre: the original pop-rock score by Duncan Sheik favored atmosphere over earworms, Steven Sater's poetic lyrics revealed the inner states of characters rather than propelling the plot forward, and Michael Mayer's directorial concept sat some audience members onstage to watch as the cast starkly toggled back and forth between rock concert song delivery and the stilted, formal language and setting of the production's source material, Frank Wedekind's 1891 play of the same name. The source material itself was difficult, fraught with plot points revolving around sexual violence and physical harm. Many production choices disrupted narrative momentum in a fragmented dramaturgy that responded to the central characters' feelings of isolation and the sharp edges of their community. Sater recalled that while he and Sheik were collaborating on the musical, "I felt I did not want to write lyrics which would forward the plot, and so chose not to follow that golden rule of musicals." Instead, the songs would be opportunities wherein "each student would give voice to his or her inner landscape."[22] The notion that art reveals inner truths is compatible with dance modernism—as Martha Graham frequently said, "movement never lies"—but within the context of this musical, Sater's approach fragments the narrative point of view and disrupts the forward momentum of the plot, thus aligning with postmodern dance values of fragmentation, multiple truths, and nonlinearity. Sheik's pop-rock score likewise favors atmospheric sound over more traditional musical theatre forms, an approach that supports a postmodern aesthetic of tone, atmosphere, and "happening" rather than narrative clarity and presentation.

Director Michael Mayer approached Jones about joining the creative team as *Spring Awakening* was moving from workshops to a full production at the Atlantic Theater Company in 2006. Mayer noted how the unusual dramaturgical structure of *Spring Awakening* affected the choreographic process, recalling that in his early communications with Jones he explained that the show's songs "interrupt the actions rather than continue it. So I told him I would stage the whole thing and leave empty spaces for him where the choreography needed to be."[23] Jones, used to directing his own company and being much more involved in the creative process, had to reset his expectations around how a choreographer contributes to a collective endeavor like musical theatre. Resetting expectations was also part of Jones's experience working with the actors. There is no dance chorus in *Spring Awakening*; the actors are responsible for executing the choreography. Jones came into the process with some choreographic tools of postmodernism, including contact improvisation, but the demand on the actors in terms of delivering the vocal score was too great to accommodate complex, virtuosic movement approaches.[24] Jones relied on postmodern dance's appreciation of gesture and sequencing (similar to what we see in Rainer's *Trio A*) to create atmosphere through movement in ways that would support the physical requirements of the score and the overall dramaturgy of the production.

Despite *Spring Awakening* being heralded as the "new," Jones brought what for him were well-worn techniques of movement generation: "at that time I was an unknown in

---

[22]Steven Sater, *Spring Awakening: A New Musical* (New York: Theatre Communications Group, 2007), viii.
[23]Quoted in Sulcas, "It Takes a Rule Breaker to Create Dance for Rebels."
[24]Sulcas.

Broadway world. . . . I offered things that we do all the time in downtown dance, you know, discontinuous movement, gesture that's not connected to narrative."[25] One clear example of this is in "The Word of Your Body," as the teenage lovers execute a simple exercise of maintaining a connection point between two bodies, familiar to anyone who has studied modern dance or contact improvisation. As a whole, the production offered aesthetics of discontinuity and disruption in its score, staging, and choreography, emphasizing the sharp edges of Wedekind's drama. Written in 1891, Wedekind's play was initially banned because of its controversial content and social critique and was not performed until 1906. Subtitled *The Tragedy of Childhood*, the play criticizes bourgeois society and its moralistic righteousness, religiosity, and conservatism as it tells the story of children becoming young adults and the failures of the adults around them to mentor them, particularly on issues of sexuality. The child characters experience many kinds of violence—emotional, physical, sexual—at the hands of the adults around them, and as they go through young adulthood their sexual encounters with one another are marked by dysfunction, shame, and aggression. At the heart of Wedekind's play is the tyranny of the "normal," when to be normal is to be kept in a state of ignorance. With this play as the source material for the musical *Spring Awakening*, the drama's inherent rebellion against the status quo, both artistic and social, makes space for aesthetic values that push against Broadway's status quo of prioritizing storytelling above all.

As presented at the Atlantic Theater Company, the production features intimate staging: a square stage with a single chair, surrounded on three sides by the audience.[26] The fourth, upstage side houses the band (guitar, bass, percussion, and cello) and a set list scrawled on a blackboard, a set design choice that helps establish the antiauthoritarian, rebel-yell ethos (if not material reality) of rock music. Members of the cast enter and sit among the audience. Wendla, the female protagonist, then enters and stands on the chair. Played by Lea Michele, she is dressed in a white romper and black tights, deliberately childlike. Wendla is one of three protagonists, joined by Melchior (Jonathan Groff) and Moritz (John Gallagher Jr.) as they try to navigate their sexual awakenings in a society that denies sexual desire. The production maintains the historical period of its source material, though its use of rock music and postmodern choreography suggests the ongoing resonance of its themes. By the end of the show, Moritz has died by suicide, Wendla, carrying Melchior's child, has died from a botched abortion, and Melchior contemplates taking his own life at her graveside. The plot emphasizes the violent consequences of keeping people ignorant in order to maintain a veneer of moralism, and Mayer's production offers glimpses into young people's repressed inner states by having the musical numbers voice the subtext directly to the audience through score, lyric, and choreography.

Jones's now iconic gestural sequences for the production are introduced in its opening number, "Mama Who Bore Me." This number establishes the production's toggling

---

[25]Quoted in Neal Conan, "Bill T. Jones Takes Broadway Hit Fela! on Tour," *Talk of the Nation*, NPR, September 21, 2011, http://www.npr.org/2011/09/21/140672965/bill-t-jones-takes-fela-nationwide. For more analysis of this point, see Ariel Nereson, "Allergies, Allegiances, and Authenticity: Bill T. Jones's Choreography for Broadway," *Studies in Musical Theatre* 13, no. 1 (2019): 23–36.
[26]All descriptions of the production come from my viewing of the archival video at the New York Public Library for the Performing Arts. The video was filmed August 3, 2006, at the Atlantic Theater Company.

mechanism—moving swiftly between atmospheric inner worlds embodied in song and movement and dramatic scenes lifted from Wedekind and played realistically. As Wendla, Lea Michele, standing on a chair, looks out at the audience, and begins a gestural sequence that functions as the choreographic DNA for the entire production. As she sings the opening lyrics, one hand rests gently on her face as the other hand wraps around her neck then scans down her chest, tracing a breast with a quality of curiosity rather than desire. The opening song and scene foreshadow the harms that come from denying the truth, and Michele raises her hands up in front of her eyes before again tracing her chest, singing, "Mama who bore me. / Mama who gave me / No way to handle things. Who made me so bad."[27] Her arms wrap around her waist, gently pulling at the childish romper. Jones leaned into the introspective intention behind the musical numbers with a guiding question: "How can she absentmindedly introduce these gestures that speak about her body, the questions it has, the desires it has, that maybe she's not yet aware of."[28] Jones's choreography is resolutely abstract—the gestures neither directly relate to the content of the lyrics nor advance the plot—and, while stylized, is unshowy and does not require virtuosic technical training to execute, all qualities found in postmodern dance.

As the song transitions into the opening scene between Wendla and her mother, Michele transitions seamlessly from tracing her abdomen to pulling up her romper and getting dressed. Her manner is completely pedestrian and unstylized, in clear contrast to the abstract gestures. Her mother, Frau Bergman (played by Mary McCann), enters and chastises her for her childish clothing. The hypocrisy of the adult world is made immediately clear as Frau Bergman simultaneously criticizes her daughter's childlike choices and refuses to answer her questions about how a child is conceived. As Frau Bergman continues to deflect Wendla's anguished queries, the women of the company enter the stage with handheld microphones to begin the reprise of "Mama Who Bore Me," strutting and stomping around the stage like they are at a rock concert. Frau Bergman freezes in mid action as the girls strut around her. While Jones's choreography throughout *Spring Awakening* tends toward abstraction, there are more referential moments, such as the performer in the "Mama Who Bore Me" reprise who executes a back *attitude* as she stomps around McCann's frozen figure, mocking the elitism, formality, and propriety of bourgeois society.[29] As the reprise continues, Jones's choreography doubles down on a rejection of stereotypically "feminine" movement, be it either overly delicate or hypersexual, in favor of gender-neutral pedestrian stomps layered with abstract upper-body gestures. The scene ends with the women promising "No sleep in heaven, or Bethlehem," predicting the rebellion to come, and abruptly transitions to the world of the play's male characters, a world of similarly harsh judgment sited in the local school.[30] This opening shift from Wendla's intimate curiosities to a shared frustration establishes the malleability of the gestural sequence and suggests how it might serve a variety of dramaturgical needs.

---

[27]Sater, *Spring Awakening*, 15.
[28]Quoted in Gennaro, *Making Broadway Dance*, 194.
[29]An *attitude* position is from the ballet vocabulary where a leg is extended behind the dancer and raised to a ninety degree angle. The move is similar to an *arabesque*, however the leg is bent demonstrating the turnout or rotation from the hip.
[30]Sater, *Spring Awakening*, 18.

Image 13.1 *Spring Awakening* (2007). Photo by Bryan Bedder.

Jones's gestural sequence for "Mama Who Bore Me" reverberates through the production, creating a shared movement vocabulary that is both evocative and practical. The gestures are simple and thus allow for actors to layer characterization on top of them; simultaneously, the simplicity of the gestural vocabulary facilitates the actors' vocal performances. Jones also layered complexity onto the simplistic gesture score using choreographic tools like timing, facing, levels, effort qualities, and partnering. While it is true, as Liza Gennaro notes, that "establishing a movement vocabulary in an opening number is not a new idea. . . . Jones did something different," creating a single gesture score that "eschews the dominant dance number approach in which new movement vocabulary is created for each number."[31] For example, during "Touch Me," Moritz repeats Wendla's opening gestures, but his movement is facilitated by Melchior, who gently cups his hands over Moritz's as he traces his abdomen. Later in the number, the full cast lies on the floor supine, and repeats the tracing sequence lying down. The cast then walks the perimeter of the stage, layering the gestural sequence on top of pedestrian movement (and those familiar with Jones's choreography for his own company will recognize this gesture processional tactic as one of Jones's favorites). The first act closing number, "The Mirror-Blue Night," uses the gesture sequence as a point of departure to support the first act climax. Melchior establishes the gesture sequence and then, as tension builds surrounding a possible sexual encounter with Wendla, his gestures become more continuous and rhythmic, departing from the sequence

---

[31]Gennaro, *Making Broadway Dance*, 194.

in order to heighten the audience's attention to the significance of the moment—this is one of the production's more traditional uses of choreography in terms of overall dramaturgy.

The high-energy number "Totally Fucked" brings the gesture sequence back at a fever pitch, its frenetic, uncontrolled energy matching the production's swift sequence of tragedies in the second act. A dissonant guitar chord pauses the scene as Melchior, confronted by his teacher and accused of depravity (following Moritz's death by suicide, adults find among his belongings a drawing by Melchior illustrating sexual encounters), discovers he is, indeed, totally fucked. Groff performs the gestural sequence on fast-forward, abandoning gentleness and fluidity in favor of choppy, half-completed gestures. The entire cast picks up the sequence, each on their own timing. There is no visible canon or other temporal organization, though they share a frenzied quality. The concept of performers moving on their own timing, irrespective of a musical score or relationships with other performers, is a hallmark of postmodern choreography. We see a series of postmodern tactics in the production's closing number, "Purple Summer." The cast perambulates around the stage with pedestrian walks, and you can almost hear Jones coaching them in rehearsal as performers complete a now-classic modern dance warm-up: see an opening, go there, find a partner, find a new level, find a moment to kneel, and so on. This structured improvisation approach supports individualized expressions of choreography on the part of the performers as well as the production's unusually open-ended finale.

The gesture DNA of the production partners with additional postmodern aesthetics to demonstrate how *Spring Awakening*'s choreography is postmodern in product, in what we see on the stage. Yet there are also glimpses of how the choreography is postmodern in *process* as well. This is particularly clear in the first act number "The Bitch of Living," which follows "Mama Who Bore Me." "The Bitch of Living" is one of few numbers that does not recycle the gesture sequence, and by design it contrasts the female and male casts, creating aesthetic juxtaposition to support social constructions of rigid gender roles defined through opposition. Both numbers share a commitment to movement as metaphorical, atmospheric, and quality driven rather than illustrative. The process of creating this number partook of postmodern choreographic approaches, approaches that are more democratic than is typically associated with both commercial and elite art spaces. Generally speaking, as Maiya Murphy observes, postmodern dance "sought not a superficial change of style, but a much deeper change within the process of creating art itself."[32] We can see some values of this change in Jones's description of his own process for *Spring Awakening*: "I'm not a George Balanchine who walks in and says, 'Now, dear, you do this, you do this,' and, boom, it's genius. I come in and say, 'I like this movement at the beginning. Let's work awhile and see what you do with variations on that.'"[33] Jones's description reveals several values of postmodern choreographic processes, and begins with contrasting them to more modernist approaches (characterized here in the person of Balanchine, who also worked across concert and Broadway stages) that designate the choreographer as genius, and the performers as those who execute the genius's vision. Jones's ventriloquism of "now, dear" subtly underscores the paternalism and sexism of traditional choreographic approaches.

---

[32]Murphy, "Fleshing Out," 132.
[33]Quoted in Sulcas, "It Takes a Rule Breaker to Create Dance for Rebels."

Instead, Jones owns his perspective as one of many rather than as the genius: "*I* like this movement." He includes the performers as collaborators in movement generation—"let's work awhile"—whose individual choices are valued in the creative process.

For "The Bitch of Living," Groff remembered that in early rehearsals, "Bill asked us what the word bitch meant to us as young men. . . . He made us say it over and over, stand up and scream the word into his face, and see what it was doing to our bodies. Then that became the basis for the choreography. As nondancers it was so exciting to be able to express ourselves clearly in a nonverbal way."[34] This isolated example points to postmodern values in process (and indeed, while Jones's own work with his company is less and less postmodern in product, his process retains these values), where performers are asked to be cocreators and to bring in their individuality. "The Bitch of Living" begins with six boys in six chairs, dressed in school uniforms. They sit with their knees closely together and hands interlaced, appearing both solid and shrinking. Moritz takes a microphone out to sing, sharply breaking with the droning schoolteacher and the drudgery of the Latin lesson. As he croons into the mic, we see toe taps from the cast. As they build to the chorus, they add the right shoulder to their kinesthetic time-keeping. These rhythmic cues continue throughout the number as different performers reveal their inner fantasies. When the chorus kicks in, the rhythm starts from the knees down in a flat-footed stomp, then from the hip down as some performers move their whole legs. In order to execute this progression, they have to spread their legs, expand their stance—a choice that clearly differentiates masculine movement qualities from socially approved feminine qualities. During the song's second chorus, performers jump up and down, stand on chairs to jump off, and chug around the stage. Their choreography aligns with the short vocal phrases of the chorus and their anguished delivery: "It's the bitch of living / With nothing going on. / Just the bitch of living / Asking: 'What went wrong?' / Do they think we want this? / Oh—who knows?"[35] The boys' movements throughout are filled with frustrated energy, anger, rebellion, and force.

In this way, Jones's work on *Spring Awakening* demonstrates what Jose L. Reynoso characterizes as "notions of democratic, nonhierarchical dance practices, one of the *recognizable* core values of contemporary post/modern dance practices."[36] Importantly, this kind of process takes *time*, and in the commercial theatre, time is money. Time, particularly longer durations, affected both Jones's product and his process. When Jones joined *Spring Awakening*, he immediately realized that his artistic collaborators "don't really know the values of the contemporary dance world, that gesture doesn't have to correspond to a meaning or a character or music. They don't know that specific gestures accrue meaning over time and in context."[37] In other words, the significance of the gesture may not immediately hit the spectator but may instead be revealed through its repetition, a challenge to the ultralegibility demanded by a corporatized, neoliberal funding environment. Jones was, however, also self-aware about his own expectations coming into the process, recognizing that commercial spaces have different, not lesser, demands on the artist: "In

---

[34]Quoted in Sulcas.
[35]Sater, *Spring Awakening*, 24.
[36]Reynoso, "Democracy's Body, Neoliberalism's Body," 49 (original emphasis).
[37]Quoted in Gold, "On Broadway," 83.

rehearsal with my company . . . we can spend two hours on 30 seconds of movement. Here you have musicians, actors learning their stuff—everything is gonna stop while Bill figures out how these three people will manage the next five seconds? That's too expensive."[38] Thus we see postmodern process as the exception in Jones's work on *Spring Awakening*, rather than the rule. Yet even this small change to Broadway's regular operating procedures had huge ripple effects as producers, audience members, and critics considered the production as a whole, and the new direction it heralded for musical theatre.

Reception and Legacy

After transferring to Broadway, *Spring Awakening* ran for 859 performances at the Eugene O'Neill Theatre and received overwhelmingly positive reviews (and, importantly for producers, easily recouped its initial investment). The production received eight Tony Awards, including Jones's award for Best Choreography. In a characteristic review, David Rooney wrote in *Variety* that "the most arresting element is inarguably the collaboration of Mayer and Jones in a show driven by movement both contemplated and viscerally spontaneous."[39] The choreography was a visually clear departure from traditional Broadway offerings, even if its abstraction did not prioritize legibility. The fervent fandom that greeted the production affirmed Jones's approach, as CNN reported: "'People are ready for this, for a gesture, for the abstract,' Jones says, happy to find that theater audiences follow the intent of the movement, as dance audiences are more accustomed to doing."[40] Even more atypically, it wasn't just critics and artists who embraced this new approach. Producers, perhaps the most conservative category of Broadway participants, were willing to adjust their expectations, as producer Scott Morfee told *Variety*: "'Spring Awakening' proved that audiences—and producers—are being less conventional and taking more chances. . . . For a commercial producer, the success of a show like 'Spring Awakening' gives hope."[41] Rooney, Morfee, and Jones himself refer to the choreography as product, not process, in their summations of the value of *Spring Awakening*'s avant-garde approach. Yet, while Jones's postmodern aesthetics profoundly affected the success of *Spring Awakening*, we have seen little continuing influence on Broadway dance.

While several of Jones's contemporaries in the avant-garde dance scene have choreographed for Broadway, including Karole Armitage, Lar Lubovitch, Mark Morris, and Twyla Tharp, very few of them have translated postmodern aesthetics onto the musical theatre stage, preferring instead to choreograph (often very successfully) within the bounds of more traditional dramaturgies that prioritize narrative and characterization.[42] Even following Jones's reception in 2006, few choreographers interpreted postmodern aesthetics in their

---

[38]Quoted in Gold, 83.

[39]David Rooney, review of *Spring Awakening*, dir. Michael Mayer, *Variety*, June 15, 2006.

[40]Anderson, "Bill T. Jones."

[41]Quoted in David Mermelstein, "'Spring' Has Sprung New Breed of Tuner," *Variety*, April 22, 2008.

[42]Armitage choreographed the 2009 revival of *Hair;* Lubovich has done numerous Bradway musicals including, but not limited to, the original *Into the Woods* (1987), *The Red Shoes* (1998), *High Society* (1998), *The King and I* (1994); Tharp has numerous Broadway credits some of which i include *Movin' Out* (2002), *Come Fly Away* (2010), *Singin' in the Rain* (1986).

work for Broadway, and choreographers like Christopher Gattelli, Sergio Trujillo, and Andy Blankenbuehler found success in innovating within musical theatre's more established traditions. Steven Hoggett's atmospheric stagings share a more abstract orientation, if not postmodern choreographic tactics, with Jones's work on *Spring Awakening*.[43] Jones himself, departing from a consistent use of postmodern dance, utilized several choreographic methods and movement practices in his second foray on Broadway, 2009's *Fela!*, for which he received his second Tony for Best Choreography. Working with highly trained dancers on *Fela!* allowed Jones to set a lot of movement quickly and trust performers' skills, fitting more efficiently into Broadway's production model. As Elizabeth Wollman writes, "A more holistic approach to the stage musical—one that takes into consideration the commerce side of the equation alongside the artistic one—might result in a more honest, equitable reflection of Broadway and its output."[44] Considering the commerce side of the equation helps us make sense of why Jones's choreography for *Spring Awakening*, particularly its postmodern process and product, was heralded as a game changer. It also helps us make sense of why, in fact, we did *not* see postmodern aesthetics take over the Broadway stage. At the time of this writing (early 2022), Jones is back on Broadway again as a Tony nominee for *Paradise Square*, where his choreography features several historically specific, and legible, movement practices.

An important part of the legacy of Jones's choreography for *Spring Awakening*, and the overall success of the original production, is its groundbreaking 2015 revival by Deaf West Theatre, which ran for 135 performances at New York's Brooks Atkinson Theatre. Los Angeles–based Deaf West Theatre stages works that incorporate both English and American Sign Language (ASL) and are performed by Deaf actors and hearing actors. The revival's creative team included choreographer Spencer Liff as well as ASL masters, consultants, and rehearsal translators. While Deaf West's bilingual approach to theatrical production was well suited to a story about communication failures, Liff and the ASL team's contributions reminded many viewers of the original Broadway production's choreography. As Isherwood wrote, "the use of sign language . . . is intriguingly reminiscent of Bill T. Jones's superb work the first time around."[45] I want to be clear that I am not equating ASL with postmodern abstract gestures. Indeed, the dramaturgical function is opposite, with ASL directly expressing language through what are often mimetic actions. What I do think connects Jones's choreography to Liff's collaboration with the ASL team is that they both establish a willingness for the (hearing) Broadway spectator to encounter movement material that they don't immediately understand. Deaf West's revival challenges, in Sarah Wilbur's analysis, "hegemonic norms around learning, literacy, and ability" through how ASL communicates via gesture.[46] This is a political project in both process and product, and Wilbur also documents how the combination of Deaf and hearing performers necessitated additional rehearsal elements that concerned producers in terms of possibly slowing down a typical

---

[43]For this analysis, see Gennaro, *Making Broadway Dance*; Gennaro and Wolf, "Dance in Musical Theater."
[44]Wollman, "How to Dismantle a [Theatric] Bomb," 2.
[45]Charles Isherwood, "'Spring Awakening' by Deaf West Theater Brings a New Sensation to Broadway," *New York Times*, September 27, 2015.
[46]Sarah Wilbur, "Gestural Economies and Production Pedagogies in Deaf West's *Spring Awakening*," *TDR: The Drama Review* 60, no. 2 (2016): 149.

Broadway production schedule (harking back to Jones's observation about the time pressures that his postmodern approach activated in a commercial environment).

Without likening ASL to postmodern dance or claiming that postmodernism was a useful set of aesthetics for Deaf West, I am reminded of how Marcia Siegel characterizes "one of postmodernism's most consistent projects, to subvert received ideas about society and art."[47] Postmodern dance works on this project via the body in motion. Susan Leigh Foster extends Siegel's assertion into the body-based domain of choreography, writing, "In the wake of this riotous play of heterogeneous forms and formats, bodies—other than those of white, bourgeois, heterosexuals—have begun to articulate their identities and concerns."[48] Indeed, from the earliest days of their company Jones and Zane welcomed a diverse range of dancers to their process. We can see the prioritization of Global Majority and queer perspectives in recent (and still rare) incorporations of postmodern aesthetic values on the Broadway stage, from John Heginbotham in the 2019 *Oklahoma!* revival and from Raja Feather Kelly in the 2022 Broadway premiere of *A Strange Loop*. Both productions were recognized with Tony Awards for their innovations, and both Heginbotham and Kelly included postmodern movement specifically to articulate the inner worlds of Black and queer characters.

Like the 2006 *Spring Awakening*, Daniel Fish's *Oklahoma!* was meant to upend expectations about what musical theatre could be, this time by taking on one of its most sacred texts, the Golden Age stalwart *Oklahoma!*, originally choreographed by Agnes de Mille. Heginbotham joined the workshop team for the revival while directing his own modern dance company, Heginbotham Dance, which was founded in 2012 after Heginbotham's performing career with Mark Morris. The choreography shifted frequently in workshop, off-Broadway, Broadway, West End, and touring contexts; for the Broadway production at Circle in the Square Theatre, Heginbotham reserved postmodern aesthetics for what is often described as de Mille's most significant innovation, the dream ballet. Other dance numbers, like "Kansas City" and "The Farmer and the Cowman" were, in Heginbotham's design, straightforward in terms of setting a tone that drew from vernacular dance forms like the Texas two-step and other country social dances.

Played by Rebecca Naomi Jones, the 2019 revival's Laurey was the sole Black female character, with Dream Laurey danced by Gabrielle Hamilton and Demetia Hopkins-Greene. "Laurey Makes Up Her Mind," the dream ballet, prioritized Laurey's story and what happens when that story is communicated through a Black woman's experience. Like 2006's *Spring Awakening* but unlike nearly every other production of *Oklahoma!*, Heginbotham's version includes no dance chorus, a choice that emphasizes Laurey's social and psychological isolation. Staged in a similarly intimate fashion to the 2006 *Spring Awakening*, the seventeen-minute dream ballet that opens act 2 (a shift from closing act 1, its traditional placement) partakes of a noncontinuous movement score designed to fragment the dramaturgical support that the choreography plays in other scenes. The dream ballet begins with the cast storming the stage, shouting, "Hold bottle two inches from nostrils! Close your eyes and inhale! Ask your heart what you really want! Wait for the answer!" The set has been cleared

---

[47]Quoted from Daly, "What Has Become of Postmodern Dance?," 51.
[48]Quoted from Daly, 68.

of the picnic tables from the first act, and the score is distorted as it cycles through numbers from act 1. These staging choices create an unfamiliar space with few referents to the real world. Into this space, Dream Laurey dances movement that, in its nonnarrative abstraction, its confrontation with the audience, its toggling between pedestrian walks, runs, and gallops and virtuosic extensions, uses the aesthetic trappings of postmodernism to comment on social expectations of feminine gender expression and sexuality. Narrative clarity is rejected in favor of assembling a variety of movements whose connections to one another and to the world of *Oklahoma!* are not immediately obvious. This critical opacity functions, like much of Jones's choreography, as a political refusal of the legibility demanded of queer, femme, and Global Majority performers in exchange for merely existing in the predominantly white spaces of both commercial and concert dance.

Another choreographer bringing postmodern aesthetic values to Broadway, and in doing so celebrating Black queer world-making, is Raja Feather Kelly. Kelly's choreography for the 2022 *A Strange Loop* marks similarities between Kelly's and Jones's careers, and indeed, the two choreographers are professionally linked. Like Jones, Kelly has choreographed for the dramatic theatre as well as experimental dance venues, and Kelly was the 2019–20 Randjelovic/Stryker Resident Commissioned Artist at New York Live Arts, the presenting entity for which Jones serves as artistic director and the space that houses his company. While Kelly's choreographic product for dramatic and musical theatre emphasizes theatrical and exaggerated behavior (a departure from the pedestrian approaches of postmodernism), his choreographic process is clearly influenced by the world of experimental downtown dance that Jones helped reimagine. In Kelly's own words, "I don't prepare or prestage. . . . I enjoy interacting with the people with whom I'm collaborating. Together, we find out if the movement fits who they are or feels inspired—not by the way I've imagined it but by the way I'm seeing it play out in real time."[49] The sense of a more democratic or egalitarian process is part of postmodernism's legacy as taken up by minoritarian choreographers and combined with social values that prioritize community-building and mutual support. Kelly's choreography for *A Strange Loop*'s opening number, "Intermission Song," showcases individualized gestural and behavioral choreography for each of the Thoughts, physicalized fragments of the main character Usher's mental landscape. Interestingly, Kelly incorporates step vocabulary at the end of the number to both celebrate and satirize stereotyped Black popular culture (a through line of the musical as a whole): as the six Thoughts flank Usher, each completes their own unique step rhythm, forming a cacophony of both virtuosic and decidedly apathetic gestures and sounds that align in intention but not manifestation. This polyvocal choreography invites performers to layer characterization onto a collective that is ambivalent, even in conflict, rather than representing a single, unified Black community.

The critical reception of the 2019 *Oklahoma!* and 2022 *A Strange Loop* productions uses similar language to the awe that met the Broadway premiere of *Spring Awakening* in 2006. Ben Brantley's review of *Oklahoma!* gleefully describes the production as "the coolest new show on Broadway . . . wide-awake, jolting, and altogether wonderful," singling out

---

[49]Quoted in Coco Romack, "Raja Feather Kelly: Waiting for the Subway," *New York Times Magazine*, April 21, 2022.

Heginbotham's "radically reconceptualized" dream ballet.[50] *A Strange Loop* was praised as "radical" by Maya Phillips, who also noted Kelly's "uninhibited" choreography.[51] While the narratives of these productions are strikingly divergent, the critical perception that each offers a challenge to musical theatre's status quo is a shared result of how each production incorporates postmodern dance among other design elements. In the case of *Spring Awakening* in both 2006 and 2015, heterogeneity, individuality, and uniqueness were celebrated choreographically even as they instigated punishment in Wedekind's narrative. Jones established the value of bringing disparate approaches and allegedly oppositional aesthetics together, telling CNN in 2007 that Broadway must evolve to serve the public: "There's an audience now that's younger. It has fewer biases. Maybe they can go in different directions—if we have the work there for them to see."[52] *A Strange Loop* and 2019's *Oklahoma!* are providing this work. Studying the moment of *Spring Awakening* and its use of postmodern values may give us additional tools for making this work, for welcoming a broader swath of spectators, and for voicing a wider range of the human experience.

Bibliography

Anderson, Porter. "Bill T. Jones: Narrative of Trauma." *CNN*, May 22, 2007. https://www.cnn.com/2007/US/02/20/bhm.billtjones/index.html.

Banes, Sally. *Terpsichore in Sneakers: Post-Modern Dance*. Middletown, CT: Wesleyan University Press, 1987.

Banes, Sally, and Susan Manning. "Terpsichore in Combat Boots." *TDR: The Drama Review* 33, no. 1 (1989): 13–16.

Brantley, Ben. "A Smashing 'Oklahoma!' Is Reborn in the Land of Id." *New York Times*, April 7, 2019.

Conan, Neal. "Bill T. Jones Takes Broadway Hit Fela! on Tour." *Talk of the Nation*, NPR, September 21, 2011. http://www.npr.org/2011/09/21/140672965/bill-t-jones-takes-fela-nationwide.

Daly, Ann, ed. "What Has Become of Postmodern Dance? Answers and Other Questions by Marcia B. Siegel, Anna Halprin, Janice Ross, Cynthia J. Novack, Deborah Hay, Sally Banes, Senta Driver, Roger Copeland, and Susan L. Foster." *TDR: The Drama Review* 26, no. 1 (1992): 48–69.

Gennaro, Liza. *Making Broadway Dance*. New York: Oxford University Press, 2022.

Gennaro, Liza, and Stacy Wolf, "Dance in Musical Theater." In *The Oxford Handbook of Dance and Theater*, edited by Nadine George-Graves, 148–68. New York: Oxford University Press, 2015.

Gold, Sylviane. "On Broadway." *Dance Magazine*, November 2006.

Isherwood, Charles. "In 'Spring Awakening,' a Rock 'n' Roll Heartbeat for 19th-Century German Schoolboys." *New York Times*, June 16, 2006.

Isherwood, Charles. "Sex and Rock? What Would the Kaiser Think?" *New York Times*, December 11, 2006.

Isherwood, Charles. "'Spring Awakening' by Deaf West Theater Brings a New Sensation to Broadway." *New York Times*, September 27, 2015.

---

[50]Ben Brantley, "A Smashing 'Oklahoma!' Is Reborn in the Land of Id," *New York Times*, April 7, 2019.
[51]Maya Phillips, "'A Strange Loop' Review: A Dazzling Ride on a Mental Merry-Go-Round," *New York Times*, April 26, 2022.
[52]Quoted in Anderson, "Bill T. Jones."

Mermelstein, David. "'Spring' Has Sprung New Breed of Tuner." *Variety*, April 22, 2008.

Murphy, Maiya. "Fleshing Out: Physical Theater, Postmodern Dance, and Som[e]agency." In *The Oxford Handbook of Dance and Theater*, edited by Nadine George-Graves, 125–47. New York: Oxford University Press, 2015.

Nereson, Ariel. "Allergies, Allegiances, and Authenticity: Bill T. Jones's Choreography for Broadway." *Studies in Musical Theatre* 13, no. 1 (2019): 23–36.

Phillips, Maya. "'A Strange Loop' Review: A Dazzling Ride on a Mental Merry-Go-Round." *New York Times*, April 26, 2022.

Rainer, Yvonne. "Retrospective." *The Tulane Drama Review* 10, no 5 (1965): 168–78.

Reynoso, Jose L. "Democracy's Body, Neoliberalism's Body: The Ambivalent Search for Egalitarianism within the Contemporary Post/Modern Dance Tradition." *Dance Research Journal* 51, no 1 (2019): 47–65.

Romack, Coco. "Raja Feather Kelly: Waiting for the Subway." *New York Times Magazine*, April 21, 2022.

Rooney, David. Review of *Spring Awakening*, directed by Michael Mayer. *Variety*, June 15, 2006.

Sater, Steven. *Spring Awakening: A New Musical*. New York: Theatre Communications Group, 2007.

Sulcas, Roslyn. "It Takes a Rule Breaker to Create Dance for Rebels." *New York Times*, June 7, 2007.

Wilbur, Sarah. "Gestural Economies and Production Pedagogies in Deaf West's *Spring Awakening*." *TDR: The Drama Review* 60, no. 2 (2016): 145–53.

Wollman, Elizabeth. "How to Dismantle a [Theatric] Bomb: Broadway Flops, Broadway Money, and Musical Theater Historiography." *Arts* 9, no. 2 (2020): article 66. https://doi.org/10.3390/arts9020066.

Wollman, Elizabeth. *The Theater Will Rock: A History of the Rock Musical, from "Hair" to "Hedwig."* Ann Arbor: University of Michigan Press, 2006.

14 Movement Direction in Musical Theatre: Physical Actions and Gestural Storytelling

MICHAEL D. JABLONSKI AND DUSTYN MARTINCICH

Contemporary musical theatre stories necessitate contemporary approaches to developing vocabulary and staging that support and employ thematic, metaphoric, and pedestrian movement instead of traditional "dance" choreography to communicate a character's journey or the circumstances of the world. With these new stories and the need for new vocabulary and approaches comes a need to reimagine the role of the choreographer. In building a musical production, a movement director, a role generally taken up outside the genre, can offer attention to character physicality and a repeated physical motif that lends cohesion to visual storytelling. This chapter explores approaches in movement direction that prove necessary toward building choreography for certain musical theatre productions. This has been something of an experiment in collaboration: the chapter authors worked in tandem to include co-author Michael Jablonski's own experiences alongside external critical analysis, historical contextualization, and case study analysis. Our investigation points to the physical dramaturgy that can enhance in-scene physicality, connecting it to traditional choreographed numbers, which then can be filled with gestural and character-driving vocabulary. The chapter also considers how a choreographer, applying strategies from movement direction, can bring a more precise fusion of acting and dance approaches to musical staging. This artistic choice offers movement-based or text-based performers individuality and objective-driven physicality beyond the technical virtuosity so often featured in musical theatre dance. In discussing how movement direction has worked in musical theatre productions, Jablonski's firsthand experiences provide examples of how approaches to movement direction have bolstered a performance from original casts to tours to revivals.

When I was dance captain for the national tour of *Matilda the Musical* from 2015 to 2017, I was responsible for maintaining Peter Darling's choreographic integrity and intention, and with that, translating the nuanced intersections the choreography had within each character's life, from ensemble member to lead. In rehearsals, I observed how the exchanges between the associate director (Tom Caruso) and associate choreographer (Kate Dunn) created a natural and seamless transition of acting and physical movement, scene work, and musical numbers. This collaboration allowed for directing and choreography to each contribute in a way that offered a visual fluidity in storytelling. It was apparent that the original director and choreographer, Matthew Warchus and Peter Darling, respectively, envisioned a process that developed storytelling through the integration of movement, music, text, and character. For instance, the physical stature of Miss Trunchbull, played by Bryce Ryness on the first national tour, affected the character's physical score and movement, seen in numbers like "The Smell of Rebellion." Similarly, Miss Honey, played by Jennifer Blood on the first national tour, interacted with scenic properties that carried from scene to song with precision, like the meticulous process of making tea, showing the delicate care and detail she puts into the simplest of tasks and allowing us an inner pathway to the soul of the character in the song "My House." This active yet nuanced attempt at keeping physical storytelling as the main driver in a production was different from my experiences in other musicals. For instance, when I worked on the 2010 revival of *West Side Story*, there was a clear, traditional delineation between choreographer Joey McKneely, who adapted and created movement intentionally connected to music (inspired by the original choreography of Jerome Robbins), and director Arthur Laurents, who worked exclusively on scene work. McKneely and Laurents each worked separately with actors, demarcating dance numbers from scenes. Yet, in *Matilda the Musical*, there was crossover between both creative departments, allowing a collaboration that integrated the acting intentions and directorial concepts with text and music. — Michael D. Jablonski

As we consider how more theatrical approaches have offered alternative entries to using movement to tell stories, it's useful to look to how these practices have found their ways to the musical theatre rehearsal rooms. The chapter begins by briefly pointing to a history of movement direction in musical theatre choreography through the twentieth and twenty-first century, highlighting roots in narrative dance forms like German *Ausdruckstanz* and inspiration in physical theatre practices. Special attention is given to key contributors who created a bridge for movement direction practices to musical theatre, including Kate Flatt and particularly Steven Hoggett. The chapter then turns to two contemporary case studies: Peter Darling's work on *Matilda the Musical* (2013) and Kelly Devine's work on *Come from Away* (2017). Darling's and Devine's examples demonstrate how movement direction approaches can be used to physicalize metaphor and image in order to enhance directorial concepts and create consistent motifs outside of nonliteral pantomime or traditional dance vocabulary. For *Matilda*, Jablonski's experience as dance captain and performer provides access to Darling's process from inside the rehearsal space. In contrast, the discussion of *Come from Away* approaches the musical from the outside, centering an interview Jablonski conducted with choreographer Kelly Devine to understand the approaches used for that production. Both segments share a sense of embodied knowledge that can be useful in understanding the intricacies of embedded movement in a musical production.

Roots and Lineages of Movement Direction

But first, how does movement direction differ from choreography? Rebecca Goh, artistic director of (a)basement theatre collective, defines movement direction as creating the "physical score of a production, taking into account characterization techniques, dramaturgy, text, set design, the performers' abilities & body, and the overarching aesthetic and themes of the play."[1] A movement director works closely with the director and the performers to

---

[1] "Demystifying in Process (Part 1) . . . The Role of the Movement Director," *Mrs. C's Collective* (blog), July 1, 2021, https://www.mrscscollective.co.uk/collective-blog/demystifying-in-process-the-role-of-the-movement-director.

create a physical language developed through dramaturgical research on etiquette, cultural touchstones, nonverbal communication, physical touch, gestural language, societal norms, and physical conditions important to the characters in the world of the production. Additionally, the movement director works with the director and production team to create visual flow and cohesion through physical motifs that can be employed in transitions between or within scenes or between modes of expression. In this way, the choreography for a song or production numbers is seen as an extension of the physicality of the world of the production.

Movement direction evolved as its own theatrical approach, separate from musical theatre choreography. One can see its roots in early twentieth century expressionistic dance forms from central Europe. *Ausdruckstanz*, a dance practice that developed in German-speaking Europe in the early and mid-twentieth century, "emerged from the life reform movement of the early 20th century that promoted diverse practices of physical culture as a way of contesting the industrialisation and urbanisation of modern life."[2] In *Ausdruckstanz*, feelings were an essential part of the processing tool of movement, going against the strict, rigid, and mechanical forms of traditional ballet of the period. *Ausdruckstanz* had two aims: to express one's innermost feelings and to create a form that remains reflective of the events and culture of the time period. Diane S. Howe states that "*Ausdruckstanz* choreographers wanted to find and express what draws all human beings together, and that, they felt, had to begin with honest, truthful expression of the individual being."[3] Rudolf von Laban was a leader in *Ausdruckstanz* or expressionistic dance forms, creating a method of movement analysis that he defined through explorations of modern dance. This approach extended into the actor's realm, particularly his "Eight Efforts" (Wring, Press, Flick, Dab, Glide, Float, Punch, and Slash), tools that actors could use to discover the emotional and physical elements of a character and thus explore character in the body.[4] Laban's methodologies influenced modern dance choreographers who came to work for Broadway productions, such as Hanya Holm, who trained with Laban's student Mary Wigman. Holm's choreography for *Kiss Me, Kate* (1948) was transcribed into Labanotation, a system of symbols that are meant to record human movement by tracking its direction, level, and timing, as well as the body part involved.[5]

In the 1950s, British movement director Litz Pisk developed a technique to assist actors in eliminating recurrent bodily constraints and achieving a shapable physicality, thereby

---

[2]Susan Manning, "Ausdruckstanz (1910–1950)," *The Routledge Encyclopedia of Modernism* (online), published April 26, 2018, https://doi.org/10.4324/0123456789-REM1773-1.

[3]Diane S. Howe, *Individuality and Expression: The Aesthetics of the New German Dance, 1908–1936* (New York: Peter Lang, 1996), 2–3.

[4]For further information about Laban's method, as well as its translation to theatrical training, see, e.g., Rudolf von Laban and Dick McCaw, *The Laban Sourcebook* (New York: Routledge, 2011); Brigid Panet and Fiona McHardy, *Essential Acting: A Practical Handbook for Actors, Teachers and Directors* (London: Routledge, 2009); Jean Newlove, *Laban for Actors and Dancers: Putting Laban's Movement Theory into Practice; A Step-by-Step Guide* (New York: Routledge, 2003).

[5]Using Laban transcription ultimately paved the way for Holm's choreography to be the first awarded federal copyright for an entire production in 1952. Copyrighting choreography, particularly for musical theatre dance, continues to be especially challenging. For more information, please see Anthea Kraut's *Choreographing Copyright: Race, Gender, and Intellectual Property Rights in American Dance* (Oxford: Oxford University Press, 2015).

tapping into their "transformation, imagination and the 'need' to move."[6] Pisk believed that movement is a practice of expression for the individual, where "the shape of your body and the way you stand, sit, and walk indicate your personality." She developed a series of movement progressions rooted in breath, mobilization of the spine, and physical transformation. These approaches allowed actor movement to, as Pisk describes, "spring from physical, emotional, and mental sources." She continues, "On the physical level the shape of your body is the outer boundary of inner contents. Movement, which starts from an impulse and is joined to the centre of the mover, has the power to emanate."[7] As Ayse Tashkiran asserts in the introduction to Pisk's book, her legacy for movement directors "pioneered a model of working on production where voice and movement were integrated into the rehearsal process," thereby acknowledging the body as central to storytelling and physicality as vital to conveying meaning.[8]

Other practitioners—like Jacques Copeau, who founded the Théâtre du Vieux-Colombier, and Suzanne Bing, "the muse of the Vieux-Colombier"—established the practice of working in natural settings in order to connect to deeper human emotions and gestural movement.[9] Copeau and Bing focused on chorus work, masks, mime, the use of sport and natural gymnastics, and animal work to create a new form of storytelling onstage. Bing also developed formal training that utilized isolation and improvisation to develop an actor's sensitivity to physical expressions through movement. Similarly, Jacques Lecoq developed training methods that focused on finding the physical impulse that today we call the character's intention. Lecoq "wanted to reach down, beneath the idea, beneath the word, to find the physical impulse which, he believed, could be shown to underlie all thinking, all emotion, all expression."[10] In 1956, he founded the École internationale de théâtre Jacques Lecoq, where students from around the world could intensively train in movement and gesture work through improvisation, analysis, and collaboration. Lecoq's training methods disseminated widely and became foundational in many professional theatre companies and training spaces throughout Europe and the United States.

As physical theatre training influenced the founding of professional theatre companies, choreography for actors attuned to practices of physical expression. Movement training became less about assigning movements and more about offering a framework within which performers might create specific and detailed movement vocabulary and then block it into a scene. The intersecting interests of theatre and dance and the study of the body's capacity to tell a story converged in the work of British companies like DV8, Complicité, and Frantic Assembly. Members of these companies and descendants of Lecoq training have often

---

[6]Litz Pisk, *The Actor and His Body*, 4th ed. (London: Bloomsbury, 2017), xxi.

[7]Pisk, xxxv.

[8]Ayse Tashkiran, introduction to Pisk, xxi.

[9]On Copeau, see, e.g., Mark Evans, *Jacques Copeau* (London: Routledge, 2017). On Bing, see, e.g., Jane Baldwin, "Raising the Curtain on Suzanne Bing's Life in the Theatre," in *Women, Collective Creation, and Devised Performance: The Rise of Women Theatre Artists in the Twentieth and Twenty-First Centuries*, ed. Kathryn Mederos Syssoyeva and Scott Proudfit (New York: Palgrave Macmillan, 2016), 29–50.

[10]David Bradby, editor's introduction to *Theatre of Movement and Gesture*, by Jacques Lecoq, ed. David Bradby (London: Routledge, 2006), xiii. See also Jacques Lecoq, *The Moving Body: Teaching Creative Theatre*, with Jean-Gabriel Carraso and Jean-Claude Lallias, trans. David Bradby (London: Methuen, 2000).

been invited to other theatres to work on plays with music, or scored plays (a genre that differs from musicals in that the dialogue, not the score, is primarily responsible for conveying story). At the Royal National Theatre in London, for instance, this occurred with *War Horse* (2007), with movement direction by Lecoq-trained Toby Sedgwick, and with *The Curious Incident of the Dog in the Night-Time* (2012) with movement direction by Frantic Assembly's Scott Graham and Steven Hoggett.

From Stylized Movement to "Invisible" Choreography

The collaborative structure of the British companies listed above and their commitment to employing multiple mediums in theatrical storytelling have helped evolve approaches to movement direction. This is particularly evident in contemporary plays with music, where the score is an integral dramaturgical element. For the production of *Curious Incident*, Frantic Assembly's Graham and Hoggett carefully led the cast in creating the unique reality of character Christopher Boone, an autistic young man. Through stylized movement and choreography, the cast translated what Graham described as "Christopher's take on the world" into an experience that was accessible to neurotypical and neurodiverse audiences alike.[11] As Chad Kennedy notes, "realism would only alienate Christopher by emphasizing his otherness, so the creative team developed a new stage language to enable and inspire empathy from the audience."[12] Graham and Hoggett, along with the creative team, brought interviews, autism research, and extensive dramaturgical and production analysis to the rehearsal process in order to develop a "neuro-perceptive" approach that privileged movement over speech to convey dramaturgical information. Graham continues, "Nothing really exists unless Christopher wants it to, so the company will be chaos, they will be flitting around until Christopher focuses then they will snap into position."[13]

Graham and Hoggett particularly attended to the elements of space and time, which, for those on the spectrum, feature differently. The set, designed by Bunny Christie, often offered a visual grid that the ensemble could follow, shifting neutral boxes in space. In one scene, Christopher walks on the gridlines of the wall, easily lifted by ensemble members, who help this reality play out visually for an audience that may not perceive space in such a way. At other times, the space swirls with Christopher as he darts through the shifting ensemble members. He occasionally leaps into their arms, and they lift and carry him, suspending his tempo for just a moment, and set him back down again. In the first half of act 2, Christopher is making his way from Swindon to Willesden by train. The grid and boxes convey the setting of the station and create structures found in the environment, like benches or the trains themselves. In this setting the indirect qualities of space are inhabited by the ensemble members, who walk through the space, creating the chaos of London, their tempo imitating the anxiety and panic growing in Christopher. In this sequence, Graham and Hoggett stage

---

[11]Scott Graham, "Physical Theatre: Frantic Assembly," *The Curious Incident of the Dog in the Night-Time* (website), accessed December 10, 2022, https://www.curiousonstage.com/physical-theatre/.
[12]Chad Kennedy, "From Neurotypical Curiosity to Empathetic Movement: Exploring the 'Neuro-Perceptive' Staging of *The Curious Incident of the Dog in the Night-Time*," in *Text and Presentation, 2018*, ed. Jay Malarcher (Jefferson, NC: McFarland, 2019), 154.
[13]Graham, "Physical Theatre."

the ensemble in movement that resembles what Graham calls the "habitual patterns of commuters." As Graham says, Christopher "ran away from their movement, got caught up, dodged and jumped out of their relentless process."[14] The performers thus represent not just Londoners but Christopher's *perception* of Londoners, and the staging reflects how he conceives of his interactions with them. Graham says the ensemble, "They represent his thoughts; they can be chaotic, and they can be absolutely pure and linear and precise, whatever state of mind he is in."[15] The ensemble's staging and vocabulary help translate the world of the play, creating Christopher's world through their specific physicality.

Movement direction has grown to serve musical theatre in much the same way it serves plays and devised theatre productions. Its aim to provide physical storytelling to enhance the story is fully capitalized on in musical theatre because of the genre's natural and accepted integration of movement, scene, and song. As the musical's form and content evolved over the twentieth century, so too did the choreography, both in approach and in vocabulary. Though much notable musical theatre dance generally produces spectacle, by staging physical virtuosity, movement direction approaches can be seen in choreographers who value either incorporating acting techniques into compositional strategies or building character-enhancing vocabulary. As some choreographers shift into the role of director, this work especially comes into play. For example, Jerome Robbins applied Stanislavsky's method acting principles to guide performers as well as inspire composition, often expanding on character gestures to develop a full dance vocabulary, build visual cohesion in a production, deliver subtext, and add beauty as well as depth of character. In the number "Cool" in *West Side Story* (1957), Robbins's pedestrian movement merged with dance vocabulary to assist dancers in conveying the Jets' suppression of rising anger, connecting their characters' motivations and emotional reality directly to the movement. Jablonski shares the process, giving insight from a performer's perspective:

In preparing for the 2010 revival of *West Side Story*, I met dancers who had worked with Robbins directly, and they shared some of his coaching and imagery. For instance, at one moment in the middle of "Cool," the Jets are in an inverted fourth position lunge—one leg in front of the other in a turn out—with a contraction as their arms are extended out to the front and back. They bounce in a plié on the beat and let their arms swing. This step creates a connection symbolizing the unity between the Jets, the conviction that each one would sacrifice himself to protect the others. If you take the same step and move the legs to a *sous-sus* position in relevé—one foot behind the other, while on their toes—what we see is the imagery of Jesus on the cross, connecting the movement to the metaphor of sacrifice. When the movement director shares these metaphorical images embedded in the movement with the performers, it helps them translate the movement out of simply ballet vocabulary or abstract dance, allowing them to convey subtext through dance. — Michael D. Jablonski

---

[14]Scott Graham, "An Insight into Curious Movement," *The Curious Incident of the Dog in the Night-Time: Education Resource*, National Theatre (website), accessed December 10, 2022, https://www.nationaltheatre.org.uk/sites/default/files/nt_learning_curious_an_insight_into_curious_movements.pdf.
[15]Graham, "Physical Theatre."

Movement directors in musical theatre choreography became particularly useful with the rise of vocal-dominant productions, like *Les Misérables* (1985). For example, British choreographer Kate Flatt, who choreographed the original production of *Les Misérables*, took inspiration for her movement direction from French mime Marcel Marceau and, especially, Russian choreographer Léonide Massine, whose interests in Italian commedia, folk dance, and modernism were threaded into her training at the Royal Ballet. Thus, for the "invisible" choreography in the production, Flatt set out "to discover the ensemble language and the way that the many stories . . . could be told through action."[16] As Flatt states, "Rather than choreograph numbers, I created improvisations, which became part of the language and movement material of the staging. I worked on body language for whores, convicts, the angry unemployed and malnourished beggars. I invented a way to march, which gives the illusion of advancing without going anywhere."[17] Flatt worked alongside codirectors John Caird and Trevor Nunn to evolve the complex staging from an initial, improvisatory process of "finding a sense of weight and rhythm," where "energy, emotion and different bodily states were explored and from these were developed the musical numbers."[18] In this way, Flatt's choreography derived from and supported the acting, as it originated in the impulses of the performers, offering an informative and visually spectacular way of organizing bodies dynamically onstage, most often without the use of any traditional dance vocabulary.

As musical directors began to acknowledge and employ individuality in the ensemble, the focus necessarily shifted for the choreographers. Thematic content that offered more attention to individual identity markers like race, gender, and sexuality opened up a space for choreographers to employ gestural, pedestrian-inspired, and culturally specific movement beyond traditional dance vocabulary to translate story to audiences. Furthermore, the integration of postmodern dance influences, beginning in the 1960s with the Judson Dance Theater, means that musical theatre has "embraced a wide range of performance techniques from both dance and non-dance sources," especially pedestrian gesture.[19] As Liza Gennaro traces in her history of Broadway dance, the dance theatre and postmodern choreographers of the 1980s turned to concert dance forms to "re-investigate an interest in dance storytelling shared with text." Though these concert dance forms were not as legible to Broadway audiences, they did influence approaches to how movement, text, and score intentionally intersect, albeit abstractly. Gennaro points to Bill T. Jones, who choreographed *Spring Awakening* (2006), as a key player in bringing post-modern aesthetics and creative process to Broadway-style choreography and movement direction. As Gennaro highlights, "Jones' artistic journey through post-modern abstraction to his inclusion of text and narrative, as well as his experience developing movement material on non-dancers, served him well as he entered the ultra-legible world of Broadway."[20] Jones has been joined in the past two decades by movement directors like Hoggett, who have crossed over from the world of

---

[16]Kate Flatt, *Movement Direction: Developing Physical Narrative for Performance* (Ramsbury, UK: Crowood Press, 2022), 10.
[17]Kate Flatt, "*Les Misérables*: A Very Short History on Its Invisible Choreography," *Kate Flatt* (website), accessed December 10, 2022, https://www.kateflatt.com/les-miserables/.
[18]Flatt, *Movement Direction*, 13.
[19]Liza Gennaro, *Making Broadway Dance* (Oxford: Oxford University Press, 2022), 188.
[20]Gennaro, *Making Broadway Dance*, 190, 192. On *Spring Awakening*, see also Ariel Nereson's chapter in this volume.

physical theatre to musical theatre stages, bringing with them the approach of combining expressionistic, stylized unison movement that unifies text, music, and design elements.

Stephen Hoggett's Approach to Musical Theatre Choreography

Stephen Hoggett, dubbed the "anti-dance choreographer" by Sylviane Gold,[21] has Broadway musical credits that include *American Idiot* (2010), *The Last Ship* (2014), and *Once* (2011), and scored plays like *Peter and the Starcatcher* (2011) and *Harry Potter and the Cursed Child* (2016). He rejects the label of choreographer, suggesting that what he does falls outside the realm of that label. In an interview with Steven McElroy, he explained, "Choreography often is its own entity. . . . It stands up and kind of announces itself and then it's finished." McElroy continues explaining that Hoggett defines musical staging as "more about creating movement that springs naturally,"[22] and that his approach, even for musicals, is to create movement based on the actors' facilities. He says, "I use the word 'ensemble' and I use the word 'collaborate' and I *mean* those words."[23] Without formal dance training himself, he activates each individual body to help create the story in a more abstract way, thereby expanding the world onstage. As seen in his Tony-nominated choreography for *Once*, Hoggett "dislikes big, splashy numbers where the actors, under the spell of love . . . break into song and dance."[24] For *Once*, a story about a man and woman who meet in Dublin, fall in love, write songs together, and part ways, Hoggett was inspired to create movement when watching musicians in rehearsal. He would use "the way their frames fitted around an instrument and tried to create a general language from that."[25]

Even in scenes not focused on musicians, the "physical shapes of musicians and musicianship and what it is to play music" remained core inspiration for the movement vocabulary in *Once*.[26] In the scene where the Girl and the Guy go to a bank for a loan to make their demo tape, Hoggett focused on highlighting their hope and innocence, juxtaposing these with the redundancy and coldness of commerce. The ensemble, portraying the bank clerks, performed actions and gestures one might see clerks perform at a bank while confined to their desks: filing, rubber-stamping documents, rubbing their temples to quell a headache. Hoggett then directed layers of gestures and dream-like qualities of movement, thereby turning the phrases into a semi-abstract movement sequence. The dichotomy of the staccato repetitive action and the floating and waving movements of a dream elevated the inner subtext of hope and innocence that might be alive in each character, not just the leads. Like Flatt, Hoggett invites performers to contribute to the process, empowering them to expand the narrative and give definition to the world of the production.[27]

---

[21]Sylviane Gold, "Steven Hoggett Is the Anti-Dance Choreographer," *Los Angeles Times*, April 10, 2012.
[22]Steven McElroy, "How to Throw Punches without Getting Hurt," *New York Times*, February 27, 2011.
[23]Ayse Tashkiran, *Movement Directors in Contemporary Theatre: Conversations on Craft* (London: Methuen Drama, 2020), 140.
[24]Joan Acocella, "Hit Maker: Can Boxing Be Made to Look Believable on Broadway?," *New Yorker*, March 2, 2014.
[25]Tashkiran, *Movement Directors in Contemporary Theatre*, 140.
[26]Tashkiran, 140.
[27]Acocella, "Hit Maker."

But Hoggett's use of gesture to physically draw out metaphor does more than simply offer actors options to communicate complex emotions and character objectives; it invites the audience in, allowing viewers to apply their own interpretation to what they witness. For instance, throughout the whole course of the musical, the Girl and the Guy don't embrace or even join hands. Hoggett describes this decision, saying, "That energy of holding two hands, it's a dead moment, it means that the show is going to end."[28] Instead, when they touch, they lean forward and touch foreheads, gesturing metaphorically that the songs that came out of their heads are all they will ever have to emotionally connect. This kind of gestural detail supports the needs of the moment, and Hoggett recognizes that neither literal gesture nor traditional dance vocabulary could possibly convey the emotional truth in the same way. Throughout the production, Hoggett allows all the actors, lead or ensemble, to embody the rhythmic energy of emotion, and invites the audience to feel the lack of clear resolve and lingering space between the characters at the end of the show.

Twenty-first-Century Approaches to Movement Direction for Musical Theatre

Even when the score or book does not signal a "dance" in the traditional sense of upbeat tempo or syncopated rhythm, movement is still a viable and necessary factor in communicating narrative. Twenty-first-century movement directors and choreographers like Hoggett incorporate approaches that focus on actor-driven contributions, movement tied to dramaturgical research, and the evolution of character gesture into gross motor movement. The lines are often blurred between "choreography" and "movement direction," and the chosen term for any given production is often determined by the members of the production team or simply as a formality, to align with award categories.[29] As Hoggett indicates, movement direction departs from choreography in terms of its origination and purpose, with the emphasis on staging movement that feels "natural" for the character and surrounding circumstances. Whether pedestrian or abstracted, the movement stays focused on character intention and contributes to the given circumstances of the narrative.

Outside of the score, the production's shared dramaturgical resources provide tools to maintain thematic consistency and offer actors multiple possible physical languages they can individualize according to the needs of their characters. Central imagery may be highlighted in physical motifs, and textual metaphors can be teased out, supported, and embodied through nonliteral gesture in order to create visual patterns for audiences to then interpret. Recognized dance vocabulary or cultural dance forms can be intertwined into this foundational movement vocabulary, but the primacy remains with the authentic impulses for the characters. Given this intricate and often subtle threading of physical language, much of the movement director's work may not be as obvious as with traditionally choreographed numbers. In addition to employing standard compositional strategies used in dance,

[28]Acocella.
[29]The Tony Award is for "Choreographer," for example, and so Hoggett and others who have preferred to be acknowledged as movement directors would not be considered for the Tony Award unless they are given this title.

movement directors may also employ acting or directing techniques like Uta Hagen's Six Steps for character development, Konstantin Stanislavsky's simplified approach of asking *what if*, Anne Bogart and Tina Landau's Viewpoints method, or Rasa Boxes, a performance theory developed by Richard Schechner based on eight emotional states (or "rasas") described in the Natyasastra, an ancient Indian manual of performance.[30]

Choreographing the characters' interactions with the space and others helps communicate their function, relationships, and specific wants. This strategy can distinguish ensemble characters from one another, while working in conjunction with or as a counterpoint to the rhythmic structure of the score in order to emphasize subtext and mood. Furthermore, when working with orchestrations, the movement director can treat each individual instrument as a window into the subtext of the characters, informing the story through the melodic line.

The remainder of this chapter turns to Peter Darling's work for *Matilda the Musical* and Kelly Devine's work in *Come from Away* in order to highlight the ways in which the aforementioned approaches in movement direction have been applied as foundational elements in contemporary choreography.

Peter Darling and *Matilda the Musical*

Matilda came to Broadway via Britain's Cambridge Theatre in 2013. With book by Dennis Kelly and songs by Tim Minchin, the production, based on Roald Dahl's book, stays "true to the tartness of Dahl, who reveled in the sinister."[31] Tony- and Olivier-winning choreographer Peter Darling came to the project in 2010, after finding success with *Billy Elliot* (2008). Primarily trained as an actor with physical theatre companies like Cheek by Jowl and DV8, Darling sees his job as a movement director and choreographer to be to "*always* make sure that I'm telling a story so that the story doesn't stop the moment the scene ends, and the song begins."[32] He draws on influence from directors Joan Littlewood and Declan Donnellan, as well as choreographers William Forsythe and Pina Bausch, to develop a collaborative approach to creating movement. In order to prepare for *Matilda*, he did extensive research, reading about the time period and setting, and visiting a primary school and Dahl's house.

Darling says he was attracted to Dahl because, though the story "often deals with heightened situations, the underlying themes are real."[33] *Matilda* uses fantasy to address issues like bullying, injustice, education, and family values, and Darling rooted his movement

---

[30]On the acting and directing technique listed here, see, e.g., Uta Hagen, *A Challenge for the Actor* (New York: Scribner's, 1991); Hagen, *Respect for Acting* (New York: Macmillan, 1973); Anne Bogart and Tina Landau, *The Viewpoints Book: A Practical Guide to Viewpoints and Composition* (New York: Theatre Communications Group, 2004); Richard Schechner, "Rasaesthetics," *TDR: The Drama Review* 43, no. 3 (2001): 27–50.

[31]Ben Brantley, "Sugar and Spice, and Something Sinister," rev. of *Matilda the Musical*, by the Royal Shakespeare Company, London, *New York Times*, January 31, 2012.

[32]Quoted in Tashkiran, *Movement Directors in Contemporary Theatre*, 129 (original emphasis).

[33]Peter Darling, "Face to Face: Peter Darling," interview by Jenny Dalzell, *Dance Teacher*, April 3, 2013, https://dance-teacher.com/peter-darling/.

vocabulary in this stylized world, assisting actors in crafting physicalized gestures for each role. Additionally, Darling created movement transitions to help establish the production's flow and assisted in creating visual cohesion by incorporating design elements into the physical performance. "I treat dancers like actors," he says. "I would always make sure that the dancer understood the reason why we were doing each movement, what the intention of each movement was."[34] Darling's collaborative approach enhanced the directorial conceit, further expanded engrained metaphors, and threaded specific cultural references into the movement to create visual motifs. He has developed his own unique process for working on musical theatre productions, with dancers especially, saying, "if you discover the setting/the place and what's going on in the song (that is, the action), then—combined with the objective of the character—you have everything you need to create a musical sequence."[35] For Darling, a focus on the circumstances and intention for the individual character allows him to create the larger physical world of the show.

Collaboration between director Matthew Warchus and Darling in scene work and movement can be seen in the number "Loud." In the narrative, Mrs. Wormwood is instructing Miss Honey that intelligence and knowledge are less important than looks and a loud presence. Mrs. Wormwood's movement, which is fast and twitchy, creates a facade of authority. Her movements are rhythmic, with emphasized gestures like removing Miss Honey's glasses over her head on a musical cue, or directing characters around the stage with expansive arm gestures and overindulgent leg kicks. Miss Honey, in contrast, moves very little, similarly to Matilda, and when she does, she lacks control in her movement. As Darling says, "Miss Honey is very nervous of Mrs. Wormwood, and her objective is to get away; Mrs. Wormwood's objective is to teach Miss Honey, a woman she sees as her inferior, to dance."[36] The movement vocabulary is established in the scene and threads into the musical number, which is a diegetic element of the show as it is part of Mrs. Wormwood's private dance class. Miss Honey's inability to ground herself in Mrs. Wormwood's presence, much like her inability to be grounded in her life, allows her to be thrown around the stage and lifted into the air as if a tornado of energy has overtaken her when she dances with Rudolpho, the dance instructor. Darling's choreography, though having established parameters in terms of language and style, remained open enough for any performer playing Mrs. Wormwood to develop their own interpretation of the character and style.

Darling welcomed exaggerated and avant-garde aesthetics that tied to Dahl's fictional world as well as Quentin Blake's original art from the 1988 novel. He tapped into Blake's illustrations to give a "spiky, stretched-out quality, and angular" energy to the characters and their relationships provided a thematic framework and clear central image from which Darling and the performers could draw inspiration.[37] For example, for the character of Miss Trunchbull, who has most often been played by a male-identifying performer, Darling utilized a consistent vocabulary of dynamically jagged, almost militant gestures and shapes. Along with the Trunchbull's costume, which made the character appear larger, boxier, and more cartoonish, the physicality gave the character "a gothic heft," alluding to Blake's ominous,

---

[34]Quoted in Tashkiran, *Movement Directors in Contemporary Theatre*, 131.
[35]Quoted in Tashkiran, 132.
[36]Quoted in Tashkiran, 132.
[37]Darling, "Face to Face."

grotesque drawings of her in the book.[38] This physicality informed the acting choices for performers like Bertie Carvel (who originated the role) and Bryce Ryness (who played Trunchbull on the first US tour), and the acting choices in turn carried through to the choreography. For instance, in the "The Smell of Rebellion," the Trunchbull's sharp, striking arm movements, as if waving a sword, and militaristic goose-stepping emphasized the intimidating nature of the character. In this case and others, the stylized physicality enhanced the abstraction of fictional characters living in this world.

Darling's movement direction approach also factored heavily in developing choreography for the two ensembles of children in the musical: one comprised of child performers, and the other comprised of adult performers. When Darling observed children, studying their mannerisms at a primary school in London, he settled on the action of fidgeting as a foundational movement. This dynamic was featured in the number "Bruce," where the children watch another student as he is forced to devour a chocolate cake. Darling stages the children in the ensemble with physical motions that indicate anxiety: scratching their neck or swiping the back of their leg as they strike their body forward in a flat back. This twitchy and stompy movement vocabulary created a less polished look than traditional dance vocabulary. This action was personalized, as each person twitches differently, thereby creating a texture and individuality within the imposed uniformity of the school atmosphere.

Image 14.1 *Matilda* (2013). Photo by Manuel Harlen.

---

[38]Brantley, "Sugar and Spice."

This exploration also offered a physical, bubbling tension that could erupt when the children revolt.

The ensemble of adults playing children is set apart, characterized by their obvious size and penchant for aggression and cruelty. This character choice is indicative of the kind of education the older students have received from the Trunchbull or possibly their parents. Their movement is in distinct contrast to that of the children's ensemble, though occasionally they are in unison, symbolizing how children learn and are a product of the system in which they are in. The eventual joining up of similar physicalization makes the final revolution all the more impactful. The characterization of these two distinct ensembles and the implicit themes of learning through his movement direction, can be seen in Darling's staging in numbers like "School Song." At the start of the number, Darling stages the adult ensemble upstage, on the inside of the gates, taunting the children. The key physical objective of the scene is to intimidate, but underlying the action is a goal to instruct. We first see the members of this older ensemble morbidly walking, as if progressing through a fog, passing nonverbal code through their eyes to communicate that they are there to help the children. Then, as if their arms were laser beams shooting out from their shoulders angled downward, they reach toward the children, penetrating the gate, to inform them that there are scanners watching their every move. At one point, the disembodied limbs take hold of two students, signaling the force and violence expected to take place inside the school. At first, the movement of the children's ensemble lacks the structure and rigidity of the adult ensemble's movement; the youngsters move in a more pedestrian and free-flowing manner, while clutching their bags and scuffling their feet. As they are pulled through the gates and enter the school, there is a visible shift within the scene, and the children and adult ensembles work in a more unison physical structure, symbolizing how quickly children overcome the blocks of fear and learn to assimilate. This final driving, percussive march accents the community that builds as the show progresses forward and remains consistent throughout the production, both in the score and in the movement.

"School Song" also offers an example of Darling and Warchus's collaboration with set and costume designer Rob Howell, and the way intentional, character-driven movement helps create scenic transitions. The number moves with the first-year students as they await their first day of school, enter the gates of Crunchem Hall, and then enter their classroom. The choreography makes use of the gate as industrial playground equipment: cold, dangerous, but still climbable. As the gates open, the young students enter and the full ensemble begins the labor of stacking colorful blocks with letters of the alphabet into the holes of the gate, symbolizing the building of a language or code that will be used to communicate. Two featured ensemblists continue more complex climbing choreography on the extended boxes and steel, often shifting as if to avoid the blocks knocking them off or to dodge security lasers. Once the alphabet is completed, the gates open, allowing the students to enter safely. This thematic counterpoint helps set up the facade of conflict and foreshadows the later scenes when the students will band together. The walls part and shift smoothly offstage as rows of desks and a chalkboard shift on in parallel tracks. The set pieces shift with the driving rhythm of the score as the ensemble sings in round while performing corresponding canons in the choreography. The students then enter the classroom, quickly marching, standing at attention, lining up, and performing small gestures associated with school (pointing an index finger to the sky, writing on a chalkboard). Their movement incorporates the changing set pieces as the lines of students reflect the rows of desks, and the final, repeated *Why?* is further emphasized by the adult ensemble reaching out their arms in an extended V, the younger ensemble now seated at their desks poring over their books. A bell brings the students to attention, and class begins. The flow of this midscene transition ensures continuous energy, harmonizing the performers' movements with scenic elements and shifts. Each character and object has a track, which is visually enhanced with choreographed gestures and patterns.

In their collaboration, Darling and Howell centered the narrative from the viewpoint of a child, and incorporated playful pieces like swings, scooters, and ribbons into the choreography to not only offer visual and physical spectacle, but also enhance metaphors in the narrative. In the song "When I Grow Up," Darling uses swings to explore the ability to fly away free from our troubles. He uses a physicalized movement that he called a "superman" where the actor would run and dive onto the swing on their sternum, allowing them to fly over the audience, or metaphorically out over the world.

Darling's choreography, rooted in principles of movement direction, proved crucial for *Matilda*'s success in transferring from performer to performer, sit-down show to tour, because it offered performers structure and flexibility in translating the vocabulary. The musical remained truthful to its intention, whether stemming from keen observations of children's behaviors or incorporating ritual cultural dances that signal battle (as in the New Zealand Māori Haka dance forms in the number "Revolting Children"). As seen in how associate choreographer Kate Dunn translated the information to the touring cast, Darling's choreography clearly helped convey the directorial intention and Dahl's world of magical realism. In particular, his creation of dynamic differences and similarities between the adults playing children and the child performers supported the intended symbolism. In the integration of scenic pieces and the smoothness of transitions, Darling's movement direction made possible strong, character-based movement that constantly energizes the space.

Kelly Devine and *Come from Away*

Unlike *Matilda*, which is based on a beloved, fanciful children's book, *Come from Away* is based on the real-life accounts of citizens of the Canadian town of Gander, Newfoundland, and the seven thousand United States–bound airplane passengers who were unexpectedly grounded there on September 11, 2001. The musical, with book, music, and lyrics by David Hein and Irene Sankoff, requires a minimalist visual aesthetic on which the many stories and the quick chaos of the day can be centered. Choreographer Kelly Devine joined director Christopher Ashley and the creative team in the show's early development at Sheridan College in Toronto in the inaugural year of the Canadian Music Theatre Project, which allowed movement to be factored into the story early in the process. As described by Phoebe Rumsey earlier in this collection, Devine's choreography incorporated nods to social dances, pedestrian movement, and dynamic tableaus to enhance underlying themes of community. Nothing in the movement vocabulary could be considered traditionally dance technique. Devine focused on the physical interpretation of source material to tell a truthful story, and incorporated approaches aligned with movement direction instead of traditional dance choreography to set forth the heartbeat of the community.

Unlike Darling, Kelly Devine trained in dance, and began choreographing early in her career, so her approach to building choreography has frequently involved dance vocabulary.

She choreographed for commercials, television, and music videos, becoming interested in stage choreography after seeing a tour of Susan Stroman's *Contact* (1999) in her hometown of Los Angeles. Her work for the stage, while often integrating dance elements, is rooted in bringing authentic, character-dominant movement into the bigger stage picture. After working as an associate choreographer to Sergio Trujillo on *Memphis* (2009) and *Jersey Boys* (2005), she choreographed *Rock of Ages* (2009), *Doctor Zhivago* (2015), and *Rocky the Musical* (2014) (for this last, Hoggett also came on as fight choreographer). For the Tony-winning *Come from Away*, Devine stuck to her approach: using movement to create "a deeper emotional response past words."[39]

Devine's choreography was a central factor in providing fluid transitions between quickly shifting scenes; assisting actors in transforming into characters; and rooting the physical shape of the production in a common vocabulary, tapping into the score's rhythmic drive to translate the chaotic energy while maintaining a visual organization so the audience could follow the story without being overwhelmed. As Devine said in an interview with Jablonski, "If you think of the show as a whole, it is as if we are creating one big production number," with movement that transitions from text to song to dance.[40] This kind of integration is established from the opening number, "Welcome to the Rock," which Rumsey so vividly describes in her chapter of this collection. The number is indicative of the way Devine, working alongside the director, integrated movement vocabulary to support the larger world of the play, threading it into the musical staging.

To begin the process, Devine recalls, the director tasked her to keep twelve chairs, twelve performers, and two tables in use onstage at all times. This kept the stage mostly bare, with the performers placed in control of transforming the world at any moment, where one scene would be set in the airplane and another at one of several locations in Gander. Devine explains, "the whole show is total transitions, and it's very hard on the actors mentally." In rehearsals, Ashley and Devine would direct the cast to move the chairs into different formations. Devine would ask the ensemble, "Does this look like a plane? What if we put it on the diagonal?"[41] Without an extensive set, the characters and their stories are at the forefront of the narrative, and the performers' physical labor manifests as a metaphor for one's need to make sense of a situation and the coming together of a community during a crisis—a story Hein and Sankoff describe as "numerous tales of ordinary people and extraordinary generosity."[42] As performers fill the bare stage, they also physicalize the act of making meaning when recalling a story or memory. Stringing these stories together helped support a full account of the chaos of the day.

Devine tracked the set pieces and their transitions from scene to scene, including the way each chair or table was handled, adding frenetic energy and anxiety to the space or helping ground a space in calm. Shifts of location often come within a scene or number, and in some numbers these shifts happen almost every fifteen seconds. For example, in the

[39]Ruthie Fierberg, "25 Days of Tonys: Why Kelly Devine Needed to Tell *Come from Away*'s Story through Movement," *Playbill*, June 2, 2017.
[40]Kelly Devine, interview by Michael D. Jablonski, 2021.
[41]Devine.
[42]"*Come from Away*: Study Guide," *Come from Away* (website), accessed December 10, 2022, https://comefromaway.com/incl/CFA_P146_study_guide_LO_M2B.pdf.

transition before the number "28 Hours/Wherever We Are," the actors, who are staged to be sitting in a Tim Hortons coffee shop, grab chairs and props that are labeled in the back with a number so they can track each item. Over the next fifteen seconds the chairs get assembled into six rows of two seats, each on a long diagonal, then each actor presets a piece of clothing or prop that they need for the next sequence. Then all twelve actors sit on the exact same count, and we are suddenly in the cabin of the plane. Devine describes this as one of the most complicated transitions, because each actor was given at least three tasks to complete. It is also the first major transition in the show, the first time the audience gets a sense of how many voices and characters are accounted for in this story.

The number "28 Hours/Wherever We Are" follows the passengers of the grounded planes who are devolving into states of panic as they try to reach their families by phone, all the while being plied with alcohol by the flight attendants. After the actors sat in their "plane seats," Devine focused on isolated gestures, like pushing a seat, opening the air vent, or shifting to try and find sleep, utilizing compositional tools like canons to create texture and repetition in space. As she described to Jablonski, it is like "catching snapshots of people where they are at in that moment. . . . Stuck doing the same exact thing because there's nowhere to go."[43] The gestures of restlessness shift from stunted, sharp movements in near space, showing the containment of the plane seats, to larger, more fluid movement after the passengers are served alcohol. Devine capitalizes on unison movements as the passengers simulate a drop in the plane, look out the windows, or try to get the attention of the flight attendant. In the middle of the number, the chairs release into the space to a formation that indicates a quickly established town meeting in Gander, and then once again re-form as the plane—but this reset further condenses the rows of chairs, now rows of three instead of rows of two, signaling the greater intimacy between the passengers.

Devine organized the space in a split focus, with internal moments happening downstage while the chaos in movement occurs upstage. Putting these movements together built energy, and the moments of stillness elevated the internal conflict that each character endures. Each character was able to express their emotional states of frustration, boredom, curiosity, and fear in how they approached the gesture. The way an actor picked up a chair and moved around another character demonstrated their skepticism of the other or their efforts at camaraderie. These careful decisions helped thread together the patchwork of stories and translate subtextual themes throughout the production. It was essential that the audience was able to navigate the transitions and find focal points from moment to moment. Each transition employed props and costume elements like hats and coats to help the audience follow individual characters. In rehearsal, Devine built each transition around the featured actor who was speaking, working slowly to orchestrate the right musical timing for the trading of props and shifting in space.

While characters make frequent mention of the logistical timeline of September 11, the timeline does not play out in an orderly fashion onstage. The casting of just twelve performers to represent the multitude of characters whose stories formed the book challenged Devine to offer consistent vocabulary that performers could access as any character by adding their own nuanced gesture and dynamic energy. As she explained in an interview for *Entity*

---

[43]Devine, interview by Jablonski.

magazine, the cast was "a very talented group of actors but dance would not be their first strength so I had to hold a 'Kelly Boot Camp' to find what they were good at and expand on that."[44] Devine supported the cast members with limited dance experience by incorporating actor- and character-based movement creation in collaboration with the performers, connecting the meaning and intention with the impulses through the text and music.

Devine's simple, naturalistic movement vocabulary allowed the cast to build community through the movement process and, as she describes, "it kept me in check for a show that needed to be grounded."[45] It also offered a universal language for the townsfolk of Gander and the passengers. As the character Claude says in "Welcome to the Rock," "you probably understand about a half of what we say," meaning that this Newfoundland community's dialect, which is highlighted often in the text, is distinct, and requires translation at times for the passengers. In conversations with the real-life people of Gander, Devine learned that they often have parties where guests break into folk dancing in the middle of their kitchens. This image and vocabulary became key source material for the production and is seen throughout, beginning in "Welcome to the Rock." In rehearsal, Devine tried a variety of stomping movement sequences, adding dimensions of level and depth by having actors get up on chairs and tables. While such sequences were visually appealing, Devine ultimately edited the opening movement to the actions of stomping and pointing to the floor, which for her signaled the appropriate energy, demonstrating the pride these Newfoundlanders have for their community and the bond they share, which is essential to communicate in the opening number. The compositional flourish of jumping on tables and chairs did not serve the needs of the characters, who would soon be thrust into a staged chaos with the events of the planes grounding in Gander. Devine's editing, which attends to the characters and truth of world, aligns her approach with movement direction rather than traditional Broadway choreography.

For research, Devine watched people who were stuck on a plane or bus, passengers bound by a common circumstance of a confined space and growing tension. She would analyze their movements and gestures, focusing on the minutiae of these moments, such as "turning the knob to crank the air or just fiddling around to get comfortable in your seat."[46] To Jablonski, Devine described taking inspiration from a film of a subway station with everybody frozen in time, waiting for the train as the camera kept moving. She posed questions like, "What happens to your body, and how do you move when you are immersed in these types of moments?"[47] When she took this inspiration to the actors, they created vocabulary for sequences such as that in "28 Hours/Wherever We Are." In this sequence, the gestures, ranging from minimal adjustments of posture to large, full-bodied reactions, helped enhance the sense of increasing frustration for the passengers, who are forced to stay inside planes on the tarmac for an extended period of time.

Like many musicals, Come from Away did not call for traditional dance-based vocabulary. However, choreography was essential in organizing and translating so many stories in less

---

[44]Sandro Monetti, "Breaking Broadway's Glass Ceiling: 'Come from Away' Choreographer Kelly Devine," Entity, March 25, 2017, https://www.entitymag.com/come-from-away-choreographer-kelly-devine/.
[45]Devine, interview by Jablonski.
[46]Devine.
[47]Devine.

than two hours. Devine's work gave visual structure, where the movement was often minimal but layered, offering texture that was both visually interesting and allowed for physical metaphors to play out. The way she worked with the set and prop pieces helped establish the minimal and selective realism in the scenic design, and contributed a sense of the surreal that must have been felt by the people in this compilation of true stories. Featured townsfolk, plane passengers, and airline crew shifted into focus with the help of spotlights but also Devine's staging and use of levels, foreground, and background.

Conclusion

As Steven Hoggett has said, "movement direction or choreography . . . is a joyous work experience because it's about bringing inherent quality out of people's bodies."[48] The movement in musical theatre has evolved new ways to incorporate storytelling with fluid energy into a production. With a meld of dance composition, acting, and directing techniques, movement direction approaches can be useful in their application for creating vocabulary and organizing movement for musical theatre productions. Movement directors' approaches allow for the implementation of themes, metaphors, and naturalistic gesture to create a more vivid picture of character intention throughout an entire production.

Though movement direction and choreography both develop and shape movement, the former centers characters' wants and needs instead of a visual aesthetic. The attention to gesture (instead of specific dance styles) as a foundational vocabulary and the collaboration with actors in rehearsal allow for movement to seamlessly integrate into the storytelling, working in tandem with music, design, and direction as a tool of expression.

As seen in Peter Darling's choreography for *Matilda*, abstract and gestural movement shapes the world of the production, codified thematically and woven into the intentions of the characters onstage, accentuating the connection to the beloved children's book and highlighting the archetypes of child, teacher, parent, villain. Conversely, in *Come from Away*, Kelly Devine elevates the pedestrian and everyday world we inhabit. The quick tempo of movement and shifting scenes, signaling urgency and a community working together, keeps the audience engaged throughout the play from the first downbeat until the final blackout. More contemporary choreographers have dug into approaches of movement direction. For instance, Camille A. Brown, whose work on *Choir Boy* (2012) garnered her a Tony nomination for Best Choreography, brings cultural narratives to reclaim African American identity though staging Black diasporic movement traditions. The staging and vocabulary in *Choir Boy* elevated the inner turmoil that the characters endured, allowing them to speak through movement even when they could not raise their voices directly.[49]

As Hoggett mentions, the "tricky aspects" of the opposing labels of movement direction and choreography "start at the contractual level and go right through to awards."[50] Kate Flatt's invisible choreography for *Les Misérables* was not, in fact, invisible, especially because it provided meaning and structure for the performers. At the time it might have been thought

---

[48]Quoted in Tashkiran, *Movement Directors in Contemporary Theatre*, 137.
[49]On Brown, see Dustyn Martincich and Alexandra Joye Warren's chapter in this volume.
[50]Quoted in Tashkiran, *Movement Directors in Contemporary Theatre*, 137.

invisible because the other elements of the production were thought to be primary—the score, the set, and the sheer amount of people in the cast. Flatt's choreography, with its integrated approach to movement direction, organized the spectacle of staging many bodies, activating the stage to physically support the intense emotionality of the score.

Productions that incorporate complex dramaturgical strategies can rely on movement to be the balancing factor between all narrative elements, particularly ones that are founded on classic or image-based material, that deal with subtextual concepts, or that work through nontraditional casting or nonlinear plot lines. Additionally, contemporary efforts to further integrate physicality into a production can be seen in rehearsal practices that use physical dramaturgy to begin developing foundational vocabulary for a musical.[51] Movement direction approaches, particularly those that engage the ensemble in ways that support the driving premise of the story, are activated by considering choreography that exists beyond recognizable dance techniques.

Bibliography

Acocella, Joan. "Hit Maker: Can Boxing Be Made to Look Believable on Broadway?" *New Yorker*, March 2, 2014.

Baldwin, Jane. "Raising the Curtain on Suzanne Bing's Life in the Theatre." In *Women, Collective Creation, and Devised Performance: The Rise of Women Theatre Artists in the Twentieth and Twenty-First Centuries*, edited by Kathryn Mederos Syssoyeva and Scott Proudfit, 29–50. New York: Palgrave Macmillan, 2016.

Bogart, Anne, and Tina Landau. *The Viewpoints Book: A Practical Guide to Viewpoints and Composition*. New York: Theatre Communications Group, 2004.

Bradby, David. Editor's introduction to *Theatre of Movement and Gesture*, by Jacques Lecoq, edited by David Bradby, xii–xvi. London: Routledge, 2006.

Brantley, Ben. "Sugar and Spice, and Something Sinister." Review of *Matilda the Musical*, by the Royal Shakespeare Company, London. *New York Times*, January 31, 2012.

"*Come from Away*: Study Guide." *Come from Away* (website). Accessed December 10, 2022. https://comefromaway.com/incl/CFA_P146_study_guide_LO_M2B.pdf.

Darling, Peter. "Face to Face: Peter Darling." Interview by Jenny Dalzell. *Dance Teacher*, April 3, 2013. https://dance-teacher.com/peter-darling/.

"Demystifying in Process (Part 1) . . . The Role of the Movement Director." *Mrs. C's Collective* (blog), July 1, 2021. https://www.mrscscollective.co.uk/collective-blog/demystifying-in-process-the-role-of-the-movement-director.

Evans, Mark. *Jacques Copeau*. London: Routledge, 2017.

Fierberg, Ruthie. "25 Days of Tonys: Why Kelly Devine Needed to Tell *Come from Away*'s Story through Movement." *Playbill*, June 2, 2017.

Flatt, Kate. "*Les Misérables*: A Very Short History on Its Invisible Choreography." *Kate Flatt* (website). Accessed December 10, 2022. https://www.kateflatt.com/les-miserables/.

Flatt, Kate. *Movement Direction: Developing Physical Narrative for Performance*. Ramsbury, UK: Crowood Press, 2022.

Gennaro, Liza. *Making Broadway Dance*. Oxford: Oxford University Press, 2022.

---

[51]For more information on physical dramaturgy in musical theatre, see, e.g., Annette Thornton, "Quadruple Threat Musical Theatre: Adding the Physical Dramaturg," in *Physical Dramaturgy: Perspectives from the Field*, ed. Rachel Bowditch, Jeff Casazza, and Annette Thornton (London: Routledge, 2018), 146–53.

Gold, Sylviane. "Steven Hoggett Is the Anti-Dance Choreographer." *Los Angeles Times*, April 10, 2012.

Graham, Scott. "An Insight into Curious Movement." *The Curious Incident of the Dog in the Night-Time: Education Resource*, National Theatre (website). Accessed December 10, 2022. https://www.nationaltheatre.org.uk/sites/default/files/nt_learning_curious_an_insight_into_curious_movements.pdf.

Graham, Scott. "Physical Theatre: Frantic Assembly." *The Curious Incident of the Dog in the Night-Time* (website). Accessed December 10, 2022. https://www.curiousonstage.com/physical-theatre/.

Hagen, Uta. *A Challenge for the Actor*. New York: Scribner's, 1991.

Hagen, Uta. *Respect for Acting*. New York: Macmillan, 1973.

Howe, Diane S. *Individuality and Expression: The Aesthetics of the New German Dance, 1908–1936*. New York: Peter Lang, 1996.

Kennedy, Chad. "From Neurotypical Curiosity to Empathetic Movement: Exploring the 'Neuro-Perceptive' Staging of *The Curious Incident of the Dog in the Night-Time*." In *Text and Presentation, 2018*, edited by Jay Malarcher, 154–64. Jefferson, NC: McFarland, 2019.

Laban, Rudolf von, and Dick McCaw. *The Laban Sourcebook*. New York: Routledge, 2011.

Lecoq, Jacques. *The Moving Body: Teaching Creative Theatre*. With Jean-Gabriel Carraso and Jean-Claude Lallias. Translated by David Bradby. London: Methuen, 2000.

Manning, Susan. "Ausdruckstanz (1910–1950)." *The Routledge Encyclopedia of Modernism* (online), published April 26, 2018. https://doi.org/10.4324/0123456789-REM1773-1.

McElroy, Steven. "How to Throw Punches without Getting Hurt." *New York Times*, February 27, 2011.

Monetti, Sandro. "Breaking Broadway's Glass Ceiling: 'Come from Away' Choreographer Kelly Devine." *Entity*, March 25, 2017. https://www.entitymag.com/come-from-away-choreographer-kelly-devine/.

Newlove, Jean. *Laban for Actors and Dancers: Putting Laban's Movement Theory into Practice; A Step-by-Step Guide*. New York: Routledge, 2003.

Panet, Brigid, and Fiona McHardy. *Essential Acting: A Practical Handbook for Actors, Teachers and Directors*. London: Routledge, 2009.

Pisk, Litz. *The Actor and His Body*. 4th ed. London: Bloomsbury, 2017.

Schechner, Richard. "Rasaesthetics." *TDR: The Drama Review* 43, no. 3 (2001): 27–50.

Tashkiran, Ayse. Introduction to *The Actor and His Body*, 4th ed., by Litz Pisk, iv–xxxi. London: Bloomsbury, 2017.

Tashkiran, Ayse. *Movement Directors in Contemporary Theatre: Conversations on Craft*. London: Methuen Drama, 2020.

Thornton, Annette. "Quadruple Threat Musical Theatre: Adding the Physical Dramaturg." In *Physical Dramaturgy: Perspectives from the Field*, edited by Rachel Bowditch, Jeff Casazza, and Annette Thornton, 146–53. London: Routledge, 2018.

15 Everybody Cancan: Contemporary Musical Theatre Dance

DUSTYN MARTINCICH AND ALEXANDRA JOYE WARREN

In 2022, Camille A. Brown became the first Black female choreographer-director of a Broadway show since 1955, heading the Tony Award–nominated Broadway revival of Ntozake Shange's *for colored girls who considered suicide / when the rainbow was enuf*, a choreopoem that centers on Black womanhood through the sharing of seven women's stories. As the choreographer for the Public Theater's 2019 production, Brown used her signature movement vocabulary, "known for an introspective approach to cultural themes through visceral movement and socio-political dialogues," to convey the breadth of Black female experiences.[1] Brown's choreographic signature also threaded the characters' monologues together throughout the production to offer visual harmony. These transitions provided what Lovia Gyarkye describes as a "fertile terrain," where audiences find "a shadow language that bolsters Shange's rhythmic poems."[2] As Soyica Diggs Colbert describes, "Shange's work is meant to unfold through dance," and it does so in Brown's staging, which includes references to circle dances, double Dutch jump rope, collective hand- and foot-made rhythms, and unifying compositional staging built within thematic physical motifs.[3]

Brown began her professional career as a dancer with Ronald K. Brown / Evidence dance company and trained at the University of North Carolina School of the Arts. She has created for concert dance, opera, play, and musical stages, and her work exemplifies trends practiced among contemporary Broadway choreographers. She thrives in collaborative environments where she not only builds work with production and associate artist teams as well as performers, but also publicly acknowledges their collective contributions. In her creative process, she "leads her dancers through excavations of ancestral stories, encouraging each dancer to embrace their unique embodiment of the artistic vision and gestural vocabulary."[4] Whether it is incorporating American Sign Language, as seen in *for colored girls . . .*, or furthering dramaturgical information and embodied history, as seen in *Once on This Island* (2017), Brown's process of collective creativity makes space for inclusive and culturally conscious practices. In creating her unique vision for a piece, she centers

---

[1]"Camille A. Brown & Dancers (CABD)," *Camille A. Brown* (website), accessed November 1, 2022, http://www.camilleabrown.org/overview-dance.
[2]Lovia Gyarkye, review of *For Colored Girls*, dir. Camille A. Brown, *Hollywood Reporter*, April 20, 2022.
[3]Soyica Diggs Colbert, "'Told It Like It Was': Ntozake Shange's Tales of Black Womanhood," *New York Times*, March 30, 2022.
[4]"Camille A. Brown & Dancers (CABD)."

history-infused, identity-driven movement vocabulary, bringing authenticity to the characters and creating a unified world in which they share space with the audiences. Brown describes her eclectic style, saying, "It's everything. It's modern, it's hip-hop, it's tap, it's jazz, it's ballet, it's social dance. I call it a jambalaya. You stir it up in a pot and you put your own seasoning on it. And then when it comes out into the bowl, it's who you are."[5]

* * *

This approach to choreography and aesthetic—fusing genres, engaging in an inclusive process, maintaining a unique style—is necessary for contemporary musical theatre storytelling, as it gives space for more stories and storytellers in Broadway productions. This is particularly important if musical theatre is meant to reflect its audiences and the time period in which it is created. This chapter uses close readings of dance numbers and insights from collaborators to highlight contemporary choreographers and their productions, particularly Camille A. Brown, Sonya Tayeh, Spencer Liff, Sam Pinkleton, and Sidi Larbi Cherkaoui. It identifies movement trends in twenty-first-century contemporary musical theatre dance, centering these choreographers' use of signature movement vocabulary (i.e., style), composition, genre influences, and attention to the body and its conveyance of identity markers. Additionally, attention is given to the changing quality and function of social dance forms used in musical theatre choreography.

Likewise, this chapter examines the sociopolitical issues that contemporary musical theatre choreography tackles and looks at how dance is employed to address topics such as abuse or addiction. To borrow from Ann Cooper Albright's work, we suggest that with contemporary dance approaches and choreography carrying "the intriguing possibility of being both very abstract and very literal, dance can foreground a body's identity differently," and therefore offer space for more diverse bodies.[6] In this manner, we explore how movement preserves identities and confronts stereotypes of the racialized body.

Recent first-class revivals such as *for colored girls . . .* have given way to choreographic approaches that emphasize more truthful, identity-driven storytelling.[7] In addition to providing subtext, style, and visual narrative, new choreographic approaches encourage embodied character language that enhances the emotional and social truth of the world of the play, for example, by embedding period-specific movement into choreography or highlighting cultural signifiers within movement. This is not so much a departure from previous choreographic approaches seen in Broadway musicals as it is an evolution of those approaches, one that would not be possible without the infusion of perspectives from outside the "standard" Broadway choreography fare. Choreographers featured in this chapter came to Broadway with fully developed careers in other performance mediums. They have worked relatively outside the common Broadway trajectory, which tracks a budding choreographer from dancer to dance captain to assistant to associate to choreographer to choreographer-

[5]Mark Kennedy, "Pioneering Camille A. Brown Creates a Broadway Rainbow," *AP News*, May 26, 2022.

[6]Ann Cooper Albright, *Choreographing Difference: The Body and Identity in Contemporary Dance* (Hanover, NH: Wesleyan University Press, 1997), 3.

[7]We recognize that *for colored girls . . .* is not acknowledged as a musical according to the American Theatre Wing award designations. However, as chapter 14 in this collection suggests, there is a connection between the choreographic approaches to movement-driven plays with music and approaches to contemporary musical theatre choreography.

director. This chapter highlights choreographers who are not cuffed to traditions of musical theatre dance or to the conventions of the form, who instead apply concert and commercial dance practices and aesthetics as well as performance art in order to better reflect the society in which the work is created. Though their work remains in service of the story, it engages in innovative methods of practice and execution in order to address, captivate, inspire, and maybe even activate audiences through movement rooted in cultural embodiment.

Beyond the goals of entertaining, conveying the story, transitioning between scenes, and bringing the music, costumes, and set to life, contemporary musical theatre dance aims to encourage audiences to become active participants who will go beyond watching, to what Ann Cooper Albright calls "witnessing." As she posits, "this is particularly true of dances that foreground issues of social, political, and sexual difference in ways that make the spectator aware of the performer's cultural identity as well as his or her own cultural positioning."[8] By situating contemporary choreographers in the history of musical theatre dance and defining "contemporary" trends, this final chapter establishes markers by which work may continue to evolve and looks to future possibilities in practice and performance for inclusivity and artistry in this foundational American art form.

Defining Contemporary Dance in Musical Theatre Dance History

As many chapters in this book highlight, musical theatre dance aesthetics and approaches have evolved as stories have changed to suit the times. Choreographers such as Jerome Robbins, Bob Fosse, Gower Champion, Katherine Dunham, Agnes de Mille, and Michael Bennett often trained budding choreographers who worked for them as dancers first. Choreographer and director Jerry Mitchell, for instance, got his start in Bennett's *A Chorus Line* (1975) and assisted Jerome Robbins in *Jerome Robbins' Broadway* (1989). Mitchell names two dominant choreographic approaches that influenced the next generation of choreographers: Robbins/Bennett and Fosse. For him, Robbins's and Bennett's "styles were dictated by each piece," whereas Fosse, "had a specific style present in every piece he worked on."[9] Rising choreographers in the 1990s and 2000s like Mitchell, Susan Stroman, Graciela Daniele, and Rob Ashford followed Robbins and Bennett, with choreography that primarily supports character and given circumstances of a production, while specific attributes of style remain secondary. Conversely, Ann Reinking, Chet Walker, Wayne Cilento, and Rob Marshall tend to follow Fosse and Gwen Verdon in style and approach, prioritizing specific, detailed movement vocabulary and form over the plot narrative.[10]

Additionally, concert dance choreographers from ballet and modern traditions including Twyla Tharp, Garth Fagan, Matthew Bourne, and Christopher Wheeldon have continued the trajectory of George Balanchine, Katherine Dunham, and Hanya Holm through productions where choreography has been built to showcase dancers who are highly trained in specific

---

[8]Albright, *Choreographing Difference*, xxiii.

[9]Quoted in Lauren Kay, "Face to Face: Jerry Mitchell," *Dance Teacher*, March 1, 2011, https://dance-teacher.com/face-to-face-jerry-mitchell/. For more on Robbins/Bennett and Fosse's approaches, please see chapter 5 in this collection.

[10]Bob Fosse and Gwen Verdon's specific contributions are being preserved in the Verdon Fosse Legacy project and can be seen in the remounting of shows like *Dancin'* (2023), which premiered at San Diego's Old Globe Theatre in spring 2022.

concert dance disciplines. Postmodern concert dance choreographers like Bill T. Jones, for example, offer a more abstract approach to musical theatre dance, creating intricate, nonliteral, physical vocabularies rooted in identity and gesture, approaches used in creating work for the Bill T. Jones/Arnie Zane Dance Company.

Inspired by choreographers such as those listed above, musical theatre dance has become its own genre, employing dancers who will perform movement that has "the same possibility of impact on a character" as a script.[11] Contemporary choreographers, many of whom come from commercial or concert dance backgrounds, merge elements of these previous choreographic approaches. While they use dance to activate the entire cast and create physical specificity for ensemble characters, they also maintain a focus on style in order to enhance spectacle and communicate narrative. The term *contemporary* has been adopted by other genres of dance ("contemporary jazz," "contemporary ballet," "contemporary Asian dance") to distinguish a style from its *classical* or *traditional* method of study. For the purposes of this chapter, we follow dance scholar SanSan Kwan in our usage of the term, seeking to "align the 'contemporary' with a series of aesthetic preoccupations while also reckoning with it as the dance that is happening now."[12] Contemporary musical theatre dance, then, is a departure from the classical expectations of its form and training, reflecting the movement styles and circumstances of current stories.

Contemporary musical theatre in the twenty-first century shares similar aspects to the contemporary commercial and concert dance that Kwan examines in her article "When Is Contemporary Dance?" Like contemporary commercial dance, made popular in competition circuits such as *So You Think You Can Dance* (2005–), contemporary musical theatre dance can be "emotive, dramatic, and virtuosic." Moreover, the work can also be "narrative or character driven."[13] For example, Sonya Tayeh's core vocabulary for *Moulin Rouge* (2019) showcases her experience in film and commercial dance.[14] Tayeh's choreography is rooted in the Detroit club scene, and so it exists in the balance between tension and release of the body, empowers sensuality of movement, and uplifts individuality within group choreography. These stylings are seen in the tight formations with gestural, dynamic movement staged in photographic tableaus in *Moulin Rouge*. Tayeh's personal style of "pile on a lot" suits the aesthetic of this show, with its color-filled excess and intensity. For her, dancers who "[hold] onto their characters inside the unison moments" and also leave the work with "a grit and a roughness to it" are as essential as the excess.[15] She wants dancers to "use what they had been training for all these years," and so employs ballet-based lines adopted by jazz technique alongside hip-hop elements in her emphasis on leg movement, quick isolations, and distinct rhythmic patterns, finding ways that the body can move as swiftly as a camera on rails.

Similar to Kwan's description of contemporary concert dance, contemporary musical theatre dance, can also be "conceptual and anti-spectacle" or "excessively

---

[11]Kay, "Face to Face."

[12]SanSan Kwan, "When Is Contemporary Dance?," *Dance Research Journal* 49, no. 3 (2017): 39.

[13]Kwan, 41.

[14]Tayeh's work on the television show *So You Think You Can Dance* was nominated for an Emmy in 2013. She has also worked in national tours of music artists such as Florence and the Machine and Miley Cyrus, as well as with concert dance companies like Malpaso Dance Company and Martha Graham Dance Company.

[15]Quoted in Courtney Escoyne, "Sonya Tayeh Is on the Move," *Timeout*, November 14, 2019.

expressive."[16] Both forms can purposefully employ pedestrian gestural movement vocabulary to enhance subtext or can intentionally distance the audience with abstraction—a way for the audience to witness the story instead of becoming immersed in it. For both forms, movement vocabulary is not bound to a definitive genre; it aims instead to incorporate the kind of dance that is necessary for the storytelling. The movement can be identified by its application of abstract and pedestrian gesture, classical and nonclassical lines and shapes, weightedness, floor work, partnering that utilizes weight sharing, nonheteronormative pairings, and structured improvisations.[17] While contemporary dance has become known as its own genre, contemporary *musical theatre* dance means that elements of other genres, like hip-hop and street dance, voguing, West African dance, release-based vocabulary, and various non-Western cultural dances or African American vernacular social dance traditions can be accessed in order to tell more specific stories. Choreographers can incorporate asymmetrical patterns to enhance narrative discord or employ theme and variation to intentionally create meaning, just as a composer might insert a familiar melody or leitmotif throughout a show. Dynamic irregularities in music may also emphasize the activation and articulation of the torso, as a means of highlighting a performer's emotionally driven expression, in contrast to the once-common employment of strict unison formations. In short, the palette of "acceptable" vocabulary in musical theatre dance has widened. The following case studies illustrate these aspects of musical theatre choreography.

To start, Camille A. Brown's choreography for Kirsten Childs's *Bella: An American Tall Tale*, which premiered at Playwrights Horizons in 2017, demonstrates how multiple dance genres, including recognizable social dances, blend together to amplify character and narrative. *Bella* is a musical comedy set in the American West during the 1870s, and it follows the adventures of its eponymous heroine as she travels by train to meet her fiancé, who is a Buffalo soldier. Childs's libretto uniquely centers the narrative of a Black woman during the American Reconstruction period. Brown as the choreographer plays with the spontaneously joyful moments sprinkled through this production: a dance battle arises between men and women; a Chinese American cowboy performs with backup dancers reminiscent of the Motown era. During the song "White People Tonight," Brown harkens back to a vaudevillian-era minstrel performance. The Buffalo soldiers march with a weightedness, in a polyrhythmic step that is fused with contemporary West African movement. From the robbers on the train, we witness hand gestures from Beyoncé's "Single Ladies" music video (2008), a motif that adds a contrasting comedic moment during a harrowing scene.[18] Throughout the production, Brown draws on diverse and recognizable

---

[16]Kwan, "When Is Contemporary Dance?," 40, 41.

[17]Weightedness here refers not only to movement through a pelvic center that gathers energy from the floor, but also to "get down" as Robert Farris Thompson describes in his book *African Art in Motion: Icon and Act in the Collection of Katherine Coryton White* (Los Angeles: University of California Press, 1974). "Get down" as Julie Kerr-Berry describes it is "giving weight in which the knees act as springs that release into and rebound from the earth." Kerr-Berry, "Africanist Elements in American Jazz Dance," in *Rooted Jazz Dance: Africanist Aesthetics and Equity in the Twenty-First Century*, ed. Lindsay Guarinao, Carlos R. A. Jones, and Wendy Oliver (Gainesville: University Press of Florida, 2022), 85.

[18]In the musical video for "Single Ladies," Beyoncé and two dancers place one hand on their hip and hold the other hand bent, the elbow with the fingertips aiming upward, and then flip the hand facing the body and facing the away from the body multiple times, isolating the hand with emphasis on the ring finger as it rotates.

Image 15.1 Actors performing Camille A. Brown's choreography in *Bella: An American Tall Tale* (2017). Photo by Joan Marcus.

genres, from flamenco to cakewalk, to connect physical vocabulary to the combined lineage of African American vernacular dance and African diasporic movement.

Brown's use of recognizable motifs intentionally enriches the plot and heightens the humor. This is evident in the characters' physicalities as well. In the libretto text, Childs, in her author's note, states, "This American tall tale is a big-assed lie created to point out outrageous American home truths. So please, my dear actors, put your booty in it."[19] This important direction is carried out through Brown's choreography, where the movement is often subtle and loose, like the groove from the edge of the dance floor. When Bella is feeling good, she breaks into a swing of the arms, opening the chest; the pleasurable fun Bella experiences in these moments is elevated through Brown's choreography. Bella uses her hips and "booty" to fight against the oppressive experiences that she faces. Bella's booty is big and unapologetic about its possibility and its impact. Brown smartly crafts movement starring a liberated pelvis. This pelvis moves like a warrior; it's enticing, life saving, astute, and yet vulnerable. Bella's body is full of agency, and Brown's work allows performer Ashley D. Kelley to fulfill the libretto directive.

Sam Pinkleton's choreography for *Natasha, Pierre, and the Great Comet of 1812* (2016) exhibits another aspect of Kwan's description of contemporary musical theatre choreography that resonates with Kwan's understanding of contemporary concert dance: it can fit in "nontraditional spaces and nontraditional spectator-performer relationships."[20] This musical was staged on platforms and staircases built in and around the audience, and Pinkleton's choreography assisted the ensemble members in creating and sustaining the 3 a.m. party vibe of the production. His style, which includes exuberant individuality, regular kinesthetic quotation of media and pop culture references, and high-energy vocabulary, creates the

[19]Kirsten Childs, *Bella: An American Tall Tale* (New York: Samuel French, 2019), 5.
[20]Kwan, "When Is Contemporary Dance?," 41.

foundation for what Courtney Bowers describes as "captivating chaos."[21] The choreography employs a mash-up of social dance forms (Russian folk dance, waltz, rave, house), commercial jazz, and hip-hop to create a vibrant vocabulary for the party and party-like sequences. The mash-up gives texture and energy to the scenes, as well as signals location and mood. For Pinkleton, it was important that every person of the thirty-member cast do "slightly different choreography in their own way. It isn't about unison and lines, necessarily, it's about people expressing themselves at the absolute height of emotion."[22] Performers traverse the multiple stair units, creating play space in most areas of the theatre. Granted permission to interpret the choreography, they are allowed to remain open to interactions with audience members, including them in the unfolding melodrama and allowing them access to the story through an individual point of view.

Likewise, contemporary interpretations of dream ballets, dance breaks, and diegetic uses of dance in a musical follow trends in contemporary concert and commercial dance in approach and aesthetic. Brown's work as co-director and choreographer of the contemporary opera *Fire Shut Up in My Bones*, which premiered at the Metropolitan Opera in 2021, provides another example. The opera, based on the memoir of the same name by Charles M. Blow and with libretto by Kasi Lemmons, is set over the span of the 1970s–90s in rural Louisiana, and follows the story of Charles, a man battling the trauma of childhood sexual abuse. In the plot-driving dream sequence at the opening of act 2, the adult Charles is processing what happened to him, wrestling with how his feelings of same-sex attraction are manifesting as he matures. As Brown describes in the program note, her intention was to "play with abstraction and time travel, capturing the psyche of Charles, his inner turmoil, and his tussles with Destiny and Loneliness." This intention manifests in the staging and movement vocabulary, as she "treated each scene as though it were one of those aged Polaroid pictures—static in time, with the only breath being Charles, walking us through his journey, the pictures shapeshifting as we follow him along."[23]

The act 2 opening begins as Charles, lit with bright, almost iridescent light, tosses and turns in his bed. His head is orientated downstage; his headboard is designed with five bars between two posts, further reiterating his internal prison. A chorus of male dancers enter in silhouette, running and falling, reaching and tripping, undulating the body down and the arms sharply flying up, arms curl with fists, hands gently graze their own chests and drop. The torsos heave. The dancers are shaped in their own solo trajectories and pathways and yet at unexpected moments turn in unison. The back panel upstage left lifts to reveal a duet performed by Tim Edwards and Juel D. Lane. The two face each other. They gesture to each other in friendly greeting, their movements denoting warm conversation. The other dancers continue in solos in the foreground with full body and limbs, in release, their bodies curving with tension in one moment and striking in the next. As the duet continues

---

[21]Courtney Bowers, "Inside Broadway's 'Great Comet' with Choreographer Sam Pinkleton," *Dance Spirit*, May 7, 2017, https://dancespirit.com/inside-broadways-great-comet-with-choreographer-sam-pinkleton/.
[22]Bowers.
[23]Camille A. Brown, author's note, in *Fire Shut Up in My Bones* (program, October 1, 2021), p. 38B, Metropolitan Opera, New York, https://www.metopera.org/season/2021-22-programs/fire-shut-up-in-my-bones/.

downstage, Charles sits up and follows the two; they tussle and adjust their shirts, which are unbuttoned. They show off for each other, gesturing toward one another, as if to "check" each other or size up their authority and evaluate their masculine prowess. The other dancers melt to a low shape and pause their movement. The duet dancers begin to beat on each other's chests slowly, as if to affirm their strength, but then the beat slows further as they become more drawn into each other, a hand pulling in another's jaw. The music swells, and the intimacy is interrupted by the chorus of dancers spinning across the stage, turning and then slightly airborne. Yet, what is most critical to the unfolding of the narrative in this dream ballet sequence is the intensity of the duet in the dream and Charles's relationship to it.

The duet between Edwards and Lane moves apart, and they continue moving toward downstage. Charles is now out of bed as if he is walking around in his own dream, in his white tank and boxer briefs in contrast to the chorus of male dancers in shades of soft flowy brown. The chorus of dancers are at varying levels, writhing, some individually, some intertwined with others; their arms sweep, reach up, and yet they remain anchored to the floor. The duet continues with an embrace that swiftly becomes intense groping, across the back, along the thigh, around the shoulders, while the other dancers one at a time interact with Charles by swirling in and then away from him. He witnesses the other dancers in duet with one another, grasping one arm around the back, folding gently along with another. From among this chorus, one dancer's arms reach up slowly, his shirt tied around his waist, his chest bare. As he reaches up, Charles gently hovers at his chest and rests his head there. The dancer brings his arms down and cradles Charles's head like a motherly ghost.

This contemporary dream ballet moves the story forward without lyric. It defines where the lead character is in his personal journey, brings the audience up to speed, and sets up the scenes to come. Tapping into Charles's struggles and isolation "both spiritually and physically," Brown shows Charles's "longing for peace, and his search for a savior—only to realize that his savior was himself."[24] As other forms of contemporary dance reimagines previous structures, so too does Brown with the dream ballet, trusting that narrative can indeed be communicated through abstract movement sequences that are grounded in themes of connection, themes that are demonstrated through the acceptance or rejection of touch. As the next section of this chapter makes clear, this question of touch is no less crucial when social dance is incorporated into musical theatre.

Rethinking Social Dance

The application of social dance has also seen contemporary adjustments in musical theatre choreography. The use of social dance in musical theatre choreography has previously invited the audience into the music, to see themselves dancing in space, while physically establishing time, place, character traits, cultural affiliation, and relationships. Contemporary musical theatre choreographers have further pushed the function and concept of social dance by changing who is doing it and how and where it is done. Social dances are still used

---

[24]Brown, 38B.

as identity markers in contemporary choreography, offering visual cues that indicate character identity and relationships. Additionally, references to a particular social dance can be threaded into choreography or musical staging to show community connection, cultural consciousness, the humanity or pedestrian nature of movement, or even satire.

For example, from the start of *Moulin Rouge*, Tayeh's choreography and staging establish a world that is dangerous, sexually free, and queer, one where stakes for each character are high. Audiences are greeted by the Lady Ms, originally played by Robyn Hurder, Holly James, Jeigh Madjus, and Jacqueline B. Arnold, who inhabit the bohemian world of 1899 Paris with a wholistic feminine energy and range of skin tones, shapes, sizes, and genders. With the ensemble, they perform Tayeh's reimagined cancan, who employs it as both a historical reference and a social dance. The dance maintains its historical relationship to spectacle by commanding audience attention with its thirty-nine kicks through explicit sexuality (the legs separating in kicks and splits) and lifted skirts, Tayeh empowers the performers to capitalize on their characters' sense of urgency by allowing for individual expression and community connection to exist between moments of the unison kick line. Where the use of touch in the production can signal temptation, violence, or consensual pleasure, Tayeh's choreography's employs it in the opening as a way for the community to establish a bond. Instead of a purely presentational caress intended to arouse a viewer, the full, weighted touch between all members of the cast signals freedom of identity expression, collective support, and personal connection. In this way, this new kind of cancan sets the tone for the whole show.

More contemporary social dances have become regularly integrated in musical choreography. For instance, voguing, historically rooted in queer communities of color in underground house clubs and the ballroom scene, is purposely entwined in Spencer Liff's choreography in *Head over Heels* (2019) as Arcadia citizens journey to find their missing beat. Kate Prince roots the youthful, upbeat, and rhythmic movement vocabulary of hip-hop and club dance in *Everybody's Talking About Jamie* (2017) to signal camaraderie and a shared need for physical expression among the high school characters. *A Strange Loop* (2022) is infused with Raja Feather Kelly's style of "audacious maximalism and his witty, cerebral deconstructions of pop culture." He uses Motown, Lindy, and voguing as physical signifiers of Black life and culture in order to intentionally dramatize the performance of Black life.[25] In externalizing the fantastical strange loop composed by the lead player, Usher, and performed by his Thoughts, Kelly uses movement as a means of satire and alienation, a tool for audiences to reflect instead of escape.[26]

Social dances can clearly display complex conflict, narrative, and emotional connections, and though having become abstracted, contemporary applications of social dance in musical theatre still serve diegetic functions. For example, Camille A. Brown employs step, a social dance with its own African diasporic journey and evolution, in the third act of *Fire Shut Up In My Bones*. Brown reflects that "at one point in history, Black people were not

---

[25]Courtney Escoyne, "Raja Feather Kelly Makes the Strange Leap to Broadway," *Timeout*, April 21, 2022.
[26]Usher's Thoughts, originally played on Broadway by L Morgan Lee, James Jackson Jr., John-Michael Lyles, John-Andrew Morrison, and Antwayn Hopper, are characters who "inhabit Usher's inner psyche, along with standing in as his family members, agent, strangers on a subway, and a myriad other presences." Logan Culwell-Block, "'Thoughts' on *A Strange Loop*," *Playbill*, May 6, 2022.

allowed to perform on the Met stage and even more so, were not able to authentically portray our own narratives."[27] The step dance performed by the fraternity that Charles pledges illustrates and intensifies the journey of what his body endures. The step style indicates the personality, values, strength, and character of the fraternity, and also of what Charles was hoping to absorb and transform his own body into.

Social dance and concert dance partnering have long been entwined to serve musical theatre productions. This kind of partnering appears more organic and sequential, uses full-body touch, and is not confined to heteronormative pairings. This choice offers more narrative potential in translating character interiority and relationships than do spectacular and period-specific disco or Lindy lifts.

An example of this can be seen in the couch pas de deux for "Uninvited" in *Jagged Little Pill* (2019). Choreographer Sidi Larbi Cherkaoui worked with director Diane Paulus, the performers, and the production team to, as he says, "analyze how to physically portray the transformations of these layered characters . . . through movement and through the body, find ways to speak about the unspeakable."[28] Cherkaoui's work is influenced by his eclectic background, including his time with Les Ballets C de la B, a Belgian company known for "pushing the edges of theatrical realism."[29] His varied vocabulary—including hip-hop, West African, jazz, ballet, modern, and moshing—creates a contemporary aesthetic most visible in solos performed by featured dancers in transitional scenes, and also enhances the ensemble's intensity, the individuality expressed within a collective frustration at the lack of understanding, action, and communication in the world of the play.[30] The use of touch throughout the production is especially deliberate, as the story unfolds with two instances of sexual assault.

For "Uninvited," Mary Jane battles her internal demons as she struggles with addiction to the point of overdose. Cherkaoui created the "raw, visceral, tragic, detailed and delicate" duet with Elizabeth Stanley and Heather Lang, who played the original Mary Jane and Mary Jane's doppelgänger, asking them to embody "the stillness, the tension, the knots, the attraction and the repulsion" of the moment.[31] Mary Jane at times watches this other version of herself flail, perch, or slide on and off the couch, and at other times joins her, with mirrored hand gestures (tracing the arms, head in hands, prayer hands, hands reaching) that are performed in unison. The music bursts when her doppelgänger refuses touch, throwing Lang's character into a solo fit before she crawls to sit quietly next to Mary Jane again, lip-synching beside her. The piece culminates in a full-contact battle where Mary Jane fights the doppelgänger off before sliding limply off the couch into unconsciousness. The use of

[27]Brown, author's note, in *Fire Shut Up in My Bones* (program, October 1, 2021), p. 38C.
[28]Quoted in Jerry Portwood, "'Jagged Little Pill': Sidi Larbi Cherkaoui on Inspiration for 'Uninvited' Movement," *Rolling Stone*, March 3, 2021.
[29]Albright, *Choreographing Difference*, xxi.
[30]Moshing, like slam dancing, is a popular dance from the 1980s and 1990s modified from the early punk pogo dance. Though the dances are different, characteristics of both moshing and slam dancing include fast movement and a formation of a "pit" where dancers "slam into people and then quickly push them away," with swinging arm movement. William Tsitsos, "Rules of Rebellion: Slamdancing, Moshing, and the American Alternative Scene," *Popular Music* 18, no. 3 (1999): 122.
[31]Portwood, "Jagged Little Pill."

release, in actions of either letting go or throwing, allows for visualizing the music and its social dance—moshing. The full-body contact in partnering evokes a visceral uneasiness and the unrelenting pressure and weight of the inner voice embodied by another dancer, one who is dressed identically. In "Uninvited," Cherkaoui accesses contemporary dance partnering practices to stage a variation on a duet. The use of touch and staging that oscillates between face-off and presentational focus can be viewed as a stylized modern-day social dance between Mary Jane and herself.

In this example from *Jagged Little Pill*, the duet exists beyond a diegetic structure, manifesting in a dream ballet space. Where musical theatre dance has often had diegetic structures like a show or school dance to support it, contemporary dance in musical theatre may not rely on those structures explicitly. In many ways, vocabulary created from pedestrian gesture evolves from diegetic impulses in the scene. Through the abstraction of recognizable movement, the essence of that history, who is dancing and where, can exist without explicit explanation. Furthermore, social dance forms and structures can exist, as Ariel Nereson describes in relation to postmodern dance in musical theatre, less "legibly."[32] Social dance and partnering, then, can be repurposed, as postmodern choreographers repurpose gesture, where elements of cakewalk and tango do not explicitly define race or gender and voguing isn't assigned to indicate sexuality. Instead, choreographers, particularly those examined in this chapter, often abstract or apply social dance movements beyond diegetic use in scenes, in the process offering deeper characterization and establishing community as a whole.

Seeing More Bodies Dance

As the look of musical choreography changes to suit the needs of the stories being produced, so too does the identity of who is dancing.[33] As all cast members sing, all cast members also can dance, thereby offering more diverse audiences a chance to see themselves in the story in a more complete way. For example, as mentioned above, the Lady Ms of *Moulin Rouge* convey a spectrum of feminine representation in body shape, size, and gender expression, while Tayeh's choreography enhances their unified sexuality, confidence, and beauty. In the example of *Kinky Boots* (2013), Jerry Mitchell imbues Lola and the Angels, who are drag queen performers, with the core physical language that reflects Cyndi Lauper's lyrics proclaiming acceptance of self and others. With house- and drag-infused choreography, numbers like "Sex Is in the Heel" feature the Angels subliminally inviting the factory community of all ages, shapes, and sizes to share in their movement and message of acceptance. The community gradually picks up the Angels' full choreography through the show, culminating in a unison performance where everyone wears the red boots in "Raise You Up." The movement, a follow-along line dance featuring struts, a series of step touches and poses, and outstretched arms, becomes a symbol of unity, similar to how Mitchell employs choreography in *Hairspray* (2002). In these musicals, the sight of diverse bodies dancing

---

[32]See Ariel Nereson's chapter in this book.
[33]For more about the history of bodies and dance in musical theatre, see Ryan Donovan, *Broadway Bodies: A Critical History, 1970–2020* (Oxford: Oxford University Press, 2023).

unironically alongside one another signals a departure from certain expectations of who gets to dance in a Broadway musical.

Choreography that acknowledges and centers physical disability can be seen (albeit minimally) in some contemporary musical theatre performances. To return to the opening example of Brown's *for colored girls* . . ., Alexandria Wailes, a Deaf actor-dancer and accessibility advocate, weaves American Sign Language (ASL) into the choreography with the assistance of ASL movement directors throughout her performance as the Lady in Purple. This action normalizes Deafness as well as physical language potential outside of dance. In Deaf West's *Spring Awakening* (2015), Deaf and hearing, able and disabled bodies share in a collective physical vocabulary established through the collaboration of choreographer Spencer Liff and ASL consultants. As seen in numbers like "Touch Me," the movement communicates human desire, arousal, and awakening sexuality. The ensemble members perform their personal sexual exploration in solos, duos, and full unison staging. When the company moves collectively, they lift the lead, a wheelchair-bound actor, literally elevating and centering disability, as hearing and nonhearing performers continue to artfully sign.[34]

Liff's repertoire of musical choreography often celebrates difference and individuality while creating collective movement language that more bodies can perform. For *Head over Heels*, eighteen songs by the Go-Go's are set to a modern adaptation of Sir Philip Sidney's sixteenth-century *The Countess of Pembroke's Arcadia*. Liff's movement motifs and vocabulary outwardly celebrate queerness, sex positivity, and the range of sexual and gender identities. He describes his inspiration as "born of the queer club world of the 1980s . . . there are touches of voguing and touches of tutting," with "all the angularness and the posing of . . . [Renaissance] sculptures," and shapes from costume designer Arianne Phillips's vintage Tudor research. Liff's own club experience became a basis for the ensemble characters, rooting them in, for Liff, "the most glamorous, fabulous people . . . and that gorgeous, sparkly world they lived in."[35] From the opening number, a rendition of the Go-Go's song "We Got the Beat," this common physical vocabulary is performed across the cast regardless of role.

In this iconic Go-Go's song, Liff's movement is rhythmic, full body, and energetic, acting as a symbol of Arcadian culture and lifestyle. Performers of various ages, sizes, races, and gender expressions perform collective choreography that includes rhythmic body percussion, posing, and quick shifts of formation. More traditionally trained ensemble members perform virtuosic kicks and pirouettes as well as an impressive dance break featuring "the beat" — executed in unison, in a line, as a complex game of syncopated percussive rhythms played out behind a table. Bodies strike impressive shapes with long limbs that accentuates the rhythms, alongside vocal improvisation that establishes a sense of joy and play, as if this was the joyful task they execute every day. This dancing ensemble frequently takes foundational movement performed by everyone in the cast and adds complicated rhythms,

---

[34]For more on Deaf West's *Spring Awakening* and the use of ASL in Liff's choreography, see Ariel Nereson's chapter in this book.

[35]Quoted in Curtis M. Wong, "How Spencer Liff Helped Broadway's 'Head over Heels' Find a Beat," *HuffPost*, August 1, 2018.

transforming the movement into spectacle with virtuosic timing, flexibility, and camp attitude.

When Pythio, originated by Peppermint, the first transgender actor cast in a trans role on Broadway, joins the community, some of the initial choreography is repeated, intentionally pointing the audience toward both feminine and masculine elements of the movement and its roots in queer social dances. For Liff and these characters, dance doesn't have to exaggerate or stereotype, it is simply rooted in movement performed in queer spaces.

Cultural Competency in Musical Theatre Dance

Whether it's an industry-wide change or something that individual company practices have incorporated, creating inclusive, culturally competent spaces for performers to work in collaboration with the creative team enhances visual cohesion in a show.[36] Additions to the creative team like intimacy choreographers, physical dramaturgs, or cultural consultants may assist contemporary choreographers in addressing issues of trauma, offering historical and cultural context, and creating consent-based, antiracist practices in rehearsals where the physical performance of emotional processing through dance may be triggering. For example, in developing "Uninvited" for *Jagged Little Pill*, the creative team employed specialists from the nonprofit organization Learn to Cope, which focuses on addiction services, to ensure the movement remained sensitive and authentic to an addict's experience. These resources supported the actors' preparation and Cherkaoui's mindful staging. While, in the past, choreographers may have set work on the actors and dancers without their input, Cherkaoui's collaborative approach to develop the pas de deux with the actors created stronger performances and connections between actors and audiences in this intense scene.

The abstract quality of dance has historically made difficult or taboo topics more palatable for wider audiences (narrative examples might include "Laurey Makes Up Her Mind" in *Oklahoma!* [1943] discussed earlier in this book, or "Roxanne" in *Moulin Rouge*, where sexual abuse and violence are key to the story). The representation of acts of violence can be traumatizing not only for audience members to witness, but also for the actors to perform. Tayeh's use of the tango and apache in "Roxanne" harks back to "Slaughter on 10th Avenue" from *On Your Toes* (1936), which features an aggressive pas de deux accompanied by other male characters of the show.[37] In "Roxanne" the characters Nene and Santiago, originally played by Robyn Hurder and Ricky Rojas, are stand-ins for Christian and Satine, as Christian decides to rescue Satine from the Duke. Underlying tango rhythms drive the movement vocabulary, building tension toward a stand-off between the courtesan, the Duke, and the anguished lover. Tayeh worked to create a supportive experience for the performers by

---

[36]Cultural competency, mentioned in this section title, refers to a pedagogical practice where theatremakers, especially white artists, engage in actions that actively decolonize material in order to make it more inclusive. In this common practice, theatremakers who do not identify with the culture or identity markers expressed in the production would bring in consultants not only to create more authentic storytelling, but also to support artists of color who are performing in the piece.

[37]Historically, tango is an explicitly sexual, forceful social dance, performed by women employed in brothels and local male laborers. The apache, performed in Paris in the early 1900s, is a social dance featuring domestic violence disputes between two lovers. It's recognized by its virtuosic drops, grabs, and throws in partnering. Both dance forms found popularity in the ragtime and vaudeville eras. On "Slaughter on 10th Avenue," see Nathan James's chapter in this book.

encouraging conversation and understanding of technical partnering. For Hurder especially, Tayeh focused on the technical aspects of momentum and groundedness that are necessary to sustain the intensity of the number's extreme positions, abrupt stops, and quick releases for seven to eight shows a week, while wearing a corset. Hurder uses opposing force to protect herself and stay in physical and emotional control while delivering strong, direct, explosive energy in this physical, "sparring" movement.

Additionally, cultural competency in musical theatre choreography, as in other theatre productions, aims to support truthful storytelling when creative teams are predominately artists who do not identify culturally with the characters in the show. The nuances of physicality that dance provides can emphasize identity markers, but this is sometimes to a detriment, when exaggerated physical performances signaling race or gender feed into perpetuated stereotypes and therefore contribute to continued bias.[38] Directors and choreographers have employed consultants to assist in the rehearsal process to foster more mindful creative development and supportive rehearsal practices. For example, in creating choreography for Pulitzer Prize–nominated *Soft Power* (2019), a musical-within-a-play written by David Henry Hwang and Jeanine Tesori, Sam Pinkleton, a white American choreographer, researched and consulted with experts in Chinese theatre styles, and he worked with the cast of Asian American performers to create choreography that aided in translating the complexity of the satire and social commentary. Pinkleton and his collaborators found nuances between physical stereotype and authenticity that would best translate the story.

Musical theatre references are central to *Soft Power*, though told through the lens of a Chinese musical production, complete with blonde wigs on characters who play Westerners/Americans. Dorinne Kondo, in conversation with Hwang, describes the musical as "a creative vision that upends whiteness and theatre's Eurocentricity, allowing white audience members to see themselves from a Chinese perspective."[39] The musical is a story of an Asian American writer who, while lying unconscious after being attacked, dreams of an alternative version of *The King and I* (1951), from China's point of view, where a Chinese man, Xue Xing, comes to a violent, excessive America, teams up with Hillary Clinton, and teaches the nation about democracy after the 2016 election.

In working toward Hwang's vision to "create that complicated feeling of watching stereotypical or inauthentic work which is also executed so artfully that it sucks us in nonetheless," Pinkleton used his talent for tackling subversive themes in movement and drawing from elements of the absurd to heighten the intended satire.[40] Employing a collaborative approach, Pinkleton would, as he says, have "people build things, and then I sculpt from there. Or I'll have one phrase that I mutate."[41] For the production, Pinkleton focused on the "big Golden Age style musical that is told using the styles and forms that

---

[38]Examples of this process are interrogated by Kim Varhola in her chapter in this book.
[39]Quoted in Dorinne Kondo, "Casting, Cross-Racial Performance, and the Work of Creativity," in *Casting a Movement: The Welcome Table Initiative*, ed. Claire Syler and Daniel Banks (London: Routledge, 2020), 186.
[40]Quoted in Kondo, 187.
[41]Quoted in Bowers, "Inside Broadway's 'Great Comet.'"

have made up a century of American musical theatre," and gathered dance references from twentieth century movie musicals, social dance styles, music videos, and Tai Chi.[42] He and associate choreographer Sunny Hitt would then share these videos—featuring Gene Kelly, Fred Astaire and Ginger Rogers, Gower Champion, Agnes de Mille, Salt-N-Pepa, Missy Elliott, or Backstreet Boys—with the cast and ask for their reinterpretation of segments, to, as Pinkleton describes, "pluck out the bold, signifying impressions that people remember from dance numbers or dance moves."[43]

Each dance number was then given a core inspiration, intentionally drawing from American and Western musical theatre as well as Chinese traditions. For example, the dance for "I'm with Her" has recognizable references to *The Music Man* (1957), Eleanor Powell, Liza Minnelli, and *The Tap Dance Kid* (1983), but also draws from real-life moments when Clinton tried to appeal to the American people through movement (for instance, when she learned to dab on the television show *Ellen* in 2016). The song "Fuxing Park" was created based on videos of dancers in Fuxing Park, where there's "a rich tradition of line dancing and group exercise," and "The New Silk Road" was inspired by official propaganda ballets created in mid-twentieth century China.[44]

Pinkleton is open about his collaborative process, giving large credit to associate choreographer Sunny Hitt, the contributions from the all–Asian American cast, the director, and Hwang. As a white choreographer communicating stories from Asian and Asian American histories and experiences, Pinkleton is working toward what Dorinne Kondo describes as "creative labor that showcases the artistry of people of color, and welcoming into the rehearsal room multiple points of view that can offer perspectives on race and power (*the work of creativity*)."[45] Incorporating culturally competent practices, expanding the credit of collaborators, and citing cultural references in ways that aim to destigmatize and avoid appropriation are vital elements that signal that contemporary choreography in musical theatre is working to serve the needs of a production and acknowledge the responsibility of physical storytelling. Research, transparency, and a collective agreement on the part of the creative team and performers are not always associated with musical theatre development or choreography, but in the era where physical dramaturgy is becoming more of a common practice, more contemporary choreographers can offer authenticity to the creative process, as the bodies performing movement harbor culture and cultural expression.

To return once more to the impact and contribution of Brown: her process of integrating Haitian folkloric dance into the choreography for the revival of *Once on This Island* highlights her commitment to bringing authentic movement to the stage and honoring culture. In an interview, Maxine Montilus, who worked with Brown as the Afro-Cuban/Haitian choreographic consultant on the production, stated in an interview with Alexandra Warren, "I appreciate the fact that she takes the time, to do the research. . . . Camille wants to be more genuine and authentic in her presentation of the culture." She describes Brown's work as "rooted in

---

[42]Quoted in Ruthie Fierberg, "Inside the Making of the Deeply Meta Choreography for Off-Broadway's *Soft Power*," *Playbill*, November 12, 2019.
[43]Quoted in Fierberg.
[44]Quoted in Fierberg.
[45]Kondo, "Casting, Cross-Racial Performance, and the Work of Creativity," 188 (original emphasis).

Image 15.2 The touring production of *Once on This Island* (2019). Photo by Joan Marcus.

African American social dance and African American traditions."[46] Written by Lynn Ahrens and Stephen Flaherty and based on the novel *My Love, My Love* by Trinidadian-born Rosa Guy, *Once on This Island* is not set in Haiti, though its location shares many similarities to Haitian culture.[47] Montilus worked with Brown on Haitian folkloric dances "that I thought would help enhance that particular aspect of the storyline. . . . Then, she [Brown] on her own, figured out ways to incorporate what I taught into the choreography."[48]

The work with Montilus offered Brown a further understanding of the "social, historical, and political context of the dances." For example, "One of the dances I showed her was Elegua from the Afro Cuban lineage because Elegua is an orisha in Cuba or Santeria or Lucumí that lives at the crossroads, the one that opens the way to opportunities and prosperity and he's also a trickster."[49] The lead character, Ti Moune, aims for a life with Daniel, her love interest and the male protagonist of this story. Referencing the dance of Elegua, Montilus reflects, "makes sense in terms of her wanting to access the energies that would take away whatever was blocking her path toward a life with Daniel."[50]

---

[46]Maxine Montilus, pers. comm., March 3, 2022.
[47]The original 1990 production was directed and choreographed by Graciela Daniele. The movement was rooted in general Caribbean dance aesthetics, ranging from African diasporic traditions to colonial waltzes.
[48]Montilus, pers. comm.
[49]The author writes this description based on the *Once on This Island* performance from the 2018 Tony Awards.
[50]Montilus, pers. comm.

During the 2018 Tony Awards the company performed a mash-up of two numbers "We Dance" and "Mama Will Provide." This performance captures how dance "strengthens the sense of community at the very core of the play."[51] Ti Moune as a young girl is carried through the stage space by the people embodying an ocean tide. When she reappears as a more mature girl she is encouraged and supported by this intergenerational community through movement. As the "storytellers" come together, in unison, one foot steps out as hips undulate back, one foot steps with the pelvis rocking in place, and the arms flow forward and back smoothly in opposition of the pelvis movement. The feet come together, and the arms float up above the head, while the hips circle together and shift direction. As the storytellers begin to walk, the hands come together with the fingertips extended and pointing forward, undulating from the shoulders down to the fingertips still held together, waving through the upper body as they spread out into a circle around the shipwrecked boat Ti Moune stands on. They break into individual movement, which takes on the quality of the words mentioned in the song: *moss*, arms spread across a center plane as the hips fluidly circle; *rocks*, arms opening up with fist; *sand*, arms floating up, letting the sand on the stage floor trickle down between the fingers; *plantain*, hands behind the back with palm out, elbows out to the side with a playful shake of the shoulders and torso, emphasizing the abdomen.

Daniel enters. Exposing a defined torso, he begins to move, dropping down in the pelvis from standing up tall to a medium-low level. He rocks side to side and then undulates his torso while moving backward. On the stage there is a shallow pool of water that is happily being kicked up, sand, a goat being pulled in through the audience. The ensemble moves to a circle and in unison they sweep the arms forward and up, then drop, rocking in the pelvis, letting the energy in the body flow up through the fingertips and trickle down through the body to the toes. They move away from the unison movement but individually maintain the celebratory energy.

Brown's use of traditional Haitian and Afro-Cuban movement in *Once on This Island* honors traditional forms and is expanded on and reimagined in her own choreographic style. Her choreographic signature lends an authenticity to the storytelling, deepening the backstories of the characters, and engaging in diasporic traditions that signal how cultural identity is part of an everyday language of all the characters, both humans and gods. Brown's work on this musical is exemplary from process to product. Her research, collaborative approach, and movement vocabulary that draws on authentic methods and her unique aesthetic all work together to elevate its choreographic significance in the musical theatre canon.

Conclusion

Dance remains central to innovative, evocative, and emotional storytelling in musical theatre. It conveys meaning beyond the limits of lyrics because it activates the body's narrative power, offers spectacle that can help digest difficult topics, and invites audiences to draw connections and make meaning. Musical theatre dance has necessarily had to evolve with each period to better support the stories of the era and connect to audiences. Barbara

---

[51]Anouk Bottero, "'A Play That Provides': The 2017 Broadway Revival of *Once on This Island*," *Miranda* 17 (2018): par. 18, https://doi.org/10.4000/miranda.13878.

Cohen-Stratyner notes that audiences have long "consumed musicals about people like themselves," just as they do other popular arts and culture forms of their time (magazines, novels, and film).[52] As this chapter claims, Camille A. Brown and her contemporaries are creating dance for musical theatre stages that offers integral support for new story formations, using their own style and approach to evolve traditional practices of musical theatre choreography. These contemporary musical theatre choreographers incorporate movement vocabulary from other mediums and from current dance trends, and they privilege stage compositions that allow for individualized movement within a group in order to signify identity and convey subtext and the emotional world of the play.

Brown and her contemporaries are situated in a musical theatre dance tradition that, as Liza Gennaro says, is rooted in "Robbins' methods and . . . de Mille's drive to create original movement."[53] However, Brown's lineage is indeed separate from and unencumbered by musical theatre dance traditions, coming from a historical line whose influence and value must be acknowledged. Contemporary musical choreographers like Brown can stay true to their personal style, which often exists outside musical theatre stages, because the style is part of the value added to the movement vocabulary in a production, something that is necessary to the storytelling. Though the choreographers' unique style can be seen in their vocabulary, the successful application of contemporary choreography in musical theatre means pairing the right choreography with the right project, so that the aesthetic of the choreographer serves the needs of the specific narrative. As "an ever-changing, evolving dance form, egalitarian in its embrace of any and all dance genres," first-rate musical theatre dance must continue to enlist artists who specialize in concert dance and performance art, like Annie-B Parsons from post-modern dance (*American Utopia*, 2020) and concert tap dance's Michelle Dorrance (*Flying over Sunset*, 2021).[54] Choreographers who specialize in postmodern pedestrian styles, multimedia performance art, or concert tap dance can introduce the language necessary to communicate a character's narrative or a community's struggle or joy. When the language is paired with the story, tradition and expectations are usurped by authenticity and narrative connection.

Contemporary musical choreographers like Brown bring new and inclusive methods to employ the body as primary communicator and dance as its key translator of meaning, working within the parameters of a tradition but remaining unbound by its past expectations. Through more integrative and individualized rehearsal practices that honor and humanize performers as contributors and invite specialists and consultants into the creative process, contemporary choreography in musical theatre also aims to deliver authenticity in storytelling. As creative teams for musicals have become more inclusive of artists from the Global Majority, audiences have begun to see cultural codes from within their communities on the stage. Choreographers' potential impact extends beyond the dance and ensemble, then, into casting, direction, and other parts of the creative process.

After all, musical theatre dance has long been associated with the cultural and social norms of a period, particularly with regard to ideas of beauty. As the trailer for the *Ziegfield*

---

[52]Barbara Cohen-Stratyner, "Social Dance in Broadway Musical Comedy," in *Ballroom, Boogie, Shimmy Sham, Shake*, ed. Julie Malnig (Urbana: University of Illinois Press, 2009), 231.
[53]Liza Gennaro, *Making Broadway Dance* (Oxford: Oxford University Press, 2021), 212.
[54]Gennaro, 218.

Follies (1946) film proclaimed, the show was filled with "music and magic, laughter and romance, and America's most beautiful girls," and was reflective of "a startling new era in the world of entertainment."[55] In this contemporary moment, Brown is helping usher in an era in which beauty is redefined, centering stories previously relegated to the margins, and offering a more inclusive and reflective picture of communities and audiences. She employs contemporary practices in choreographic composition by using everything at her fingertips, bringing all of herself and her experiences and the experiences of her collaborators to the work. She weaves classical, traditional, and social dance into her storytelling to create contemporary movement for musical stages. Her process involves "asking questions, investigating, and listening," which helps the work remain authentic on the bodies of performers and connected to the needs of the show. By asking herself questions to center her process—"How could I make sure that the gestures and movements stayed true to the intentions of the composer? How could my direction amplify the voice and the heart of this piece?"—Brown ensures the choreography remains collaborative and in service of a cohesive product.[56]

Successful contemporary musical theatre choreography is mindful that while movement can be useful for its beauty and awe, it also can push audiences to sit with discomfort, whether by disrupting expectations of the body in performance or abstracting gesture and composition. As Ann Cooper Albright acknowledges, as the dance is "simultaneously registering, creating, and subverting cultural conventions, embodied experience is necessarily complex and messy."[57] For example, in Kelly's work for *A Strange Loop*, he is mindful of the physical stereotypes of the Black body and subverts or exploits them in ways that force audiences to reconsider the stereotype, as demonstrated in the number "Inwood Daddy." Similarly, Pinkleton uses physical satire in *Soft Power* to destabilize audiences, keeping them from receding into a place of escapism or voyeurism.

If the future of musical storytelling means to tackle difficult topics or access marginalized cultural narratives, choreographers must be equipped to implement practices that support performers and audiences alike. As Montilus offers, "the onus is on choreographers . . . to do the research and make sure we're representing cultures in a very genuine way. . . . If they're going to showcase cultures that have often been ignored, make sure that they do their due diligence to represent the culture, the best way possible."[58] Accessing research, resources, and tools to effectively practice cultural competency and building mindful rehearsal practices are necessary steps in communicating more authentic stories through the body.

Contemporary musical theatre dance can be inherently open to more dancing bodies, and therefore opens up the possibility for a range of bodies to be read through dance language. Though classical Western dance styles and contemporary concert dance forms continue to be the dominant aesthetic seen in musical theatre choreography, the wide palette of genres and dance forms offer possibilities for more diverse casting in terms of

[55]"Ziegfeld Follies—Trailer," uploaded by TheJudyRoomVideos, April 9, 2013, YouTube video, 2:32, https://www.youtube.com/watch?v=yfetvN_GWFc.
[56]Brown, author's note, in *Fire Shut Up in My Bones* (program, October 1, 2021), p. 38B.
[57]Albright, *Choreographing Difference*, 5.
[58]Montilus, pers. comm.

ability, experience, age, and size.[59] Representation matters, and not just the sight of different bodies onstage, but the sight of those bodies moving truthfully. "They're not placeholders. They are *dancing*," Tayeh says in an interview, touting the dancing ensemble in *Moulin Rouge*. For Tayeh, the ensemble "can carry the story. You can feel emotional content and intention, *by dancing*."[60] As musical theatre continues to evolve and meet the needs of emerging audiences, it's hopeful that dance will be a foundational consideration in storytelling for the future, and that innovative choreographers, including movement directors, cultural consultants, intimacy choreographers, and fight choreographers will continue to offer their unique perspectives to the bodies translating stories and entertaining audiences.

Bibliography

Albright, Ann Cooper. *Choreographing Difference: The Body and Identity in Contemporary Dance*. Hanover, NH: Wesleyan University Press, 1997.

Bottero, Anouk. "'A Play That Provides': The 2017 Broadway Revival of *Once on This Island*." *Miranda* 17 (2018). https://doi.org/10.4000/miranda.13878.

Bowers, Courtney. "Inside Broadway's 'Great Comet' with Choreographer Sam Pinkleton." *Dance Spirit*, May 7, 2017. https://dancespirit.com/inside-broadways-great-comet-with-choreographer-sam-pinkleton/.

"Camille A. Brown & Dancers (CABD)." *Camille A. Brown* (website). Accessed November 1, 2022. http://www.camilleabrown.org/overview-dance.

Childs, Kirsten. *Bella: An American Tall Tale*. New York: Samuel French, 2019.

Cohen-Stratyner, Barbara. "Social Dance in Broadway Musical Comedy." In *Ballroom, Boogie, Shimmy Sham, Shake*, edited by Julie Malnig, 217–33. Urbana: University of Illinois Press, 2009.

Colbert, Soyica Diggs. "'Told It Like It Was': Ntozake Shange's Tales of Black Womanhood." *New York Times*, March 30, 2022.

Culwell-Block, Logan. "'Thoughts' on *A Strange Loop*." *Playbill*, May 6, 2022.

Donovan, Ryan. *Broadway Bodies: A Critical History, 1970–2020*. Oxford: Oxford University Press, 2023.

Escoyne, Courtney. "Raja Feather Kelly Makes the Strange Leap to Broadway." *Timeout*, April 21, 2022.

Escoyne, Courtney. "Sonya Tayeh Is on the Move." *Timeout*, November 14, 2019.

Fierberg, Ruthie. "Inside the Making of the Deeply Meta Choreography for Off-Broadway's *Soft Power*." *Playbill*, November 12, 2019.

Fire Shut Up in My Bones. Program, October 1, 2021. Metropolitan Opera, New York. https://www.metopera.org/season/2021-22-programs/fire-shut-up-in-my-bones/.

Gennaro, Liza. *Making Broadway Dance*. Oxford: Oxford University Press, 2021.

Gyarkye, Lovia. Review of *For Colored Girls*, directed by Camille A. Brown. *Hollywood Reporter*, April 20, 2022.

Kay, Lauren. "Face to Face: Jerry Mitchell." *Dance Teacher*, March 1, 2011. https://dance-teacher.com/face-to-face-jerry-mitchell/.

---

[59]For more on casting and body types in Broadway musical theatre see Ryan Donovan's *Broadway Bodies: A Critical History of Conformity*. Oxford University Press, 2023.
[60]Escoyne, "Sonya Tayeh Is on the Move" (original emphasis).

Kennedy, Mark. "Pioneering Camille A. Brown Creates a Broadway Rainbow." *AP News*, May 26, 2022.

Kerr-Berry, Julie. "Africanist Elements in American Jazz Dance." In *Rooted Jazz Dance: Africanist Aesthetics and Equity in the Twenty-First Century*, edited by Lindsay Guarinao, Carlos R. A. Jones, and Wendy Oliver, 79–92. Gainesville: University Press of Florida, 2022.

Kondo, Dorinne. "Casting, Cross-Racial Performance, and the Work of Creativity." In *Casting a Movement: The Welcome Table Initiative*, edited by Claire Syler and Daniel Banks, 176–89. London: Routledge, 2020.

Kwan, SanSan. "When Is Contemporary Dance?" *Dance Research Journal* 49, no. 3 (2017): 38–52.

Portwood, Jerry. "'Jagged Little Pill': Sidi Larbi Cherkaoui on Inspiration for 'Uninvited' Movement." *Rolling Stone*, March 3, 2021.

Thompson, Robert Farris. *African Art in Motion: Icon and Act in the Collection of Katherine Coryton White*. Los Angeles: University of California Press, 1974.

Tsitsos, William. "Rules of Rebellion: Slamdancing, Moshing, and the American Alternative Scene." *Popular Music* 18, no. 3 (1999): 397–414.

Wong, Curtis M. "How Spencer Liff Helped Broadway's 'Head over Heels' Find a Beat." *HuffPost*, August 1, 2018.

"Ziegfeld Follies—Trailer." Uploaded by TheJudyRoomVideos, April 9, 2013. YouTube video, 2:32. https://www.youtube.com/watch?v=yfetvN_GWFc.

Index

Figures are indicated by *f* following the page number.